Clockwise, Roasted Turkey Breast with Winter Vegetables, page 184; No-Cook Cranberry-Ginger Relish, page 183; Bourbon-Glazed Baby Carrots, page 185; and Steamed Broccoli with Buttery Herb Crumbs, page 185

Meet the Good Housekeeping Foods Staff

Match the names and faces of the people behind your favorite recipes.

Susan Westmoreland,
Food Department Director

Food Director Susan Westmoreland and the Food Department at *Good Housekeeping* magazine continue a tradition of excellence. As a part of the Good Housekeeping Institute, the food department is responsible for developing recipes that assure success. Each recipe is triple-tested and comes with the Good Housekeeping Seal of Approval. As a result, every recipe you'll find in this book is guaranteed to earn rave reviews.

Look for Susan Westmoreland's "Food Editor's Q & A" throughout the book. She will answer your cooking questions with her test-kitchen secrets. You'll also find food editors' tips and techniques that accompany many of the recipes.

Want the inside scoop from the foods staff? Flip to page 9 to find a list of the food department's favorite recipes from this year's annual.

Sharon Franke,
Food Appliances Director

Debby Goldsmith,
Food Department Associate Director

Lori Conforti,
Associate Food Editor

Lisa Troland,
Associate Food Editor

Cathy Lo,
Assistant Food Editor

Caramel-Pecan Bars,
Cranberry-Cheesecake
Fingers, page 204

Good Housekeeping
2002 ANNUAL RECIPES

Oxmoor
House®

Published by Oxmoor House, Inc.
Book Division of Southern Progress Corporation
P.O. Box 2463, Birmingham, Alabama 35201

ISBN: 0-8487-2553-0
ISSN: 1537-6478

Printed in the United States of America
First printing 2002

To order additional publications, call 1-205-445-6560.

For more books to enrich your life, visit
oxmoorhouse.com

For more Good Housekeeping recipes, visit
goodhousekeeping.com

Good Housekeeping®
Editor in Chief: Ellen Levine
Executive Editor: Judith Coyne
Senior Deputy Editor: Evelyn Renold
Managing Editor: Sarah Scrymser
Art Director: Gina Davis
Special Projects Director: Richard Eisenberg

The Good Housekeeping® Institute
Food Director: Susan Westmoreland
Associate Director: Susan Deborah Goldsmith
Associates: Lori Conforti, Lisa Troland
Assistant: Catherine Lo
Food Appliances Director: Sharon Franke
Nutrition Director/Associate Institute Director:
    Delia A. Hammock, M.S., R.D.
Food Associate: Beverlie Sinclair
Assistant: Samantha Buckanoff, M.S., R.D.

Oxmoor House, Inc.
Editor-in-Chief: Nancy Fitzpatrick Wyatt
Executive Editor: Susan Carlisle Payne
Art Director: Cynthia R. Cooper

Good Housekeeping Annual Recipes 2002
Editor: Allison Long Lowery
Editorial Assistant: Diane Rose
Designer: Carol Damsky
Publishing Systems Administrator: Rick Tucker
Director, Production and Distribution: Phillip Lee
Books Production Manager: Theresa L. Beste
Production Assistant: Faye Porter Bonner

Contributor
Copy Editor and Indexer: Keri Bradford Anderson

Cover: French Lemon Tart (page 58)

Contents

our year at
Good Housekeeping

Dear Readers,

Welcome to *Good Housekeeping Annual Recipes,* our yearly anthology of great cooking. This year, more than ever, gathering family and friends around the table has become an important part of our lives. The twelve months of recipes in this book will help you serve delicious, easy-to-prepare food for every occasion. Whether you're baking a fancy birthday cake, hosting family for Thanksgiving, or trying to get Tuesday night dinner on the table fast, our recipes and menu plans will guide you. *Good Housekeeping 2002 Annual Recipes* is not merely a year's worth of delicious recipes—it's also packed with all the hints, tips, and techniques you have come to expect from us.

"The twelve months of recipes in this book will help you serve delicious, easy-to-prepare food for every occasion."

In the *Good Housekeeping* test kitchens, we not only develop and triple-test dozens of recipes each month, we also take our reader service to the next level. For example, in the tip boxes that accompany "A Month of Guilt-Free Dinners," you'll learn more about ingredients like buttermilk that are surprisingly good for you, and if you are in the market for a new skillet, our Institute Report on "New Skillets: How Do They Pan Out?" will tell you about innovations that just might make you a better cook.

One of the things that allows us to provide this in-depth information—and that makes us, and this book, special—is our access to all the other departments in the Good Housekeeping Institute. With the Institute's expertise, and extensive laboratory and product-testing facilities, we can do everything from putting lemon gadgets and cherry pitters through their paces to conducting a blind taste-test to tell you which lowfat ice cream rated best—even alongside full-fat premium brands.

Occasionally, we invite chefs to come to the *Good Housekeeping* kitchens and cook a meal that they would do at home for friends. For a cozy winter menu, Rick Bayless, of Chicago's Frontera Grill and Topolobampo, made us his Tomatillo-Braised Pork Loin (which all of us in the food department have since made at home to rave reviews). Jean-Georges Vongerichten, of Jean-Georges, JoJo, and Mercer Kitchen in New York, and Prime in Las Vegas, taught us how to make a steak with shiitake mushrooms that will make any steak-lover swoon.

We want you to enjoy the process as much as the food—so you'll find the book peppered with how-to photos that demonstrate new techniques. We hope you'll get as much satisfaction from using this collection of *Good Housekeeping* recipes and kitchen wisdom as we did in creating it for you.

Susan Westmoreland
Food Department Director

our favorite recipes

The *Good Housekeeping* Food Editors have chosen their favorites from a year's worth of taste-testing. We think you'll agree that these recipes deserve their highest ratings.

Pork Tenderloin with Dijon-Fennel Rub & Sweet-Potato Fries (page 12) Homemade oven-baked sweet-potato fries and steamed green beans accompany a flavorful spice-rubbed tenderloin for an inviting supper suitable for a quick weeknight meal or a special dinner.

Super Bowl Chili (page 22) Have friends over for the game and serve this Texas-style chili. Rather than ground beef, this recipe uses chunks of stew meat and adds red kidney beans for a low-fat alternative to a winter favorite.

Teriyaki Salmon (page 32) A Japanese-style teriyaki glaze tops salmon fillets, brown rice, and spinach for an elegant dinner that's ready in fifteen minutes or less.

Creamy Flan with Ginger & Lime (page 45) Award-winning chef Rick Bayless spices up this popular Mexican dessert with fresh ginger and lime zest.

Lentil & Bacon Soup (page 56) Lentils cook up faster than other legumes, making this soup a quick fix for a hearty family meal.

French Lemon Tart (page 58) This classic European-style tart has a lemon-cream filling resting in a crispy pastry crust. Look for the dessert garnished with baby kiwifruit and lemon leaves pictured on the cover of this cookbook.

Lemon Upside-down Cake (page 58) Tangy lemons offer a new approach to this refreshing upside-down cake that's delicious served warm or cool.

Pinto-Bean Burgers (page 69) Meatless burgers have never tasted so good! Top them with salsa, sour cream, and cilantro for an updated version of a family favorite.

Chicken Breasts with Raspberry-Balsamic Sauce (page 71) Basic chicken gets a flavor boost from pan sauce made from raspberry jam and balsamic vinegar.

Gift-Box Cake (page 72) This surprisingly simple dessert transforms layer cake made from a mix into an impressive package. From a whimsical birthday party to an elegant holiday gathering, you can personalize the decorations to suit the occasion.

Thai Salad with Roast Pork (page 82) Fresh springtime flavors of watercress, cilantro, and mint doused in a lime-soy sauce pair well with roasted pork tenderloin in this eye-pleasing arranged salad.

Roasted Asparagus (page 93) Roasting enhances the natural sweetness of asparagus. Toss with a little olive oil, salt, and pepper, and this simple side shares sophisticated flavor.

Lemon-Lime Coolers (page 96) Unwind on a hot summer's day with this refreshing cross between lemonade and limeade.

Plum-Glazed Ribs (page 99) Star anise lends its distinctive licorice flavor to these glazed and grilled baby back ribs.

Ginger-Jalapeño Slaw (page 104) Red and green cabbage combine for a colorful side to a backyard barbecue menu. Jalapeño chiles spice up the dish.

Sugar & Spice Blueberry Crisp (page 105) Juicy, sweet blueberries bubble beneath a crunchy layer of buttery brown sugar-oat topping. Scoop vanilla ice cream over the warm crisp or chill and serve later—either way, it's sure to please.

Cajun Shrimp with Rémoulade Sauce (page 108) This entrée is a busy person's dream. The spicy shrimp will be on and off the grill in less than four minutes, and you can make the creamy Rémoulade Sauce up to three days ahead.

Chile-Rubbed Ham with Peach Salsa (page 109) Rub ham steak with paprika and smoky chiles and throw it on the grill for a quick sear. A soothing salsa made from peaches and lime juice tames the spice for a complete balance of flavors.

Jeweled Fruit Galettes (page 124) Savor the bounty of summer with these individual fruit tarts. Choose a combination of your favorites—fresh peaches, plums, apricots, or berries—to be wrapped in a tender pastry.

Bow Ties with Salmon & Peas (page 132) Salmon and dill make a perfect marriage and vibrant green peas add color and texture in this elegant pasta dish.

Thin Spaghetti with Pesto & Tomatoes (page 134) Put garden-fresh basil to good use for this classic pesto. Yellow and red cherry tomatoes add sweetness and beautiful color, making this dish a delight for the senses.

Frozen Mochaccino Bars (page 139) A coffee-lover's delight, these bars combine a thick layer of vanilla and coffee ice cream over a decadent chocolate cookie crust.

Cinnamon Poached Plums (page 146) Enrich ripe, firm plums with deep flavor by cooking them in spiced poaching liquid until tender.

Gruyère Garden Frittata (page 146) Make this Italian-style omelette the centerpiece for a Sunday brunch. Robust garlic, basil, and nutty cheese pair well with ripe melon on the side.

Roasted Red Pepper Dip (page 150) Enhance regular red peppers by roasting them in the oven and lacing them with Middle Eastern spices. Dip with toasted pita wedges for a fabulous low-fat appetizer or snack.

Turkey Cutlets with Chopped Salad (page 161) Enjoy these crispy pan-fried turkey cutlets over tomato-arugula salad for a hearty main-dish salad.

Apple and Thyme Roast Chicken (page 162) Granny Smith apples, herbs, and spices impart fragrant flavor to classic roasted chicken.

Steak with Shiitake Mushrooms & Soy-Shallot Sauce (page 187) Chef Jean-Georges Vongerichten shows off his culinary genius with this impressive entrée. You can get a head start on this dish by preparing the sauce ahead and chilling it overnight.

Baked Brie with Lemon & Herbs (page 191) Begin a holiday open house with warm herbed Brie served with fresh fruit and crackers.

Baked Chocolate-Hazelnut Puddings (page 208) Your guests will delight in these soufflelike desserts baked in individual ramekins. Top them off with a dollop of whipped cream and listen as the raves pour in.

Sour Cream Nut Rolls (page 217) Rich walnut filling is rolled up in moist sour cream-yeast dough. These spiraled treats are pretty enough for holiday cookie swaps or gift-giving.

January

A Month of Guilt-Free Dinners

a month of guilt-free dinners

Yummy entrées—and desserts—that will make this year's resolutions a snap to keep.

TUESDAY, JANUARY 1

Pork Tenderloin with Dijon-Fennel Rub*& Sweet-Potato Fries*

Steamed Green Beans

Pork Tenderloin with Dijon-Fennel Rub & Sweet-Potato Fries

An easy rub seasons this lean and tender cut of pork.

PREP **15 minutes**
ROAST **about 25 minutes**
MAKES **4 main-dish servings**

Sweet-Potato Fries
   nonstick cooking spray
2 medium sweet potatoes (about 1¼ pounds)
½ teaspoon salt

Dijon-Fennel Pork
1 tablespoon Dijon mustard
2 teaspoons fennel seeds, crushed
1 garlic clove, crushed with garlic press
½ teaspoon dried thyme
½ teaspoon salt
½ teaspoon ground black pepper
1 whole pork tenderloin (1 pound)

recipe given

1. Prepare Sweet-Potato Fries: Preheat oven to 475°F. Spray 15½" by 10½" jelly-roll pan or large cookie sheet with nonstick cooking spray.
2. Scrub potatoes well but do not peel. Slice each potato lengthwise in half. Holding each potato half cut side down, cut lengthwise into ¼-inch-thick slices. Place potatoes in jelly-roll pan; sprinkle with salt and lightly coat with nonstick cooking spray.
3. Prepare Dijon-Fennel Pork: In small bowl, mix all ingredients except pork. Rub pork with Dijon mixture. Place pork on rack in small roasting pan (14" by 10").
4. Place potatoes and pork on 2 oven racks, and roast about 25 minutes or until pork is still slightly pink in the center (internal temperature of meat should be 155°F. on meat thermometer) and potatoes are tender and lightly browned. Transfer pork to cutting board and thinly slice. Transfer potatoes to serving bowl.

■ Each serving: About 300 calories, 27 g protein, 36 g carbohydrate, 5 g total fat (2 g saturated), 5 g fiber, 67 mg cholesterol, 670 mg sodium.

WEDNESDAY, JANUARY 2

Whole Wheat Pita Pizzas with Vegetables*

Italian-Style Green Salad

Low-Fat Rice Pudding

Whole Wheat Pita Pizzas with Vegetables
pictured on page 39

We topped whole wheat pitas with ricotta cheese, garbanzo beans, and sautéed vegetables for a fast dinner the whole family will love.

PREP **25 minutes**
BAKE **about 10 minutes**
MAKES **4 main-dish servings**

1 teaspoon olive oil
1 medium red onion, sliced
2 garlic cloves, crushed with garlic press
¼ teaspoon crushed red pepper
8 ounces broccoli flowerets (half 16-ounce bag), cut into 1½-inch pieces
½ teaspoon salt
1 can (15 to 19 ounces) garbanzo beans, rinsed and drained
1 cup part-skim ricotta cheese
4 whole wheat pitas (6 inches each), split horizontally in half
½ cup grated Parmesan cheese
2 medium plum tomatoes, cut into ½-inch chunks

1. Preheat oven to 450°F. In nonstick 12-inch skillet, heat oil over medium-high heat until hot. Add onion and cook 7 to 10 minutes or until golden, stirring occasionally. Add garlic and crushed red pepper, and cook 30 seconds, stirring. Add broccoli flowerets, ¼ teaspoon salt, and ¼ *cup water;* heat to boiling. Reduce heat to medium and cook, covered, 5 minutes or until broccoli is tender-crisp.

2. Meanwhile, in small bowl, with potato masher or fork, mash beans with ricotta and remaining ¼ teaspoon salt until almost smooth.

3. Arrange pita halves on 2 large cookie sheets. Bake 3 minutes or until lightly toasted. Spread bean mixture on toasted pitas. Top with broccoli mixture and sprinkle with Parmesan. Bake 7 to 10 minutes longer or until heated through. Sprinkle with tomatoes to serve.

■ Each serving: About 510 calories, 27 g protein, 77 g carbohydrate, 13 g total fat (6 g saturated), 13 g fiber, 27 mg cholesterol, 1,155 mg sodium.

THURSDAY, JANUARY 3

Steamed Scrod
Fillets*

Quick-Cooking
White Rice

Nonfat Yogurt with
Crystallized Ginger

Steamed Scrod Fillets

These fresh fillets are steamed on a bed of bok choy and carrots with a drizzle of a ginger-soy mixture.

PREP *15 minutes*
COOK *about 10 minutes*
MAKES *4 main-dish servings*

  4 pieces scrod fillet (6 ounces each)
  3 tablespoons reduced-sodium soy
      sauce
  2 tablespoons seasoned rice
      vinegar
  1 tablespoon finely chopped, peeled
      fresh ginger
  1 garlic clove, crushed with garlic
      press
  1 pound bok choy, coarsely chopped
1¾ cups (half 10-ounce package)
      shredded carrots
  3 green onions, sliced

---

food editor's Q&A SUSAN WESTMORELAND

Q Packages of dried fruit marked SULFITES ADDED contain fruit that is a lot brighter and fresher-looking than the fruit in packages labeled NATURAL, but aren't sulfites bad for you?

a Sulfiting agents (which are used to preserve the color of dried fruit) are safe for most people to eat. Some individuals, however, are sensitive to these additives; reactions range from minor breathing difficulties to a severe asthma attack. If you have a problem, choose only name-brand packages labeled NO SULFITES. Federal law requires that sulfite information be clearly stated on the label, but a few years ago we investigated how strictly this rule is enforced. Our findings? The New York City stores we visited were buying dried fruit in bulk and then repackaging it or selling it from bins without labeling. More than half of the samples we tested at that time contained sulfites, and, we suspect, that's probably still the case.

Q What is light or extra-light olive oil? The label says it has just as many calories as other olive oils.

a "Light" refers to the oil's color and mildness of flavor, not its calorie count (all olive oils are 100 percent fat and contain about 115 calories per tablespoon). Made with an extremely fine filtration process, light olive oil has a more neutral flavor and is the perfect choice for baked goods such as our Chewy Oatmeal-Raisin Cookies, page 28, or our Carrot Cake, page 24. You can also use light olive oil for sautéing or browning in recipes in which you don't want the oil to impart its flavor to the dish. For salad dressings and other recipes in which you do want the oil's characteristic flavor, reach for the more pungent extra virgin oil. It is made from the first pressing of the olives, with no filtering, and it is the fruitiest (and deepest colored) of the olive oils.

---

1. With tweezers, remove any small bones from scrod fillets.

2. In small bowl, combine soy sauce, vinegar, ginger, and garlic.

3. Toss bok choy and carrots in 12-inch skillet. Fold thin end of scrod fillets under to create even thickness. Place scrod over vegetables. Pour soy-sauce mixture over scrod; sprinkle with green onions.

4. Cover skillet and heat to boiling over high heat. Reduce heat to medium and cook about 10 minutes or until scrod flakes easily when tested with a fork.

■ Each serving: About 200 calories, 34 g protein, 12 g carbohydrate, 2 g total fat (0 g saturated), 3 g fiber, 73 mg cholesterol, 820 mg sodium.

FRIDAY, JANUARY 4

Oven-Roasted
Meatballs
with Spaghetti*

Steamed Broccoli
Flowerets

Italian Bread

Ripe Pears

Oven-Roasted Meatballs with Spaghetti

Weeknight-fast and diet-friendly, these turkey meatballs can even be made and frozen up to one month ahead.

PREP *20 minutes*
BAKE *18 to 20 minutes*
MAKES *6 main-dish servings*

  2 slices firm white bread, coarsely chopped
  1 small zucchini (8 ounces), shredded
  1 large egg white
  ⅓ cup grated Romano or Parmesan cheese
  1 garlic clove, crushed with garlic press
  1 teaspoon salt
  ¼ teaspoon ground black pepper
  1 pound lean ground turkey breast
  1 package (16 ounces) whole wheat spaghetti
  1 jar (about 26 ounces) pasta sauce chopped parsley for garnish

1. Preheat oven to 450°F. In large bowl, with hand, mix bread, zucchini, egg white, Romano, garlic, salt, and pepper until evenly moistened. Add ground turkey and mix just until evenly combined.
2. With wet hands, shape turkey mixture into twelve 2-inch meatballs. Place meatballs in 15½" by 10½" jelly-roll pan and bake 18 to 20 minutes or until cooked through and lightly browned.
3. Meanwhile, heat large saucepot of *salted water* to boiling over high heat; add spaghetti and cook as label directs.

4. While spaghetti is cooking, in 2-quart saucepan, heat sauce over medium-low heat until simmering, stirring occasionally.
5. Drain spaghetti. Serve spaghetti with sauce and meatballs. Sprinkle with parsley if you like.

■ Each serving: About 460 calories, 33 g protein, 70 g carbohydrate, 6 g total fat (2 g saturated), 9 g fiber, 44 mg cholesterol, 1,090 mg sodium.

Portobello Pasta

A delicious sauté of mushrooms, red pepper, and onion tossed with bow-tie pasta and baby spinach.

PREP *10 minutes*
COOK *about 20 minutes*
MAKES *4 main-dish servings*

     salt
  1 tablespoon olive oil
  1 large onion, cut in half and thinly sliced
  1 large red pepper, thinly sliced
  2 garlic cloves, crushed with garlic press
  1 package (16 ounces) bow-tie pasta
  2 packages (6 ounces each) sliced portobello mushrooms, each halved
  1 tablespoon balsamic vinegar
  ¼ teaspoon ground black pepper
  1 bag (6 ounces) baby spinach

1. Heat large saucepot of *salted water* to boiling over high heat. While water is heating, in nonstick 12-inch skillet, heat oil over medium heat until hot. Add onion and red pepper, and cook 10 to 12 minutes or until vegetables are tender and golden, stirring often. Add garlic and cook 30 seconds, stirring.
2. Add pasta to boiling water in saucepot and cook as label directs.
3. Meanwhile, to onion mixture in skillet, add mushrooms, vinegar, black pepper, and 1¼ teaspoons salt, and cook over medium-high heat about 10 minutes or until mushrooms are tender, stirring often.
4. When pasta has cooked to desired doneness, remove ½ *cup pasta cooking water* and reserve. Drain pasta. Return pasta to saucepot; stir in mushroom mixture, spinach, and reserved cooking water.

■ Each serving: About 515 calories, 20 g protein, 96 g carbohydrate, 5 g total fat (1 g saturated), 11 g fiber, 0 mg cholesterol, 1,000 mg sodium.

MONDAY, JANUARY 7

Macaroni & Cheese
on the Light Side*

Iceberg Lettuce
Wedges with
Light Italian
Dressing

Breadsticks

Lime Sherbet

Macaroni & Cheese on the Light Side

Our pasta recipe is amazingly creamy, and it sneaks vegetables into the kids' dinner without a lot of fuss.

PREP *20 minutes*
COOK *about 20 minutes*
MAKES *8 main-dish servings*

salt
1 package (16 ounces) cavatelli pasta
2 tablespoons margarine or butter
3 tablespoons all-purpose flour
¼ teaspoon ground black pepper
pinch ground nutmeg
3½ cups low-fat (1%) milk
6 ounces (1½ cups) reduced-fat
sharp Cheddar cheese, shredded
⅓ cup grated Parmesan cheese
1 package (10 ounces) frozen
mixed vegetables

1. Heat large saucepot of *salted water* to boiling over high heat; add pasta and cook as label directs.
2. Meanwhile, in 3-quart saucepan, melt margarine over medium heat. With wire whisk, stir in flour, pepper, nutmeg, and ½ teaspoon salt; cook 1 minute, stirring constantly. Gradually whisk in milk and, stirring constantly,

cook over medium-high heat until sauce boils and thickens slightly. Boil 1 minute, stirring.
3. Remove saucepan from heat; stir in cheeses just until melted. Following manufacturer's directions, use immersion blender to blend mixture in saucepan until smooth. (Or, in blender at low speed, with center part of cover removed to allow steam to escape, blend sauce mixture in small batches until smooth. Pour sauce into bowl after each batch.)
4. Place frozen vegetables in colander; drain pasta over vegetables. Return pasta mixture to saucepot; stir in cheese sauce.

■ Each serving: About 340 calories, 18 g protein, 43 g carbohydrate, 11 g total fat (4 g saturated), 2 g fiber, 32 mg cholesterol, 585 mg sodium.

new skillets: how do they pan out?

Do you really need high-tech cookware? Our food appliance experts think the answer might be yes. Each piece of **Thermospot nonstick-cookware from T-Fal** has a visual heat indicator in the surface to let you know when the pan is hot enough for browning or searing. Although it's not precise, the red-dot feature is helpful, especially for inexperienced cooks. Our experts also found Thermospot's nonstick finish worked well, releasing food and cleaning easily. The cookware is available in 2 product lines: The Hard Enamel collection, sold in department stores, features a black or gray porcelain exterior. Thermospot Total Non-Stick, available in mass merchandise outlets such as Target, Kmart, and Sears, has a nonstick-finish exterior as well as interior. For either style, prices range from

about $25 for a 9½-inch skillet to $140 for a 9-piece set. Contact 800-395-8325 or www.t-fal.com.

Cybernox from Sitram is a line of skillets with an interior cooking surface of a unique stainless steel that makes it stick resistant. Foods release, and the pan cleans far more easily than with ordinary stainless (though not quite as well as other nonsticks). In addition, you never have to worry about the finish scratching or wearing off. You can also use metal utensils. The pans themselves are heavy, with solid aluminum bases for even heat distribution. Skillets range from $79.95 to $99.95 for models with heat-resistant plastic handles, $97.50 to $136.50 for stainless-steel handles. Available at specialty stores or contact 800-515-8585.

TUESDAY, JANUARY 8
Pan-Roasted Chicken
& Vegetables*
"Baked" Apples*
(recipe, page 27)

Pan-Roasted Chicken & Vegetables
pictured on page 40

Boneless chicken thighs, red potatoes, onion wedges, and spinach are roasted together for an easy one-dish meal.

PREP *15 minutes*
ROAST *about 45 minutes*
MAKES *4 main-dish servings*

1½ pounds red potatoes, cut into
1½-inch chunks
1 jumbo onion (1 pound), cut into
12 wedges
4 garlic cloves, peeled
2 tablespoons olive oil
1¼ teaspoons salt
½ teaspoon ground black pepper
½ teaspoon dried rosemary
1 pound skinless, boneless chicken
thighs, each cut into quarters
1 bag (10 ounces) spinach, stems
discarded
fresh rosemary sprigs for garnish

1. Preheat oven to 475°F. In large roasting pan (17" by 11½"), combine potatoes, onion, garlic, oil, salt, pepper, and rosemary; toss to coat.
2. Roast vegetables 25 minutes, stirring once. Add chicken, tossing to coat; roast 15 minutes longer or until juices run clear when thickest part of chicken is pierced with tip of knife.
3. Place spinach over chicken mixture and roast 5 minutes longer or until spinach wilts. Toss before serving. Garnish with rosemary sprigs.

■ Each serving: About 440 calories, 34 g protein, 48 g carbohydrate, 13 g total fat (2 g saturated), 11 g fiber, 118 mg cholesterol, 930 mg sodium.

WEDNESDAY, JANUARY **9**

Steak with
Mushroom Sauce*

Steamed Asparagus

Crusty Dinner Rolls

Raspberry Soufflé*
(recipe, page 28)

Steak with Mushroom Sauce

pictured on page 38

Tender, lean filet mignon steaks are panfried, then smothered in a mushroom, shallot, and port wine sauce. Either ruby or tawny port works well in this recipe.

PREP **10 minutes**
COOK **about 20 minutes**
MAKES **4 main-dish servings**

- 4 well-trimmed beef tenderloin steaks (filet mignon), ¾ inch thick (about 4 ounces each)
- ½ teaspoon salt
- ¼ teaspoon ground black pepper
- 1 tablespoon olive oil
- 1 large shallot, minced (¼ cup)
- 1 package (10 ounces) sliced white mushrooms
- 1 package (4 ounces) assorted sliced wild mushrooms (gourmet blend)
- ¼ cup port wine

1. Sprinkle steaks on both sides with ¼ teaspoon salt and ⅛ teaspoon pepper. Heat nonstick 12-inch skillet over medium-high heat until very hot. Add steaks and cook 8 to 10 minutes for medium-rare or until desired doneness, turning steaks over once. Transfer steaks to platter; keep warm.
2. To drippings in skillet, add oil and shallot, and cook 1 minute, stirring often. Add mushrooms and remaining ¼ teaspoon salt and ⅛ teaspoon pepper, and cook until liquid evaporates and mushroom mixture is golden, 8 to 10 minutes, stirring frequently.

Add port and ¼ *cup water;* cook 30 seconds, stirring constantly. Spoon mushroom sauce over steaks.

■ Each serving: About 265 calories, 27 g protein, 7 g carbohydrate, 13 g total fat (4 g saturated), 2 g fiber, 70 mg cholesterol, 365 mg sodium.

THURSDAY, JANUARY **10**

Eggs
Florentine*

Mixed Green
Salad

Orange Slices

Eggs Florentine

This slimmed-down recipe is every bit as satisfying as the calorie-laden classic.

PREP **25 minutes**
BAKE **about 20 minutes**
MAKES **6 main-dish servings**

- 1 log (16 ounces) precooked polenta
- 6 slices Canadian-style bacon (about 4 ounces)
- 1½ cups low-fat (1%) milk
- 1 tablespoon cornstarch
- ½ teaspoon salt
  pinch ground red pepper (cayenne)
- 1 package (10 ounces) frozen chopped spinach, thawed and squeezed dry
- ¼ cup grated Parmesan cheese
- 6 large eggs

1. Preheat oven to 400°F. Grease shallow 2½-quart casserole. Cut polenta log crosswise in half, then cut each half lengthwise into 3 slices. Place polenta slices in single layer in casserole. Bake polenta slices 15 minutes or until heated through. Top each polenta slice with 1 slice bacon; return to

oven and bake 5 minutes longer. Keep warm.
2. Meanwhile, in 2-quart saucepan, with wire whisk, mix milk, cornstarch, salt, ground red pepper, and ½ *cup water* until blended. Cook over medium-high heat until mixture thickens and boils; boil 1 minute, stirring. Stir in spinach and Parmesan; heat through.
3. Poach eggs: In 12-inch skillet, heat 1½ *inches water* to boiling over medium-high heat. Reduce heat to medium to maintain water at a gentle simmer. Break cold eggs, 1 at a time, into cup; holding cup close to surface of water, slip in each egg. Cook eggs 3 to 5 minutes, until whites are set and yolks begin to thicken. With slotted spoon, lift out each egg; quickly drain in spoon on paper towels.
4. To serve, place a bacon-topped polenta slice on each of 6 plates. Spoon spinach mixture over bacon and polenta; top each with a poached egg. Serve immediately.

■ Each serving: About 215 calories, 16 g protein, 18 g carbohydrate, 8 g total fat (3 g saturated), 2 g fiber, 226 mg cholesterol, 995 mg sodium.

the perfect poached egg

- Start with fresh, cold eggs; the whites are thicker and less likely to spread in water.
- In saucepan or deep skillet, bring 1 to 3 inches of water, milk, low-salt broth, or other liquid to boiling. Just before adding eggs, reduce heat to a gentle simmer; if liquid is boiling rapidly, whites may separate into shreds.
- Break the eggs, 1 at a time, into a custard cup. Gently slip each egg into the simmering liquid and cook until whites are completely set and the yolks begin to solidify but are not hard, 3 to 5 minutes. Spooning poaching liquid over tops of eggs will help them set faster. (Swirling the water into a well before slipping in the eggs helps them retain their roundness.)
- Remove eggs from poaching liquid with a slotted spoon and drain on paper towels.
- Don't add vinegar or salt to the poaching liquid. You may have heard that adding vinegar allows the whites to coagulate at a lower temperature, helping them stay intact, but the experts at the American Egg Board say it toughens the white. The same is true of salt.
- To ensure pretty eggs when serving a crowd, cook them in advance. To stop cooking, plunge eggs into cold water, then trim off the ragged edges with kitchen shears. When ready to serve, reheat eggs in simmering water for 30 seconds.

FRIDAY, JANUARY 11

Eat Out

SATURDAY, JANUARY 12

Pizza Night

SUNDAY, JANUARY 13

Chicken with Pears*

Angel-Hair Pasta

Sliced Tomato Salad

Chicken with Pears

This recipe offers an easy way to make an elegant fruit sauce that saves time and calories. Quickly sauté sliced pears, then finish with chicken broth and a splash of raspberry vinegar.

PREP *10 minutes*
COOK *about 20 minutes*
MAKES *4 main-dish servings*

- 4 medium skinless, boneless chicken-breast halves (about 1¼ pounds)
- ¼ teaspoon ground black pepper
- ½ teaspoon salt
- 1 teaspoon vegetable oil
- 2 teaspoons margarine or butter
- 2 ripe large pears (about 1 pound), peeled, cored, and thinly sliced
- 2 tablespoons brown sugar
- ¼ teaspoon dried thyme
- ¼ cup chicken broth
- 1 tablespoon raspberry vinegar

1. Sprinkle chicken with pepper and ¼ teaspoon salt.

2. In nonstick 12-inch skillet, heat oil over medium-high heat until hot. Add chicken and cook 6 minutes. Reduce heat to medium; turn chicken over and cook 6 to 8 minutes longer or until juices run clear when thickest part of breast is pierced with tip of knife. Transfer chicken to plate; cover with foil to keep warm.

3. In same skillet, melt margarine. Add pears, sugar, thyme, *¼ cup water,* and remaining ¼ teaspoon salt; cook 3 to 5 minutes or until pears are tender, stirring occasionally. Stir in broth and vinegar. Heat to boiling; boil 1 minute.

4. To serve, arrange chicken on plates and pour pear sauce over chicken.

■ Each serving: About 270 calories, 33 g protein, 22 g carbohydrate, 5 g total fat (1 g saturated), 3 g fiber, 82 mg cholesterol, 435 mg sodium.

MONDAY, JANUARY 14

Curried Carrot
Soup*

Whole Wheat Rolls

Romaine Salad

Warm Chocolate-
Banana Cake*
(recipe, page 27)

Curried Carrot Soup

A creamy soup spiced with curry and sweetened with apples. Start with peeled baby carrots to save time.

PREP *15 minutes*

COOK *about 35 minutes*

MAKES *about 7 cups or 4 main-dish servings*

- 1 tablespoon olive oil
- 1 medium onion, chopped
- 1 tablespoon grated, peeled fresh ginger
- 1 teaspoon curry powder
- 1 bag (16 ounces) peeled baby carrots
- 2 Golden Delicious apples (1 pound), peeled, cored, and cut up
- 1 can (14½ ounces) chicken broth (1¾ cups)
- ¾ teaspoon salt
- 1 can (5 ounces) evaporated nonfat milk

1. In 4-quart saucepan, heat oil over medium heat until hot. Add onion and cook 8 minutes or until tender, stirring occasionally.

2. Add ginger and curry; cook 1 minute, stirring constantly. Add carrots, apples, broth, salt, and *2 cups water*; heat to boiling over high heat. Reduce heat to medium; cover and cook 25 minutes or until carrots are very tender, stirring occasionally.

3. In blender, with center part of blender cover removed to allow steam to escape, blend soup at low speed in small batches until pureed. Pour pureed soup into large bowl after each batch.

4. Return soup to saucepan; stir in undiluted evaporated milk and heat over medium heat until soup is hot, stirring often.

■ Each serving: About 175 calories, 5 g protein, 29 g carbohydrate, 5 g total fat (1 g saturated), 4 g fiber, 1 mg cholesterol, 945 mg sodium.

TUESDAY, JANUARY 15

Tossed Green Salad

Vegetarian Souvlaki*

Green Grapes

Vegetarian Souvlaki

No one will miss the meat in these sandwiches. Make the filling by cutting up your favorite veggie burgers.

PREP *15 minutes*

COOK *about 20 minutes*

MAKES *4 main-dish servings*

- 1 tablespoon olive oil
- 1 large onion, cut in half and thinly sliced
- 4 frozen vegetarian soy burgers (10- to 12-ounce package), cut into 1-inch pieces
- ¼ teaspoon ground black pepper
- ½ teaspoon salt
- 8 ounces plain nonfat yogurt
- 8 ounces English (seedless) cucumber, cut into ¼-inch dice
- 1 teaspoon dried mint
- 1 small garlic clove, crushed with garlic press
- 4 pitas (6 to 7 inches each), warmed
- 1 medium tomato, cut into ½-inch dice
- 1 ounce feta cheese, crumbled

1. In nonstick 12-inch skillet, heat oil over medium heat until hot. Add onion and cook 12 to 15 minutes or until tender and golden, stirring occasionally. Add burgers, pepper, and

¼ teaspoon salt, and cook 5 minutes or until heated through.

2. Meanwhile, in medium bowl, stir yogurt with cucumber, mint, garlic, and remaining ¼ teaspoon salt. Add burger mixture and toss gently to combine.

3. Cut 1-inch slice from each pita to make opening. Reserve cut-off pitas for crumbs another day. Spoon one-fourth burger mixture into each pita. Sprinkle with tomato and feta.

■ Each serving: About 390 calories, 24 g protein, 45 g carbohydrate, 13 g total fat (3 g saturated), 6 g fiber, 9 mg cholesterol, 945 mg sodium.

WEDNESDAY, JANUARY 16

Soy-Glazed Salmon
with Spinach*

Brown Rice with
Green Onions

Fresh Strawberries

Soy-Glazed Salmon with Spinach

Salmon steaks are roasted with an Asian glaze, with no added fat. Pre-washed, bagged baby spinach leaves need no cooking—the heat of the salmon served on top wilts them.

PREP *15 minutes*

ROAST *about 10 minutes*

MAKES *4 main-dish servings*

- 4 salmon steaks, ¾ inch thick (6 ounces each)
- ¼ cup reduced-sodium soy sauce
- 2 tablespoons seasoned rice vinegar
- 1 garlic clove, crushed with garlic press
- 1 tablespoon grated, peeled fresh ginger
- 1 tablespoon dark brown sugar
- 2 teaspoons cornstarch
- ⅛ teaspoon crushed red pepper
- 1 bag (6 ounces) baby spinach

1. Preheat oven to 450°F. Place salmon steaks in 13" by 9" glass baking dish. Roast 5 minutes.

2. Meanwhile, in small bowl, whisk soy sauce, vinegar, garlic, ginger, sugar, cornstarch, red pepper, and *2 tablespoons water* until blended. Pour glaze over salmon. Roast about 5 minutes longer or until salmon flakes easily when tested with a fork and glaze thickens.

3. To serve, arrange spinach on plates. Top spinach with salmon and drizzle with remaining glaze.

■ Each serving: About 280 calories, 33 g protein, 10 g carbohydrate, 11 g total fat (3 g saturated), 4 g fiber, 72 mg cholesterol, 895 mg sodium.

THURSDAY, JANUARY 17

Skillet Chicken Parmesan*

Thin Spaghetti

Lemon Ice

Skillet Chicken Parmesan

We sautéed thinly sliced chicken breasts in just a teaspoon of olive oil and used part-skim mozzarella to lighten up this family favorite.

PREP *10 minutes*

COOK *about 10 minutes*

MAKES *4 main-dish servings*

1 teaspoon olive oil
1 pound thin-sliced skinless, boneless chicken breasts
1 container (15 ounces) refrigerated marinara sauce
1 cup shredded part-skim mozzarella cheese (4 ounces)
2 plum tomatoes, chopped
2 tablespoons grated Parmesan cheese
1 cup loosely packed fresh basil leaves, sliced

1. In nonstick 12-inch skillet, heat oil over medium-high heat until hot. Add half of chicken to skillet and cook 4 minutes, turning once halfway through cooking time, until browned on both sides and just cooked through. Remove cooked chicken to plate, and repeat with remaining chicken.

2. Reduce heat to medium. Return chicken to skillet; top with marinara sauce and mozzarella. Cover skillet and cook 2 minutes or until sauce is heated through and mozzarella melts. Sprinkle with tomatoes, Parmesan, and basil.

■ Each serving: About 295 calories, 36 g protein, 10 g carbohydrate, 11 g total fat (4 g saturated), 2 g fiber, 84 mg cholesterol, 660 mg sodium.

FRIDAY, JANUARY 18

After-Work Chicken Soup*

Toasted Whole Wheat Bread

Apple Wedges Dipped in Honey

After-Work Chicken Soup

You can whip up this homey chicken soup, made with leeks and tiny bow-tie pasta, in just minutes!

PREP *15 minutes*

COOK *about 15 minutes*

MAKES *8 cups or 4 main-dish servings*

1 medium leek (about 8 ounces)
1 tablespoon olive oil
2 medium carrots, each cut lengthwise in half, then crosswise into ¼-inch-thick slices
1 medium celery stalk, thinly sliced
¼ teaspoon dried thyme
1 bay leaf
1 can (14½ ounces) chicken broth (1¾ cups)
½ cup small bow-tie pasta (2 ounces)
½ teaspoon salt
⅛ teaspoon ground black pepper
12 ounces skinless, boneless chicken-breast halves, cut crosswise into very thin slices

1. Cut off root and leaf ends from leek. Discard any tough outer leaves. Cut leek lengthwise in half, then crosswise into ¼-inch-thick slices. Place leek into bowl of *cold water;* swish leek around to remove any sand. With hand, transfer leek to colander. Repeat process, changing water several times, until all sand is removed. Drain and set aside.

2. In 4-quart saucepan, heat oil over medium-high heat until hot. Add leek, carrots, celery, thyme, and bay leaf, and cook 5 to 7 minutes or until leek wilts and vegetables are tender-crisp.

3. Add broth, pasta, salt, pepper, and *3 cups water;* heat to boiling over high heat. Reduce heat to medium-low; simmer, covered, 5 minutes or until pasta is just cooked. Increase heat to medium; add chicken pieces and cook, uncovered, 3 minutes or until chicken loses its pink color. Discard bay leaf before serving.

■ Each serving: About 220 calories, 23 g protein, 17 g carbohydrate, 6 g total fat (1 g saturated), 2 g fiber, 63 mg cholesterol, 800 mg sodium.

SATURDAY, JANUARY 19

Make-Your-Own
Burritos

SUNDAY, JANUARY 20

Jerk Pork with
Pineapple Salsa*

Red-Skinned
Potatoes

Chewy Oatmeal-
Raisin Cookies*
(recipe, page 28)

Jerk Pork with Pineapple Salsa

Store-bought seasoning mixes offer a convenient way to add an exotic touch to many dishes. Here, we've rubbed boneless chops with Jamaican jerk seasoning before a quick pan-grilling.

PREP *15 minutes*
GRILL *about 7 minutes*
MAKES *4 main-dish servings*

Pineapple Salsa
2   limes
2   cans (8 ounces each) crushed pineapple in juice, drained
½   cup loosely packed fresh cilantro leaves, chopped
1   pickled jalapeño chile, minced

Jerk Pork
4   boneless pork loin chops, ¾ inch thick (5 ounces each), well trimmed
1¼ teaspoons jerk seasoning
¼   teaspoon salt

1. Prepare Pineapple Salsa: From limes, grate ½ teaspoon peel and squeeze 2 tablespoons juice. In medium bowl, mix pineapple, cilantro, jalapeño, lime peel, and lime juice; set aside. Makes about 2 cups.
2. Prepare Jerk Pork: Rub pork chops with jerk seasoning and salt. Heat grill

pan over medium-high heat until hot. Add pork and cook 4 minutes; turn pork over and cook 3 to 4 minutes longer or until lightly browned on the outside and still slightly pink on the inside. Serve pork with salsa.

■ Each serving: About 265 calories, 34 g protein, 13 g carbohydrate, 8 g total fat (3 g saturated), 1 g fiber, 85 mg cholesterol, 360 mg sodium.

MONDAY, JANUARY 21

Soba Noodles
Primavera with
Miso*

Green Tea Ice Cream

Soba Noodles Primavera with Miso

A quick and easy Asian-inspired pasta primavera made with packaged broccoli flowerets and carrots. For a nutritional boost, we used soba noodles (Japanese buckwheat noodles) and miso (concentrated soybean paste).

PREP *20 minutes*
COOK *about 20 minutes*
MAKES *4 main-dish servings*

1   package (15 ounces) extrafirm tofu, rinsed, drained, and patted dry
    salt
1   package (8 ounces) soba noodles
1   tablespoon olive oil
1   medium red pepper, thinly sliced
1   large onion, sliced
2   garlic cloves, crushed with garlic press
1   tablespoon grated, peeled fresh ginger
¼   teaspoon crushed red pepper
1   bag (16 ounces) broccoli flowerets, cut into 1½-inch pieces
1   bag (10 ounces) shredded carrots
¼   cup red (dark) miso paste
2   green onions, thinly sliced

1. Cut tofu horizontally in half. Cut each half into 1-inch chunks; set aside.
2. Heat large saucepot of *salted water* to boiling over high heat; add noodles and cook as label directs.
3. Meanwhile, in nonstick 5- to 6-quart Dutch oven, heat oil over medium-high heat until hot. Add red pepper and onion, and cook 10 minutes or until golden, stirring occasionally. Add garlic, ginger, crushed red pepper, and tofu, and cook 1 minute, stirring.
4. To tofu mixture, add broccoli, carrots, and ¼ *cup water;* heat to boiling over medium-high heat. Reduce heat to medium; cook, covered, 7 minutes or until vegetables are tender.
5. When noodles have cooked to desired doneness, remove ¾ *cup noodle cooking water* and reserve. Drain noodles and return to saucepot. With wire whisk, mix miso paste into reserved noodle cooking water until blended.
6. To serve, toss noodles with tofu mixture, green onions, and miso-paste mixture.

■ Each serving: About 455 calories, 26 g protein, 68 g carbohydrate, 11 g total fat (2 g saturated), 11 g fiber, 0 mg cholesterol, 1,290 mg sodium.

Sweet-Potato & Black-Bean Stew

A vegetable stew that's fragrant with orange and oregano. It's cooked in a pressure cooker, which allows you to have dinner on the table in minutes.

PREP *20 minutes*
COOK *4 minutes plus bringing up to pressure*
MAKES *about 8 cups or 4 main-dish servings*

 1 medium orange
 2 pounds sweet potatoes (about 4 medium), peeled and cut into 1½-inch chunks
 2 cans (15 to 19 ounces each) black beans, rinsed and drained
 1 can (14½ ounces) vegetable broth or chicken broth (1¾ cups)
 1 large onion, cut in half and thinly sliced
 2 medium peppers (red and/or green), thinly sliced
 2 garlic cloves, crushed with garlic press
 ½ teaspoon salt
 ½ teaspoon dried oregano
 ⅛ teaspoon crushed red pepper
 1 cup loosely packed fresh cilantro leaves, chopped

1. From orange, grate ½ teaspoon peel and squeeze 2 tablespoons juice.
2. In 6-quart pressure cooker, place orange peel and remaining ingredients except cilantro and orange juice. Following manufacturer's directions, cover pressure cooker, bring up to pressure, and cook under pressure

4 minutes. Release pressure quickly, as manufacturer directs. Stir in cilantro and orange juice.

■ Each serving: About 400 calories, 16 g protein, 93 g carbohydrate, 1 g total fat (0 g saturated), 19 g fiber, 0 mg cholesterol, 1,305 mg sodium.

Indian-Style Shrimp

What makes this dish so deceptively rich-tasting? The secret ingredient is evaporated nonfat milk with a touch of cornstarch added for more body.

PREP *20 minutes*
COOK *about 20 minutes*
MAKES *4 main-dish servings*

    salt
 8 ounces (1⅓ cups) orzo pasta
 1 can (14½ ounces) chicken broth (1¾ cups)
 1 cup undiluted evaporated nonfat milk
 2 teaspoons cornstarch
 1 tablespoon olive oil
 1 medium onion, cut into ¼-inch dice
1½ teaspoons curry powder
 ½ teaspoon ground cumin
 1 pound shelled and deveined fresh or frozen (thawed) shrimp
 1 package (10 ounces) frozen peas
 ½ cup packed fresh cilantro leaves, chopped
    nonfat yogurt (optional)

1. Heat large saucepot of *salted water* to boiling over high heat; add orzo and cook as label directs. In small bowl, stir broth, milk, and cornstarch until blended; set aside.
2. Meanwhile, in nonstick 12-inch skillet, heat oil over medium heat until hot. Add onion and cook 8 minutes or until tender, stirring occasionally. Add curry, cumin, and ½ teaspoon salt, and cook 1 minute. Increase heat to medium-high; add shrimp and cook 4 minutes or just until shrimp turn opaque throughout, stirring often. Stir broth mixture to blend, then pour mixture into skillet; heat to boiling. Boil 1 minute.
3. Place peas in colander; drain orzo over peas. Transfer orzo mixture to shallow serving bowl; top with shrimp mixture and chopped cilantro, and toss gently to combine. Serve with yogurt if you like.

■ Each serving: About 500 calories, 41 g protein, 66 g carbohydrate, 8 g total fat (1 g saturated), 6 g fiber, 175 mg cholesterol, 1,135 mg sodium.

THURSDAY, JANUARY 24

Leftovers

FRIDAY, JANUARY 25

Fiesta Potatoes*

Coleslaw with
Vinaigrette Dressing

Dulce de Leche
Frozen
Lowfat Yogurt

Fiesta Potatoes

Salsa and black beans add no-fat flavor to microwaved "baked" potatoes.

PREP **20 minutes**
MICROWAVE **10 to 12 minutes**
MAKES **4 main-dish servings**

    4   medium baking potatoes
         (about 10 ounces each)
    2   teaspoons olive oil
    1   medium onion, chopped
    2   teaspoons ground cumin
    1   garlic clove, crushed with
         garlic press
    1   jar (16 ounces) mild salsa
    1   can (15 to 19 ounces) black
         beans, rinsed and drained
   ½   cup packed fresh cilantro
         leaves, chopped
         plain nonfat yogurt (optional)
         diced avocado (optional)

1. With fork or paring knife, pierce potatoes several times to allow steam to escape during cooking. Place potatoes on paper towel in microwave oven. Cook on High 10 to 12 minutes or until potatoes are fork-tender.
2. Meanwhile, in 2-quart saucepan, heat oil over medium heat until hot. Add onion and cook 10 minutes or until tender and golden. Add cumin and garlic, and cook 1 minute, stirring. Add salsa and beans, and cook 5 minutes or until heated through.
3. Cut each potato lengthwise almost in

half. Top each with one-fourth of bean mixture; sprinkle with cilantro. Serve with yogurt and avocado if you like.

■ Each serving: About 400 calories, 13 g protein, 88 g carbohydrate, 3 g total fat (0 g saturated), 15 g fiber, 0 mg cholesterol, 795 mg sodium.

SATURDAY, JANUARY 26

Rotisserie Chicken
Night

GREAT FOR
SUPER BOWL SUNDAY
JANUARY 27

Avocado & Pea
Guacamole*

Super Bowl Chili*

Spicy Corn Bread*

Romaine & Cherry-
Tomato Salad with
Buttermilk Dressing*
(recipe, page 24)

Carrot Cake*
(recipe, page 24)

Avocado & Pea Guacamole

pictured on page 37

Guests will gobble up this dip and never know it's low fat. Serve with baked tortilla chips and fresh veggies.

PREP **15 minutes**
MAKES **about 2½ cups**

    1   package (10 ounces) frozen peas,
         thawed
    1   ripe avocado, peeled and pitted
   ⅓   cup plain nonfat yogurt
   ⅓   cup jarred medium-hot salsa
    3   tablespoons fresh lime juice
   ½   cup loosely packed fresh cilantro
         leaves, chopped
   ½   teaspoon salt

1. In food processor, with knife blade attached, pulse peas until almost smooth; set aside.
2. In medium bowl, with fork, mash avocado. Add peas and remaining ingredients to mashed avocado; stir until evenly mixed. Cover and refrigerate if not serving right away.

■ Each tablespoon: About 15 calories, 1 g protein, 2 g carbohydrate, 1 g total fat (0 g saturated), 1 g fiber, 0 mg cholesterol, 45 mg sodium.

Super Bowl Chili

pictured on page 37

This recipe for Texas-style chili contains small *chunks* of beef, not ground. The classic version doesn't contain beans, but we replaced a portion of the meat with red kidney beans to cut some fat.

PREP **30 minutes**
COOK **about 2 hours**
MAKES **about 14 cups or 12 main-dish servings**

    2   tablespoons olive oil
    2   pounds boneless beef for stew, cut
         into ½-inch chunks
    4   garlic cloves, crushed with garlic
         press
    2   red peppers, cut into ½-inch dice
    2   jalapeño chiles, seeded and minced
    1   large onion, chopped
   ⅓   cup chili powder
    2   cans (28 ounces each) whole
         tomatoes in puree
    1   can (6 ounces) tomato paste
   ¼   cup sugar
    2   teaspoons salt
    2   teaspoons dried oregano
    2   cans (15 to 19 ounces each) red
         kidney beans, rinsed and drained

1. In 8-quart saucepot or Dutch oven, heat 1 teaspoon oil over high heat until hot. Add one-third of beef and cook until browned on all sides and liquid evaporates, 6 to 8 minutes, stirring often. With slotted spoon, transfer beef to bowl. Repeat with remaining beef, using 1 teaspoon oil per batch; set aside.

2. Add remaining 1 tablespoon oil to drippings in saucepot and heat over medium-high heat until hot. Stir in garlic, red peppers, jalapeños, and onion; cook until vegetables are tender, about 10 minutes, stirring occasionally. Stir in chili powder; cook 1 minute.

3. Return beef to saucepot. Stir in tomatoes with their puree, tomato paste, sugar, salt, oregano, and *2 cups water,* breaking up tomatoes with side of spoon. Heat to boiling over high heat. Reduce heat to low; cover and simmer 1 hour and 30 minutes. Stir in beans and cook 10 to 30 minutes longer or until meat is fork-tender, stirring occasionally.

■ Each serving: About 275 calories, 25 g protein, 30 g carbohydrate, 7 g total fat (2 g saturated), 11 g fiber, 36 mg cholesterol, 1,115 mg sodium.

Spicy Corn Bread
pictured on page 37

This deliciously moist and tender bread is best served warm. If you like, you can make it ahead and reheat it right in the baking pan, covered, at 400°F. for 20 minutes.

PREP *10 minutes*
BAKE *25 minutes*
MAKES *24 servings*

1¾ cups all-purpose flour
  2 cups yellow cornmeal
  ¼ cup sugar
  1 tablespoon plus 1 teaspoon
     baking powder
  ¾ teaspoon salt
  ½ teaspoon ground black pepper
  6 tablespoons cold butter or
     margarine (¾ stick), cut up
  1 can (14 ounces) cream-style corn
  2 large eggs, beaten
  4 green onions, sliced

1. Preheat oven to 400°F. Grease 13" by 9" metal baking pan.

2. In large bowl, mix flour, cornmeal, sugar, baking powder, salt, and pepper. With pastry blender or 2 knives used scissor-fashion, cut in butter until mixture resembles fine crumbs. With fork, stir corn, eggs, and green onions into flour mixture just until blended (batter will be very stiff).

3. Spoon batter into baking pan; spread evenly. Bake corn bread 25 minutes or until toothpick inserted in center comes out clean. Cool in pan on wire rack 10 minutes to serve warm, or cool completely in pan to serve later.

4. Cut lengthwise into 4 strips, then cut each strip crosswise into 6 pieces. Reheat before serving if you like.

■ Each serving: About 130 calories, 3 g protein, 21 g carbohydrate, 4 g total fat (2 g saturated), 1 g fiber, 24 mg cholesterol, 235 mg sodium.

surprising good-for-you foods

BUTTERMILK Originally, buttermilk was the liquid remaining after cream was churned into butter, but today it's made by adding lactic acid–producing bacteria and nonfat milk solids to pasteurized milk. Buttermilk can be made from whole milk, but the more popular varieties are low-fat (1% fat) and reduced-fat (1.5% fat).

CREAM-STYLE CORN There was cream in your great-grandma's recipe, but the liquid in today's cans is actually a component of the corn kernels themselves and other ingredients such as starch. If you look at calories and fat, canned cream-style and whole-kernel corn are identical.

PORK Lean cuts (tenderloin, boneless loin chops) compare favorably with skinless chicken. So, if your family is crying "fowl," vary the menu with these healthy cuts of pork.

SALMON Yes, half of its calories come from fat, but it's the heart-healthy omega-3 type (often called fish oil). Some studies indicate omega-3 fats reduce the likelihood of blood clots that can lead to heart attacks or stroke.

EGGS One large egg is a significant source of a number of vitamins and minerals, and contains only 75 calories and 5 grams of fat. Moreover, most of this fat is the healthy, unsaturated variety. (Eggs are high in cholesterol, but the chief villain in raising blood-cholesterol levels is not the cholesterol in our diets, but saturated fats.) Also, egg yolks are rich in the pigment zeaxanthin, which seems to help protect eyes from macular degeneration, a leading cause of blindness in people older than 65.

CHICKEN THIGHS They are higher in fat and calories than breasts, but as long as you remove the skin and any excess fat, economical thighs fit into a good-for-you diet. They also provide 25 percent more iron and more than twice as much zinc as the same amount of breast meat.

FROZEN/CANNED FRUITS AND VEGETABLES We agree that fresh, locally grown produce can't be beat, but frozen and canned fruits and vegetables compare favorably (in terms of nutrition), providing an array of vitamins, minerals, and phytochemicals, as well as fiber.

BEEF TENDERLOIN STEAKS Ounce for ounce, this tender cut has about the same calorie and fat content as skinless chicken thighs. The key is portion size. At home, count a ¾-inch-thick steak (about 3½ ounces) as a single serving. At steak houses, order the petit filet mignon.

Romaine & Cherry-Tomato Salad with Buttermilk Dressing

pictured on page 37

Combining packaged prechopped romaine with shredded carrots and red cabbage makes this recipe a snap to toss together for your party.

PREP *10 minutes*
MAKES *20 cups or 12 accompaniment servings*

Buttermilk Dressing
¾ cup buttermilk
¼ cup light mayonnaise
1 tablespoon lemon juice
1 large bunch chives, chopped (⅓ cup)
½ teaspoon salt
¼ teaspoon ground black pepper

3 bags (10 ounces each) romaine lettuce salad
1 pint (12 ounces) cherry tomatoes, each cut in half

1. Prepare Buttermilk Dressing: In small bowl, with wire whisk, mix buttermilk, mayonnaise, lemon juice, chopped chives, salt, and pepper until blended. Refrigerate dressing until ready to serve or up to 2 days. Makes about 1 cup.
2. To serve, in large bowl, toss romaine salad and tomatoes with Buttermilk Dressing.

■ Each serving: About 45 calories, 2 g protein, 5 g carbohydrate, 2 g total fat (0 g saturated), 1 g fiber, 2 mg cholesterol, 160 mg sodium.

the healthiest cooking methods

Grilling and **broiling** are the only methods that use direct heat. When food is grilled, it's cooked above the heat source, for example on a rack over coals or on a stovetop grill; it requires no additional fat. (See Jerk Pork with Pineapple Salsa, page 20.) When food is broiled, it's cooked below the heat source. These methods are best for items less than 1 inch thick; thicker foods may burn on the outside before they cook through. In addition to traditional beef and chicken, try grilling seafood, vegetables, fruits, flat breads, and pizzas.

Roasting uses dry heat to cook foods in an enclosed environment (oven). It's usually done at a high temperature (450°F. or more) to create a golden-brown crust on food while also cooking the center. (See Soy-Glazed Salmon with Spinach, page 18.) **Baking** is typically done at a lower temperature.

Steaming is the best method for retaining a food's color, texture, and nutrients. Food items are placed in a wire steaming basket or on a rack over boiling or simmering liquid in a covered pot. For pan-steaming, you cook the food item in a small amount of simmering, flavorful liquid. By the time the food has finished cooking, the reduced liquid has become a fat-free sauce. Pan-steaming is usually used for vegetables, but you can try the technique for fish fillets too. (See Steamed Scrod Fillets, page 13.)

Poaching gently cooks food in liquid (usually water, broth, wine, juice, or milk) kept just below the boiling point (between 160° and 180°F.). Fish and chicken breasts are popular choices, but poaching also works well with pork or beef tenderloins or eye-round roasts. (See Poached Chicken Piccata, page 26.)

Carrot Cake

We took one of our favorite carrot cake recipes and reduced the oil by half—but didn't even miss it because we added crushed pineapple for moistness. If you want to cut calories and fat even more, omit the frosting and sprinkle cake with confectioners' sugar when ready to serve. You will save 50 calories and 3 grams of fat per serving.

PREP *20 minutes plus cooling*
BAKE *50 to 55 minutes*
MAKES *20 servings*

Carrot Cake
2¼ cups all-purpose flour
2 teaspoons baking soda
2 teaspoons ground cinnamon
1 teaspoon baking powder
1 teaspoon salt
½ teaspoon ground nutmeg
2 large eggs
2 large egg whites
1 cup granulated sugar
¾ cup packed light brown sugar
1 can (8 to 8¼ ounces) crushed pineapple in juice
½ cup vegetable oil
1 tablespoon vanilla extract
1 bag (10 ounces) shredded carrots (about 3 cups)

Cream-Cheese Frosting
4 ounces light cream cheese (Neufchâtel)
1 cup confectioners' sugar
2 tablespoons margarine or butter, softened
1 teaspoon vanilla extract

1. Prepare Carrot Cake: Preheat oven to 350°F. Grease 13" by 9" metal baking pan. Line bottom with waxed paper; grease paper and dust with flour.

2. In medium bowl, combine flour, baking soda, cinnamon, baking powder, salt, and nutmeg.

3. In large bowl, with mixer at medium speed, beat eggs and egg whites until blended. Gradually add sugars. Increase speed to medium-high; beat 2 minutes, frequently scraping bowl with rubber spatula. Beat in pineapple with its juice, oil, and vanilla. Reduce speed to low; add flour mixture and beat 1 minute to blend. Fold in carrots.

4. Pour batter into pan. Bake 50 to 55 minutes or until toothpick inserted in center of cake comes out clean with a few moist crumbs attached. Cool cake in pan on wire rack 10 minutes. Invert cake onto rack and remove waxed paper. Cool cake completely on rack.

5. Meanwhile, prepare Cream-Cheese Frosting: In small bowl, with mixer at low speed, beat cream cheese, confectioners' sugar, margarine, and vanilla until blended. Increase speed to medium; beat until smooth.

6. Transfer cake to large platter or tray. Spread frosting over top of cake. If not serving cake right away, store in refrigerator until ready to serve. Let cake stand at room temperature 30 minutes before serving.

■ Each serving: About 240 calories, 3 g protein, 38 g carbohydrate, 9 g total fat (2 g saturated), 1 g fiber, 26 mg cholesterol, 320 mg sodium.

MONDAY, JANUARY 28
Chinese Takeout

TUESDAY, JANUARY 29
Potato-Dill Frittata*
Spinach Salad
Broiled Grapefruit Halves

Potato-Dill Frittata

Made with almost all egg whites, this baked omelet is filled with Yukon gold potatoes, peas, cottage cheese, and fresh dill. Enjoy it without feeling guilty. Complete the meal with a salad and fruit for a family-pleasing dinner.

PREP *25 minutes*
BAKE *about 15 minutes*
MAKES *4 main-dish servings*

- 2 teaspoons olive oil
- 1 medium onion, chopped
- 2 medium Yukon gold potatoes (about ¾ pound), unpeeled and cut into ½-inch pieces
- ⅛ teaspoon ground black pepper
- ¾ teaspoon salt
- 1 cup frozen peas
- 8 large egg whites (1 cup)
- 2 large eggs
- 1 container (8 ounces) low-fat (1%) cottage cheese
- ⅓ cup nonfat milk
- 2 tablespoons chopped fresh dill

1. Preheat oven to 425°F. In nonstick 10-inch skillet with heat-safe handle (or, wrap handle with double thickness of heavy-duty foil for baking in oven later), heat oil over medium heat until hot. Add onion, potatoes, pepper, and ¼ teaspoon salt, and cook,

covered, about 8 minutes or until potatoes are tender, stirring occasionally. Stir in frozen peas.

2. Meanwhile, in large bowl, with wire whisk or fork, beat egg whites, whole eggs, cottage cheese, milk, dill, and remaining ½ teaspoon salt until blended.

3. Pour egg mixture over potato mixture; cover and cook 5 to 7 minutes or until set around edge. Uncover skillet and place in oven. Bake 12 to 15 minutes or until frittata is set in center. If you like, invert frittata onto round platter. Cut into wedges to serve.

■ Each serving: About 250 calories, 22 g protein, 28 g carbohydrate, 6 g total fat (2 g saturated), 4 g fiber, 109 mg cholesterol, 865 mg sodium.

WEDNESDAY,
JANUARY 30

Turkey Cutlets
à l'Orange*

Rice & Peas

"Baked" Apples*
(recipe, page 27)

Turkey Cutlets à l'Orange

You can have dinner on the table in less than 30 minutes with this delicious dish. A brandy-spiked orange sauce adds the right touch to quick-cooking turkey cutlets. A side dish of rice and peas accompanies the saucy dish nicely.

PREP *10 minutes*
COOK *about 10 minutes*
MAKES *4 main-dish servings*

2 large navel oranges
½ cup chicken broth
2 tablespoons brandy
2 tablespoons orange marmalade
1½ teaspoons cornstarch
2 teaspoons olive oil
4 turkey-breast cutlets (about 1 pound)
½ teaspoon salt
¼ teaspoon ground black pepper
parsley sprigs for garnish

1. From 1 orange, squeeze ⅓ cup juice. Cut remaining orange into ¼-inch-thick slices. In cup, stir orange juice, broth, brandy, marmalade, and cornstarch until blended; set aside.

2. In nonstick 12-inch skillet, heat oil over medium-high heat until hot. Add turkey cutlets; sprinkle with salt and pepper. Cook cutlets 5 to 8 minutes or until lightly browned on the outside and no longer pink on the inside, turning over once. Transfer cutlets to platter; keep warm.

3. Add orange slices to skillet; cook 2 minutes. Transfer orange slices to platter with cutlets. Stir juice mixture to blend; add to skillet and heat to boiling. Boil orange sauce 1 minute; pour over cutlets. Garnish with parsley sprigs.

■ Each serving: About 210 calories, 29 g protein, 14 g carbohydrate, 3 g total fat (1 g saturated), 1 g fiber, 70 mg cholesterol, 480 mg sodium.

THURSDAY, JANUARY 31

Poached
Chicken Piccata*

Steamed Frozen
Mixed Vegetables

Whole Wheat
Couscous

Poached Chicken Piccata

Poaching keeps these chicken breasts moist and juicy. Reserve the flavorful poaching broth to use as the base for making the piquant lemon-and-caper sauce.

PREP *10 minutes*
COOK *about 12 minutes*
MAKES *4 main-dish servings*

1 bay leaf
½ teaspoon salt
4 small skinless, boneless chicken-breast halves (1 pound)
1 lemon, thinly sliced
2 teaspoons cornstarch
3 tablespoons capers, drained
2 teaspoons margarine or butter (optional)

1. In 10-inch skillet, heat *1½ cups water* to boiling over high heat. Add bay leaf, salt, chicken, and 2 lemon slices; heat to boiling. Reduce heat to low; cover and simmer 10 to 12 minutes or until chicken loses its pink color throughout. With slotted spoon, transfer chicken to platter; keep warm.

2. Drain poaching liquid through coarse sieve set over medium bowl; discard solids. Return poaching liquid to skillet. In cup, mix cornstarch with *1 tablespoon water.* With wire whisk, beat cornstarch mixture into poaching liquid until blended; heat to boiling over high heat. Add capers; cook 1 minute, stirring constantly. Stir in margarine if you like. Pour caper sauce over chicken and garnish with remaining lemon slices.

■ Each serving: About 130 calories, 26 g protein, 2 g carbohydrate, 2 g total fat (0 g saturated), 0 g fiber, 66 mg cholesterol, 555 mg sodium.

light desserts

Finish off your meals with guilt-free desserts that skimp on calories and fat, but not on flavor.

Warm Chocolate-Banana Cake

Chocolate lovers won't feel deprived when they indulge in this rich-tasting brownielike cake. It comes hot from the oven with a fudgy sauce on top made from brown sugar and cocoa. Serve the warm cake with fat-free vanilla ice cream, if you like.

PREP **15 minutes**
BAKE **35 minutes**
MAKES **8 servings**

- 1 cup all-purpose flour
- ½ cup granulated sugar
- 1 teaspoon baking powder
- ½ teaspoon salt
- ¼ teaspoon ground cinnamon
- ¾ cup plus ¼ cup unsweetened cocoa
- 2 tablespoons butter or margarine
- 1 ripe large banana, mashed (½ cup)
- 1 large egg, beaten
- 1 teaspoon vanilla extract
- ½ cup packed dark brown sugar

1. Preheat oven to 350°F. In large bowl, combine flour, granulated sugar, baking powder, salt, cinnamon, and ¾ cup cocoa.

2. In 1-quart saucepan, melt butter over medium heat. Remove saucepan from heat and stir in banana, egg, vanilla, and *¼ cup water* until blended.

3. Stir banana mixture into flour mixture just until blended (batter will be thick). Spoon batter into ungreased 8" by 8" glass baking dish; spread evenly.

4. In same bowl, with wire whisk, beat brown sugar, remaining ¼ cup cocoa, and *1¼ cups boiling water* until well blended. Pour mixture over chocolate batter in baking dish; do not stir.

5. Bake 35 minutes (dessert should have some fudgy sauce on top). Cool in pan on wire rack 5 minutes. Serve cake warm.

■ Each serving: About 235 calories, 5 g protein, 47 g carbohydrate, 5 g total fat (3 g saturated), 4 g fiber, 35 mg cholesterol, 240 mg sodium.

"Baked" Apples

Cooking these plump, fruit-filled apples in the microwave oven saves lots of time without sacrificing a bit of flavor—and provides a delicious, warm, low-fat dessert in the middle of winter.

PREP **10 minutes**
MICROWAVE **8 minutes**
MAKES **4 servings**

- 4 large Golden Delicious apples (about 8 ounces each)
- ¼ cup pitted prunes, chopped
- 2 tablespoons golden raisins
- 2 tablespoons brown sugar
- 2 teaspoons margarine or butter, softened
- ½ teaspoon ground cinnamon pinch salt

1. Core apples, cutting a 1¼-inch diameter cylinder from center of each, almost but not all the way through to bottom. Place apples in 8" by 8" glass baking dish or shallow 1½-quart microwave-safe casserole.

2. In small bowl, combine prunes, raisins, sugar, margarine, cinnamon, and salt. Fill each cored apple with equal amounts of prune mixture.

3. Cook apples, covered, in microwave oven on High 8 minutes or until tender. Spoon any juices from baking dish over apples before serving.

■ Each serving: About 185 calories, 1 g protein, 44 g carbohydrate, 3 g total fat (0 g saturated), 6 g fiber, 0 mg cholesterol, 65 mg sodium.

Chewy Oatmeal-Raisin Cookies

We made these cookies with olive oil and egg whites, but no one will guess these cookie-jar treats are guilt-free.

PREP *30 minutes plus cooling*
BAKE *10 to 12 minutes per batch*
MAKES *about 3½ dozen cookies*

    nonstick cooking spray
2 cups all-purpose flour
1 cup quick-cooking or old-fashioned oats, uncooked
1 cup dark seedless raisins
¾ cup packed dark brown sugar
½ cup granulated sugar
1 teaspoon baking soda
½ teaspoon salt
¼ cup extralight olive oil
2 teaspoons vanilla extract
4 large egg whites

1. Preheat oven to 375°F. Coat large cookie sheet with nonstick cooking spray.
2. In medium bowl, combine flour, oats, raisins, sugars, baking soda, and salt; set aside. With spoon, stir in oil, vanilla, and egg whites, and mix just until evenly moistened.
3. Drop dough by level tablespoons (dough will be sticky), 2 inches apart, on cookie sheet. Bake cookies 10 to 12 minutes or until lightly browned around the edges. Transfer cookies to wire rack to cool completely. Repeat with remaining dough. Store cookies in tightly covered container up to 1 week.

■ Each cookie: About 85 calories, 2 g protein, 16 g carbohydrate, 2 g total fat (0 g saturated), 1 g fiber, 0 mg cholesterol, 65 mg sodium.

Raspberry Soufflé

pictured on page 39

This impressive fat-free dessert is easier to make than you think; just fold store-bought raspberry fruit spread into beaten egg whites and bake. To do ahead, prepare and refrigerate soufflé mixture in soufflé dish up to three hours, then bake as directed just before serving.

PREP *20 minutes*
BAKE *15 to 18 minutes*
MAKES *6 servings*

⅔ cup seedless raspberry spreadable fruit (no-sugar-added jam)
1 tablespoon fresh lemon juice
4 large egg whites (½ cup)
½ teaspoon cream of tartar
1 teaspoon vanilla extract
2 tablespoons sugar

1. Preheat oven to 375°F. In large bowl, with wire whisk, beat raspberry fruit spread with lemon juice; set aside.
2. In small bowl, with mixer at high speed, beat egg whites and cream of tartar until whites begin to mound. Beat in vanilla. Gradually add sugar, beating until sugar dissolves and whites stand in stiff peaks when beaters are lifted.
3. With rubber spatula, fold one-third of whites into raspberry mixture until well blended, then fold in remaining whites. Spoon mixture into 1½-quart soufflé dish; gently spread evenly.
4. Bake 15 to 18 minutes or until soufflé is puffed and lightly browned. Serve immediately.

■ Each serving: About 75 calories, 3 g protein, 16 g carbohydrate, 0 g total fat, 1 g fiber, 0 mg cholesterol, 35 mg sodium.

February

15 minutes to dinner

Fast, fresh, home-cooked meals with the help of a few convenience foods

If you're preparing fewer and fewer meals from scratch, you're not alone. Although American families aren't eating out any more than we did ten years ago, we're not sitting down to home-cooked dinners either. Instead, we're relying on takeout, reheatable entrées, and those ever-dependable cans of soup. It all comes down to time: You'd like to serve fresh meals, you tell us, but you just don't have the hours it takes to shop, chop, and cook.

You don't need hours. The *Good Housekeeping* food department has scouted out the best shortcuts—foods and tools—to get you out of the kitchen fast. To hold to our promise of flavorful recipes that you can make in 15 minutes, we shopped regular supermarket aisles, testing (and tasting) all manner of "helpers." You'll find old standbys—fresh pasta, bagged slaw mix—used in new ways. And you'll find recipes featuring products recently introduced to the market: marinated meats, flavored sauces, spice blends, canned seasoned tomatoes. On page 34, we list our favorite convenience foods and give you tips on ways to use them for fast meals.

Thai Shrimp & Noodles

pictured on page 42

Frozen shrimp and a Thai seasoning blend make it possible to whip up this homemade soup in no time.

TOTAL TIME *15 minutes*
MAKES *8 cups or 4 main-dish servings*

- 1 container (32 ounces) chicken broth
- 1 tablespoon Thai seasoning
- 4 ounces thin rice noodles (⅛ inch thick)
- 12 ounces fresh or frozen shelled and deveined raw shrimp
- ¼ cup fresh lime juice
- 2 green onions, thinly sliced lime wedges (optional)

1. In 3-quart saucepan, heat broth, Thai seasoning, and 2 cups water to boiling over high heat.
2. Add rice noodles and shrimp; heat to boiling. Stir in lime juice and green onions. Serve with lime wedges.

■ Each serving: About 225 calories, 20 g protein, 28 g carbohydrate, 4 g total fat (1 g saturated), 0 g fiber, 129 mg cholesterol, 1,385 mg sodium.

Fettuccine with Creamy Tomato Sauce & Peas

Fresh pasta is tossed with tomato sauce simmered with heavy cream.

TOTAL TIME *15 minutes*
MAKES *4 main-dish servings*

- 2 packages (9 ounces each) fresh (refrigerated) fettuccine
- 2 teaspoons salt
- 1 can (14½ ounces) seasoned chunky tomatoes for pasta
- 1 can (15 ounces) tomato sauce
- ⅓ cup heavy or whipping cream
- 1 package (10 ounces) frozen peas grated Parmesan cheese (optional)

1. In large saucepot, heat *5 quarts water* to boiling over high heat. Add pasta and salt; cook as label directs.
2. Meanwhile, in 2-quart saucepan, heat tomatoes, tomato sauce, and cream to boiling over medium-high heat. Reduce heat to medium and cook 2 minutes, stirring.
3. Place frozen peas in colander. Drain fettuccine over peas. In large serving bowl, toss fettuccine and peas with tomato mixture. Serve with Parmesan if you like.

■ Each serving: About 575 calories, 22 g protein, 96 g carbohydrate, 13 g total fat (6 g saturated), 9 g fiber, 158 mg cholesterol, 1,375 mg sodium.

Couscous with Garbanzo Beans

A vegetarian entrée fragrant with the flavors of Morocco—warm spices, green olives, and garlic—gets a quick start from seasoned couscous mix.

TOTAL TIME *15 minutes*
MAKES *4 main-dish servings*

- 1 box (5.6 ounces) couscous (Moroccan pasta) with toasted pine nuts
- ⅓ cup dark seedless raisins
- 1 tablespoon olive oil
- 1 medium zucchini (about 10 ounces), cut lengthwise in half, then crosswise into ½-inch pieces
- 1 garlic clove, crushed with garlic press
- ¾ teaspoon ground cumin
- ¾ teaspoon ground coriander
- ⅛ teaspoon ground red pepper (cayenne)
- 2 cans (15 to 19 ounces each) garbanzo beans, rinsed and drained
- ½ cup salad olives, drained, or chopped pimiento-stuffed olives
  parsley sprigs for garnish

1. Prepare couscous as label directs except add raisins to cooking water.
2. Meanwhile, in nonstick 12-inch skillet, heat oil over medium-high heat until hot. Add zucchini and cook 5 minutes, stirring occasionally. Add garlic, cumin, coriander, and pepper, and cook 30 seconds, stirring. Add beans, olives, and *¼ cup water,* and cook 5 minutes to heat through, stirring often.
3. Add cooked couscous to bean mixture and toss gently. Spoon into serving bowl; garnish with parsley sprigs.

■ Each serving: About 555 calories, 20 g protein, 101 g carbohydrate, 10 g total fat (1 g saturated), 15 g fiber, 0 mg cholesterol, 1,110 mg sodium.

food editor's Q&A

Q The baby spinach leaves sold in bags in the supermarket are so flat and delicate. Are they the same as the coarse, curly spinach leaves sold in bunches?

a There are 2 basic varieties of spinach. One has a thicker leaf that is crinkled (curly), and the other has a smaller, smooth leaf. Bagged baby spinach could be either variety harvested at a young age. Because they're tender and have a mild flavor, they're the perfect choice for a spinach salad or quick sauté.

Q If I buy quick-cooking brown rice, will I be sacrificing nutrients?

a Not at all. Instant brown rice—ready to eat in 10 minutes—and the longer-cooking version are both whole grains. Compared with refined grains (including white rice), they contain more antioxidants, such as vitamin E and selenium; more minerals, such as potassium, magnesium, copper, and zinc; and more fiber. Because instant brown rice is parboiled, the outer husk or bran is open, which makes the grains more porous. That enables water to be absorbed quickly the second time around. It is lighter in color and has a fluffier texture.

Q I'm confused. What's the difference among the varieties of smoked salmon you find in the market?

a Nova is cold-smoked (using relatively low temperatures ranging from 70° to 90° F.) for anywhere from 1 day to 3 weeks. Because this process doesn't fully cook the salmon, it's cured beforehand with salt and sometimes sugar. The result is a shiny, translucent fish with a mild flavor. Lox is cured in sugar and brine and sometimes lightly smoked as well, producing the saltier, Jewish-American style of smoked salmon. Both are delicious eaten on bagels spread with cream cheese. Scottish-style salmon is cold-smoked for a longer period of time, yielding a firmer outer flesh that makes it ideal for serving in thin slices on brown bread. The hot-smoking process (at 120° to 180° F.) takes 6 to 12 hours, producing a cooked salmon, known as Northwest-style, that is firm and opaque with a flaky texture. Serve on crackers as an appetizer or use in a fresh fish pâté. Whatever type of salmon you buy, unless it's vacuum-packed, store it in the refrigerator and use within a week. Salmon can also be frozen, tightly wrapped, for up to a month, but its texture may change slightly.

Curried Pork Medallions

A simple skillet dinner: Tender slices of pork are flavored with curry and apple, and tossed with baby carrots.

TOTAL TIME *15 minutes*
MAKES *4 main-dish servings*

- 1 bag (16 ounces) peeled baby carrots
- 1 tablespoon olive oil
- 1 medium Gala or Golden Delicious apple, unpeeled, cored, and cut into ½-inch dice
- 2 teaspoons curry powder
- 1 garlic clove, crushed with garlic press
- 1 pork tenderloin (about 1 pound), cut into ¾-inch-thick slices
- ½ teaspoon salt
- ¼ cup apple cider or apple juice

1. Place carrots in covered microwavable dish with *¼ cup water*. Cook in microwave oven on High 6 minutes or until carrots are tender.
2. Meanwhile, in nonstick 12-inch skillet, heat oil over medium-high heat. Add apple, curry powder, and garlic, and cook 1 minute, stirring.
3. Add pork and salt, and cook 6 to 8 minutes or until pork is still slightly pink in center. Add cider and cooked carrots with any liquid, and heat to boiling; cook 1 minute.

■ Each serving: About 250 calories, 25 g protein, 17 g carbohydrate, 9 g total fat (2 g saturated), 3 g fiber, 71 mg cholesterol, 390 mg sodium.

Teriyaki Salmon

A luscious topping for salmon, this Japanese-style glaze also partners well with brown rice and spinach.

TOTAL TIME *15 minutes*
MAKES *4 main-dish servings*

- ¼ cup plus 2 tablespoons bottled teriyaki baste and glaze sauce
- 4 pieces skinless salmon fillet (about 6 ounces each)
- 1 package (10 ounces) frozen chopped spinach
- 1½ cups instant brown rice
  parsley sprigs for garnish

1. Preheat oven to 475°F. Line bottom of 15½" by 10½" jelly-roll pan with foil. Pour ¼ cup teriyaki glaze into center of pan. Place salmon in pan, turning to coat with glaze. Bake about 10 minutes or until fish flakes easily when tested with a fork.
2. Meanwhile, in 3-quart saucepan, heat frozen spinach and *1½ cups water* to boiling over high heat (spinach will not thaw completely). Stir in rice and cook, covered, 10 minutes or until all liquid is absorbed.
3. In cup, mix remaining 2 tablespoons teriyaki glaze with *¼ cup water* until blended. Pour teriyaki mixture into cooked rice mixture and toss to combine. Garnish salmon with parsley sprigs; serve with rice mixture.

■ Each serving: About 460 calories, 42 g protein, 35 g carbohydrate, 16 g total fat (3 g saturated), 3 g fiber, 117 mg cholesterol, 800 mg sodium.

Linguine with Tuna & Broccoli

Instead of white clam sauce, substitute canned tuna cooked with garlic, hot pepper, and white wine for a savory pasta dish.

TOTAL TIME *15 minutes*
MAKES *4 main-dish servings*

- 2 packages (9 ounces each) fresh (refrigerated) linguine
- 2 packages (10 ounces each) frozen broccoli cuts
  salt
- 2 tablespoons olive oil
- 3 garlic cloves, crushed with garlic press
- ¼ teaspoon crushed red pepper
- ¼ cup dry white wine
- 1 can (12 ounces) tuna packed in water, drained

1. In large saucepot, heat *5 quarts water* to boiling over high heat. Add pasta, broccoli, and 2 teaspoons salt; cook 2 to 3 minutes or until linguine and broccoli are tender.
2. Meanwhile, in nonstick 10-inch skillet, heat oil over medium-high heat until hot. Add garlic and crushed red pepper, and cook 1 minute, stirring. Add wine and heat to boiling; boil 1 minute, stirring. Stir in tuna and cook 30 seconds.
3. When linguine is cooked, remove *½ cup pasta cooking water;* reserve. Drain linguine and broccoli and return to saucepot. Add tuna mixture, *½ teaspoon salt,* and reserved pasta cooking water; toss until well mixed.

■ Each serving: About 595 calories, 36 g protein, 79 g carbohydrate, 15 g total fat (3 g saturated), 7 g fiber, 174 mg cholesterol, 800 mg sodium.

Fast Fried Rice

pictured on page 43

The secrets to this dish are quick-cooking brown rice, precut frozen vegetables, and ready-to-use stir-fry sauce.

TOTAL TIME *15 minutes*
MAKES *4 main-dish servings*

1½ cups quick-cooking brown rice
1 pound firm tofu, drained and cut into 1-inch cubes
6 teaspoons olive oil
1 package (16 ounces) frozen vegetables for stir-fry
2 large eggs, lightly beaten
⅓ cup stir-fry sauce

1. Prepare rice as label directs.
2. Meanwhile, in medium bowl, place 3 layers paper towels. Place tofu on towels and top with 3 more layers paper towels. Gently press tofu with hand to extract excess moisture.
3. In nonstick 12-inch skillet, heat 2 teaspoons oil over medium-high heat until hot. Add frozen vegetables; cover and cook 5 minutes, stirring occasionally. Transfer vegetables to bowl; keep warm.
4. In same skillet, heat remaining 4 teaspoons oil until hot. Add tofu and cook 5 minutes, gently stirring. Stir in rice and cook 4 minutes longer.
5. With spatula, push rice mixture around edge of skillet, leaving space in center. Add eggs to center of skillet; cook 1 minute, stirring eggs until scrambled. Add stir-fry sauce, vegetables, and ¼ *cup water;* cook 1 minute, stirring.

■ Each serving: About 360 calories, 17 g protein, 41 g carbohydrate, 15 g total fat (2 g saturated), 5 g fiber, 106 mg cholesterol, 760 mg sodium.

Pierogi & Sauerkraut-Slaw Casserole

This recipe couldn't be easier—just toss coleslaw mix with sauerkraut and seasonings, top with mini pierogi, then let the microwave do all the work!

TOTAL TIME *15 minutes*
MAKES *4 main-dish servings*

1 bag (16 ounces) shredded cabbage mix for coleslaw
1 bag (16 ounces) sauerkraut, drained
¼ cup apple cider or apple juice
½ teaspoon caraway seeds
⅛ teaspoon ground black pepper
1 box (12 ounces) frozen mini pierogi
2 tablespoons chopped fresh dill
2 tablespoons margarine or butter, cut up

1. In shallow 3-quart microwave-safe casserole, stir cabbage mix, sauerkraut, cider, caraway seeds, and pepper. In microwave oven, cook coleslaw mixture, covered, on High 5 minutes, stirring once halfway through cooking.
2. Arrange frozen pierogi over coleslaw mixture (it's OK if they overlap slightly). Sprinkle pierogi with dill and top with margarine.
3. Return casserole to microwave oven and cook, covered, on High 5 to 7 minutes longer or until pierogi are hot. Toss before serving.

■ Each serving: About 260 calories, 7 g protein, 37 g carbohydrate, 10 g total fat (3 g saturated), 7 g fiber, 49 mg cholesterol, 855 mg sodium.

Pork BBQ

We used ready-made shredded barbecued pork, sold in tubs in the meat department, for the base and added beans and fresh tomatoes for extra flavor and fiber. Serve with store-bought corn bread.

TOTAL TIME *15 minutes*
MAKES *6 cups or 4 main-dish servings*

16 ounces fully cooked barbecue sauce with shredded pork (half 32-ounce container)
1 can (15 to 19 ounces) red kidney beans, rinsed and drained
1 can (15 to 19 ounces) black beans, rinsed and drained
2 large plum tomatoes, cut into ¼-inch dice

In 3-quart saucepan, heat pork mixture with beans, tomatoes, and *1 cup water* to boiling over medium-high heat. Reduce heat to low; cover and simmer 5 minutes to blend flavors, stirring occasionally.

■ Each serving: About 380 calories, 29 g protein, 60 g carbohydrate, 6 g total fat (2 g saturated), 18 g fiber, 30 mg cholesterol, 1,245 mg sodium.

FRESH PASTA

Cooking times vary from 1 minute (angel hair) to 5 minutes (tortellini), but all boil up faster than dried pasta.

• Toss fresh fettuccine or linguine with ready-made pesto, canned cannellini beans (rinsed and drained), and grated Parmesan.

• Heat a jar of white clam sauce, splash in a little white wine and add some chopped fresh parsley, then toss with angel-hair pasta.

FLAVORED SPICE BLENDS

These small jars are available from several different spice manufacturers and come in a variety of flavors, including Cajun, Indian, Southwestern, Szechuan, and Thai.

• Mix with ground meat for extraflavorful meatballs or burgers.

• Whisk into canned chicken broth along with frozen (or leftover) vegetables and pasta.

COUSCOUS

Sometimes called precooked Moroccan pasta, it's found near the rice mixes on supermarket shelves. Couscous cooks in 5 minutes and works either as an entrée (mixed with meat, fish, or vegetables) or as an almost instantaneous side dish.

• Blend prepared couscous with scrambled eggs, a dash of soy sauce, and sliced green onions to make a mock fried-rice dish.

• Toss couscous with golden raisins and a dash each of cinnamon and cumin for an exotic accompaniment to plain broiled meat or poultry.

SALAD DRESSING

That bottle has a life beyond greens and marinades.

• Spoon creamy-style dressing onto mashed potatoes instead of sour cream or butter.

• Skip the oil—sauté fresh vegetables with a tablespoon of vinaigrette-style dressing.

QUICK-COOKING BROWN RICE

All the nutrition and flavor of the longer-cooking variety, but ready in just 10 minutes.

• Add to canned soups to make a filling meal.

• Roll up in a tortilla with canned refried beans, corn, and a spoonful of salsa for a quick burrito.

PACKAGED GREENS & VEGETABLES

To save even more time, make sure you choose prewashed varieties.

• Sauté baby spinach and minced garlic in olive oil and toss with toasted pine nuts and raisins.

• Make a no-prep stir-fry with shredded carrots, broccoli flowerets, and sliced mushrooms. Add a couple of tablespoons of soy sauce at the end.

MARINATED OR PRECOOKED MEATS & POULTRY

Most markets sell packages of seasoned or marinated pork, lamb, chicken, and beef—in cuts ranging from roasts to prepared kabobs. You'll also find meat and poultry that have already been cooked—simply heat and serve.

• Grill or broil marinated pork tenderloins or chicken breasts, then slice and serve fajita-style with sautéed peppers and onions in a flour tortilla.

• Slice precooked pot roast and heat with its gravy in the microwave; serve over warm, soft sandwich buns.

FLAVORED CHEESES

Add a boost to recipes without the mess of mixing.

• Use garlic-flavored spreadable cheese (thinned with a little milk) to make a creamy sauce for pasta or vegetables.

• Substitute flavored cream cheese for sour cream or butter as a topping for baked potatoes.

FROZEN VEGETABLE MIXES

Packages come in a variety of combinations. Some are based on ethnic mixes such as Mediterranean.

• Toss a broccoli-based mix with hot pasta, olive oil, strips of smoked turkey or ham, and a sprinkling of grated Parmesan.

• Add Asian mixed vegetables to ramen noodle soup along with a splash of Asian sesame oil.

PRESLICED MEATS & POULTRY

Presliced turkey, chicken, veal, or beef can be seasoned in myriad ways, then cooked in minutes.

• Sauté thinly sliced poultry cutlets in a little olive oil, then deglaze the pan with equal amounts of soy sauce, balsamic vinegar, and brown sugar.

• In a deep skillet or wok, cook beef or pork, presliced for stir-frying, and add frozen mixed vegetables and a few tablespoons of stir-fry or sweet-and-sour sauce.

Black-Bean
& Corn Burritos

These hearty burritos stuffed with black beans, corn, and pickled jalapeño chiles are an excellent choice for people on the go.

TOTAL TIME *15 minutes*
MAKES *4 main-dish servings*

- 2 teaspoons chili powder
- 1 can (15 to 19 ounces) black beans, rinsed, drained, and coarsely mashed
- 1 can (15¼ ounces) whole-kernel corn, drained
- 3 tablespoons sliced pickled jalapeño chiles, drained and chopped (optional)
- 4 burrito-size flour tortillas, warmed
- 2 cups thinly sliced or chopped lettuce
- 2 medium tomatoes, chopped
- 1 cup shredded Mexican-blend cheese*
  sour cream (optional)

1. In 3-quart saucepan, toast chili powder over medium heat 1 minute or until fragrant. Stir in black beans, corn, and jalapeño chiles; cook 3 to 4 minutes or until mixture is hot, stirring occasionally.
2. Place one-fourth of bean mixture in center of each tortilla; top each with one-fourth of lettuce, tomatoes, and cheese. Fold 2 opposite sides of each tortilla over filling, then fold over other sides to form a package. Serve with sour cream if you like.

■ Each serving: About 490 calories, 20 g protein, 75 g carbohydrate, 15 g total fat (7 g saturated), 12 g fiber, 25 mg cholesterol, 985 mg sodium.

* Mexican-blend cheese is a mixture of Cheddar and jack cheese. If unavailable, substitute either of the cheeses.

Smoked Salmon
Omelet

Perfect for a light meal, this omelet pairs prepared chive-and-onion cream cheese with slivers of rich smoked salmon.

TOTAL TIME *15 minutes*
MAKES *4 main-dish servings*

- 8 large eggs
- 1 tablespoon margarine or butter
- 4 ounces chive-and-onion cream cheese (half 8-ounce container)
- 4 ounces smoked salmon, cut into thin strips
- 1 medium tomato, chopped
- 2 tablespoons capers, drained
- 4 slices pumpernickel or rye bread, toasted

1. In large bowl, with wire whisk or fork, beat eggs with *½ cup water.*
2. In nonstick 12-inch skillet, melt margarine over medium-high heat. Pour egg mixture into skillet and cook 2 to 3 minutes or until set around edge.
3. With spatula, gently lift edge as it sets, tilting skillet to allow uncooked egg mixture to run under omelet. Repeat until omelet is set but still moist on top.
4. Over half of omelet, place spoonfuls of cream cheese; top with salmon, tomato, and capers; cook 1 minute longer. Tilt skillet and, with spatula, fold omelet in half. Slide omelet onto platter. Serve with toasted bread.

■ Each serving: About 395 calories, 22 g protein, 20 g carbohydrate, 24 g total fat (10 g saturated), 3 g fiber, 459 mg cholesterol, 855 mg sodium.

Spinach Salad with
Warm Bacon Dressing

Cut hours off the prep time for this main-dish salad by buying already roasted and sliced chicken breast to toss with a homemade warm-from-the-skillet dressing. Serve with a French baguette, and you'll think it's just like dinner at your favorite bistro.

TOTAL TIME *15 minutes*
MAKES *4 main-dish servings*

- 6 slices bacon (4 ounces)
- ¼ cup cider vinegar
- 1 tablespoon sugar
- 2 tablespoons olive oil
- 2 teaspoons Dijon mustard
- ¼ teaspoon ground black pepper
- 1 can (11 ounces) mandarin-orange segments, drained
- 1 package (10 ounces) carved cooked chicken breast
- 1 bag (6 to 7 ounces) baby spinach

1. In 10-inch skillet, cook bacon over medium heat 8 minutes or until browned, turning once. Transfer bacon to paper towels to drain. Discard all but 1 tablespoon bacon fat from skillet.
2. Into fat in skillet, stir vinegar, sugar, oil, mustard, and pepper until blended. Heat dressing over medium-low heat 1 minute.
3. In large bowl, toss orange segments, chicken, and spinach with warm dressing until salad is evenly coated. Crumble bacon over salad.

■ Each serving: About 275 calories, 24 g protein, 10 g carbohydrate, 17 g total fat (4 g saturated), 5 g fiber, 61 mg cholesterol, 725 mg sodium.

Southwest Chicken Tenders with Slaw & Oven Fries

Thanks to some of our favorite convenience products, you can have this entire dinner ready in a snap.

TOTAL TIME *15 minutes*
MAKES *4 main-dish servings*

12 ounces frozen shoestring-potato fries (about 4 cups)
⅔ cup cornflake crumbs
2 teaspoons chili powder
½ teaspoon salt
1 pound chicken tenders
1 tablespoon olive oil
⅓ cup bottled citrus dressing
3 tablespoons reduced-fat sour cream
1 bag (16 ounces) shredded cabbage mix for coleslaw

1. Preheat oven to 450°F.
2. Place fries on large cookie sheet; bake 15 minutes until crisp and golden.
3. Meanwhile, in self-sealing plastic bag, combine cornflake crumbs, chili powder, and salt. In jelly-roll pan, toss chicken with oil. Add chicken to bag; shake bag until chicken is coated. Return chicken to pan.
4. Place jelly-roll pan with chicken in oven with fries and bake 10 minutes or until juices run clear when thickest part of chicken is pierced.
5. While chicken and fries are baking, mix citrus dressing and sour cream in large bowl; stir in shredded cabbage mix. Serve chicken with fries and slaw.

■ Each serving: About 460 calories, 32 g protein, 47 g carbohydrate, 18 g total fat (4 g saturated), 6 g fiber, 77 mg cholesterol, 750 mg sodium.

home on the range: twice as fast

The **Maytag Accellis 2X** is one of a new breed of electric appliances called speed cookers. The Accellis 2X combines microwave energy with conventional heat to cook twice as quickly, although it also has all the traditional cooking, baking, and broiling capabilities. Programming is simple; in the speed-cook mode you select from 4 options (main and side dishes, baked goods or eggs, defrost, or frozen meals) and enter the conventional cooking time. The oven then automatically sets itself for speed cooking. Lasagna bakes in 25 minutes, meat loaf in 30, and a 13-pound turkey roasts up picture-perfect in a mere hour and a half. The Accellis 2X comes in white, black, bisque, and brushed chrome, and has a smooth top and self-cleaning oven; $1,299. www.maytag.com

Super Bowl Chili, page 22;
Romaine & Cherry-Tomato
Salad with Buttermilk
Dressing, page 24;
Avocado & Pea
Guacamole, page 22;
Spicy Corn Bread, page 23

Steak with Mushroom
Sauce, page 16

Whole Wheat Pita Pizzas
with Vegetables, page 12

Raspberry Soufflé,
page 28

Pan-Roasted Chicken
& Vegetables, page 15

Mushroom-Studded
Tortilla Soup, page 46

Tomatillo-Braised
Pork Loin, page 49

Thai Shrimp &
Noodles, page 30

Fast Fried Rice,
page 33

Creamy Flan with
Ginger & Lime, facing page

In the
GH Kitchen with
RICK BAYLESS

Beyond tacos: hearty Mexican food from the
award-winning chef and cooking-show host

Creamy Flan with Ginger & Lime
pictured on facing page

Based on the classic baked vanilla custard with caramel, this version of the popular Mexican dessert is spiced with fresh ginger and lime zest.

PREP *30 minutes plus cooling*
BAKE *35 to 40 minutes*
MAKES *8 servings*

Caramel
¾ cup sugar

Custard
¾ cup sugar
1⅓ cups whole milk
1⅓ cups half-and-half or light cream
10 to 12 slices (each ¼ inch thick) peeled fresh ginger
4 strips lime peel (each 2" by 1")
3 large eggs
5 large egg yolks
2 teaspoons vanilla extract

1. Prepare Caramel: In 1-quart saucepan, heat sugar and ⅓ *cup water* to boiling over high heat. Reduce heat to medium; boil, without stirring, 7 to 10 minutes or until mixture becomes light amber in color.
2. Remove saucepan from heat and swirl pan until caramel becomes deep amber in color. Pour caramel into eight 6-ounce ramekins or custard cups. Immediately tilt ramekins to coat bottom evenly with caramel.
3. Prepare Custard: Preheat oven to 325°F. In 3-quart saucepan, heat sugar, milk, half-and-half, ginger, and lime peel to simmering over medium-high heat. Remove saucepan from heat; cover and let stand 10 minutes.
4. In large bowl, with wire whisk, beat eggs, egg yolks, and vanilla until blended. Gradually whisk hot milk mixture into egg mixture. Pour custard mixture through strainer into 8-cup liquid measuring cup or another large bowl. Pour or ladle custard mixture into prepared ramekins.
5. Place ramekins in medium roasting pan (15½" by 10½"); place pan on rack in oven. Carefully pour enough *boiling water* into roasting pan to come halfway up sides of ramekins.
6. Bake 35 to 40 minutes or until custards are barely set in the centers. Remove roasting pan with custards from oven. Let custards cool in water in roasting pan 1 hour.
7. Remove ramekins from water. Refrigerate custards at least 2 hours or up to 4 days. To unmold, run small metal spatula around top ½ inch of each ramekin. Invert each custard onto a dessert plate, allowing caramel syrup to drip from ramekin onto custard.

■ Each serving: About 285 calories, 7 g protein, 40 g carbohydrate, 11 g total fat (5 g saturated), 0 g fiber, 233 mg cholesterol, 65 mg sodium.

"Silky, delicious, and so easy to make!" says GH Food Director Susan Westmoreland. Bayless begins by caramelizing sugar in a saucepan (1), then swirls the syrup in each ramekin (or custard cup) to coat the bottom (2). He pours the custard over the syrup (3) and bakes the cups. After the flan has cooled, he loosens each cup with a small knife (4) and inverts each flan onto a plate so the syrup flows over the sides (opposite page).

Mushroom-Studded Tortilla Soup

(Sopa de Tortilla y Hongos)

pictured on page 41

Homemade or canned chicken stock works equally well in this brothy tomato soup. If you prepare the soup a day or two ahead, the flavor develops into an even tastier version. Just reheat and add the toppers to serve.

PREP *about 30 minutes*

COOK *about 1 hour 10 minutes*

MAKES *about 7 cups or 8 first-course servings*

Soup

¼ cup vegetable oil

4 garlic cloves, peeled

1 small white onion, sliced

1 can (14½ ounces) tomatoes in juice, drained

6 cups chicken broth

8 ounces shiitake mushrooms, stems discarded, caps thinly sliced

½ teaspoon salt

Soup Toppers

6 corn tortillas

1 tablespoon vegetable oil

2 to 3 canned chipotle chiles in adobo sauce

4 ounces goat cheese, cut or broken apart into roughly ½-inch pieces

1 large ripe avocado, peeled and cut into ½-inch cubes

1 large bunch watercress, stems discarded

1. Prepare soup: In 4-quart saucepan, heat oil over medium heat until hot.

Add garlic and onion and cook 10 to 12 minutes or until golden, stirring frequently. With slotted spoon, remove garlic and onion; drain well over saucepan. Transfer garlic and onion to food processor, with knife blade attached, or to blender; set aside saucepan with oil. Add tomatoes to garlic and onion, and blend until smooth. (Reserve tomato juice for use another day.)

2. Heat oil remaining in saucepan over medium-high heat until hot. Reduce heat to medium; add tomato mixture and cook 20 to 25 minutes or until thickened to the consistency of tomato paste, stirring frequently (you should have about 1 cup mixture). Stir in broth, mushrooms, and salt; heat to boiling over high heat. Reduce heat to medium-low and simmer, partially covered, 30 minutes.

3. Prepare toppers: Meanwhile, preheat oven to 375°F. Cut each tortilla in half, then cut each half crosswise into ¼-inch-thick strips. In 15½" by 10½" jelly-roll pan, toss tortilla strips with oil; arrange in single layer. Bake 10 minutes, stirring twice during baking, until golden and crisp.

4. While tortillas are baking, slice open chipotle chiles; scrape out seeds and discard. Cut chiles into thin strips.

5. To serve, into each of 8 soup bowls, place equal amounts of cheese, avocado, watercress leaves, and chipotle chiles. Ladle broth into bowls; top with tortilla strips.

■ Each serving: About 320 calories, 10 g protein, 29 g carbohydrate, 20 g total fat (2 g saturated), 6 g fiber, 0 mg cholesterol, 1,375 mg sodium.

"Mexican food is fun and flavorful—perfect for entertaining a crowd of friends."

CHEF RICK BAYLESS

Crispy Potato Boats with Salsa & Goat Cheese

(Sopes de Papa con Salsa y Queso de Cabra)

These tartlike appetizers are best served as soon as they are fried to ensure crispness. To get a head start, prepare the "boats" through step 5, up to several hours ahead, then cover to keep them from drying out.

PREP *1 hour*

COOK *about 14 minutes*

FRY *about 6 minutes*

MAKES *18 sopes*

1 medium baking potato (8 ounces), peeled and cut into 1-inch chunks

8 ounces Mexican instant corn masa mix* or masa harina (1 cup)

1 teaspoon salt
about 2½ cups vegetable oil

2 tablespoons balsamic vinegar

¾ cup Red Chile–Tomatillo Salsa (page 50)

2 cups loosely packed torn herb leaves (such as watercress, arugula, mizuna, and/or basil)

2 ounces dried (aged) goat cheese or ricotta salata, crumbled (about ½ cup)

1. In 1-quart saucepan, place potatoes and enough *water* to cover; heat to boiling over high heat. Reduce heat to low; cover and simmer 10 minutes or until potatoes are fork-tender; drain. Press potatoes through ricer or medium-mesh sieve into medium bowl (you should have about 1 cup mashed potato).

2. In small bowl, with fork, stir masa mix with *½ cup plus 2 tablespoons water* until blended. With hands, knead reconstituted masa and salt into the potato until dough forms (it should be the consistency of soft cookie dough).

3. Divide dough into 18 portions. With hands, shape each portion into a ball; cover with plastic wrap to keep dough from drying out. Cut 2 squares (each about 4 inches) from heavy-weight plastic storage bag or waxed paper; set aside.

4. Heat well-seasoned or nonstick griddle or nonstick 12-inch skillet over medium heat until hot. Meanwhile, with hands, gently press 1 ball of dough between sheets of plastic to about 2½ inches in diameter. Peel off the top sheet of plastic. Use thumb and index finger to pinch edge of dough all around into ½-inch-high border to form the sope. Flip the sope, uncovered side down, onto the fingers of 1 hand, then gently peel off the second piece of plastic. Now, flip the sope over onto the griddle or skillet, flat side down. Cook about 1 minute or until the bottom of sope is lightly browned. With wide metal spatula, transfer sope to cookie sheet or large plate. (This cooking is just to set the bottom surface, not to cook the masa all the way through.)

5. While the first sope is cooking, continue shaping and adding others to the griddle or skillet. After cooking, to keep them from puffing oddly during frying, prick bottom of each with a fork, being careful not to go all the way through. Cool sopes, then cover with plastic wrap to keep them from drying out.

6. Preheat oven to 250°F. In deep 12-inch skillet, heat oil over medium-high heat to 350°F. on deep-fry thermometer. Add 6 sopes to oil and fry about 2 minutes, turning sopes over once during cooking, until golden brown. Drain sopes upside down on tray lined with paper towels. Transfer fried sopes to 15½" by 10½" jelly-roll pan and keep warm in oven. Repeat with remaining sopes.

7. To serve, arrange sopes on platter. Stir vinegar into Red Chili–Tomatillo Salsa. Spoon 1 to 2 teaspoons salsa into each sope; top with some herbs and sprinkle each with about 1 teaspoon cheese.

■ Each sope: About 165 calories, 2 g protein, 9 g carbohydrate, 3 g total fat (0 g saturated), 1 g fiber, 0 mg cholesterol, 195 mg sodium.

* Mexican instant corn masa mix or masa harina is used here as a substitute for fresh, ground corn masa. It can be purchased at most Mexican groceries or by mail order from the CMC Company, 800-cmc-2780.

Crispy Potato Boats

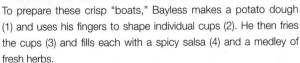
To prepare these crisp "boats," Bayless makes a potato dough (1) and uses his fingers to shape individual cups (2). He then fries the cups (3) and fills each with a spicy salsa (4) and a medley of fresh herbs.

We dished with this talented chef, TV personality, and cookbook author (and husband and father) to learn the ingredients of his success.

Who inspired you to learn to cook? My grandmother. For four generations, my family has run a restaurant/catering business in Oklahoma City. I grew up with many cooks, but it was my grandmother who taught me the importance of food in bringing people together.

What are some of your earliest cooking memories? Every summer, all the grandkids would help my grandma with the peach harvest. My job was to collect all the bruised fruit so we could make peach butter—a thick jam. We also pickled peaches, and put up enough in syrup to make peach cobbler—our family's favorite dessert—all winter.

How did you become interested in Mexican food? For my tenth birthday my next-door neighbor gave me an international cookbook. I made every single recipe in the book, but the ones that called out to me the most were the Mexican dishes. I was fascinated by the whole culture. When I was 14, I dreamed up a trip to Mexico. I did all the booking and convinced my parents we could afford it. It was our first airplane vacation, and we flew to Mexico City. I remember sitting by the hotel window, looking out to the bright lights below, and thinking, *Wow, this is for me.* After college, where I majored in Spanish and Latin American culture, I decided to put my love for food and my love for Mexico together.

Do you have an ace-in-the-hole dessert? At home I'm a pie person. In fact, I have Northern Spy apples from the farmers' market in my refrigerator waiting for my attention this weekend.

Is there a special tool you always travel with? I'm not a gadget person, but I do usually pack my knife case. It makes me feel that I can cook in anyone's kitchen.

Is there any secret junk food you can't resist? Doughnuts. I'm wild about doughnuts. I don't eat them very often, but they're something that I'll even make for myself once in a while.

When you're home with your wife, Deann, and your nine-year-old-daughter, Lanie, what do you like to do? Believe it or not, the three of us love to cook together. We usually make something that we can all participate in, such as fresh pasta from scratch, or grilled pizzas, or homemade ice cream. We like to make fairly simple things, but not always quick things, because we enjoy the time that we spend doing it.

How do you relax? One night a week, Deann and I have dinner at Topolobampo, one of my restaurants in Chicago. We'll make reservations just like regular guests for a Friday or Saturday night. It's really very nice to just sit there with a glass of wine and enjoy the experience instead of having to worry about the mechanics of running the restaurant. It puts it all in perspective for me.

Do you like to have friends over for dinner? What do you cook? I love to. I won't do anything formal at home because that's too much like work. Everything is served family-style. And since I like to spend my time with my friends in the kitchen, I'll get them involved in the process. We have a big garden, and we grow greens from the very earliest days of springtime through fall. So I'll ask the guests to pick the lettuce and make the vinaigrette. That way, they feel like they had a part in making the dinner. During the winter, I'll do one thing that's grilled in the fireplace, sometimes even just grilled bread. Then we'll all relax and have a really good bottle of wine.

Who are your heroes in the food world? Without Julia Child, I probably wouldn't be doing what I'm doing now. I started watching her cook on TV when I was eight or nine, and I was captivated with the world she opened up for me. In later years, I was inspired by Diana Kennedy, whose early work in Mexican cooking really laid down the road map for me.

You've received many awards. Which are you most proud of? Winning the James Beard Humanitarian Award meant a great deal to me because giving back to the community has always been a big focus of my life. I was also thrilled to win the Book of the Year Award from the International Association of Culinary Professionals for *Mexican Kitchen.* I pour a lot of my soul into my writing, and it was so exciting to be recognized.

Tomatillo-Braised Pork Loin

(Lomo de Puerco en Salsa Verde)

pictured on page 41

A boneless pork roast braised in a spicy puree of roasted tomatillos and jalapeños. You can make the sauce a day ahead, but braise the pork just before serving for best texture.

PREP *1 hour*
BAKE *about 50 minutes*
MAKES *8 main-dish servings*

- 2 tablespoons olive oil
- 1 boneless pork loin roast (about 3 pounds)
- 1½ pounds tomatillos, husked and rinsed
- 2 jalapeño chiles
- 1 large onion (12 ounces), thinly sliced
- 5 large garlic cloves, minced
- 1 cup loosely packed fresh cilantro leaves, chopped, or 2 large sprigs epazote
- salt
- 2 pounds small red potatoes, each cut into quarters
- cilantro leaves for garnish

1. In 8-quart Dutch oven, heat oil over medium-high heat until hot. Add pork and brown on all sides, about 10 minutes. Transfer pork to plate.
2. Meanwhile, preheat broiler. Place tomatillos and jalapeños in broiling pan (without rack). Place pan in broiler at closest position to source of heat, and broil until tomatillos are blackened in spots and blistering, and jalapeños are tender, about 10 minutes, turning vegetables over once.
3. Transfer broiled vegetables and any remaining juice in broiling pan to food processor, with knife blade attached, or to blender and pulse until pureed, occasionally scraping down side of food processor or blender; set aside. Turn oven control to 325°F.

4. To drippings in Dutch oven, add onion and cook over medium heat until golden, about 7 minutes, stirring often. Stir in garlic; cook 1 minute. Increase heat to medium-high; when onion mixture is sizzling, stir in tomatillo puree and cook 4 minutes or until thickened. Add chopped cilantro or epazote sprigs, 1½ teaspoons salt, and *2¼ cups water;* stir until well blended.
5. Return pork to Dutch oven with vegetable sauce; heat to boiling. Cover and bake 30 minutes.
6. While pork is cooking, in 3-quart saucepan, place potatoes, 1 teaspoon salt, and enough *water* to cover; heat to boiling over high heat. Reduce heat to low; cover and simmer 5 minutes or until potatoes are barely tender. Drain potatoes.

7. After cooking pork 30 minutes, turn pork over and add the cooked potatoes to the sauce around the pork. Cover and bake 20 minutes longer or until temperature on meat thermometer, inserted in center of roast, reaches 145°F. Internal temperature of meat will rise 5° to 10°F. upon standing.
8. Transfer pork to cutting board. Let stand 15 minutes to set juices for easier carving; keep warm.
9. Skim fat from sauce; discard. Spoon sauce and potatoes onto warm deep platter. Cut pork into ¼-inch-thick slices and arrange over sauce. Garnish with cilantro leaves.

■ Each serving: About 500 calories, 37 g protein, 32 g carbohydrate, 25 g total fat (8 g saturated), 5 g fiber, 93 mg cholesterol, 525 mg sodium.

Bayless dishes up a savory meal for a cold winter's night. He first browns a pork loin (1) while he removes the husks from each tomatillo (2). He roasts the tomatillos (3) and purees them in a food processor to make a sauce (4). He then braises the pork in the sauce with potatoes (5) before cutting the pork into slices (6).

Red Chili-Tomatillo Salsa

(Salsa Roja)

This sauce is called for in Crispy Potato Boats with Salsa & Goat Cheese (page 46), but it also can add great flavor to burritos and quesadillas. If you'd like to try a milder version, cut back on the dried chiles.

PREP *about 45 minutes*
BROIL *about 10 minutes*
MAKES *about 1½ cups*

½   ounce small hot dried chiles, stemmed*
6   large garlic cloves, unpeeled
1   pound tomatillos, husked and rinsed
1   teaspoon salt
½   teaspoon sugar

1. In small skillet, toast chiles over medium heat until aromatic and browned in spots, about 5 minutes, stirring occasionally. Transfer chiles to medium bowl. Cover chiles with *boiling water* and let stand 30 minutes to rehydrate.

2. Meanwhile, in same skillet, cook garlic cloves over medium heat until soft and browned, about 20 minutes, turning garlic often. Remove skillet from heat. Cool garlic until easy to handle, then remove papery skin and discard.

3. Preheat broiler. Place tomatillos in broiling pan (without rack). Place pan in broiler about 4 inches from source of heat and broil tomatillos until they are blackened in spots and blistering, about 10 minutes, turning tomatillos over once. Transfer tomatillos and any juice in broiling pan to food processor, with knife blade attached, or to blender.

4. Drain chiles. Add chiles, garlic, salt, and sugar to tomatillos. Pulse mixture until almost smooth, occasionally scraping down side of food processor or blender. Transfer tomatillo salsa to medium bowl. If needed, stir in *¼ cup water,* 1 tablespoon at a time, until salsa is a spoonable consistency. Cover and refrigerate salsa up to 3 days.

■ Each tablespoon: About 10 calories, 0 g protein, 2 g carbohydrate, 0 g total fat, 1 g fiber, 0 mg cholesterol, 100 mg sodium.

* You can choose from among a wide variety of small hot, dried chiles to make this salsa. As a rough guide, ½ ounce dried chiles equals 6 red chipotles, 4 tan chipotles, 16 árbols, 3 cascabels, or ¼ cup pequín.

March

QUICK STEWS & SOUPS

A ZEST FOR LEMONS

quick stews & soups

These hearty dinners are ready in 30 minutes
and offer (almost) instant gratification.

Moroccan-Style Chicken Stew

Our version of this long-simmering stew, called a tagine, with its blend of spices, olives, and raisins, is fast thanks to small chunks of tender chicken and canned beans. Garnish the delicious stew with fresh cilantro leaves before serving.

TOTAL TIME *30 minutes*

MAKES *about 8 cups or 6 main-dish servings*

- 1 tablespoon olive oil
- 1 medium onion, chopped
- 1 tablespoon all-purpose flour
- 1 teaspoon ground coriander
- 1 teaspoon ground cumin
- ½ teaspoon salt
- ¼ teaspoon ground red pepper (cayenne)
- ¼ teaspoon ground cinnamon
- 1½ pounds skinless, boneless chicken thighs, cut into 2-inch chunks
- 2 garlic cloves, crushed with garlic press
- 1 can (28 ounces) whole tomatoes in puree
- 1 can (15 to 19 ounces) garbanzo beans, rinsed and drained
- ⅓ cup dark seedless raisins
- ¼ cup salad olives (chopped pimiento-stuffed olives)
- ½ cup loosely packed fresh cilantro leaves

1. In nonstick 5- to 6-quart Dutch oven, heat oil over medium heat until hot. Add onion and cook 5 minutes or until light golden.

2. Meanwhile, in pie plate, mix flour with coriander, cumin, salt, pepper, and cinnamon. Toss chicken with flour mixture to coat evenly.

3. Add chicken to Dutch oven and cook 7 minutes or until lightly browned, turning chicken over halfway through cooking time. Add garlic and cook 1 minute.

4. Stir in tomatoes with their puree, beans, raisins, olives, and *1 cup water.* Simmer, uncovered, 5 minutes or until chicken is cooked through, breaking up tomatoes with side of spoon. Garnish with cilantro.

■ Each serving: About 305 calories, 29 g protein, 28 g carbohydrate, 9 g total fat (2 g saturated), 5 g fiber, 94 mg cholesterol, 890 mg sodium.

Coq au Vin

This hearty stew, like its namesake, is made with red wine but takes about two hours less to prepare. We used small pieces of chicken and vegetables that cook more quickly. Use two pans to do two cooking tasks simultaneously. Serve over noodles or with crusty bread.

TOTAL TIME *30 minutes*

MAKES *4 main-dish servings*

- 1 tablespoon olive oil
- 2 carrots, chopped
- 1 medium onion, chopped
- 1 package (10 ounces) sliced mushrooms
- 2 garlic cloves, crushed with garlic press
- 2 pounds small bone-in chicken thighs, skin removed
- 2 slices bacon
- 1 cup dry red wine
- 2 tablespoons brandy
- 3 tablespoons all-purpose flour
- 1 can (14½ ounces) chicken broth (1¾ cups)
- ¼ teaspoon salt
- 2 tablespoons chopped fresh parsley leaves for garnish

1. In nonstick 12-inch skillet, heat oil over medium-high heat until hot. Add carrot, onion, and mushrooms; cook 15 minutes or until vegetables are lightly browned, stirring. Add garlic and cook 30 seconds, stirring often. Remove skillet from heat.

2. Meanwhile, heat nonstick 5- to 6-quart Dutch oven over medium-high heat until hot. Add chicken and bacon, and cook 12 to 13 minutes or until chicken is tender and golden, turning chicken over halfway through cooking time. When bacon is browned, transfer to paper towels to drain; crumble when cool.

3. Stir wine and brandy into Dutch oven with chicken; heat to boiling. Boil 1 minute.

4. In 2-cup liquid measuring cup,

with wire whisk or fork, mix flour with broth until blended. Add broth mixture, salt, and mushroom mixture to Dutch oven; heat to boiling over medium-high heat. Reduce heat to medium; cook 5 minutes or until chicken is cooked through. Sprinkle with crumbled bacon and garnish with parsley.

■ Each serving: About 395 calories, 32 g protein, 16 g carbohydrate, 21 g total fat (6 g saturated), 3 g fiber, 120 mg cholesterol, 840 mg sodium.

Hungarian Pork Stew

Quick-cooking pork tenderloin (we used a preseasoned one) is simmered in a sauce reminiscent of goulash.

TOTAL TIME *30 minutes*
MAKES *4 main-dish servings*

- 1 package (12 ounces) wide egg noodles
- 1 tablespoon olive oil
- 1 large onion, cut in half and thinly sliced
- 3 tablespoons sweet paprika
- 1 garlic clove, crushed with garlic press
- 1 package lemon-pepper seasoned pork tenderloin (about 1 pound), cut lengthwise in half, then crosswise into ½-inch-thick slices
- ½ teaspoon salt
- 1 can (14½ ounces) stewed tomatoes
- ½ cup reduced-fat sour cream

1. Heat large saucepot of *salted water* to boiling over high heat. Add noodles and cook as label directs.
2. Meanwhile, in nonstick 12-inch skillet, heat oil over medium heat until hot. Add onion and cook until golden, about 15 minutes, stirring occasionally. Stir in paprika and garlic; cook 1 minute, stirring.

3. Increase heat to medium-high. Add pork and salt, and cook 2 minutes, stirring often. Add tomatoes and ½ *cup water;* heat to boiling. Reduce heat to low; cover and simmer 10 minutes or until pork is cooked through, stirring occasionally.
4. Remove skillet from heat, and stir in sour cream until blended. Drain noodles. Spoon pork mixture over noodles.

■ Each serving: About 620 calories, 39 g protein, 77 g carbohydrate, 19 g total fat (6 g saturated), 5 g fiber, 165 mg cholesterol, 680 mg sodium.

Sweet-Potato & Peanut Stew

A tasty vegetarian dish with tomatoes, spices, and a touch of peanut butter. Microwaving the sweet potatoes helps you finish in a flash.

TOTAL TIME *30 minutes*
MAKES *about 8 cups or 4 main-dish servings*

- 3 medium sweet potatoes (about 12 ounces each), well scrubbed and each cut into 1½-inch chunks
- 1 tablespoon olive oil
- 2 garlic cloves, crushed with garlic press
- 1½ teaspoons ground cumin
- ½ teaspoon salt
- ¼ teaspoon ground cinnamon
- ⅛ teaspoon crushed red pepper
- 2 cans (15 to 19 ounces each) garbanzo beans, rinsed and drained
- 1 can (14½ ounces) vegetable broth (1¾ cups)
- 1 can (14½ ounces) diced tomatoes
- ¼ cup creamy peanut butter
- ½ cup loosely packed fresh cilantro leaves, chopped

1. Place potatoes in 2½-quart microwave-safe dish. Cover dish and

microwave on High about 8 minutes or until fork-tender.
2. Meanwhile, in 5- to 6-quart saucepot, heat oil over medium-high heat. Add garlic, cumin, salt, cinnamon, and crushed red pepper, and cook 30 seconds, stirring. Stir in beans, broth, tomatoes, and peanut butter until blended; heat to boiling and cook 1 minute, stirring occasionally.
3. Reduce heat to medium-low; add sweet potatoes to bean mixture and simmer 2 minutes, stirring occasionally. Stir in cilantro.

■ Each serving: About 585 calories, 22 g protein, 92 g carbohydrate, 16 g total fat (2 g saturated), 18 g fiber, 0 mg cholesterol, 1,725 mg sodium.

Quick Cassoulet

We cut the prep time of this slow-baked French casserole by calling for store-bought roast chicken and canned beans.

TOTAL TIME **30 minutes**
MAKES **6 main-dish servings**

- 1 tablespoon olive oil
- 8 ounces Italian-style turkey-sausage links, cut into 1-inch pieces
- 8 ounces peeled baby carrots (half 16-ounce bag), each cut into thirds
- 2 medium celery stalks, chopped
- 1 medium onion, chopped
- ¼ teaspoon dried thyme
- 3 cans (15 to 19 ounces each) white kidney beans (cannellini), rinsed and drained
- 1 can (14½ ounces) chicken broth (1¾ cups)
- 2 packages (about 4 ounces each) roasted chicken-breast halves, skin and bones discarded, meat torn into 1-inch pieces

1. In nonstick 5- to 6-quart Dutch oven, heat oil over medium-high heat until hot. Add sausage, carrots, celery, onion, and thyme, and cook 12 to 15 minutes or until lightly browned.
2. Add beans, broth, chicken pieces, and *½ cup water* to Dutch oven; heat to boiling over high heat, stirring gently to combine. Reduce heat to low; cover and simmer 5 minutes to blend flavors.

■ Each serving: About 365 calories, 26 g protein, 44 g carbohydrate, 9 g total fat (2 g saturated), 12 g fiber, 42 mg cholesterol, 965 mg sodium.

Fisherman's Stew

Our recipe is a speedy version of cioppino—a California specialty of fish simmered in a garlicky tomato broth. We cut back on the variety of seafood usually called for, helping us shave off a considerable amount of prep time.

TOTAL TIME **30 minutes**
MAKES **about 12 cups or 6 main-dish servings**

- 1 tablespoon olive oil
- 1 medium red pepper, finely chopped
- 1 medium red onion, cut in half and thinly sliced
- 2 garlic cloves, crushed with garlic press
- ⅛ teaspoon crushed red pepper
- ½ cup dry white wine
- 2 cans (14½ ounces each) diced tomatoes
- ½ teaspoon salt
- 1 pound cod fillet, cut into 2-inch pieces
- 1 pound large mussels, scrubbed and beards removed
- ½ pound shelled and deveined large shrimp, with tail part of shell left on if you like
- ¼ cup loosely packed fresh basil or parsley leaves, chopped

1. In nonstick 5- to 6-quart Dutch oven, heat oil over medium-high heat until hot. Add chopped pepper and onion, and cook 6 to 8 minutes or until tender, stirring occasionally. Add garlic and crushed red pepper, and cook 1 minute, stirring. Add wine and heat to boiling; boil 2 minutes.
2. Stir in tomatoes, salt, and *½ cup water;* heat to boiling over medium-high heat. Add cod, mussels, and shrimp; heat to boiling. Reduce heat to medium-low and simmer, covered, 8 to 9 minutes or until cod and shrimp turn opaque throughout and mussel shells open. Remove Dutch oven from heat; sprinkle with basil.

■ Each serving: About 190 calories, 26 g protein, 10 g carbohydrate, 4 g total fat (1 g saturated), 2 g fiber, 98 mg cholesterol, 915 mg sodium.

shoring up on mussels

Types There are 2 species of mussels normally eaten in the United States. The blue or common mussel is the more widely available, and, despite its name, it has a glossy, almost black shell. The beautiful blue-green New Zealand mussel is somewhat larger than the 2- to 3-inch blue and can be prepared in the same ways.

Safety Cultivated mussels are grown in ocean waters that have been certified safe. For wild mussels, it's important to verify that they've been harvested from clean waters that have been tested for contaminating pollutants and red tide.

Storing Always purchase live mussels. (If they are open slightly, tap them—they should begin to close.) Discard any that gape wide open, have broken shells, are extra heavy (they are probably filled with mud), or do not close when tapped. Store mussels in a bowl covered loosely with a damp towel for no longer than 2 days in the refrigerator. Do not seal them in a plastic bag or in an airtight container, and don't store them in water; the mussels can suffocate.

Cleaning Scrub wild mussels well with a kitchen brush to remove grit. Cultivated varieties just need to be rinsed in cold water. If you purchase mussels with their "beard" or byssus (hairlike threads the mussel uses to attach itself to rocks or other surfaces) intact, remove it with a strong tug, no more than an hour or 2 before cooking.

Cooking Mussels are delicious in stews (such as our Fisherman's Stew, above) and soups. Their shells pop open when they're cooked (about 5 to 10 minutes), so it's easy to tell when they're done. Once steamed open, they may be fried, broiled, or simply served with a light tomato sauce.

White-Bean & Tomatillo Chili

Try this spicy vegetarian chili made with fresh tomatillos—tart, green, tomato-like fruits (with papery husks) that are staples in Southwestern cuisine. For this recipe, we used canned, not dry, white kidney beans as a time-saver. Serve the flavorful chili with warm tortillas and a dollop of plain yogurt.

TOTAL TIME **30 minutes**
MAKES **about 9 cups or 4 main-dish servings**

  2 tablespoons olive oil
  3 garlic cloves, crushed with garlic press
  1 small onion, cut in half and thinly sliced
  1 jalapeño chile, seeded and minced
  1 teaspoon ground cumin
  1 pound tomatillos, husked, rinsed, and coarsely chopped
1¼ teaspoons salt
  ½ teaspoon sugar
  1 can (14½ ounces) vegetable broth (1¾ cups)
  1 can (4 ounces) chopped mild green chiles
  2 cans (15 to 19 ounces each) white kidney beans (cannellini), rinsed, drained, and coarsely mashed
  1 cup loosely packed fresh cilantro leaves, chopped

1. In nonstick 10-inch skillet, heat oil over medium heat until hot. Add garlic, onion, jalapeño, and cumin, and cook 7 to 10 minutes or until light golden, stirring often.
2. Meanwhile, in 5- to 6-quart saucepot, heat tomatillos, salt, sugar, broth, green chiles, and *1 cup water* to boiling over high heat.
3. Reduce heat to low. Add onion mixture to saucepot; cover and simmer 15 minutes. Stir in beans and cilantro; heat through.

■ Each serving: About 335 calories, 13 g protein, 50 g carbohydrate, 10 g total fat (1 g saturated), 15 g fiber, 0 mg cholesterol, 1,610 mg sodium.

Corn & Shrimp Chowder

Topped with bacon and chives, this rich and tasty soup makes a delightfully satisfying meal on a cold night. We save time by boiling the potatoes while the bacon-and-onion mixture cooks. Buying cleaned shrimp can also help speed up the preparation time.

TOTAL TIME **30 minutes**
MAKES **about 10½ cups or 6 main-dish servings**

  1 pound red potatoes (3 medium), cut into ½-inch chunks
  1 can (14½ ounces) chicken broth (1¾ cups)
  1 teaspoon salt
  ¼ teaspoon ground black pepper
  2 packages (10 ounces each) frozen whole-kernel corn
  2 slices bacon
  1 medium onion, chopped
  1 pound shelled and deveined large shrimp
  1 cup half-and-half or light cream
    fresh chives for garnish

1. In 4-quart saucepan, heat potatoes, broth, salt, pepper, and *1 cup water* to boiling over high heat. Reduce heat to medium; cover and cook 10 minutes. Add 1 package frozen corn and cook 5 minutes longer or just until potatoes are fork-tender.
2. Meanwhile, in 12-inch skillet, cook bacon over medium heat 5 minutes. Add onion and cook 10 minutes longer or until onion is golden and tender. When bacon is browned, transfer to paper towels to drain; break into pieces when cool.
3. Add *1 cup water* and remaining package frozen corn to skillet with onion; heat to boiling over high heat. Add shrimp; cook 4 to 5 minutes or until shrimp turn opaque.
4. When potatoes are tender, remove 2 cups potato mixture to blender. At low speed, with center part of cover removed to allow steam to escape, blend mixture until pureed. Return pureed mixture to saucepan. Add shrimp mixture and half-and-half; heat through (do not boil or soup may curdle). Top with bacon, and garnish with chives.

■ Each serving: About 370 calories, 23 g protein, 39 g carbohydrate, 15 g total fat (6 g saturated), 3 g fiber, 138 mg cholesterol, 915 mg sodium.

Pasta e Fagioli

A fast-lane version of our favorite Italian bean soup.

TOTAL TIME *30 minutes*
MAKES *about 8 cups or 4 main-dish servings*

- 1 tablespoon olive oil
- 1 small onion, sliced
- 1 large celery stalk, sliced
- 1 can (14½ ounces) chicken broth (1¾ cups)
- 1 can (15 to 19 ounces) white kidney beans (cannellini), rinsed and drained
- 1 can (14½ ounces) diced tomatoes
- 2 garlic cloves, crushed with garlic press
- 1 teaspoon sugar
- ¼ teaspoon salt
- ¼ teaspoon ground black pepper
- ¼ cup tubettini or ditalini pasta
- 1 package (10 ounces) frozen chopped spinach

1. In 5- to 6-quart Dutch oven, heat oil over medium heat until hot. Add onion and celery and cook until vegetables are tender, about 10 minutes.
2. Meanwhile, in 2-quart saucepan, heat broth and *2 cups water* to boiling over high heat.
3. To Dutch oven, add beans, tomatoes, garlic, sugar, salt, and pepper; heat to boiling over high heat. Add broth mixture and pasta; heat to boiling. Reduce heat to medium and cook 5 minutes. Add frozen spinach; cook 3 to 4 minutes longer, stirring often to separate spinach.

■ Each serving: About 220 calories, 10 g protein, 33 g carbohydrate, 5 g total fat (1 g saturated), 8 g fiber, 0 mg cholesterol, 1,265 mg sodium.

Lentil & Bacon Soup

We chose lentils, one of the fastest-cooking dried legumes, and bacon instead of a ham bone, to speed up this hearty soup.

TOTAL TIME *30 minutes*
MAKES *about 9 cups or 6 main-dish servings*

- 1 bag (16 ounces) dry lentils (2½ cups), rinsed
- 1 container (32 ounces) chicken broth
- 2 bay leaves
- 4 slices bacon
- 1 medium onion, chopped
- 2 medium carrots, cut into ¼-inch-thick slices
- 2 medium celery stalks, cut into ¼-inch-thick slices
- 1 garlic clove, crushed with garlic press
- 1 teaspoon salt
- ¼ teaspoon ground black pepper
- ¼ teaspoon dried thyme

1. In covered 4-quart saucepan, heat lentils, broth, bay leaves, and *4 cups water* to boiling over high heat. Reduce heat to low; simmer, covered, 15 minutes.
2. Meanwhile, in nonstick 12-inch skillet, cook bacon over medium-high heat until browned; transfer to paper towels to drain.
3. Discard all but 1 tablespoon fat from skillet. Add onion, carrots, and celery, and cook 5 minutes, stirring occasionally. Add garlic and cook 1 minute longer, stirring.
4. Crumble bacon into lentil mixture; stir in salt, pepper, thyme, and vegetable mixture. Cover and cook 5 minutes or until lentils are tender. Discard bay leaves.

■ Each serving: About 335 calories, 24 g protein, 48 g carbohydrate, 6 g total fat (2 g saturated), 24 g fiber, 6 mg cholesterol, 1,110 mg sodium.

Hot & Sour Soup

We streamlined seasonings to help get this popular Asian soup on the table in record time—without sacrificing the great taste.

TOTAL TIME *30 minutes*
MAKES *about 8 cups or 4 main-dish servings*

- 1 tablespoon vegetable oil
- 4 ounces shiitake mushrooms, stems discarded, caps thinly sliced
- 3 tablespoons reduced-sodium soy sauce
- 1 package (15 to 16 ounces) extrafirm tofu, drained, patted dry, and cut into 1-inch cubes
- 2 tablespoons cornstarch
- 1 container (32 ounces) chicken broth (4 cups)
- 3 tablespoons seasoned rice vinegar
- 2 tablespoons grated, peeled fresh ginger
- 1 tablespoon Worcestershire sauce
- ½ teaspoon Asian sesame oil
- ¼ teaspoon ground red pepper (cayenne)
- 2 large eggs, beaten
- 2 green onions, sliced

1. In nonstick 5-quart saucepot, heat vegetable oil over medium-high heat until hot. Add mushrooms, soy sauce, and tofu, and cook 5 minutes or until liquid evaporates, gently stirring often.
2. In cup, with fork, mix cornstarch with *¼ cup water;* set aside. Add broth and *¾ cup water* to tofu mixture; heat to boiling. Stir in cornstarch mixture and boil 30 seconds, stirring. Reduce heat to medium-low; add vinegar, ginger, Worcestershire, sesame oil, and pepper, and simmer 5 minutes.
3. Remove saucepot from heat. Slowly pour beaten eggs into soup in a thin, steady stream around the edge of the

saucepot. Carefully stir the soup once in a circular motion so egg separates into strands. Sprinkle with green onions.

■ Each serving: About 280 calories, 18 g protein, 17 g carbohydrate, 15 g total fat (3 g saturated), 1 g fiber, 106 mg cholesterol, 1,790 mg sodium.

Salsa Beef Stew

We used a jar of mild salsa to add a south-of-the-border flavor to this chililike entrée and substituted ground beef for cubes of meat to help speed up the cooking. Sprinkle the stew with cilantro leaves and serve it with crunchy tortilla chips on the side.

TOTAL TIME *30 minutes*
MAKES *about 10 cups or 8 main-dish servings*

1½ pounds lean ground beef
  1 large onion, chopped
  3 tablespoons chili powder
  1 tablespoon olive oil
  1 carrot, chopped
  1 jar (16 ounces) mild salsa
  1 can (14½ ounces) chicken broth (1¾ cups)
  1 can (15 to 19 ounces) no-salt-added black beans, rinsed and drained
  1 can (11 ounces) no-salt-added whole-kernel corn, drained
  1 can (14½ ounces) diced tomatoes in puree
½ cup loosely packed fresh cilantro leaves

1. Heat nonstick 12-inch skillet over medium-high heat until very hot but not smoking. Add ground beef and half of onion and cook 8 minutes or until liquid evaporates and beef is browned, stirring occasionally to break up beef. Stir in chili powder and cook 2 minutes.

2. Meanwhile, in 5- to 6-quart Dutch oven, heat oil over medium-high heat. Add carrot and remaining onion, and cook 5 minutes or until golden, stirring occasionally. Stir in salsa, chicken broth, beans, corn, and tomatoes with their juice; cook 5 minutes, stirring occasionally.

3. Stir beef mixture into bean mixture; heat through. Sprinkle with cilantro to serve.

■ Each serving: About 415 calories, 23 g protein, 35 g carbohydrate, 21 g total fat (8 g saturated), 8 g fiber, 64 mg cholesterol, 940 mg sodium.

Osso Buco Express

For this Italian dish, usually made with thick veal shanks, we call for thinner—and less expensive—veal shoulder arm steaks. They may be labeled chops but either way, be sure to look for the small round bone.

TOTAL TIME *30 minutes*
MAKES *6 main-dish servings*

  1 tablespoon olive oil
  2 pounds bone-in veal shoulder arm steaks
  1 bag (16 ounces) peeled baby carrots
  8 ounces frozen small onions (half 16-ounce bag)
  1 medium celery stalk, cut crosswise into ½-inch pieces
  3 garlic cloves, minced
½ teaspoon salt
¼ teaspoon ground black pepper
¼ teaspoon dried thyme
  1 can (14½ ounces) diced tomatoes
¼ cup dry white wine
½ cup loosely packed fresh parsley leaves, chopped
  2 teaspoons grated fresh lemon peel

1. In 6-quart pressure cooker, heat oil over high heat. Add half the veal and

cook until browned on both sides. Transfer veal to bowl; repeat with remaining veal.

2. Add carrots, onions, celery, garlic, salt, pepper, and thyme, and cook 1 minute, stirring. Stir in tomatoes, wine, and *¼ cup water;* heat to boiling over high heat.

3. Return veal to pressure cooker. Following manufacturer's directions, cover pressure cooker, bring up to pressure, and cook under pressure 15 minutes. Release pressure quickly, as manufacturer directs.

4. In cup, mix parsley with lemon peel; sprinkle over stew.

■ Each serving: About 220 calories, 29 g protein, 13 g carbohydrate, 6 g total fat (1 g saturated), 3 g fiber, 114 mg cholesterol, 625 mg sodium.

a zest for lemons

How sweet they are:
Pies, crepes, cookies, cakes, and other citrusy creations deliver big flavor with the fresh taste of lemon.

French Lemon Tart

pictured on cover

Your guests will enjoy this classic European-style tart with a thin, piquant lemon layer on top of a crisp pastry crust. Serve the elegant dessert garnished with kiwifruit, lemon leaves, and a light dusting of confectioners' sugar.

PREP *30 minutes plus chilling and cooling*
BAKE *about 55 minutes*
MAKES *8 servings*

Crust
1 cup all-purpose flour
¼ teaspoon salt
6 tablespoons cold butter or margarine, cut up
1 tablespoon vegetable shortening

Lemon-Cream Filling
4 to 6 lemons
3 large eggs
¾ cup granulated sugar
¼ cup heavy or whipping cream

baby kiwifruit or sliced kiwifruit, lemon leaves, and confectioners' sugar for garnish

1. Prepare Crust: In large bowl, mix flour and salt. With pastry blender or 2 knives used scissor-fashion, cut in butter and shortening until mixture resembles coarse crumbs. Sprinkle about *3 tablespoons ice water*, 1 tablespoon at a time, into flour mixture, mixing lightly with fork after each addition until dough is just moist enough to hold together. Shape dough into a disk; wrap with plastic wrap and refrigerate 30 minutes or until firm enough to roll.

2. Preheat oven to 425°F. On lightly floured surface, with floured rolling pin, roll dough into 11-inch round. Press dough onto bottom and up side of 9" by 1" round tart pan with removable bottom. Fold overhang in and press against side of tart pan to form a rim ⅛ inch above edge of pan. With fork, prick bottom and side of tart shell at 1-inch intervals to prevent puffing and shrinking during baking. Refrigerate or freeze tart shell 10 to 15 minutes to firm pastry before baking.

3. Line tart shell with foil; fill with pie weights or dried beans. Bake tart shell 20 minutes; remove foil with weights and bake 10 minutes longer or until golden. Transfer to wire rack. Turn oven control to 350°F.

4. Meanwhile, prepare Lemon-Cream Filling: From lemons, grate 1½ teaspoons peel and squeeze ½ cup juice. In medium bowl, whisk eggs, granulated sugar, lemon peel, and juice until blended; whisk in cream.

5. Pour lemon mixture into warm tart shell. Place on cookie sheet and bake 23 to 25 minutes or until just set. Cool tart in pan on wire rack.

6. When tart is cool, carefully remove side of pan. To serve, garnish with kiwifruit and lemon leaves; sprinkle with confectioners' sugar.

■ Each serving: About 280 calories, 4 g protein, 32 g carbohydrate, 16 g total fat (8 g saturated), 1 g fiber, 115 mg cholesterol, 195 mg sodium.

Lemon Upside-down Cake

Brown sugar and tangy lemons combine to make a deliciously different upside-down cake. You can serve this cake warm or cool.

PREP *30 minutes plus cooling*
BAKE *45 to 50 minutes*
MAKES *12 servings*

¾ cup butter or margarine (1½ sticks), softened
1 cup packed light brown sugar
6 lemons
1⅓ cups all-purpose flour
¼ cup yellow cornmeal
2 teaspoons baking powder
½ teaspoon salt
¾ cup granulated sugar
2 large eggs
1 teaspoon vanilla extract
½ cup whole milk

1. Preheat oven to 350°F. In nonstick 10-inch skillet with oven-safe handle (or wrap handle in double thickness of foil), melt 4 tablespoons butter with brown sugar over medium heat, stirring often. Cook brown sugar mixture 2 minutes or until melted, stirring constantly. Remove skillet from heat.

2. From lemons, grate 2 teaspoons peel. With knife, remove peel and white pith from lemons. Slice lemons crosswise into ¼-inch-thick slices.

With tip of knife, remove seeds. Arrange lemon slices in skillet.

3. On waxed paper, combine flour, cornmeal, baking powder, and salt.

4. In large bowl, with mixer at medium speed, beat granulated sugar and ½ cup butter until creamy. Beat in eggs, 1 at a time, until well blended. Beat in vanilla and lemon peel.

5. Reduce speed to low. Beat in flour mixture alternately with milk just until blended. Spoon batter over lemons and spread evenly.

6. Bake 45 to 50 minutes or until toothpick inserted in center comes out clean. Cool cake in skillet on wire rack 10 minutes. Invert cake onto plate. Cool 30 minutes to serve warm or cool completely to serve later.

■ Each serving: About 315 calories, 4 g protein, 46 g carbohydrate, 14 g total fat (8 g saturated), 1 g fiber, 70 mg cholesterol, 310 mg sodium.

Lemon Crème Brûlée

We added lemon and cinnamon to enhance the flavor of this silky restaurant-style dessert.

PREP *35 minutes plus chilling*
BAKE *35 to 40 minutes*
BROIL *1 to 2 minutes*
MAKES *6 servings*

2 lemons
1½ cups heavy or whipping cream
1 cinnamon stick (3 inches long), broken in half
4 large egg yolks
⅓ cup plus 1 tablespoon sugar
pinch salt
¼ teaspoon ground cinnamon

1. Preheat oven to 325°F. From lemons, remove 6 strips peel (3" by 1" each) and squeeze 2 tablespoons juice.

2. In 1-quart saucepan, heat cream, cinnamon stick, and lemon peel over medium-high heat just until simmering. Remove saucepan from heat; cover and let stand 15 minutes. (Cream will develop a thin skin on top; whisk in when mixing into egg yolks.) Remove cinnamon stick and lemon peel; discard.

3. In large bowl, with wire whisk or fork, beat egg yolks, ⅓ cup sugar, and salt until blended. Beat in warm cream mixture and lemon juice. Pour custard into six 3-ounce broiler-safe ramekins or custard cups.

4. Place ramekins in 13" by 9" baking pan; place pan in oven. Carefully pour *boiling water* into baking pan to come halfway up sides of ramekins. Bake 35 to 40 minutes or just until mixture is set (mixture will still be slightly soft in center). Carefully remove ramekins from baking pan; cover and refrigerate at least 2 hours or until well chilled.

5. Up to 4 hours before serving, preheat broiler. In small bowl, mix cinnamon and remaining 1 tablespoon sugar. Sprinkle tops of chilled custards with sugar mixture to cover.

6. Place ramekins on small cookie sheet for easier handling. Place cookie sheet with ramekins in broiler at closest position to source of heat and broil 1 to 2 minutes or just until sugar melts and browns slightly. Serve immediately or cover and refrigerate up to 4 hours. If not served within 4 hours, sugar topping will lose its crispness.

■ Each serving: About 295 calories, 3 g protein, 15 g carbohydrate, 26 g total fat (15 g saturated), 0 g fiber, 224 mg cholesterol, 50 mg sodium.

fresh uses for lemons

More than just another tasty ingredient, lemons do double duty cleaning and freshening your home—and you.

• Neutralize the odors of fish or onions on your hands by rubbing them with slices of lemon.

• Deodorize the garbage disposal with leftover lemon peels. Simply drop in, turn on disposal, and flush with water.

• Polish unlacquered brass and copper. Sprinkle a little salt on the cut side of half a lemon and rub it on the tarnished item. Rinse and dry with a soft cloth.

• Clean the microwave with this tip from Heloise's new book, *In the Kitchen with Heloise* (Perigree): Using a microwave-safe bowl, stir 2 tablespoons of lemon juice into a cup of water. Let the mixture boil in the microwave for 5 minutes, then wipe off the condensed steam.

• Bleach tomato stains from plastic storage containers. *In the Kitchen with Heloise* recommends rubbing the cut side of a lemon over the stained areas of the container; leave the container in the sun for a few hours for extra lightening.

• Remove rust stains from washable fabric by applying lemon juice and salt to the fabric and placing it in the sun. Keep the stained area moist with lemon juice until the spot disappears. Brush away dried salt, and wash as the label directs.

Lemon Crumble Bars

A quick brown-sugar dough is made in the food processor and spread with some lemon curd and almonds for delicious, crumbly treats.

PREP *25 minutes plus cooling*
BAKE *35 to 40 minutes*
MAKES *24 bars*

1¼ cups all-purpose flour
½ cup packed light brown sugar
¼ teaspoon baking soda
½ cup cold butter or margarine
   (1 stick), cut up
¼ cup whole natural almonds,
   coarsely chopped
½ cup jarred lemon curd
½ teaspoon grated fresh lemon peel

1. Preheat oven to 350°F. In food processor, with knife blade attached, blend flour, sugar, and baking soda until mixed. Add butter and pulse just until mixture resembles coarse crumbs. Transfer ½ cup dough to small bowl and stir in almonds; reserve.
2. Press remaining dough firmly onto bottom of ungreased 9" by 9" metal baking pan. In another small bowl, mix lemon curd and lemon peel; spread mixture over dough up to ¼ inch from edges. Crumble reserved dough over curd.
3. Bake 35 to 40 minutes or until browned. Cool completely in pan on wire rack. Cut into 8 strips, then cut each strip crosswise into 3 bars.

■ Each bar: About 105 calories, 1 g protein, 15 g carbohydrate, 5 g total fat (3 g saturated), 0 g fiber, 11 mg cholesterol, 60 mg sodium.

Sour Cream-Lemon Tea Loaf

This moist cake, with a texture similar to pound cake's, gets brushed with a lemony-sugar syrup for extra zest after it's baked.

PREP *30 minutes plus cooling*
BAKE *50 to 55 minutes*
MAKES *1 loaf, 16 servings*

Tea Loaf
2½ cups all-purpose flour
1½ teaspoons baking powder
½ teaspoon baking soda
½ teaspoon salt
1 container (8 ounces) sour
   cream
1 teaspoon vanilla extract
1¼ cups sugar
½ cup butter or margarine
   (1 stick), softened
1 tablespoon grated lemon peel
2 large eggs

Lemon-Sugar Syrup
⅓ cup sugar
¼ cup fresh lemon juice

1. Preheat oven to 350°F. Grease 9" by 5" loaf pan; dust with flour.
2. Prepare Tea Loaf: On waxed paper, combine flour, baking powder, baking soda, and salt. In small bowl, with wire whisk or fork, mix sour cream and vanilla.
3. In large bowl, with mixer at low speed, beat sugar, butter, and lemon peel until smooth. Increase speed to high; beat until creamy. Reduce speed to low; add eggs, 1 at a time, beating well after each addition, scraping bowl occasionally with rubber spatula. Add flour mixture alternately with sour-cream mixture, beginning and ending with flour mixture.
4. Spoon batter into prepared pan; spread evenly. Bake 50 to 55 minutes or until toothpick inserted in center of loaf comes out clean. Cool loaf in pan on wire rack 10 minutes.

5. Meanwhile, prepare Lemon-Sugar Syrup: In small bowl, mix sugar and lemon juice. Remove loaf from pan; place on wire rack set over sheet of waxed paper (to catch dripping syrup). With skewer, prick top and sides of loaf in many places. With pastry brush, brush top and sides of warm loaf with syrup; cool on wire rack.

■ Each serving: About 240 calories, 3 g protein, 35 g carbohydrate, 10 g total fat (6 g saturated), 1 g fiber, 49 mg cholesterol, 225 mg sodium.

Lemon-Sugar Crepes

These delicate crepes are perfect for a brunch menu or a light (and do-ahead) dinner party finale.

PREP *10 minutes plus chilling*
COOK *about 30 minutes*
MAKES *12 crepes or 6 servings*

3 lemons
3 large eggs
1½ cups whole milk
⅔ cup all-purpose flour
½ teaspoon salt
3 tablespoons butter or margarine,
   melted
¾ cup granulated sugar
   candied lemon peel (optional)

1. From lemons, grate ½ teaspoon peel and squeeze ¾ cup juice. Cover and refrigerate juice to use later.
2. In blender at medium speed, mix eggs, milk, flour, salt, lemon peel, and 2 tablespoons melted butter until batter is completely smooth.
3. Transfer batter to medium bowl; cover and refrigerate at least 1 hour or overnight. Whisk batter thoroughly before using.
4. Heat nonstick 10-inch skillet or crepe pan over medium-high heat until hot. Brush pan lightly with some melted butter. Pour scant ¼ cup batter into pan, swirling to evenly coat

bottom. Cook crepe 1½ minutes or until top is set and underside is lightly browned.

5. With spatula, loosen crepe; turn and cook other side 30 seconds (be gentle, crepes are delicate). Slip crepe onto sheet of waxed paper. Repeat with remaining batter, placing waxed paper between each crepe and brushing pan lightly with butter before cooking each crepe. If not serving crepes right away, wrap with plastic wrap and refrigerate.

6. When ready to serve, preheat oven to 350°F. Grease 13" by 9" glass baking dish. Sprinkle each crepe with 1 tablespoon sugar and 1 tablespoon lemon juice. Fold each crepe into quarters; place in baking dish, overlapping slightly. Cover dish with foil; heat crepes in oven 12 minutes or until hot. Top with candied lemon peel and serve.

■ Each serving: About 290 calories, 7 g protein, 40 g carbohydrate, 12 g total fat (7 g saturated), 1 g fiber, 136 mg cholesterol, 340 mg sodium.

Editor's note: Crepes can be prepared and frozen up to 2 months ahead. To freeze, stack crepes, placing waxed paper between crepes. Wrap stacked crepes tightly in foil; label and freeze. To use, place wrapped, frozen crepes on cookie sheet and heat in preheated 350°F. oven until heated through, about 20 minutes. To serve, follow step 6.

food editor's Q&A

Q I've heard that Meyer lemons are the most delicious variety. What are they, and where can I find them?

a The Meyer lemon (named for Frank N. Meyer, who first imported the fruit from China in 1908) is not actually a true lemon. Rather, it's a hybrid, probably a cross between a lemon and a mandarin orange. Its light orange-yellow flesh is sweeter than a lemon's, and it has a thin, smooth skin. Meyer lemons are not always easy to find outside of California (where they're the most popular variety for home growing), but they can be found in some specialty food stores around the country. At one time, they carried a virus that had the potential to damage other citrus crops, so their sale was restricted. Now, a new virus-free strain has been developed, and hopefully they will become more widely available.

Q Can you substitute a sweet onion, such as a Vidalia, for a regular yellow onion in a recipe?

a You can, but you'll probably need to cook the onions slightly longer because sweet varieties (such as Vidalias, Walla Wallas, and Texas Spring Sweet Onions) have a naturally higher water content. Your dish may also have a little less bite; these onions contain more sugar and fewer of the sulfuric acid compounds that give onions their characteristic flavor.

Be careful, too, when you're storing sweet onions—they're more susceptible to bruising and nicks. All onions should be kept in a cool, dry environment that allows for adequate air circulation. You can also use a pair of clean, sheer pantyhose (a great way to recycle those with a run): Place an onion in the toe, tie a small knot, then drop in another, make a knot, and so on, until you fill the leg of the hose. When you need an onion, simply cut below a knot. I don't recommend storing onions in the refrigerator, but if you do, wrap each one separately in a paper towel to absorb moisture and ensure adequate air circulation.

Q My supermarket is selling chicken broth in 32-ounce packages—similar to juice-box containers. The price of the soup is very reasonable, but is it a good idea to buy such a large container if I won't be using it all at one time?

a Aseptic packaging (as it's called) extends a product's shelf life by months or even years. Once opened, though, the broth will stay fresh for only 14 days in the refrigerator. If you're not going to be able to use the 4 cups of broth within that time, freeze the remainder to use at a later date. Quick tip: Purchase an ice-cube tray to be used only for chicken broth (you won't want to use the tray for making ice cubes because they'll absorb the broth flavor). Once they're frozen, place the cubes in a plastic bag or container. When I'm pressed for time, such as on a busy weeknight, I just pop out a cube and make a quick pan sauce.

easy as pie: lemon meringue

When lemon meringue pie is done right, it's a slice of heaven. Here are our secrets.

PASTRY

• For the flakiest crust, use butter or margarine right from the refrigerator.

• To prevent sticking when rolling out the dough, flour the surface well, work quickly, and turn dough after each roll.

• Gently ease dough into the pie plate. If you stretch it too much, it will shrink and crack while baking.

• Let crust cool completely before adding the lemon filling.

LEMON FILLING

• Thoroughly blend the cold water into the cornstarch mixture to prevent lumps.

• Occasionally stir the cornstarch and water mixture while it comes to a boil, making sure to scrape the pan's interior edges so the mixture doesn't burn. (As it reaches a boil, it will thicken considerably—don't panic!)

• Cold eggs will curdle (scramble) if added directly to a hot mixture; to avoid this, first stir a small amount of boiled cornstarch mixture into the yolks, then add them slowly to the remaining hot cornstarch mixture, stirring rapidly as an added precaution.

• The egg-yolk mixture must be heated to a gentle boil for the filling to thicken properly. Don't worry about curdling the yolks; at this point, the cornstarch will prevent it.

MERINGUE

• Separate the eggs straight from the refrigerator; the yolks are less likely to break when cold.

• Even a trace of yolk in the whites will make it difficult, if not impossible, to beat the egg whites to full volume. Use 3 bowls to separate eggs: Crack an egg and let the white drip into the first small bowl. Drop yolk into another small bowl, then transfer the white into your large mixing bowl. That way, if a yolk breaks while cracking an egg, you can set it aside to use another day, rather than running the risk of "infecting" the whole batch of whites.

• Let the egg whites come to room temperature before beating—you'll get more volume in less time. Just remember not to leave them out longer than 2 hours, for food safety reasons.

• Bowls and beaters must be clean and dry. Use a copper, glass, ceramic, or metal bowl. Plastic is hard to clean and there may be traces of oil on the surface.

• Beat the egg whites just until stiff peaks form when the beaters are lifted (if you overbeat them, they'll lose their stability). Make sure the sugar is completely blended. Test by rubbing a small amount of beaten whites between two fingers. You shouldn't feel any granules of sugar.

• The beaten whites must be spread on the warm lemon filling in order to fully cook the meringue and prevent it from becoming watery, or "weeping." Also, spread the meringue completely to the perimeter of the filling (it should touch the crust all around); otherwise, it may shrink while baking and weep as it cools, causing a watery layer to form between the meringue and lemon filling.

• Beware of overcooking; it will cause "beading" (little spots of sugary moisture) to appear on the meringue.

Lemon Meringue Pie

Weep no more: Our luscious no-fail recipe for this all-American classic is a cinch to make.

PREP *about 1¼ hours plus cooling*
BAKE *about 25 minutes*
MAKES *10 servings*

Crust

1¼ cups all-purpose flour
¼ teaspoon salt
4 tablespoons cold butter or margarine, cut up
2 tablespoons vegetable shortening

Lemon Filling

5 to 6 medium lemons
1 cup sugar
⅓ cup cornstarch
¼ teaspoon salt
3 large egg yolks
2 tablespoons butter or margarine

Meringue Topping

4 large egg whites
¼ teaspoon cream of tartar
pinch salt
½ cup sugar

1. Prepare Crust: In large bowl, mix flour and salt. With pastry blender or 2 knives used scissor-fashion, cut in butter and shortening until mixture resembles coarse crumbs. Sprinkle *4 to 5 tablespoons ice water,* 1 tablespoon at a time, into flour mixture, mixing lightly with fork after each addition, until dough is just moist enough to hold together. Shape dough into a disk; wrap with plastic wrap and refrigerate 30 minutes or until firm enough to roll.

2. Preheat oven to 425°F. On lightly floured surface, with floured rolling pin, roll dough into a round 1½ inches larger in diameter than inverted 9-inch pie plate. Gently ease dough into pie plate, and trim edge, leaving 1-inch overhang. Fold overhang under; bring up over pie-plate rim and pinch to form high decorative edge. With fork, prick bottom and side of pie shell at 1-inch intervals to prevent puffing and shrinking during baking. Refrigerate or freeze pie shell 10 to 15 minutes to firm pastry before baking.

3. Line pie shell with foil; fill with pie weights or dried beans. Bake pie shell 20 minutes; remove foil with weights and bake 5 to 7 minutes longer or until golden. Cool on wire rack. Turn oven control to 400°F.

4. Prepare Lemon Filling: From lemons, grate 1 tablespoon peel and squeeze ¾ cup juice. In 2-quart saucepan, mix sugar, cornstarch, and salt; stir in *1½ cups cold water* until well blended. Cook over medium-high heat until mixture thickens and boils, stirring occasionally. Boil 1 minute, stirring. Remove saucepan from heat.

5. In small bowl, whisk egg yolks. Stir in ½ cup hot cornstarch mixture until blended; slowly pour egg-yolk mixture back into cornstarch mixture in saucepan, stirring rapidly to prevent curdling. Place saucepan over medium-low heat and cook until mixture comes to a gentle boil, stirring constantly. Cook 2 to 3 minutes or until filling is very thick, stirring. Remove saucepan from heat; stir in butter until melted. Stir in lemon juice and peel (mixture will thin out). Pour into pie shell.

6. Prepare Meringue Topping: In small bowl, with mixer at high speed, beat whites, cream of tartar, and salt until frothy. Gradually sprinkle in sugar, 2 tablespoons at a time, beating until sugar completely dissolves and egg whites stand in stiff, glossy peaks when beaters are lifted.

7. Spread meringue over warm filling. To keep meringue from shrinking during baking, make sure it seals in the filling completely, touching edge of crust all around. Swirl meringue with back of spoon to make attractive top. Bake 6 to 8 minutes or until meringue is golden. Cool pie on wire rack away from draft. Refrigerate at least 1 hour before serving.

■ Each serving: About 300 calories, 4 g protein, 47 g carbohydrate, 12 g total fat (6 g saturated), 1 g fiber, 84 mg cholesterol, 230 mg sodium.

If life hands you lemons . . . try these

Strips of citrus make elegant cake decorations. Of the 12 strippers we tested, the **Citrus Stripper, $6,** was our favorite—it cuts easily and gives a neat length of rind without any bitter white pith. Sold at Williams-Sonoma. Also available by catalog (800-541-2233) or at www.williams-sonoma.com.

When you want finely grated lemon peel to add to a batter or dough, the best option is the **Microplane Fine Grater, $16.50,** also from Williams-Sonoma. With barely any effort, it produces a cloud of zest so fine it melts away—leaving only its tantalizing flavor and aroma in the finished cake or cookies.

A zester is a handy way to peel curls of lemon rind for garnishes and to add punch to salad dressings, Asian soups, and beverages. Look for a model that won't bend when pulled firmly against the fruit's skin. Our recommendation: the stainless-steel **Chantal Zester, $12.99,** with a comfortable curved handle; sold at specialty stores.

Fresh juice, anyone? The plastic **Oxo Good Grips Citrus Juicer, $11.99,** is perfect when you need to juice just a small amount of lemon. It sits above a 1-cup measure so you can tell how much you've squeezed. (The reamer reverses to a larger size for oranges.) Available in housewares stores.

But if you plan to juice regularly and in larger quantities, the new electric **Philips Juicer, $59.99,** can do the job quietly and exceptionally well. It handles anything from small lemons to mammoth grapefruits. Available at Target stores; for information, visit www.target.com.

Lemon Cornmeal Thins

These crunchy cookies were inspired by an Italian recipe called *zaleti*. You can keep them frozen until ready to slice and bake.

PREP *30 minutes plus chilling and cooling*
BAKE *16 to 18 minutes per batch*
MAKES *about 4½ dozen cookies*

 1 cup sugar
 ¾ cup butter or margarine
     (1½ sticks), softened
 2 large eggs
 1 tablespoon grated fresh lemon peel
 2 teaspoons vanilla extract
1½ cups all-purpose flour
1½ cups yellow cornmeal
 ¾ teaspoon baking powder
 ½ teaspoon salt

1. In large bowl, with mixer at medium speed, beat sugar with butter until creamy. At low speed, beat in eggs, lemon peel, and vanilla (mixture may look curdled). Gradually beat in flour, cornmeal, baking powder, and salt just until dough is evenly moistened.
2. With floured hands, divide dough in half. Shape each half into a 7" by 2" brick. Wrap each brick in plastic wrap and refrigerate overnight. Or, place dough in freezer 1 hour. (If using margarine, you must *freeze* dough at least 6 hours.)
3. Preheat oven to 350°F. Grease large cookie sheet. With serrated knife, cut 1 brick crosswise into ¼-inch-thick slices. Place slices, 1 inch apart, on cookie sheet. Bake cookies 16 to 18 minutes or until golden around the edges. Transfer cookies to wire rack to cool. Repeat with remaining brick.

■ Each cookie: About 70 calories, 1 g protein, 9 g carbohydrate, 3 g total fat (2 g saturated), 0 g fiber, 15 mg cholesterol, 55 mg sodium.

Lemon-Buttermilk Pudding Cake

This cake bakes into two separate layers: a light sponge cake on top and a rich lemon pudding on the bottom.

PREP *20 minutes*
BAKE *40 minutes*
MAKES *8 servings*

 3 lemons
 1 cup buttermilk
 3 large eggs, separated
 4 tablespoons butter or margarine,
     melted
 ¾ cup sugar
 ¼ cup all-purpose flour
 ⅛ teaspoon salt

1. Preheat oven to 350°F. Grease 8" by 8" glass or ceramic baking dish. From lemons, grate 1 tablespoon peel and squeeze ⅓ cup juice.
2. In large bowl, with wire whisk or fork, beat buttermilk, egg yolks, melted butter, lemon peel, lemon juice, and ½ cup sugar. Beat in flour and salt until blended.
3. In small bowl, with mixer at high speed, beat egg whites until foamy. Gradually beat in remaining ¼ cup sugar until soft peaks form when beaters are lifted. With rubber spatula, gently fold beaten egg whites into lemon mixture, one-third at a time, just until combined. Pour cake batter into prepared baking dish.
4. Place dish in 13" by 9" metal baking pan, and place on rack in oven. Carefully pour *boiling water* into baking pan to come halfway up sides of dish.
5. Bake pudding cake 40 minutes or until top is golden and set (batter will separate into cake and pudding layers). Transfer dish from pan to wire rack to cool 10 minutes. Serve cake warm.

■ Each serving: About 180 calories, 4 g protein, 24 g carbohydrate, 8 g total fat (5 g saturated), 0 g fiber, 97 mg cholesterol, 155 mg sodium.

April

dinner from the refrigerator door

Horseradish. Tomato paste. Salad dressing.
When you're out of ideas for dinner, the condiments on your fridge
shelf offer amazing inspiration.

Creamy Parmesan Twice-Baked Potatoes

We microwaved the potatoes and used a creamy Parmesan-peppercorn salad dressing in this easy version of twice-baked potatoes. Reheat the stuffed potatoes in the oven for a crispy top. If you're short on time, just pop them in the microwave.

PREP **20 minutes**
COOK **about 25 minutes**
MAKES **4 main-dish servings**

    4 medium baking potatoes
       (about 10 ounces each)
  ½ **cup bottled creamy Parmesan
       with cracked peppercorn salad
       dressing***
    1 green onion, sliced
  ¼ **cup grated Parmesan
       cheese**
       green-onion tops (optional)

1. Pierce potatoes with fork in several places. Place potatoes on paper towel in microwave oven. Cook potatoes on High 10 to 12 minutes or until fork-tender, turning potatoes over once halfway through cooking; cool slightly.
2. Meanwhile, preheat oven to 450°F.

*** Bold** *type found in ingredient lists indicates items that can be stored in the refrigerator door.*

In medium bowl, mix salad dressing and sliced onion; set aside.
3. When potatoes are cool enough to handle, slice each potato lengthwise in half. With spoon, carefully scoop out flesh from each potato half, leaving ¼-inch-thick shell and making sure potato-skin shells are intact. Place flesh in bowl with dressing mixture. Place shells on small cookie sheet.
4. With potato masher or fork, mash potato mixture in bowl until almost smooth. Spoon mashed-potato mixture into shells, and sprinkle with Parmesan.
5. Bake potatoes 12 to 15 minutes or until heated through and golden on top. Arrange potatoes on bed of green-onion tops if you like.

■ Each serving: About 420 calories, 8 g protein, 61 g carbohydrate, 18 g total fat (4 g saturated), 5 g fiber, 4 mg cholesterol, 440 mg sodium.

Horseradish & Cheddar Twice-Baked Potatoes

Prepare recipe as above, except in step 2, substitute *⅔ cup reduced-fat sour cream* and *¼ cup prepared white horseradish* for salad dressing. In step 4, substitute *½ cup shredded Cheddar cheese* for Parmesan.

■ Each serving: About 370 calories, 10 g protein, 62 g carbohydrate, 10 g total fat (6 g saturated), 6 g fiber, 30 mg cholesterol, 135 mg sodium.

BBQ Sauce for Chicken or Pork

Sweet and sassy—this sauce is great whether you're grilling in your backyard or broiling in your oven. Just brush the sauce on to ribs, chicken, or pork during the last few minutes of cooking.

PREP **10 minutes**
COOK **about 20 minutes**
MAKES **about 2 cups sauce**

    1 tablespoon olive oil
    1 medium onion, chopped
    2 tablespoons grated, peeled fresh
       ginger
  ¾ **cup chili sauce**
  ½ **cup ketchup**
    1 tablespoon sugar
    2 tablespoons cider vinegar
    2 **tablespoons soy sauce**
    1 **teaspoon Worcestershire sauce**

1. In nonstick 10-inch skillet, heat oil over medium heat. Add onion and ginger; cook 10 minutes or until onion is tender and lightly browned.
2. Stir in chili sauce, ketchup, sugar, vinegar, soy sauce, Worcestershire, and *⅓ cup water*. Cook 5 minutes, partially covered, to blend flavors.
3. Brush sauce onto spareribs, pork roast, or chicken during last few minutes of cooking (makes enough for 4 pounds spareribs or 2 chickens). Cover and refrigerate sauce if not

using right away. Sauce will keep up to 1 week in refrigerator or up to 2 months in freezer.

■ Each ¼ cup: About 70 calories, 1 g protein, 13 g carbohydrate, 2 g total fat (0 g saturated), 2 g fiber, 0 mg cholesterol, 750 mg sodium.

Weeknight Barbecue Beans

These delicious stovetop "baked beans," flavored with bacon and onion, make a perfect partner for a rotisserie chicken.

PREP *10 minutes*
COOK *about 20 minutes*
MAKES *3½ cups or 6 accompaniment servings*

2 slices bacon, cut crosswise into ½-inch pieces
1 medium onion, chopped
1 can (15 to 19 ounces) black beans, rinsed and drained
1 can (15 to 19 ounces) red kidney beans, rinsed and drained
¼ **cup bottled barbecue sauce**
2 **tablespoons ketchup**

1. In 2-quart saucepan, cook bacon pieces over medium heat about 6 minutes or until bacon is browned. With slotted spoon, transfer bacon to paper towels to drain. Discard all but 1 tablespoon bacon fat from pan. Add onion and cook 6 to 8 minutes or until onion is tender and golden, stirring occasionally.
2. Return bacon to saucepan. Stir in beans, barbecue sauce, ketchup, and *¼ cup water;* heat to boiling over medium-high heat. Reduce heat to medium; cover and cook 5 minutes longer to blend flavors, stirring often.

■ Each serving: About 175 calories, 10 g protein, 30 g carbohydrate, 4 g total fat (1 g saturated), 10 g fiber, 4 mg cholesterol, 485 mg sodium.

refrigerator door: what's in, what's out

Yes, the cute little indentations in your (old-model) refrigerator door were designed to hold eggs, but it's not wise to store them there—the door isn't cold enough. For the same reason, milk shouldn't go on the door either. But this supplementary storage compartment is handy for a number of other items.

OPENED/UNOPENED

• Nuts, seeds, and their respective oils (refrigeration keeps them from going rancid)
• Red, capsicum-based spices such as paprika, cayenne, and crushed red pepper (they are more prone to infestation than other spices)
• Lemon products such as lemon-pepper spice blends and lemon extracts (flavor dissipates more quickly at room temperature)

ONCE OPENED

• mayonnaise
• mustard
• jam
• jelly
• ketchup
• relish
• pickles
• BBQ sauce
• salad dressing
• salsa
• soy sauce
• pure maple syrup
• wine
• steak sauce

The cool temperature of the refrigerator will extend the shelf life of many items, but nothing lasts forever. Make sure to use or toss items by their "best if used by" date to ensure the freshest-tasting foods.

Chutney-Glazed Shrimp with Rice Pilaf

Here's an excellent use for chutney—coat shrimp with this tangy condiment and curry powder, then broil. On the side, a homemade pilaf helps use up both chicken broth and almonds.

PREP *about 35 minutes*
BROIL *5 to 6 minutes*
MAKES *4 main-dish servings*

1 **tablespoon margarine or butter**
1 small onion, finely chopped
1 cup long-grain white rice
¾ teaspoon salt
1 **cup chicken broth**
1 cup frozen peas
¼ **cup slivered almonds, toasted**
⅓ **cup mango chutney, chunks finely chopped**
1 **teaspoon curry powder**
1¼ pounds large shrimp, shelled and deveined, leaving tail part of shell on if you like

1. In 2-quart saucepan, melt margarine over medium heat. Add onion and cook 5 minutes, stirring occasionally. Add rice and ½ teaspoon salt, and cook 1 minute, stirring. Stir in broth and *1 cup water;* heat to boiling over high heat. Reduce heat to low and simmer, covered, 15 minutes. Stir in frozen peas and cook, covered, 5 minutes longer or until rice is tender. Stir in almonds.
2. Meanwhile, preheat broiler. In medium bowl, mix chutney, curry powder, and remaining ¼ teaspoon salt. Pat shrimp dry with paper towels. Add shrimp to chutney mixture and toss until evenly coated.
3. Arrange shrimp in broiling pan (without rack). With broiling pan at closest position to source of heat, broil shrimp 5 to 6 minutes or until they turn opaque throughout. Serve with rice.

■ Each serving: About 460 calories, 31 g protein, 60 g carbohydrate, 10 g total fat (1 g saturated), 4 g fiber, 172 mg cholesterol, 940 mg sodium.

four toppings for broiled fish or chicken

We've come up with a quartet of flavors that make fish or chicken more than average fare.

PREP **15 minutes**
BROIL **12 minutes**
MAKES **4 main-dish servings**

Topping Variations

Horseradish & Sour Cream,
    Mustard & Tarragon,
    Soy Sauce & Jalapeño, and
    Chili Sauce & Sweet Pickle

Basic Broiled Fish or Chicken

  4 small fish steaks, 1 inch thick,
    or fish fillets, ¾ inch thick
    (about 6 ounces each); or
  4 medium skinless,
    boneless chicken-breast
    halves (1¼ pounds)

1. Preheat broiler.

2. Meanwhile, prepare desired Topping Variation; set aside.

3. Prepare Basic Broiled Fish or Chicken: Lightly spray rack in broiling pan with nonstick cooking spray. Place fish or chicken on rack. With broiling pan at closest position to source of heat, broil fish or chicken 5 minutes. Remove pan from broiler; turn chicken over (fish does not need to be turned over) and broil 1 to 5 minutes longer (depending on thickness) or just until fish flakes easily when tested with a fork or juices run clear when thickest part of chicken is pierced with tip of knife.

4. Remove pan from broiler. Spread topping on top of broiled fish or chicken. Return pan to broiler and broil 1 to 2 minutes longer or until mixture is lightly browned and bubbly.

■ Each serving fish only (based on lean fish): About 165 calories, 34 g protein, 0 g carbohydrate, 2 g total fat (1 g saturated), 0 g fiber, 96 mg cholesterol, 150 mg sodium.

■ Each serving chicken only: About 185 calories, 35 g protein, 0 g carbohydrate, 4 g total fat (1 g saturated), 0 g fiber, 96 mg cholesterol, 85 mg sodium.

Horseradish & Sour Cream Topping

In small bowl, with spoon, mix *¼ cup light mayonnaise, 1 tablespoon sour cream, 1 teaspoon prepared white horseradish, ¼ teaspoon salt,* and *⅛ teaspoon cracked black pepper.* Makes about ¼ cup.

■ Each tablespoon: About 55 calories, 0 g protein, 1 g carbohydrate, 6 g total fat (1 g saturated), 0 g fiber, 6 mg cholesterol, 265 mg sodium.

Mustard & Tarragon Topping

In small bowl, with spoon, mix *¼ cup light mayonnaise, 1 teaspoon Dijon mustard with seeds, ¼ teaspoon dried tarragon, ¼ teaspoon salt,* and *⅛ teaspoon ground black pepper.* Makes about ¼ cup.

■ Each tablespoon: About 50 calories, 0 g protein, 1 g carbohydrate, 5 g total fat (1 g saturated), 0 g fiber, 5 mg cholesterol, 270 mg sodium.

Soy Sauce & Jalapeño Topping

In small bowl, with spoon, mix *¼ cup light mayonnaise, 1 tablespoon chopped pickled jalapeño chile, 1 teaspoon soy sauce,* and *¼ teaspoon Asian sesame oil.* Makes about ¼ cup.

■ Each tablespoon: About 55 calories, 0 g protein, 2 g carbohydrate, 5 g total fat (1 g saturated), 0 g fiber, 5 mg cholesterol, 245 mg sodium.

Chili Sauce & Sweet Pickle Topping

In small bowl, with spoon, mix *¼ cup light mayonnaise, 1 tablespoon chili sauce, 2 teaspoons chopped sweet pickle or pickle relish, ¼ teaspoon salt,* and *¼ teaspoon hot pepper sauce.* Makes about ¼ cup.

■ Each tablespoon: About 55 calories, 0 g protein, 3 g carbohydrate, 5 g total fat (1 g saturated), 0 g fiber, 5 mg cholesterol, 330 mg sodium.

Pinto-Bean Burgers

You can have these family-friendly burgers on the table fast.

PREP *15 minutes*
COOK *about 8 minutes*
MAKES *4 main-dish servings*

- 1 can (15 to 15½ ounces) pinto beans, rinsed and drained
- 1 teaspoon ground cumin
- **1 teaspoon minced canned chipotle chile in adobo***
- **1 slice pickled jalapeño chile, minced**
- **2 tablespoons plus ½ cup mild salsa**
- **5 tablespoons plain dried bread crumbs**
- 2 tablespoons olive oil
- 4 hamburger buns, warmed
- 4 lettuce leaves
  cilantro leaves, sliced red onion, and **sour cream** (optional)

1. In medium bowl, with potato masher, mash beans until almost smooth. Stir in cumin, chipotle, jalapeño, 2 tablespoons salsa, and 2 tablespoons bread crumbs until combined.

2. Place remaining 3 tablespoons bread crumbs on sheet of waxed paper. With floured hands, shape bean mixture into four 3-inch round burgers; coat with bread crumbs.

3. In nonstick 12-inch skillet, heat oil over medium heat until hot. Add burgers and cook about 8 minutes or until lightly browned on both sides and heated through, turning burgers over once halfway through cooking.

4. Spoon remaining ½ cup salsa on bottom halves of buns; top with lettuce and burgers. Serve burgers with cilantro, red onion, and sour cream if you like.

■ Each serving: About 350 calories, 11 g protein, 51 g carbohydrate, 11 g total fat (2 g saturated), 8 g fiber, 0 mg cholesterol, 775 mg sodium.

* Canned chipotle chiles are smoked jalapeño chiles packed in a thick vinegary sauce called adobo. Look for them in Hispanic markets.

Mussels with Capers & White Wine

These shellfish steamed with garlic, capers, and wine make a dinner that can be ready in minutes.

PREP *15 minutes*
COOK *about 10 minutes*
MAKES *4 main-dish servings*

- **1 tablespoon margarine or butter**
- 1 medium shallot, finely chopped (about 2 tablespoons)
- 2 garlic cloves, crushed with garlic press
- **½ cup dry white wine**
- **2 tablespoons drained capers**
- 3 pounds mussels, scrubbed, with beards removed
- ½ cup loosely packed fresh parsley leaves, chopped

1. In 5- to 6-quart saucepot or Dutch oven, melt margarine over medium-high heat. Add shallot and garlic, and cook 2 minutes, stirring frequently. Stir in wine and capers, and heat to boiling; boil 2 minutes.

2. Add mussels to saucepot and cook over medium-high heat, covered, 10 minutes or until shells open, stirring. Discard any unopened mussels.

3. Serve mussels in bowls with sauce. Sprinkle with parsley.

■ Each serving: About 190 calories, 21 g protein, 9 g carbohydrate, 7 g total fat (1 g saturated), 0 g fiber, 48 mg cholesterol, 655 mg sodium.

Mussels with Spicy Tomato Sauce
In 5- to 6-quart saucepot or Dutch oven, heat *1 cup jarred spaghetti sauce, ½ cup dry white wine,* and *¼ teaspoon crushed red pepper* to boiling over medium-high heat. Reduce heat to medium-low and simmer 2 minutes, stirring. Add *3 pounds mussels, scrubbed, with beards removed;* cook and serve as above in steps 2 and 3. Sprinkle with *½ cup loosely packed fresh basil leaves, chopped,* instead of parsley.

■ Each serving: About 250 calories, 22 g protein, 18 g carbohydrate, 9 g total fat (2 g saturated), 1 g fiber, 48 mg cholesterol, 830 mg sodium.

cool trends in refrigerators

Shopping for a new fridge? There are more newfangled features than ever before. Check out these:

A big burst of color Exclusively from KitchenAid, you can purchase a side-by-side model in a deep shade of cobalt blue that borders on purple.

Improved ice makers Several side-by-side models from Whirlpool, KitchenAid, and Kenmore have ice makers on the inside of the freezer door rather than in the freezer compartment itself. This translates into about 10 percent more usable freezer space. The ice bins in these ice makers are also extremely easy to remove from the door when you need to fill a bucket or a tub with ice.

Downsized models GE is offering an 18-cubic-foot refrigerator with the freezer below—which eliminates bending if you use the crispers often—that is only 31 inches wide. This makes it a viable option for apartment dwellers or anyone with limited space in the kitchen.

Increased efficiency After July 2001, all refrigerators had to be about 30 percent more energy efficient than previous models—which means that it costs less to run your new refrigerator. The cumulative reduction in energy consumption throughout the country helps decrease smog and slow down global warming. To find the most efficient models on the market, look for one with an Energy Star label. These models surpass the new federal standards by at least 10 percent.

Grilled Chicken with Red-Pepper Salsa

This zesty salsa made with roasted red peppers and olives not only enhances basic pan-grilled chicken breasts but also complements other favorite grilled meats and vegetables.

PREP *20 minutes*
GRILL *about 15 minutes*
MAKES *4 main-dish servings*

Pan-Grilled Chicken
- 4 medium skinless, boneless chicken-breast halves (about 1¼ pounds)
- ¼ teaspoon salt
- ⅛ teaspoon ground black pepper

Red-Pepper Salsa
- 1 cup drained, jarred roasted red peppers (about 6 ounces), chopped
- 2 medium celery stalks, cut into ¼-inch dice
- ¼ cup pimiento-stuffed olives, chopped
- ¼ cup minced red onion
- 1 whole pickled jalapeño chile or pepperoncini, stem discarded, minced
- 1 tablespoon fresh lemon juice
- ½ teaspoon sugar
- ¼ teaspoon salt
    lemon wedges (optional)

1. Prepare Pan-Grilled Chicken: Lightly grease grill pan; heat until hot over medium heat. Add chicken and sprinkle with ¼ teaspoon salt and pepper; cook 12 to 15 minutes or until juices run clear when thickest part of chicken is pierced with tip of knife, turning chicken over once.
2. Meanwhile, prepare Red-Pepper Salsa: In small bowl, combine all salsa ingredients except lemon wedges; stir until blended. Makes about 2 cups.
3. Cut chicken breasts into thick slices. Spoon salsa over chicken. Serve with lemon wedges if you like.

■ Each serving chicken with salsa: About 210 calories, 34 g protein, 6 g carbohydrate, 5 g total fat (1 g saturated), 1 g fiber, 91 mg cholesterol, 745 mg sodium.

■ Each ¼ cup salsa: About 30 calories, 1 g protein, 6 g carbohydrate, 1 g total fat (0 g saturated), 1 g fiber, 0 mg cholesterol, 520 mg sodium.

mix it up: 12 dressings & dips

Caesar dressing Blend mayonnaise with milk, grated Parmesan cheese, Dijon mustard, anchovy paste, lemon juice, and minced garlic. Toss with romaine lettuce and croutons; use to top baked potatoes.

Russian dressing Mix mayonnaise with chili sauce, prepared white horseradish, Worcestershire sauce, and chopped pickle. Spread on sandwiches; use as a dip for raw vegetables or cooked shrimp.

Asian sesame dip Combine peanut butter with soy sauce, seasoned rice vinegar, Asian sesame oil, minced garlic, and grated ginger. Serve with chicken fingers or steamed shrimp.

Berry-yogurt dip Mix plain or vanilla yogurt with milk, your favorite berry jam (such as strawberry or blueberry), and chopped mint. Use for dunking whole strawberries, banana chunks, and grapes; mix with granola.

Green goddess dip In a blender, combine mayonnaise with sour cream, parsley leaves, red wine vinegar, anchovy paste, and minced garlic. Serve with endive leaves and cherry tomatoes.

Blue-cheese dressing Mix mayonnaise with sour cream, milk, and crumbled blue cheese. Toss with mixed greens or serve with oven-fried chicken or raw veggies.

Roasted-pepper dip In a blender, mix jarred roasted red peppers with mayonnaise, sour cream, and minced garlic; stir in chopped basil leaves. Serve with crunchy breadsticks or pita bread crisps; use as a sauce for broiled fish.

Honey-Dijon dressing Mix mayonnaise with Dijon mustard, honey, and snipped chives. Use as a dip for french fries.

Avocado dressing In a blender, mix cut up avocado with mayonnaise, sour cream, lime juice, pickled jalapeño chiles, cilantro, and green onion. Drizzle over tacos or burritos.

Mango-chutney dip Stir chopped mango chutney with mayonnaise, plain yogurt, curry powder, and minced green onions. Serve as a dip with apples or cucumbers, or spoon over sliced cold chicken.

Sun-dried tomato dressing In a blender, mix jarred sun-dried tomatoes packed in seasoned olive oil with red wine vinegar and additional olive oil; stir in chopped parsley. Toss with baby spinach leaves and sliced mushrooms.

Lemon-poppy dressing Combine sour cream with buttermilk, lemon juice, honey, and poppy seeds. Drizzle over sliced fruit; use as a sauce for pound cake.

Maple-Glazed Salmon

This sweet, tangy glaze complements the richness of salmon. It would taste equally good on swordfish or scrod.

PREP *10 minutes*
ROAST *about 15 minutes*
MAKES *4 main-dish servings*

- 3 tablespoons pure maple syrup
- 2 tablespoons soy sauce
- 1 tablespoon grated, peeled fresh ginger
- ½ teaspoon cornstarch
- 4 pieces salmon fillet (about 6 ounces each)
- 1 green onion, thinly sliced

1. Preheat oven to 475°F. In small bowl, with wire whisk or fork, mix maple syrup, soy sauce, ginger, cornstarch, and *1 tablespoon water* until blended.
2. In shallow 1½-quart casserole, place salmon skin side down. Spoon glaze over fish and roast 15 minutes, without turning over, or until fish flakes easily when tested with a fork, basting

once halfway through cooking time. Sprinkle with green onion to serve.

■ Each serving: About 340 calories, 32 g protein, 12 g carbohydrate, 18 g total fat (4 g saturated), 0 g fiber, 89 mg cholesterol, 580 mg sodium.

Chicken Breasts with Raspberry-Balsamic Sauce

A tasty pan sauce perks up a basic chicken sauté.

PREP *10 minutes*
COOK *about 20 minutes*
MAKES *4 main-dish servings*

1 tablespoon olive oil
4 medium skinless, boneless chicken-breast halves (about 1¼ pounds)
½ teaspoon salt
¼ teaspoon ground black pepper
1 medium shallot, minced (about ¼ cup)
½ **cup chicken broth**
½ teaspoon cornstarch
3 tablespoons seedless raspberry jam
2 **tablespoons balsamic vinegar**

1. In nonstick 12-inch skillet, heat oil over medium-high heat until hot. Add chicken and sprinkle with salt and pepper; cook 8 minutes. Turn chicken over. Reduce heat to medium; cover and cook 8 minutes longer or until juices run clear when thickest part of chicken is pierced with tip of knife. Transfer chicken to plate.
2. In same skillet, cook shallot 2 minutes, stirring. In cup, mix broth and cornstarch. Add broth mixture, jam, and vinegar to skillet; heat to boiling over medium-high heat. Cook sauce 2 minutes or until slightly thickened, stirring. Return chicken to skillet; heat through.

■ Each serving: About 245 calories, 33 g protein, 13 g carbohydrate, 5 g total fat (1 g saturated), 0 g fiber, 82 mg cholesterol, 515 mg sodium.

Savory Steaks with Red Wine Sauce

This assertive sauce, made with red wine, is the perfect accompaniment to pan-seared steak. Serve the steaks with steamed vegetables and crusty bread to complete the meal.

PREP *10 minutes*
COOK *about 20 minutes*
MAKES *4 main-dish servings*

2 boneless beef top loin steaks, ¾ inch thick (about 12 ounces each), well trimmed
¼ teaspoon salt
1 tablespoon olive oil
1 medium onion, finely chopped
1 garlic clove, minced
2 **tablespoons tomato paste**
½ **cup dry red wine**
½ **cup chicken broth**
½ **teaspoon Worcestershire sauce**

1. Heat nonstick 12-inch skillet over medium-high heat until very hot but not smoking. Add steaks; sprinkle with salt. Cook 8 to 10 minutes for medium-rare or until desired doneness, turning steaks over once. Transfer steaks to plate. Cut each steak crosswise in half; cover with foil to keep warm.
2. In same skillet, in oil, cook onion over medium heat 8 minutes or until tender, stirring occasionally. Add garlic and cook 1 minute, stirring. Stir in tomato paste and wine, and heat to boiling; boil 1 minute. Add broth and Worcestershire; heat through.
3. Pour any juice on plate into sauce in skillet; spoon sauce over steaks.

■ Each serving: About 445 calories, 33 g protein, 5 g carbohydrate, 32 g total fat (12 g saturated), 1 g fiber, 108 mg cholesterol, 375 mg sodium.

Greek-Style Pasta Toss

Combine fusilli with a flavorful mixture of canned tuna, roasted red peppers, olives, and capers for a delicious Mediterranean-inspired dish.

PREP *15 minutes*
COOK *about 20 minutes*
MAKES *4 main-dish servings*

salt
1 package (16 ounces) fusilli or corkscrew pasta
1 can (6 ounces) tuna in oil
2 garlic cloves, crushed with garlic press
½ teaspoon dried oregano
¼ **teaspoon crushed red pepper**
1¼ **cups drained, jarred roasted red peppers (about 8 ounces), coarsely chopped**
¼ **cup kalamata olives, pitted and chopped**
3 **tablespoons drained capers**
½ cup loosely packed fresh parsley leaves, chopped

1. Heat large saucepot of *salted water* to boiling over high heat. Add pasta and cook as label directs.
2. Meanwhile, drain tuna, reserving 1 tablespoon oil. Set tuna aside.
3. In 10-inch skillet, heat reserved oil over medium heat until hot. Add garlic, oregano, and crushed red pepper, and cook 1 minute, stirring. Add roasted red peppers, olives, capers, and drained tuna, and cook 1 minute, stirring gently to break up tuna chunks.
4. Drain pasta, reserving *½ cup pasta cooking water*. Return pasta to saucepot. Add tuna mixture, pasta cooking water, and parsley; toss well.

■ Each serving: About 560 calories, 27 g protein, 90 g carbohydrate, 10 g total fat (2 g saturated), 4 g fiber, 7 mg cholesterol, 680 mg sodium.

Fettuccine with Mushrooms & Cream

Don't go out for pasta when you can whip up a hearty dish in your kitchen.

PREP *15 minutes*
COOK *about 15 minutes*
MAKES *4 main-dish servings*

  salt
2 packages (9 ounces each) refrigerated fettuccine pasta
1 tablespoon olive oil
1 small shallot, finely chopped (2 tablespoons)
8 ounces shiitake mushrooms, stems removed, caps thinly sliced
8 ounces white mushrooms, thinly sliced
¼ **cup Marsala wine**
1½ **cups chicken broth**
⅓ **cup heavy or whipping cream**
1 cup loosely packed fresh basil or parsley leaves, chopped
¼ **cup sun-dried tomatoes in olive oil, sliced**

1. Heat large saucepot of *salted water* to boiling over high heat. Add fettuccine and cook as label directs.
2. Meanwhile, in nonstick 12-inch skillet, heat oil over medium-high heat until hot. Add shallot and cook 1 minute, stirring occasionally. Add mushrooms and ½ teaspoon salt, and cook 10 to 12 minutes or until tender and golden, stirring occasionally.
3. Stir wine into mushroom mixture. Heat to boiling and cook 1 minute. Add broth and cream; heat to boiling and cook 3 minutes, stirring.
4. Drain fettuccine and return to saucepot. Add mushroom mixture, basil, and sun-dried tomatoes, and cook 1 minute over medium heat, tossing until evenly coated.

■ Each serving: About 560 calories, 20 g protein, 83 g carbohydrate, 18 g total fat (7 g saturated), 5 g fiber, 158 mg cholesterol, 815 mg sodium.

let them eat cake!

A little frosting, a spatula, and some imagination are all you need to prepare these party-ready confections made from a mix.

Gift-Box Cake
pictured on page 80

This layer cake makes a great canvas for any whimsical box design. If you want a different look for your party, add color to the frosting with liquid food coloring and experiment with assorted candies.

PREP *15 minutes plus cooling*
BAKE *about 25 minutes*
MAKES *12 servings*

1 package (18.25 ounces) favorite cake mix
1 can (16 ounces) vanilla frosting or 1 recipe Vanilla Frosting (right)
decorations: fruit leather rolls, or bubble gum tape, assorted gumdrops, or jelly candies, each cut horizontally in half and flattened

1. Preheat oven to 350°F. Prepare cake mix as label directs, except use two 8-inch square metal baking pans. Bake 25 minutes or until toothpick inserted in center of each cake comes out clean. Cool in pans 15 minutes. Invert cakes onto wire racks to cool completely.
2. To assemble and decorate cake, place 1 layer on cake plate. With metal spatula, spread ½ cup frosting evenly over top of layer. Place remaining cake layer on top. Spread remaining frosting over top and sides of cake.

3. Create a ribbon and bow with strips of fruit leather or bubble gum tape and decorate cake with gumdrops.

■ Each serving: About 420 calories, 3 g protein, 66 g carbohydrate, 17 g total fat (4 g saturated), 0 g fiber, 45 mg cholesterol, 315 mg sodium.

Vanilla Frosting

If you have a bit more time, try whipping up this creamy all-purpose frosting instead of buying the canned.

PREP *15 minutes*
MAKES *about 1½ cups*

2¼ cups confectioners' sugar
6 tablespoons butter or margarine, softened
3 tablespoons whole milk
1½ teaspoons vanilla extract

In large bowl, with mixer at low speed, beat sugar, butter, milk, and vanilla until blended. Increase speed to medium-high; beat until light and fluffy, occasionally scraping bowl with rubber spatula.

■ Each tablespoon: About 75 calories, 0 g protein, 11 g carbohydrate, 3 g total fat (2 g saturated), 0 g fiber, 9 mg cholesterol, 30 mg sodium.

Chocolate Frosting Prepare Vanilla Frosting as above, but beat in *3 ounces semisweet chocolate,* melted, and *1 ounce unsweetened chocolate,* melted, with sugar. Makes 1⅔ cups.

■ Each tablespoon: About 85 calories, 0 g protein, 12 g carbohydrate, 4 g total fat (3 g saturated), 0 g fiber, 8 mg cholesterol, 30 mg sodium.

Lollipop Cookies
pictured on page 79

Ask children to help dress up these adorable cookies on a stick—and let their imaginations run wild!

PREP *45 minutes*
BAKE *18 to 20 minutes per batch*
MAKES *1 dozen cookies*

- 1 package (18.25 ounces) favorite cake mix
- ½ cup butter or margarine (1 stick), melted
- 2 large eggs
- 12 wooden ice cream bar sticks
- 1 can (16 ounces) vanilla frosting or 1 recipe Vanilla Frosting (facing page)
  food coloring
  decorations: colored decors, assorted candies such as jelly beans, gumdrops, candy-coated chocolate pieces, nonpareils, black and/or red shoestring licorice

1. Preheat oven to 350°F. Grease large cookie sheet.
2. In medium bowl, with wooden spoon, stir cake mix, melted butter, and eggs until dough is blended and smooth. Drop dough by scant ¼ cups onto cookie sheet (dough will be sticky). Place one end of ice cream bar stick into dough. With hand, flatten dough into 2½-inch round. Repeat to make 4 cookies in all per cookie sheet, placing cookies about 5 inches apart.

3. Bake cookies 18 to 20 minutes or until lightly browned around edges. With wide spatula, transfer cookies to wire racks to cool. Repeat with remaining dough.
4. To decorate cookies, tint frosting with food colorings as desired. Spread about 2 tablespoons frosting on each cookie. Top frosting with decors and candies.

---

tips that make our party cakes

BAKING

- To measure the volume of a pan or bowl, simply count how many cups of water it takes to fill it to the brim. (Do this in the sink to catch any overflow.)
- A cake is done when it shrinks away from side of pan and the top springs back when lightly pressed with your finger or when a toothpick inserted into center comes out clean.

FROSTING

- Frosting can be made up to one week ahead and refrigerated, covered. (It can also be frozen for up to one month.) Let frosting come to room temperature (do not microwave) and beat with a mixer before using.
- To keep the plate clean while icing a cake, arrange 3-inch-wide strips of waxed paper to form a square covering the plate; center cake on the strips and frost, then gently pull out strips.
- Offset spatulas (the blade is lower than the handle) are handy for applying frosting; their angled shape keeps hands in a comfortable position for smoother application. Use a small one for hard-to-reach spots.
- Spread cake with a thin layer of frosting to "set" crumbs (chill in the fridge to speed up the process), then apply main frosting.
- If you're decorating with more than one frosting, keep bowls covered with plastic wrap (place directly on surface of frosting) so the frosting won't dry out.

SERVING

- Cakes can be made one day ahead and refrigerated, topped with a bowl, cake cover, or roasting pan, or loosely covered with plastic wrap. (Cake layers can be made up to two days ahead of assembling and kept, well-wrapped, in plastic wrap or foil, at room temperature. Or, layers can be frozen up to two weeks.)
- If covering a cake with plastic wrap, chill the cake first to set the frosting, then stick toothpicks into it to keep the wrap from touching the surface. Bring the cake to room temperature before serving.
- Wrap a large cutting board or heavyweight cardboard with foil to provide a surface to serve large or oddly shaped cakes (also a good way to transport a cake). A few dollops of frosting on the platter will keep the cake from slipping.
- When transporting a filled layer cake, insert a few pieces of dry spaghetti straight down through the layers to keep them from shifting.

SLICING

- A six- to eight-inch chef's knife (well-sharpened) is best for layer cakes.
- To cut, use a light, gentle sawing motion so you won't mess up the cake's shape.
- If you need to cut sticky foods like candy or fruit leather for decorating, keep dipping the knife or scissors in flour or lightly coat with nonstick cooking spray.

■ Each serving: About 430 calories, 3 g protein, 61 g carbohydrate, 20 g total fat (8 g saturated), 1 g fiber, 58 mg cholesterol, 420 mg sodium.

Gum Ball Machine Cake

pictured on page 78

Using two eight-inch cakes—one round and one square—allows you to prepare this fun party finale easily without complicated cutting.

PREP *30 minutes plus cooling*
BAKE *about 30 minutes*
MAKES *12 servings*

- 1 package (18.25 ounces) favorite cake mix
- 1 can (16 ounces) vanilla frosting or 1 recipe Vanilla Frosting (page 72) red food coloring
    decorations: 6 ounces gum balls (about 1 cup), red licorice-twist candy, fruit leather, or taffy

1. Preheat oven to 350°F. Prepare cake mix as label directs except use 1 round and 1 square 8-inch metal baking pan. Divide batter evenly between pans.
2. Bake cakes 30 minutes or until toothpick inserted in center of each cake comes out clean. Cool in pans on wire racks 15 minutes. Invert cakes onto wire racks to cool completely.
3. To assemble and decorate cake, cut ½-inch slice from edge of round layer; set aside. Place cake layers on large tray, centering cut side of round cake next to square cake. In small bowl, tint half of frosting red. With metal spatula, frost top of round cake layer with all but 3 tablespoons white frosting. Frost side of round cake layer and top and sides of square cake layer with red frosting. Cut a 2-inch strip from reserved cake; center on top edge of round cake layer. Frost piece with red frosting.
4. Place gum balls in decorative pattern on round cake. (If you want to stack gum balls for more of a 3-dimensional effect, use some of reserved white frosting to attach them.) Attach a gum ball to red knob at top of cake.
5. With small metal spatula, spread remaining white frosting in a 2-inch square at center bottom (edge farthest away from round cake) of square cake to resemble gum-ball chute. Attach several gum balls onto chute area. Use licorice to make decorative outline around chute and top edge of square cake. If you like, use fruit leather to write message such as happy birthday or 1¢ on top of square cake.

■ Each serving: About 460 calories, 3 g protein, 79 g carbohydrate, 17 g total fat (4 g saturated), 0 g fiber, 45 mg cholesterol, 310 mg sodium.

Butterfly Cake

pictured on page 79

Take this wonderful cake to a spring gathering.

PREP *30 minutes plus cooling*
BAKE *about 40 minutes*
MAKES *12 servings*

- 1 package (16 ounces) pound cake mix
- 1 can (16 ounces) vanilla frosting or 1 recipe Vanilla Frosting (page 72) yellow and blue food coloring
    decorations: 1 gummy worm, black shoestring licorice, assorted gumdrops

1. Preheat oven to 350°F. Grease and flour one 10-inch tube pan.
2. Prepare cake mix as label directs. Spoon batter into prepared pan and spread evenly. Bake cake 40 to 45 minutes or until toothpick inserted in center of cake comes out clean. Cool cake in pan on wire rack 15 minutes. Invert cake onto wire rack to cool completely.
3. To assemble and decorate cake, with serrated knife, cut cake in half from top to bottom. On large platter or tray, place cake halves with rounded sides touching and cut sides facing out to resemble butterfly wings.
4. Divide frosting in half and tint each as desired with food coloring (we used yellow and blue, but you can use any 2 colors you like or tint only half the frosting, leaving remaining frosting white). With metal spatula, frost half of each wing, top and sides, with 1 color frosting, then frost remaining half of each wing with remaining frosting. With spatula, spread frostings out toward edges of wings to create curved lines, blending frosting colors slightly to create feathered look.
5. Place gummy worm in center of halves to resemble butterfly's body. Arrange licorice at top of gummy worm to resemble antennae, inserting licorice into cake to secure. Decorate as desired with gumdrops.

■ Each serving: About 330 calories, 3 g protein, 57 g carbohydrate, 11 g total fat (4 g saturated), 0 g fiber, 37 mg cholesterol, 180 mg sodium.

Ice Cream Cone Cupcakes

These are a sweet treat that kids will want to help decorate. They're best eaten the same day they are made, or the cones will become soggy. The number of cones needed can vary depending on the brand you buy. We prefer the wider-bottomed style, which yields 24. To ensure that the cakes rise properly and do not overflow, fill each cone no more than two-thirds full.

PREP *15 minutes plus cooling*
BAKE *about 20 minutes*
MAKES *24 servings*

- 1 package (18.25 ounces) yellow or white cake mix
- 2 boxes (1¾ ounces each) waffle-style ice cream cone cups (24 cones)
- 2 cans (16 ounces each) vanilla and/or chocolate frosting or 2 recipes Vanilla Frosting and/or Chocolate Frosting (page 72) assorted sprinkles

1. Preheat oven to 350°F. Prepare cake mix as label directs. Spoon batter into cones, filling each about two-thirds full. Place cones on large cookie sheet or jelly-roll pan for easier handling.

2. Bake cones 20 to 22 minutes or until toothpick inserted in center of cake comes out clean. Cool cones completely on cookie sheet on wire rack.

3. To decorate cupcakes, with small metal spatula, spread 2 tablespoons frosting on cake in each cone; top with sprinkles.

■ Each serving: About 330 calories, 3 g protein, 55 g carbohydrate, 11 g total fat (3 g saturated), 1 g fiber, 23 mg cholesterol, 230 mg sodium.

Sunshine Cake

pictured on page 79

Create this sunny shape by cutting one of the two cake layers into eight wedges.

PREP *35 minutes plus cooling*
BAKE *about 30 minutes*
MAKES *12 servings*

    1 package (18.25 ounces) favorite
      cake mix
 1½ cans (16 ounces each) vanilla
      frosting or 1½ recipes Vanilla
      Frosting (page 72)
      yellow and red food coloring

1. Preheat oven to 350°F. Prepare cake mix and bake as label directs except use one 8-inch and one 9-inch round cake pan. Bake 25 to 30 minutes or until toothpick inserted in the center of each cake comes out clean. Cool cakes in pans 15 minutes. Invert cakes onto wire racks to cool completely.

2. To assemble cake, place 8-inch cake layer on large tray and cut 9-inch cake layer into 8 wedges. In small bowl, tint ¾ cup frosting orange. With metal spatula, spread orange frosting on top and side of

round cake layer. In another bowl, tint remaining frosting yellow. Spread yellow frosting on tops and sides of cake wedges. Place wedges, pointed tips out, around orange cake layer to resemble a sun.

■ Each serving: About 485 calories, 3 g protein, 76 g carbohydrate, 19 g total fat (5 g saturated), 0 g fiber, 45 mg cholesterol, 330 mg sodium.

food editor's Q&A

Q **You sometimes call for pink beans in your recipes. What are they? Is there a substitute?**

a Available dried or canned, smooth, pinkish-brown beans have a sweet flavor and meaty texture. You may use pinto or small red kidney beans instead. Quick tip: Most beans can be substituted successfully for one another in recipes, so it's a good idea to keep an assortment of types on hand in your pantry.

Q **When a recipe calls for large eggs, will I ruin the batter if I use medium or jumbo instead?**

a Most baking recipes call for large eggs. If you happen to have another size in your fridge, you need to be careful about substituting them when 3 or more eggs are called for. (If a recipe calls for fewer than 3, says the American Egg Board, it probably won't matter.) However, in recipes calling for 3 large eggs, use 2 jumbo, or 3 extra large or medium; for 4 large eggs, use 3 jumbo, 4 extra large, or 5 medium; for 5 large eggs, use 4 jumbo or extra large, or 6 medium; for 6 large eggs, use 5 jumbo or extra large, or 7 medium. Remember, any size may be used for frying, scrambling, or cooking eggs in the shell.

Q **With the selection of balsamic vinegars out there— aged varieties, imported types, and so on—I don't know which to buy. Do you have any tips?**

a Choosing a good imported balsamic vinegar is like buying a fine wine: You need to sample several until you find one you love. Although all varieties have a 6 percent acidity level, they vary in flavor depending on the proportion of cooked-down crushed grape to wine vinegar, the type and size of wooden casks they were aged in, and the length of time they were aged. The most refined varieties are aged for at least three years in wooden barrels, which produces an intense, woody flavor.

In an effort to boost sales, some companies may make false aging claims on their labels; others don't follow production specifications governed by Italian law (the United States doesn't oversee label claims on imported balsamic vinegar). But there is one way to know you're purchasing a quality product: Look for a seal from the Consortium for the Protection of Balsamic Vinegar of Modena (CABM). A burgundy-colored seal (you'll find it on the neck band of the bottle) guarantees product authenticity and indicates an aging period of less than three years, making these vinegars a good choice for salad dressings and pan sauces. The gold and white "Invecchiato" (aged) CABM seal guarantees that the product has been aged more than 3 years in a wooden cask, creating a more delicate (and more expensive) vinegar suitable for drizzling over vegetables, fruit, and prosciutto.

Clown Cake

pictured on facing page

This jolly clown cake will delight youngsters. A cake mix calling for oil as an "add in," not butter, will bake up better in the bowl.

PREP *1¼ hours plus cooling*
BAKE *about 65 minutes*
MAKES *12 servings*

- 1 package (18.25 ounces) favorite cake mix (calling for oil)
- 2 wooden skewers (5 to 6 inches long each)
- 1 can (16 ounces) vanilla frosting or 1 recipe Vanilla Frosting (page 72)
  blue and yellow food coloring
- 1 sugar ice cream cone
- 4 sugar wafers
  decorations: chocolate chips, gum balls, chewy orange candies, mini marshmallows, and red shoestring licorice

1. Preheat oven to 350°F. Grease 2½-quart oven-safe glass bowl (diameter of top should be 8 to 9 inches) and 6-ounce custard cup; dust both with flour.
2. Prepare cake mix as label directs. Spoon ⅓ cup batter into custard cup; spoon remaining batter into bowl. In same oven, bake cake in custard cup 25 minutes and cake in bowl 65 to 70 minutes or until toothpick inserted in center of each cake comes out clean. Cool cakes on wire racks 15 minutes. Invert cakes onto wire racks to cool completely.
3. To assemble and decorate cake, place larger cake, bottom side up, on platter. Insert skewers into top center of cake, about ½ inch apart. Press rounded edge of smaller cake into skewers to secure for clown's head, trimming skewers if necessary so that they do not protrude from cake.
4. In small bowl, tint ⅓ cup frosting light blue. Spoon ¼ cup frosting into custard cup and leave white. Tint remaining frosting yellow.

5. With a metal spatula, frost clown body yellow and clown head white.
6. With kitchen shears, cut about 2 inches from open end of ice cream cone (it's OK if cut line is a bit jagged). Frost cone and 1 wide side of each sugar wafer blue.
7. Place cone on top of clown's head for hat. Attach 2 sugar wafers, blue side out, on left side of clown body for 1 arm; attach remaining 2 sugar wafers on right side for second arm. Use chocolate chips for eyes; gum balls for nose, buttons, and top of hat. Cut orange candies into small pieces and arrange around hat for hair. With fingers, flatten 2 mini marshmallows and place 1 at end of each arm for hands. Cut licorice into short lengths; use for eyebrows and cuffs, and arrange around clown neck for collar.

■ Each serving: About 415 calories, 3 g protein, 64 g carbohydrate, 17 g total fat (4 g saturated), 0 g fiber, 45 mg cholesterol, 315 mg sodium.

the big butter test

Europeans and chefs all over the world have been using higher-fat butters for years. For one thing, the flavor is more intense; also, these butters have superior baking and cooking qualities. (The higher the fat, the less water, so pastry is flakier, sauces are richer, cakes rise higher, and crusts are more golden.)

Now that premium butters are available in U.S. supermarkets, we sampled three brands: Keller's European Style Butter (82 percent fat), Land O Lakes Ultra Creamy Butter (83 percent fat), Vermont Butter & Cheese Company's Vermont Cultured Butter (86 percent fat)—comparing them to regular Land O Lakes Sweet Cream Butter (80 percent fat). All of the samples were unsalted except Vermont Cultured Butter, which is very lightly salted. These were our favorites—by the spoon and in a recipe.

BY THE SPOON
Our first choice was Keller's, with Vermont Butter & Cheese close behind. The Keller's sample had a rich cream flavor with a slightly tangy aroma and aftertaste. The Vermont butter was extremely rich tasting, even more tangy, and the small amount of salt heightened the flavor of the cream. Land O Lakes Ultra Creamy Butter was fresh-tasting but without the tang, and the traditional Land O Lakes came across as relatively bland.

IN A RECIPE
Then, using a classic shortbread recipe, we found that the Keller's, Vermont Butter & Cheese, and Land O Lakes Ultra Creamy Butter samples baked up darker, tasted richer, had a more pronounced butter aroma during and after baking, and were decidedly crispier than the shortbread made with regular butter. In fact, there was such a high percentage of fat in the last two that they bubbled vigorously during the last five minutes of baking. We'd happily trade up to the premium brands in baking recipes where butter is the predominant flavor.

Clown Cake,
facing page

Gum Ball Machine Cake,
page 74

Butterfly Cake,
page 74

Sunshine Cake,
page 75

Lollipop Cookies,
page 73

Gift-Box Cake, page 72

May

A TASTE OF SPRING

a taste of spring

Your family will delight in these meals that feature trimmer meats, tender asparagus, and the season's freshest flavors.

Thai Salad with Roast Pork

A pretty, refreshing salad that combines easy-to-find ingredients to create an exotic dish.

PREP *about 30 minutes*
ROAST *about 20 minutes*
MAKES *4 main-dish servings*

2 to 3 limes
2 tablespoons Asian fish sauce
2 teaspoons soy sauce
1½ teaspoons sugar
¼ teaspoon crushed red pepper
1 whole pork tenderloin (about ¾ pound), trimmed
1 bunch watercress (about 4 ounces), tough stems trimmed
2 cups loosely packed fresh cilantro sprigs
1 cup loosely packed fresh mint leaves
6 radishes, trimmed and thinly sliced

1. Preheat oven to 475°F. From limes, grate ½ teaspoon peel and squeeze ¼ cup juice.
2. In small bowl, stir lime juice, lime peel, fish sauce, soy sauce, sugar, and crushed red pepper. In medium bowl, coat tenderloin with 2 tablespoons lime-juice mixture; marinate tenderloin 15 minutes at room temperature, turning occasionally.
3. Meanwhile, in bowl, toss watercress, cilantro, mint, and radishes.
4. Place tenderloin on rack in small roasting pan (14" by 10"). Tuck thin end of tenderloin under, so meat is an even thickness. Roast tenderloin 20 to 25 minutes or until internal temperature of meat reaches 150°F. on meat thermometer (temperature will rise 5° to 10°F. upon standing).
5. To serve, thinly slice tenderloin. Toss watercress mixture with remaining lime-juice mixture. Arrange salad on platter and top with tenderloin slices.

■ Each serving: About 130 calories, 20 g protein, 6 g carbohydrate, 3 g total fat (1 g saturated), 2 g fiber, 50 mg cholesterol, 915 mg sodium.

Roasted Prosciutto-Wrapped Asparagus

Perfect for a dinner party appetizer— you can oven-steam the asparagus in advance, then roast the wrapped spears just before serving. The recipe works best with medium-size asparagus spears because they're easier to handle as finger food.

PREP *30 minutes*
STEAM/ROAST *about 20 minutes*
MAKES *12 first-course servings or 24 hors d'oeuvres*

24 medium asparagus spears (about 1½ pounds), trimmed
12 thin slices prosciutto (about 8 ounces), each cut lengthwise in half
½ cup grated Parmesan cheese

1. Preheat oven to 400°F. Place asparagus and *¼ cup boiling water* in large roasting pan (17" by 11½"); cover pan with foil. Steam asparagus 10 to 15 minutes or until tender when tested with tip of knife. Transfer asparagus to paper towels to drain. Wipe pan dry.
2. On sheet of waxed paper, place 1 strip prosciutto; sprinkle with 1 teaspoon Parmesan. Place asparagus spear on 1 end of prosciutto strip. Roll prosciutto around asparagus spear, slightly overlapping prosciutto as you roll and covering most of spear. Repeat with remaining asparagus, prosciutto, and Parmesan.
3. Place wrapped asparagus in roasting pan (it's all right if spears touch), and roast 10 minutes or until asparagus is heated through and prosciutto just begins to brown.

■ Each first-course serving: About 50 calories, 7 g protein, 1 g carbohydrate, 2 g total fat (1 g saturated), 1 g fiber, 15 mg cholesterol, 540 mg sodium.

Black Forest Ham–Wrapped Asparagus
Substitute *12 thin slices Black Forest ham (about 8 ounces)* for prosciutto and use *1 cup shredded Gruyère cheese* (about 1½ teaspoons per spear) for Parmesan. Follow recipe as above.

■ Each first-course serving: About 80 calories, 8 g protein, 1 g carbohydrate, 5 g total fat (2 g saturated), 1 g fiber, 21 mg cholesterol, 315 mg sodium.

Creamy Asparagus Soup

A classic to celebrate the season!
Serve with crispy breadsticks.

PREP **10 minutes**
COOK **about 25 minutes**
MAKES **5½ cups or 4 first-course
      servings**

    1 tablespoon margarine or
       butter
    1 small onion, coarsely chopped
1½ pounds asparagus, trimmed and
       coarsely chopped
    1 can (14½ ounces) chicken broth
       or vegetable broth (1¾ cups)
 ½ teaspoon salt
 ⅛ teaspoon ground black pepper
 ¼ cup heavy or whipping cream
       sliced green onions and
       steamed thin asparagus spears
       (optional)

1. In 4-quart saucepan, melt margarine over medium heat. Add onion and cook 8 to 10 minutes or until tender and lightly golden, stirring often. Add chopped asparagus and cook 5 minutes, stirring occasionally.
2. Add broth, salt, pepper, and *1 cup water;* heat to boiling over high heat. Reduce heat to low; cover and simmer 8 to 10 minutes or until asparagus is tender. Remove saucepan from heat.
3. In blender at low speed, with center part of cover removed to allow steam to escape, blend asparagus mixture in small batches until very smooth. Pour blended soup into large bowl after each batch. (If you like, use hand blender, following manufacturer's directions, to puree mixture in saucepan until very smooth.)
4. Return blended soup to saucepan. Stir in cream and heat through. Spoon soup into 4 bowls and top with green onions and asparagus spears if you like.

■ Each serving: About 125 calories, 4 g protein, 5 g carbohydrate, 10 g total fat (4 g saturated), 2 g fiber, 21 mg cholesterol, 785 mg sodium.

food editor's Q&A

Q **When a recipe calls for green onions, can I use scallions—or is there a difference?**

a Scallion is actually the group name for many members of the onion family, including green onions, young leeks, and scallions themselves. A green onion is a new onion harvested while its top is still green and its bulb small. A scallion is younger than a green onion, and its white base (the part that would develop into a bulb) has straighter sides. A baby onion is considered a scallion until its base (bulb) matures to about three-quarters of an inch, and then it's called a green onion. Spring onion is another term for green onion and scallion, referring to immature plants that would grow to full size if left in the ground. Although true scallions are a bit milder than green onions, the two can be used interchangeably in recipes, such as our Pork Chops with Peppers & Onions (page 85) or Korean Steak in Lettuce Cups (page 89).

I also like to lightly toss green onions with olive oil and grill them to serve with beef or chicken, or chop them raw as a garnish for everything from baked potatoes to Mexican dishes.

Q **The Indian restaurant in my neighborhood serves a curry dish called vindaloo. What makes it taste so different from regular curries?**

a Vindaloo is much hotter, although it has a sweet-and-sour note, too. The original dish was a Portuguese pork stew seasoned with garlic and wine vinegar, but when it was brought to the Indian district of Goa by Portuguese colonists and made with the local ground red chiles, mustard seeds, ginger, coriander, cumin, and black peppercorns, the dish developed its distinct fiery flavor. Goa vindaloos are usually still made with pork, but you can use any meat or vegetable. And serve with rice to balance the heat.

Q **Every once in a while my supermarket carries white asparagus. Why is it so much more expensive than green? Is it worth it?**

a The higher cost has to do with its more time-consuming growing method. White asparagus is "regular" asparagus grown underground, where it doesn't get any sun. Farmers bury the young plants in plenty of dirt throughout the growing season to shield the tender shoots from sunlight, which would turn them green. This underground process yields spears that have a stronger, slightly bitter flavor (and are lower in vitamin C). Creamy spears also tend to have fewer tiny leaves at the tip and make a striking contrast next to green as a side dish or on an appetizer tray.

Seize the moment: Asparagus is at its peak through May. And the price is down from the prohibitive $3.98 or $4.98 per pound you may pay for an imported bundle in the off season. (Part of the reason this green costs more than others, even in season, is that the tender spears must be picked by hand.) To get your money's worth:

At the store Buy asparagus on the day you plan to cook it or, at most, a day ahead. Look for firm, straight spears with closed, compact tips. To test for freshness, bend a spear; it should give very little. Choose stalks that are more or less the same size to make sure they cook evenly.

In your kitchen Remove rubber bands or wires from the bundle; they cause the stalks to sweat, which can hasten rotting. Either store spears upright in the refrigerator with cut ends resting in an inch of cool water, or wrap cut ends in a moist paper towel,

cover the paper towel with a plastic bag, and refrigerate.

At the sink Rinse asparagus in cool running water. If the tips are sandy, soak them in water for a few minutes. To remove the tough, inedible ends, just bend the asparagus spears at the bottom and snap off (for larger spears, use a knife). It's not necessary to peel stalks, but if you want to, go about two-thirds of the way up the stalk, using a vegetable peeler.

On the stove No matter which method you choose—boiling, steaming, microwaving, or roasting—cook briefly (check for doneness after 3 to 5 minutes). Otherwise, asparagus becomes mushy and drab. If not serving right away, rinse under cold water to stop cooking, and refrigerate. Drizzling the asparagus with vinaigrette? Wait until just before serving; the acid will wash out the color and alter the flavor of the asparagus.

Asparagus Risotto

Sweet asparagus lends fresh spring flavor to this favorite Italian rice dish.

PREP *15 minutes*
COOK *50 minutes*
MAKES *about 8 cups or 4 main-dish servings*

1 can (14½ ounces) chicken broth or vegetable broth (1¾ cups)
1½ pounds asparagus, trimmed
2 tablespoons margarine or butter
1 small onion, finely chopped
2 cups Arborio (Italian short-grain) rice or medium-grain rice
½ cup dry white wine
¾ cup grated Parmesan cheese
¾ teaspoon salt
¼ teaspoon ground black pepper

1. In 2-quart saucepan, heat broth and *4 cups water* to boiling over high

heat. Reduce heat to low to maintain simmer; cover.

2. If using thin asparagus, cut each stalk crosswise in half and reserve halves with tips; if using medium asparagus, cut 1 inch from asparagus tops and reserve tips. Cut remaining asparagus stalks into ¼-inch pieces.

3. In deep nonstick 12-inch skillet, heat 1 tablespoon margarine over medium heat. Add chopped onion and asparagus pieces (not tips), and cook 10 minutes or until vegetables begin to soften, stirring occasionally.

4. Add rice and remaining 1 tablespoon margarine, and cook until rice grains are opaque, stirring frequently. Add wine; cook until absorbed, stirring.

5. Add about ½ cup simmering broth to rice, stirring until liquid is absorbed. Continue cooking 25 minutes, adding remaining broth, ½ cup at a time, and stirring after each addition until liquid is absorbed. Stir in

reserved asparagus when adding last ½ cup broth mixture and cook until all liquid is absorbed and rice and asparagus are tender (risotto should have a creamy consistency). Stir in Parmesan, salt, and pepper.

■ Each serving: About 590 calories, 19 g protein, 96 g carbohydrate, 11 g total fat (4 g saturated), 4 g fiber, 12 mg cholesterol, 1,245 mg sodium.

Southwestern Pork Tenderloins with Warm Corn Salad

A zesty mixture of fresh corn, red onion, chopped cilantro, and lime juice is a perfect accompaniment to chili-rubbed roasted tenderloins.

PREP *30 minutes*
ROAST *about 20 minutes*
MAKES *6 main-dish servings*

Spice-Rubbed Tenderloins
2 tablespoons chili powder
1½ teaspoons ground cumin
1½ teaspoons ground coriander
¾ teaspoon salt
½ teaspoon ground black pepper
2 whole pork tenderloins (about ¾ pound each), trimmed

Warm Corn Salad
2 teaspoons olive oil
1 small red onion, thinly sliced
3 cups fresh corn kernels (from 5 to 6 ears)
1 small jalapeño chile, seeded and minced
1 medium tomato, finely chopped
½ cup loosely packed fresh cilantro leaves, chopped
1 tablespoon fresh lime juice
½ teaspoon salt

1. Preheat oven to 475°F. Prepare Spice-Rubbed Tenderloins: In cup, blend chili powder, cumin, coriander, salt, and pepper. Rub tenderloins all over with spice mixture.

2. Place tenderloins on rack in small roasting pan (14" by 10"). Tuck thin ends of tenderloins under, so meat is an even thickness. Roast tenderloins 20 to 25 minutes or until internal temperature of meat reaches 150°F. on meat thermometer (temperature will rise 5° to 10°F. upon standing).

3. Meanwhile, prepare Warm Corn Salad: In nonstick 10-inch skillet, heat oil over medium heat until hot. Add red onion and cook 5 minutes, stirring occasionally. Add corn and jalapeño, and cook 3 minutes, stirring occasionally. Remove skillet from heat and stir in tomato, cilantro, lime juice, and salt. Makes about 4 cups salad.

4. To serve, spoon corn salad onto platter. Thinly slice tenderloins and arrange over salad.

■ Each serving: About 260 calories, 27 g protein, 25 g carbohydrate, 7 g total fat (2 g saturated), 4 g fiber, 67 mg cholesterol, 760 mg sodium.

Pork Chops with Peppers & Onions
pictured on page 117

Boneless chops are smothered in green onions and red peppers for this fast and easy skillet dinner.

PREP *10 minutes*
COOK *about 20 minutes*
MAKES *4 main-dish servings*

- 4 boneless pork loin chops, ½ inch thick (about 4 ounces each), trimmed
- ½ teaspoon salt
- ¼ teaspoon ground black pepper
- 2 teaspoons olive oil
- 1 bunch green onions, green tops cut diagonally into 3-inch pieces, white bottoms thinly sliced crosswise
- 2 medium red peppers, cut into 1½-inch pieces
- 1 garlic clove, crushed with garlic press
- ⅛ teaspoon crushed red pepper
- ½ cup chicken broth

1. Heat nonstick 12-inch skillet over medium-high heat until hot but not smoking. Add pork chops to skillet and sprinkle with salt and pepper. Cook chops about 8 minutes or until lightly browned on the outside and still slightly pink on the inside, turning chops over once (reduce heat to medium if chops are browning too quickly). Transfer pork chops to plate; keep warm.

2. To skillet, add oil and green-onion tops, and cook 4 minutes. With slotted spoon, transfer green-onion tops to small bowl. In same skillet, cook red peppers and green-onion bottoms 8 minutes, stirring occasionally. Add garlic and crushed red pepper, and cook 1 minute, stirring. Stir in broth and half of green-onion tops; heat through. Spoon pepper mixture onto platter; top with chops and remaining green-onion tops.

■ Each serving: About 210 calories, 26 g protein, 7 g carbohydrate, 8 g total fat (2 g saturated), 2 g fiber, 71 mg cholesterol, 495 mg sodium.

steamer pots: worth your green?

Good Housekeeping INSTITUTE REPORT

You've probably seen asparagus steamers in cookware stores and catalogs—narrow pots about a foot tall with a basket insert. You cook the spears stems down and they're supposed to emerge perfectly tender-crisp. But don't spend a lot of money (they cost anywhere from about $20 to $60) on this gizmo. Our food appliances team plunked bunch after bunch in the skinny steamers and found that the asparagus came out no better (or more vibrantly colored) than the samples made in a skillet with an ordinary collapsible metal steamer. What our experts did discover is that it's more difficult to arrange the stalks in the towering pot and remove them after cooking without damaging the fragile tips.

Orange Pork & Asparagus Stir-fry

pictured on page 116

Slices of lean pork tenderloin are quickly cooked with fresh asparagus and juicy orange pieces.

PREP *20 minutes*
COOK *about 6 minutes*
MAKES *4 main-dish servings*

    2 navel oranges
    1 teaspoon olive oil
    1 whole pork tenderloin
         (about ¾ pound), trimmed,
         thinly sliced diagonally
    ¾ teaspoon salt
    ¼ teaspoon ground black pepper
 1½ pounds thin asparagus, trimmed
         and each stalk cut in half
    1 garlic clove, crushed with garlic
         press
         kumquats on the stem, for
         garnish

1. From 1 orange, grate 1 teaspoon peel and squeeze ¼ cup juice. Cut off peel and white pith from remaining orange. Cut orange into ¼-inch slices; cut each slice into quarters.

2. In nonstick 12-inch skillet, heat ½ teaspoon oil over medium-high heat until hot but not smoking. Add half the pork and sprinkle with ¼ teaspoon salt and ⅛ teaspoon pepper; cook 2 minutes or until pork just loses its pink color, stirring frequently. Transfer pork to plate. Repeat with remaining ½ teaspoon oil, pork, ¼ teaspoon salt, and remaining ⅛ teaspoon pepper. Transfer pork to same plate.

3. To same skillet, add asparagus, garlic, orange peel, remaining ¼ teaspoon salt, and *¼ cup water;* cover and cook about 2 minutes or until asparagus is tender-crisp, stirring occasionally. Return pork to skillet. Add orange juice and orange pieces; heat through, stirring often. Garnish with kumquats if you like.

■ Each serving: About 165 calories, 24 g protein, 8 g carbohydrate, 4 g total fat (1 g saturated), 2 g fiber, 50 mg cholesterol, 495 mg sodium.

loving asparagus through thick or thin

Asparagus is graded by size: small, standard, large, and jumbo. The older the plant, the thicker the spear. But stalk size isn't a clue to tenderness; as long as it's fresh, jumbo asparagus can be just as sweet and buttery as young, slim varieties. And although pencil-thin spears are attractive for dipping, medium-size or thicker ones work best for some appetizers such as our Roasted Prosciutto-Wrapped Asparagus (page 82) because they hold their shape during roasting and are easier to serve as a finger food.

Asparagus & Green-Onion Frittata

Everyone loves a skillet omelet, especially when it's filled with bits of cream cheese and sautéed vegetables.

PREP *25 minutes*
BAKE *about 10 minutes*
MAKES *4 main-dish servings*

    8 large eggs
    ½ cup whole milk
    ⅛ teaspoon ground black pepper
    ¾ teaspoon salt
  12 ounces asparagus, trimmed
    1 tablespoon margarine or butter
    1 bunch green onions, chopped
    2 ounces light cream cheese
         (Neufchâtel)

1. Preheat oven to 375°F. In medium bowl, with wire whisk, mix eggs, milk, pepper, and ½ teaspoon salt; set aside. If using thin asparagus, cut stalks crosswise in half; if using medium asparagus, cut stalks into 1-inch pieces.

2. In nonstick 10-inch skillet with oven-safe handle (or wrap handle with double thickness of heavy-duty foil for baking in oven later), melt margarine over medium heat. Add asparagus and remaining ¼ teaspoon salt, and cook 4 minutes for thin stalks or 6 minutes for medium-size stalks, stirring often. Stir in green onions and cook 2 to 3 minutes longer or until vegetables are tender, stirring occasionally.

3. Reduce heat to medium-low. Pour egg mixture over vegetables in skillet; drop scant teaspoonfuls of cream cheese on top of egg mixture. Cook 3 to 4 minutes, without stirring, until egg mixture begins to set around edge. Place skillet in oven and bake 10 to 12 minutes or until frittata is set and knife inserted in center comes out clean. Cut into wedges to serve.

■ Each serving: About 250 calories, 17 g protein, 6 g carbohydrate, 18 g total fat (6 g saturated), 1 g fiber, 440 mg cholesterol, 680 mg sodium.

Lighter Beef & Broccoli

This streamlined version of the popular Chinese dish is almost as quick as ordering takeout—and it's healthy to boot.

PREP **25 minutes**
COOK **about 12 minutes**
MAKES **4 main-dish servings**

- 1 large bunch broccoli (about 1½ pounds)
- 1 pound beef tenderloin steaks, trimmed, thinly cut into ⅛-inch-thick strips
- 3 garlic cloves, crushed with garlic press
- 1 tablespoon grated, peeled fresh ginger
- ¼ teaspoon crushed red pepper
- 1 teaspoon olive oil
- ¾ cup chicken broth
- 3 tablespoons soy sauce
- 1 tablespoon cornstarch
- ½ teaspoon Asian sesame oil

1. Cut broccoli flowerets into 1½-inch pieces. Peel broccoli stems and cut stems into ¼-inch-thick diagonal slices.
2. In nonstick 12-inch skillet, heat *½ inch water* to boiling over medium-high heat. Add broccoli and cook 3 minutes, uncovered, or until tender-crisp. Drain broccoli and set aside. Wipe skillet dry.
3. In medium bowl, toss beef with garlic, ginger, and crushed red pepper. Add ½ teaspoon olive oil to skillet and heat over medium-high heat until hot but not smoking. Add half of beef mixture and cook 2 minutes or until beef just loses its pink color throughout, stirring quickly and frequently. Transfer beef to plate. Repeat with remaining ½ teaspoon olive oil and beef mixture.
4. In cup, mix broth, soy sauce, cornstarch, and sesame oil until blended. Return cooked beef to skillet. Stir in cornstarch mixture; heat to boiling. Cook 1 minute or until sauce thickens slightly, stirring. Add broccoli and toss to coat.

■ Each serving: About 245 calories, 28 g protein, 10 g carbohydrate, 11 g total fat (3 g saturated), 3 g fiber, 57 mg cholesterol, 1,010 mg sodium.

Pasta with Asparagus Pesto

pictured on page 117

Michael Chiarello, chef-owner of Tra Vigne restaurant in California's Napa Valley and author of *The Tra Vigne Cookbook,* came to the Good Housekeeping test kitchens to cook for us and inspired this pestolike sauce made with asparagus.

PREP **20 minutes**
COOK **15 minutes**
MAKES **4 main-dish servings**

- salt
- 1 pound orecchiette or medium shell pasta
- 1½ pounds asparagus, trimmed
- ¼ cup olive oil
- 2 tablespoons pine nuts (pignoli), toasted
- ¼ teaspoon ground black pepper
- 1 garlic clove, crushed with garlic press
- ¾ cup packed fresh basil leaves
- ⅓ cup grated Pecorino Romano cheese, plus additional for serving

1. Heat large saucepot of *salted water* to boiling over high heat. Add pasta and cook as label directs.
2. Meanwhile, if using thin asparagus, cut each stalk crosswise in half; if using medium asparagus, cut stalks into 1½-inch pieces. In 12-inch skillet, heat *1 inch water* to boiling over high heat. Add asparagus and cook 5 minutes or until tender. Remove and reserve *½ cup asparagus cooking water;* drain asparagus.
3. Set aside 1 cup thin asparagus stalks or ½ cup medium asparagus tips. In blender at low speed, with center part of cover removed to allow steam to escape, blend remaining asparagus with oil, pine nuts, pepper, garlic, ½ cup basil, 1 teaspoon salt, and reserved asparagus cooking water until almost smooth. Add cheese and blend until well mixed.
4. Slice remaining ¼ cup basil leaves. Drain pasta and return to saucepot. Add asparagus sauce, sliced basil, and reserved asparagus, and toss until evenly mixed. Serve with additional cheese if you like.

■ Each serving: About 620 calories, 21 g protein, 88 g carbohydrate, 20 g total fat (4 g saturated), 4 g fiber, 7 mg cholesterol, 830 mg sodium.

Springtime Lo Mein

Canadian bacon provides plenty of meaty flavor without adding a lot of fat to this Chinese restaurant-style dish.

PREP *about 30 minutes*
COOK *about 15 minutes*
MAKES *4 main-dish servings*

    salt
8 ounces spaghetti
2 teaspoons vegetable oil
1 garlic clove, minced
¾ pound napa (Chinese) cabbage (about ½ small head), thinly sliced
6 ounces shiitake mushrooms, stems discarded, caps thinly sliced
½ (10-ounce) package shredded carrots (1¾ cups)
1 yellow pepper, cut into long thin strips
6 ounces thinly sliced Canadian-style bacon, cut into long thin strips
2 tablespoons seasoned rice vinegar
2 teaspoons cornstarch
1 teaspoon Asian sesame oil
2 green onions, thinly sliced

1. Heat large saucepot of *salted water* to boiling over high heat; add spaghetti and cook as label directs.
2. Meanwhile, in nonstick 12-inch skillet, heat vegetable oil over medium heat until hot. Add garlic and cook 1 minute, stirring. Add cabbage, mushrooms, carrots, pepper, Canadian bacon, ¼ teaspoon salt, and ½ *cup water*. Increase heat to medium-high, and cook about 8 minutes or until vegetables are tender-crisp, stirring frequently. In cup, stir together vinegar, cornstarch, and sesame oil.
3. Drain spaghetti. Add spaghetti, green onions, and cornstarch mixture to vegetable mixture, and cook 2 minutes or until slightly thickened, stirring.

■ Each serving: About 390 calories, 19 g protein, 62 g carbohydrate, 8 g total fat (2 g saturated), 6 g fiber, 21 mg cholesterol, 1,075 mg sodium.

Beef & Pepper Fajitas

We seasoned a flank steak with a spicy rub before searing it in a grill pan for these tasty Mexican wraps.

PREP *30 minutes*
COOK *about 20 minutes*
MAKES *6 main-dish servings*

2 limes
1 garlic clove, crushed with garlic press
2 tablespoons plus ¾ teaspoon chili powder
1 tablespoon plus ½ teaspoon brown sugar
¾ teaspoon salt
1 beef flank steak (about 1 pound), trimmed
2 teaspoons olive oil
1 large red pepper, thinly sliced
1 large green pepper, thinly sliced
1 large red onion, cut in half and thinly sliced
6 burrito-size flour tortillas, warmed
    accompaniments: salsa, light sour cream, cilantro leaves (optional)

1. From limes, grate 1 teaspoon peel and squeeze 2 tablespoons plus 1 teaspoon juice.
2. In large bowl, mix garlic, lime peel, 2 tablespoons lime juice, 2 tablespoons chili powder, 1 tablespoon sugar, and ½ teaspoon salt until blended. Add steak to bowl and rub all over with chili-powder mixture. Marinate steak 15 minutes at room temperature or up to 1 hour in the refrigerator.
3. Heat grill pan over medium-high heat until hot. Add steak and cook 20 to 25 minutes for medium-rare or until of desired doneness, turning steak over once (reduce heat to medium if steak is browning too quickly).
4. Meanwhile, in nonstick 12-inch skillet, heat oil over medium heat until hot. Add peppers and onion, and cook, covered, 10 minutes, stirring occasionally. Add remaining ¾ teaspoon chili powder, ½ teaspoon sugar, and ¼ teaspoon salt, and cook 5 minutes longer, uncovered, or until vegetables are tender and golden, stirring occasionally. Stir in remaining 1 teaspoon lime juice.
5. Transfer steak to cutting board; let stand 10 minutes to allow juices to set for easier slicing. Thinly slice steak and wrap in tortillas with pepper mixture. Serve with salsa, sour cream, and cilantro if you like.

■ Each serving without accompaniments: About 310 calories, 23 g protein, 36 g carbohydrate, 9 g total fat (3 g saturated), 13 g fiber, 31 mg cholesterol, 710 mg sodium.

Beef Tenderloins in Marmalade Pan Sauce

Filet mignon steaks are surrounded by a delicious pan sauce of caramelized onion and orange marmalade.

PREP *10 minutes*
COOK *about 25 minutes*
MAKES *4 main-dish servings*

4 beef tenderloin steaks, 1 inch thick (about 4 ounces each), trimmed
¼ teaspoon coarsely ground black pepper
½ teaspoon salt
1 teaspoon olive oil
1 large onion, cut in half and thinly sliced
1 garlic clove, crushed with garlic press
⅓ cup chicken broth
2 tablespoons orange marmalade
2 tablespoons balsamic vinegar

1. Heat nonstick 12-inch skillet over medium-high heat until hot but not smoking. Add steaks; sprinkle with pepper and ¼ teaspoon salt, and cook about 10 minutes for medium-rare or until of desired doneness, turning steaks over once (reduce heat to medium if steaks are browning too quickly). Transfer steaks to plate.

2. In same skillet, in oil, cook onion with remaining ¼ teaspoon salt over medium heat, covered, about 10 minutes or until tender and golden, stirring often. Add garlic, chicken broth, marmalade, and vinegar; heat to boiling. Cook 1 minute, stirring. Return steaks and any juices to skillet; heat through, turning steaks to coat with sauce.

■ Each serving: About 235 calories, 24 g protein, 12 g carbohydrate, 9 g total fat (3 g saturated), 1 g fiber, 57 mg cholesterol, 440 mg sodium.

Broiled Flank Steak with Rosemary & Lemon

A fragrant rub of fresh lemon, dried herbs, and pungent garlic enhances an everyday steak.

PREP **10 minutes**
BROIL **about 15 minutes**
MAKES **4 main-dish servings**

  2 lemons
  2 garlic cloves, crushed with garlic press
  ¾ teaspoon salt
  ½ teaspoon dried rosemary
  ½ teaspoon dried oregano
  ¼ teaspoon ground black pepper
  1 beef flank steak (about 1 pound), trimmed

1. Preheat broiler. From 1 lemon, grate 2 teaspoons peel and squeeze 2 tablespoons juice. Cut remaining lemon into wedges; set aside.
2. In cup, mix lemon juice and peel with garlic, salt, rosemary, oregano, and pepper until blended.
3. Rub lemon mixture on both sides of steak. Place steak on rack in broiling pan. Place pan in broiler at closest

position to source of heat and broil steak about 15 minutes for medium-rare or until of desired doneness, turning steak over once.
4. Transfer steak to cutting board; let stand 10 minutes to allow juices to set for easier slicing. Serve sliced steak with lemon wedges.

■ Each serving: About 205 calories, 27 g protein, 3 g carbohydrate, 9 g total fat (4 g saturated), 1 g fiber, 46 mg cholesterol, 495 mg sodium.

Korean Steak in Lettuce Cups

pictured on page 117

Sliced round steak and shredded carrots are braised in a rich soy-ginger sauce and served in delicate Boston-lettuce leaves.

PREP **about 15 minutes plus standing**
COOK **about 6 minutes**
MAKES **4 main-dish servings**

  3 tablespoons soy sauce
  1 tablespoon sugar
  2 teaspoons Asian sesame oil
  1 teaspoon minced, peeled fresh ginger
  ¼ teaspoon ground red pepper (cayenne)
  1 garlic clove, crushed with garlic press
  1 beef top round steak (about 1 pound), trimmed, cut into ½-inch cubes
  4 celery stalks with leaves, thinly sliced
  ½ (10-ounce) package shredded carrots (1¾ cups)
  3 green onions, thinly sliced
  1 tablespoon sesame seeds
  1 head Boston lettuce, separated into leaves
    green-onion tops for garnish

1. In medium bowl, stir soy sauce, sugar, sesame oil, ginger, ground red pepper, and garlic until blended.

Add beef, turning to coat with soy-sauce mixture, and marinate 15 minutes at room temperature, stirring occasionally.
2. In nonstick 12-inch skillet, heat celery, carrots, and *⅓ cup water* to boiling over medium-high heat. Cook 2 to 3 minutes or until vegetables are tender-crisp, stirring occasionally. Add beef with its marinade and cook 2 minutes or until meat just loses its pink color throughout, stirring quickly and constantly. Stir in sliced green onions and sesame seeds, and cook 1 minute, stirring.
3. To serve, let each person place some beef mixture on a lettuce leaf. Garnish with green-onion tops. If you like, fold sides of lettuce leaf over filling to make a package to eat out of hand.

■ Each serving: About 250 calories, 28 g protein, 12 g carbohydrate, 10 g total fat (3 g saturated), 3 g fiber, 53 mg cholesterol, 855 mg sodium.

To keep things light, you need to start with lean varieties.

BEEF Choose round or loin (as in top loin, tenderloin, and sirloin). Rib is always high-fat, as is ground meat unless it's specifically labeled 90 to 95 percent lean. USDA Select contains the least marbling (flecks of fat within the muscle); the second leanest grade is USDA Choice. Cuts we used for our recipes this month: top round steak, tenderloin, flank steak.

PORK Because pork isn't graded in the same way as beef, you'll have to use your eye to look for lean cuts. Our picks: tenderloin, loin roast, boneless sirloin chop.

LAMB Check the label and choose leg or loin. We used leg steaks for our Middle Eastern Lamb Steaks (at right); trimmed cubes (for stew or kabobs) are also on the lean side.

VEAL All cuts, except for breast, tend to be low in fat. We used cutlets in our recipes.

Middle Eastern Lamb Steaks

Aromatic spices, including coriander, cumin, and allspice, add zip to simple pan-seared lamb steaks in a quick tomato relish. Garnish with garden-fresh baby greens.

PREP *about 15 minutes*
COOK *about 20 minutes*
MAKES *4 main-dish servings*

- 1 teaspoon dried thyme
- 1 teaspoon ground coriander
- 1 teaspoon ground cumin
- ½ teaspoon ground allspice
- ½ teaspoon salt
- ¼ teaspoon ground black pepper
- 1 can (28 ounces) whole tomatoes
- 1 teaspoon vegetable oil
- 1 medium red onion, chopped
- ¼ cup dried currants
- 1 tablespoon pine nuts (optional)
- 2 tablespoons chopped fresh parsley leaves
- 2 center-cut lamb leg steaks, ¾ inch thick (about 8 ounces each), trimmed
  baby greens for garnish

1. In small bowl, stir together thyme, coriander, cumin, allspice, salt, and pepper. Drain tomatoes, reserving ½ cup juice; chop tomatoes.
2. In nonstick 12-inch skillet, heat oil over medium heat until hot. Add chopped onion and 2 teaspoons thyme mixture, and cook 5 minutes or until onion is slightly softened, stirring occasionally. Add chopped tomatoes, reserved juice, and currants, and cook 6 minutes or until slightly thickened, stirring occasionally. Transfer tomato mixture to bowl; stir in pine nuts, if using, and 1 tablespoon parsley.
3. Coat lamb steaks with remaining thyme mixture. In same skillet, cook

Spice-Brined Pork Loin

Brining in a blend of kosher salt, sugar, and spices infuses this pork with wonderful flavor and keeps it tender and juicy. Allow the pork to soak in the brine for 18 to 24 hours before roasting.

PREP *20 minutes plus chilling and marinating 18 to 24 hours*
ROAST *about 1 hour*
MAKES *12 main-dish servings*

- ¼ cup sugar
- ¼ cup kosher salt
- 2 tablespoons coriander seeds
- 2 tablespoons cracked black pepper
- 2 tablespoons fennel seeds
- 2 tablespoons cumin seeds
  peel from 1 navel orange, white pith removed
- 1 boneless pork loin roast (about 3 pounds), trimmed
- 4 garlic cloves, crushed with side of chef's knife

1. In 2-quart saucepan, heat *1 cup water* with sugar, salt, coriander, pepper, fennel, cumin, and orange peel to boiling over high heat. Reduce heat to low, and simmer 2 minutes. Remove saucepan from heat; stir in *3 cups ice* until almost melted. Stir in *1 cup cold water*.
2. Place pork in large self-sealing plastic bag with garlic and brine. Seal bag, pressing out excess air. Place bag in bowl or small roasting pan and refrigerate 18 to 24 hours.
3. When ready to cook pork, preheat oven to 400°F. Remove pork from bag; discard brine (it's OK if some spices stick to pork). Place pork on rack in small roasting pan (14" by 10"). Insert meat thermometer into thickest part of pork. Roast about 1 hour to 1 hour 15 minutes or until thermometer reaches 150°F. (temperature will rise 5° to 10°F. upon standing). Transfer pork to cutting board and let stand 10 minutes to allow juices to set for easier slicing.

■ Each serving: About 175 calories, 24 g protein, 1 g carbohydrate, 8 g total fat (3 g saturated), 0 g fiber, 67 mg cholesterol, 445 mg sodium.

lamb over medium-high heat 8 to 10 minutes for medium-rare or until of desired doneness, turning lamb over once.

4. To serve, spoon tomato relish into deep platter; top with lamb steaks and sprinkle with remaining 1 tablespoon parsley. Garnish with baby greens.

■ Each serving: About 255 calories, 26 g protein, 17 g carbohydrate, 9 g total fat (3 g saturated), 3 g fiber, 78 mg cholesterol, 555 mg sodium.

Shortcut Asparagus Pizzas

You won't find this delicious pie—topped with shiitake mushrooms and fresh asparagus—at your local pizzeria.

PREP *30 minutes*
BAKE *about 18 minutes*
MAKES *2 pizzas or 4 main-dish servings*

1½ pounds asparagus, trimmed
  1 tablespoon olive oil
  1 large onion, cut in half and
       thinly sliced
  ¼ pound shiitake mushrooms,
       stems discarded, tops thinly
       sliced
  1 large garlic clove, minced
  ½ teaspoon salt
  ¼ teaspoon ground black
       pepper
  1 pound (1 piece) frozen bread
       dough, thawed (from 2- to
       3-pound package)*
  4 ounces Fontina cheese, shredded
       (1 cup)
  2 tablespoons grated Parmesan
       cheese

1. Preheat oven to 425°F.
2. If using thin asparagus, cut each stalk crosswise in half; if using medium asparagus, cut stalks into 1½-inch pieces. In nonstick 12-inch

skillet, heat oil over medium-high heat until hot. Add sliced onion and mushrooms, and cook 8 to 10 minutes or until vegetables are tender and golden, stirring often. Add asparagus, garlic, salt, pepper, and *¼ cup water;* cover and cook 5 minutes longer or until asparagus is tender-crisp. Remove skillet from heat.

3. Cut dough in half. On greased cookie sheet, spread and flatten 1 piece of dough to ⅛-inch thickness (about 10 inches in diameter). Pinch edges of dough to form rim. Repeat with another greased cookie sheet and second piece of dough. Sprinkle ½ cup Fontina over each piece of dough; spread equal amounts of vegetable mixture to rim of each piece of dough. Sprinkle each pizza with 1 tablespoon Parmesan.

4. Bake pizzas on 2 oven racks 18 to 20 minutes or until crust is lightly browned and cheese melts, rotating cookie sheets between upper and lower racks halfway through baking.

■ Each serving: About 505 calories, 22 g protein, 66 g carbohydrate, 18 g total fat (7 g saturated), 5 g fiber, 36 mg cholesterol, 1,230 mg sodium.

* Instead of frozen bread dough, you can use a 10-ounce package of refrigerated pizza dough (found in the dairy case of your supermarket). The crust will be thinner and bake in less time, about 12 minutes.

healthy tips

The ancient Greeks believed asparagus was an herbal medicine that would cure toothaches and prevent bee stings; the Romans grew the regal vegetable in their high-walled courtyards. And now scientists have confirmed that serving for serving, asparagus is one of the top sources of folic acid, a B vitamin that prevents certain birth defects early in pregnancy. A single helping (about 5 medium spears) provides 60 percent of the RDA for folic acid, plus vitamin C, vitamin B6, and fiber—all for a mere 20 calories. Asparagus also contains valuable phytochemicals—plant nutrients—that may play a key role in both cancer prevention and normal functioning of the immune system. To preserve the good stuff, don't overcook asparagus. And spare the tips but trim the ends; nutrient content is highest at the top and decreases as you go down.

Skillet Asparagus

A splash of lime juice and a pinch of lime zest bring out the fresh flavor of succulent asparagus spears.

PREP *10 minutes*
COOK *about 12 minutes*
MAKES *4 accompaniment servings*

    1 lime
    1 tablespoon margarine or butter
 1½ pounds asparagus, trimmed
  ¼ teaspoon salt
  ⅛ teaspoon ground black pepper

1. From lime, grate ½ teaspoon peel and squeeze 1 tablespoon juice.

2. In nonstick 12-inch skillet, melt margarine over medium-high heat. Add asparagus, lime juice, and *¼ cup water;* heat to boiling. Reduce heat to medium and cook, covered, 5 minutes.

3. Add salt, pepper, and lime peel to skillet. Increase heat to medium-high; cook, uncovered, 4 to 5 minutes or until asparagus is tender and liquid evaporates.

■ Each serving: About 55 calories, 3 g protein, 3 g carbohydrate, 4 g total fat (1 g saturated), 1 g fiber, 0 mg cholesterol, 200 mg sodium.

Veal Cutlets with Arugula & Tomato Salad

This dish is usually prepared with breaded cutlets fried in a lot of oil. To lighten it up, we sautéed the veal in just a film of oil with no coating.

PREP *25 minutes*
COOK *about 5 minutes*
MAKES *4 main-dish servings*

    1 tablespoon minced shallot
    1 tablespoon balsamic vinegar
    1 tablespoon olive oil
  ¾ teaspoon salt
  ½ teaspoon ground black pepper
    1 pound veal cutlets
    2 small bunches arugula
       (about 4 ounces each), tough
       stems removed, leaves coarsely
       chopped
    1 cup grape tomatoes, each cut
       in half
  ½ ounce Parmesan-cheese shavings

1. In large bowl, mix shallot, vinegar, 2 teaspoons oil, ¼ teaspoon salt, and ¼ teaspoon pepper until blended; set dressing aside.

2. If veal cutlets are large, cut each crosswise in half. If necessary, with meat mallet, pound cutlets to even ⅛-inch thickness.

3. In nonstick 12-inch skillet, heat ½ teaspoon oil over medium-high heat until hot. Add half of cutlets; sprinkle with ¼ teaspoon salt and ⅛ teaspoon pepper, and cook 2 minutes or until veal cutlets just lose their pink color throughout, turning over once. Transfer cutlets to platter. Repeat with remaining cutlets, ½ teaspoon oil, ¼ teaspoon salt, and ⅛ teaspoon pepper.

4. Add arugula and tomatoes to dressing in bowl, and toss to mix. Spoon salad over cutlets on platter and top with Parmesan shavings.

■ Each serving: About 225 calories, 31 g protein, 5 g carbohydrate, 9 g total fat (2 g saturated), 1 g fiber, 94 mg cholesterol, 585 mg sodium.

Asparagus & Endive Salad with Orange-Mustard Vinaigrette

This light salad is elegant enough to serve as a first course at a dinner party—and easy enough to prepare for your family as an accompaniment to a weeknight meal.

PREP *15 minutes*
COOK *about 5 minutes*
MAKES *4 first-course servings*

    1 pound asparagus, trimmed and cut
       diagonally into 2" by ¼" slices
    1 orange
    2 tablespoons seasoned rice vinegar
    1 tablespoon olive oil
    1 tablespoon minced shallot
  ½ teaspoon sugar
  ½ teaspoon salt
  ½ teaspoon Dijon mustard
  ⅛ teaspoon ground black pepper
    2 heads Belgian endive
       (about 4 ounces each), cut
       lengthwise into ¼-inch-wide
       strips

1. In 12-inch skillet, heat *½ inch water* to boiling over high heat. Add asparagus and cook 3 minutes or until tender-crisp. Drain asparagus in colander; rinse with cold water and pat dry.

2. Meanwhile, from orange, grate ½ teaspoon peel and squeeze 1 tablespoon juice. In small bowl, whisk vinegar, oil, shallot, sugar, salt, mustard, pepper, orange juice, and orange peel until blended.

3. To serve, toss asparagus and endive in large bowl with dressing until evenly coated.

■ Each serving: About 85 calories, 3 g protein, 10 g carbohydrate, 4 g total fat (1 g saturated), 4 g fiber, 0 mg cholesterol, 540 mg sodium.

Asparagus-Potato Salad

Lemony vinaigrette dresses steamed sliced asparagus and red-skinned potatoes for a great springtime accompaniment.

PREP *10 minutes*
COOK *about 15 minutes*
MAKES *10 accompaniment servings*

Potatoes & Asparagus
- 2 pounds medium red potatoes, cut into 1½-inch chunks
- 1 pound asparagus, trimmed and cut into 1-inch pieces

Lemon Vinaigrette
- 2 large lemons
- 3 tablespoons extra virgin olive oil
- 2 teaspoons sugar
- 1 teaspoon salt
- ¼ teaspoon ground black pepper

1. Prepare Potatoes & Asparagus: Add about *1 inch water* to 4-quart saucepan. Place collapsible steamer basket in saucepan. Add potatoes to steamer basket and heat water in saucepan to boiling over high heat. Reduce heat to medium; cover and cook 10 minutes or until potatoes are fork-tender. Add asparagus and cook 2 minutes longer or until tender-crisp.
2. Meanwhile, prepare Lemon Vinaigrette: From lemons, grate 2 teaspoons peel and squeeze ⅓ cup juice. In large bowl, with wire whisk, mix lemon peel and lemon juice with remaining vinaigrette ingredients.
3. Toss warm potatoes and asparagus in bowl with vinaigrette until well coated. Serve warm or cover and refrigerate up to 1 day to serve cold.

■ Each serving: About 155 calories, 3 g protein, 25 g carbohydrate, 5 g total fat (1 g saturated), 2 g fiber, 0 mg cholesterol, 300 mg sodium.

Sesame-Asparagus Stir-fry

A dash of Asian sesame oil gives this quick asparagus side special character.

PREP *10 minutes*
COOK *about 12 minutes*
MAKES *4 accompaniment servings*

- 1 tablespoon sesame seeds
- 1 tablespoon olive oil
- 1½ pounds asparagus, trimmed and cut into 1½-inch pieces
- 1 large garlic clove, minced
- 2 teaspoons soy sauce
- ½ teaspoon Asian sesame oil

1. In nonstick 12-inch skillet, cook sesame seeds over medium-high heat until fragrant and golden, about 4 minutes. Transfer to small bowl.
2. To same skillet, add olive oil and heat until hot. Add asparagus, garlic, and soy sauce, and cook 6 to 8 minutes or until asparagus is tender-crisp. Toss with sesame oil and sprinkle with sesame seeds before serving.

■ Each serving: About 75 calories, 4 g protein, 3 g carbohydrate, 6 g total fat (1 g saturated), 2 g fiber, 0 mg cholesterol, 180 mg sodium.

Roasted Asparagus

Roasting is a no-fuss way to cook asparagus—and it brings out the natural sweet flavor of the vegetable.

PREP *10 minutes*
ROAST *about 20 minutes*
MAKES *6 accompaniment servings*

- 2 pounds asparagus, trimmed
- 1 tablespoon olive oil
- ¼ teaspoon salt
- ¼ teaspoon ground black pepper

1. Preheat oven to 400°F. In broiling pan without rack or in large roasting pan (17" by 11½"), toss asparagus with oil, salt, and pepper.
2. Roast asparagus 15 to 20 minutes or until tender and lightly browned.

■ Each serving: About 45 calories, 3 g protein, 2 g carbohydrate, 3 g total fat (0 g saturated), 1 g fiber, 0 mg cholesterol, 110 mg sodium.

Lean Lemony Veal & Baby Artichokes

Take advantage of baby artichokes while they're in the market. Once trimmed, they're completely edible because they're so young and the choke hasn't developed yet. They pair perfectly with tender veal cutlets in this brothy sauce lightly flecked with tarragon.

PREP *about 30 minutes*
COOK *about 25 minutes*
MAKES *4 main-dish servings*

8   baby artichokes (about 12 ounces)
      or 2 medium artichokes*
      salt
1   pound veal cutlets
1   lemon
2   teaspoons olive oil
¼   teaspoon ground black pepper
2   medium shallots, thinly sliced
1   cup chicken broth
1   tablespoon all-purpose flour
1   teaspoon minced fresh tarragon
      leaves

1. Trim baby artichokes: Bend back green outer leaves and snap them off at base until remaining leaves are half green (at the top) and half yellow (at the bottom). Trim stem ends and cut across top of each artichoke at point where yellow meets green (about ½ inch from top).

2. In nonstick 12-inch skillet, heat ½ *inch salted water* to boiling over medium-high heat. Add artichokes; reduce heat to medium-low and cook, covered, 12 minutes or until artichokes are fork-tender. Drain in colander; cool until easy to handle. Cut each baby artichoke lengthwise into quarters. Do not discard center portion.

3. Meanwhile, if veal cutlets are large, cut each crosswise in half. If necessary, with meat mallet, pound cutlets to even ⅛-inch thickness. From lemon, grate 2 teaspoons peel and squeeze 1 tablespoon juice.

4. In same skillet, heat 1 teaspoon oil over medium-high heat until hot but not smoking. Add half of cutlets; sprinkle with ¼ teaspoon salt and ⅛ teaspoon pepper, and cook 2 minutes or until they just lose their pink color throughout, turning over once. Transfer cutlets to platter and keep warm. Repeat with remaining veal cutlets, 1 teaspoon oil, ¼ teaspoon salt, and ⅛ teaspoon pepper (reduce heat to medium if cutlets are browning too quickly).

5. To same skillet, add shallots and ½ *cup water*, and cook over medium heat 1 minute. In cup, mix broth and flour. Increase heat to medium-high; add broth mixture and lemon peel, and boil 1 minute or until slightly thickened. Add artichokes, tarragon, and lemon juice, and cook 1 minute to heat through, stirring gently.

6. To serve, spoon artichokes with sauce over veal on platter.

■ Each serving: About 180 calories, 27 g protein, 7 g carbohydrate, 5 g total fat (1 g saturated), 2 g fiber, 89 mg cholesterol, 795 mg sodium.

* If using medium artichokes, with serrated knife, cut 1 inch straight across top of each artichoke. Cut off stem; peel. Pull dark outer leaves from artichoke bottom. With kitchen shears, trim thorny tips of remaining leaves. Cut artichoke lengthwise into sixths. Scrape out choke, removing center petals and fuzzy center portion; discard. Repeat with remaining artichoke. Rinse artichokes well. Cook as in step 2.

June

The Complete Outdoor Cookbook

the complete
outdoor
cookbook

A summer's worth of quick dips, cold soups, great grills, and easy desserts—plus the Ultimate Burger

soups, dips & drinks

Lemon-Lime Coolers

A refreshing hybrid of old-fashioned lemonade and limeade—this cooler is heaven on a back porch.

PREP **10 minutes plus chilling**
COOK **5 minutes**
MAKES **about 8 cups or 8 servings**

2¾ cups sugar
1¼ cups fresh lime juice
(from about 10 medium limes)
1 cup fresh lemon juice
(from about 6 medium lemons)
ice cubes
1 lime, sliced (optional)

1. Prepare sugar syrup: In 2-quart saucepan, heat sugar and *4½ cups cold water* to boiling over high heat, stirring occasionally. Cover saucepan and boil 3 minutes; remove from heat.
2. Stir lime juice and lemon juice into sugar syrup. Pour mixture into large pitcher; cover and refrigerate until cold, about 3 hours. Add ice; stir in lime slices if using. Stir in additional *water* if flavor is too concentrated.

■ Each serving: About 140 calories, 0 g protein, 37 g carbohydrate, 0 g total fat, 0 g fiber, 0 mg cholesterol, 1 mg sodium.

Creamy Veggie Dip

Our vegetable-studded dip is best if refrigerated at least 4 hours so that the flavors will develop. Serve with crudités, bagel chips, or breadsticks.

PREP **25 minutes plus chilling**
MAKES **about 4 cups**

1 medium carrot, cut into 2-inch chunks
5 medium radishes
½ red pepper, cut into quarters
1 small celery stalk, cut into 2-inch chunks
2 green onions, cut into 2-inch pieces
1 package (3 ounces) cream cheese, softened
½ cup light mayonnaise
1 container (16 ounces) reduced-fat sour cream
1½ teaspoons grated fresh lemon peel
½ teaspoon salt
½ teaspoon ground black pepper

1. In food processor with knife blade attached, pulse carrot, radishes, red pepper, celery, and green onions until vegetables are finely minced.
2. Transfer vegetables to medium bowl. In same food processor with knife blade attached, process cream cheese and mayonnaise until smooth.

Add to bowl with vegetables. Stir in sour cream, lemon peel, salt, and pepper until well blended. Cover and refrigerate at least 4 hours or up to 2 days. Stir before serving.

■ Each tablespoon: About 20 calories, 0 g protein, 1 g carbohydrate, 2 g total fat (1 g saturated), 0 g fiber, 5 mg cholesterol, 40 mg sodium.

Guacamole

This popular Mexican specialty is a must for any summer party. Use it as a dip, spoon it over burgers, or dish it alongside sizzling steak or grilled chicken.

PREP **15 minutes**
MAKES **about 3 cups**

2 ripe medium avocados
(about 8 ounces each)
2 ripe medium tomatoes, coarsely chopped
1 jalapeño chile, seeded and minced
1 cup loosely packed fresh cilantro leaves, chopped
1 tablespoon fresh lime juice
½ teaspoon salt

Cut each avocado lengthwise in half; remove seed and peel. In medium bowl, coarsely mash avocados. Add tomatoes, jalapeño chile, cilantro, lime juice, and salt; stir gently to combine. If not serving right away, cover surface of guacamole directly with plastic wrap and refrigerate. Stir before serving.

■ Each ¼ cup: About 55 calories, 1 g protein, 3 g carbohydrate, 5 g total fat (1 g saturated), 2 g fiber, 0 mg cholesterol, 105 mg sodium.

Quick Gazpacho

Ripe, flavorful tomatoes are key to this simple version of the spicy, cool soup that's made in a food processor to speed up the chopping. For a different look, try yellow tomatoes instead.

PREP *30 minutes plus chilling*
MAKES *about 8 cups or 8 first-course servings*

3 ripe medium tomatoes (about 1 pound), cut into quarters
1 green pepper, seeded and cut into eighths
1 yellow pepper, seeded and cut into eighths
1 garlic clove
2 tablespoons sherry vinegar
2 tablespoons extra virgin olive oil
1 teaspoon salt
1 teaspoon hot pepper sauce
1 medium cucumber, peeled, seeded, and cut into 2-inch chunks
1 small red onion, cut into eighths
3 cups tomato juice
garlic croutons and sliced fresh basil leaves for garnish

1. In food processor with knife blade attached, blend half of tomatoes and half of each pepper with garlic, vinegar, oil, salt, and hot pepper sauce until pureed. Pour into large bowl.
2. In same food processor, pulse cucumber and onion with remaining tomatoes and peppers just until chopped. Stir chopped vegetables and tomato juice into pureed vegetables in bowl. Cover and refrigerate until cold, at least 3 hours.
3. To serve, ladle soup into chilled bowls. Garnish with croutons and fresh basil.

■ Each serving: About 75 calories, 2 g protein, 11 g carbohydrate, 4 g total fat (1 g saturated), 2 g fiber, 0 mg cholesterol, 630 mg sodium.

food editor's Q&A

Q Lately I've seen several types of soybeans at the store. How can I serve them?

a Fresh green soybeans, called edamame (eh-dah-MAH-meh), have a naturally sweet taste that works well in many recipes. They are sold shelled and unshelled, fresh and frozen. Try shelled beans in place of green peas in salads and entrées. Steam unshelled ones and sprinkle them with salt for a starter or snack, as a number of New York City restaurants are now doing.

Black or tan soybeans are sold in cans (and sometimes dried) in natural-food stores and supermarkets. We really like the black ones in any dish calling for black beans, such as tortilla wraps, soup, and rice and beans. All soybeans are an excellent source of protein, folic acid, and fiber, and they are very low in artery-clogging saturated fat. To try a recipe that uses edamame and black soybeans, see New Four-Bean Salad (page 103).

Q What makes fresh mozzarella so different from packaged?

a The mozzarella you see in plastic-wrapped bricks in the supermarket dairy case is typically made in a factory. It has a dry, slightly rubbery texture that's most suited for use in cooking (it has wonderful melting qualities). Fresh mozzarella, handmade in smaller batches from whole milk, has a much softer, buttery texture and a delicate flavor. It's delicious served raw with ripe, farm-fresh tomatoes or as part of an antipasto platter. It's sold—packed in whey or water—in Italian markets, cheese shops, and some supermarkets. Fresh mozzarella is best eaten the day it's made, if possible, even before chilling. It's worth splurging on for our Easy Tomato & Mozzarella Salad (page 103).

Q I can never find an avocado that's soft or even close to it at the store. What's the best way to ripen one?

a Because avocados are extremely delicate (and perishable when fully ripe), most are shipped to stores before they soften. To ripen, place the avocado in a paper bag at room temperature for 2 days, until it yields to gentle pressure when you squeeze it lightly. (Putting an apple or banana in the bag speeds up the process.) Once ripe, avocados can be stored in the refrigerator for a few days. Slice for salad, or try our great Guacamole (facing page).

Q What is London broil? Is it a special cut of beef or a specific way of preparing it?

a London broil was originally a recipe for a beef flank steak, which was marinated, broiled, or grilled, then carved across the grain into thin slices. Despite its name, the recipe is said to be American in origin. Today the term applies not only to flank steak but also to other boneless cuts of beef such as top sirloin, top round, and chuck shoulder steaks. These are also meant to be prepared in the same manner and served thinly sliced across the grain. Try our London Broil with Garlic & Herbs (page 101).

Chilled Cucumber Soup

Homemade curry oil adds a taste of the tropics to this summer favorite.

PREP *25 minutes plus chilling*
COOK *3 minutes*
MAKES *about 4 cups or 4 first-course servings*

Cucumber Soup
2   English (seedless) cucumbers (about 12 ounces each), peeled
1   small garlic clove, crushed with garlic press
1   container (16 ounces) plain low-fat yogurt (about 2 cups)
½   cup low-fat (1%) milk
1   tablespoon fresh lemon juice
1¼   teaspoons salt

Curry Oil
2   tablespoons olive oil
½   teaspoon curry powder
½   teaspoon ground cumin
¼   teaspoon crushed red pepper

Garnish
1   small tomato, chopped
1   tablespoon sliced fresh mint leaves

1. Prepare Cucumber Soup: Cut enough cucumber into ¼-inch dice to equal ½ cup; reserve for garnish. Cut remaining cucumber into chunks. In food processor with knife blade attached, or in blender, combine cucumber chunks, garlic, yogurt, milk, lemon juice, and salt; blend until almost smooth. Pour mixture into medium bowl; cover and refrigerate 2 hours or until cold.

2. Meanwhile, prepare Curry Oil: In small saucepan, combine oil, curry powder, cumin, and crushed red pepper. Cook over low heat until fragrant and oil is hot, about 3 minutes. Remove saucepan from heat; strain curry oil through sieve into cup.

3. Prepare Garnish: In small bowl, combine tomato and reserved diced cucumber. To serve, stir soup and ladle into bowls. Spoon cucumber mixture into center of soup; sprinkle with mint. Drizzle with Curry Oil.

■ Each serving: About 170 calories, 8 g protein, 15 g carbohydrate, 9 g total fat (2 g saturated), 2 g fiber, 8 mg cholesterol, 830 mg sodium.

wine online

Which goes best with pizza (such as our grilled version, page 101)? How many bottles do I need for my dinner party? What do I do when the cork falls into the bottle? At the Wine Market Council's Web site, wineanswers.com, you will find answers to questions big and small. Also useful: columns by experts, links to other sites on the topic, and a glossary of grape names.

main dishes

Best BBQ Chicken

Red wine vinegar, molasses, and red pepper give this sauce just the right balance of tangy sweetness and heat. You can try it on ribs as well as chicken.

PREP *1 hour*
GRILL *40 to 45 minutes*
MAKES *8 main-dish servings*

2   tablespoons olive oil
1   large onion, chopped
2   cans (15 ounces each) tomato sauce
1   cup red wine vinegar
½   cup light molasses
¼   cup Worcestershire sauce
⅓   cup packed brown sugar
¾   teaspoon ground red pepper (cayenne)
2   chickens (3½ pounds each), cut into quarters, skin removed if you like

1. In 10-inch skillet, heat olive oil over medium heat until hot. Add onion and cook about 10 minutes or until tender and golden, stirring occasionally. Stir in tomato sauce, vinegar, molasses, Worcestershire sauce, sugar, and ground red pepper; heat to boiling over high heat. Reduce heat to medium-low and cook, uncovered, 45 minutes or until sauce thickens slightly. If not using sauce right away, cover and refrigerate for up to 2 weeks.

2. Reserve 1½ cups sauce to serve with grilled chicken. Place chicken quarters on grill over medium heat; cook 20 to 25 minutes, turning over once. Generously brush chicken with some of the remaining barbecue sauce; cook chicken 20 minutes longer, turning pieces often and brushing with sauce frequently, until juices run clear when chicken is pierced with tip of knife. Serve with reserved sauce.

■ Each serving with skin: About 500 calories, 42 g protein, 34 g carbohydrate, 23 g total fat (6 g saturated), 2 g fiber, 158 mg cholesterol, 755 mg sodium.

■ Each serving without skin: About 395 calories, 39 g protein, 34 g carbohydrate, 13 g total fat (3 g saturated), 2 g fiber, 114 mg cholesterol, 750 mg sodium.

Plum-Glazed Ribs

pictured on page 119

Star anise, a star-shaped pod that is popular in various Asian cuisines, lends a distinctive licorice flavor to these ribs.

PREP **1 hour**
GRILL **about 15 minutes**
MAKES **6 main-dish servings**

- 4 racks pork baby back ribs (about 1 pound each)
- 12 whole black peppercorns
- 2 bay leaves
- 10 whole star anise*
- 2 cinnamon sticks (each 3 inches long)
- ¼ cup soy sauce
- 1 jar (12 ounces) plum jam (about 1 cup)
- 1 tablespoon grated, peeled fresh ginger
- 1 garlic clove, crushed with garlic press

1. In 8-quart saucepot, place ribs, peppercorns, bay leaves, 4 star anise, 1 cinnamon stick, and *enough water to cover;* heat to boiling over high heat. Reduce heat to low; cover and simmer 50 minutes to 1 hour or until ribs are fork-tender. Remove ribs to platter. If not serving ribs right away, cover and refrigerate until ready to serve.

2. Meanwhile, prepare glaze: In 1-quart saucepan, heat soy sauce, remaining star anise, and remaining cinnamon stick to boiling over high heat. Reduce heat to low; cover and simmer 5 minutes. Remove saucepan from heat; let stand, covered, 5 minutes. Strain mixture into small bowl; discard star anise and cinnamon stick. Stir in jam, ginger, and garlic.

3. Place ribs on grill over medium heat. Cook ribs 10 minutes, turning over once, until browned. Brush ribs with some glaze, and cook 5 to 10 minutes longer, brushing with remaining glaze and turning frequently. Cut each rack into 1-inch pieces and arrange on platter.

stylish outside settings: tips from the pros

One reason everyone loves outdoor dining is that it's more relaxed than a sit-down dinner. It's also a chance to stretch your creativity. We turned the tables on three of our favorite prop stylists, Betty Alfenito, Cathy Cook, and Debrah E. Donahue—they select the plates, glassware, and accessories for our GH food photographs—to find out how they entertain in the open air. Here are their tricks:

- Plant potted herbs in an old wooden tool caddy for a centerpiece.
- Fill antique bottles with field flowers—arrange 5 in the middle of the table, or put a bottle at each place setting.
- Press rosemary, basil, or wildflowers such as Queen Anne's lace under the glass of a large picture frame to make a serving tray.
- If it's really buggy out, stow everything from potato salad to pie in picnic baskets on the table and keep them closed while everyone's eating.
- Make a colorful, edible centerpiece: peaches, nectarines, and plums, with a sprinkle of berries, arranged in a footed glass bowl.
- Chill water, soda, wine, and beer in old galvanized-steel tubs filled with ice.
- Arrange long flat-bread crackers in an enamel pail or child's beach pail.
- Serve homemade whole wheat bread or muffins in vintage tin boxes from yard sales (line the boxes with waxed paper).
- Offer bread and cheese on a tray covered with pretty leaves. Make sure they aren't poisonous (mint and basil are good).
- For dessert, fill a rustic wooden box with four kinds of cookies, and serve with vanilla ice cream. Or tuck a homemade pound cake with sliced fruit in the box.

More ideas from our GH food staff

- Use colorful cotton dish towels for napkins. Slide cookie cutters (such as butterflies or flowers) over the rolled towels for napkin rings.
- Place forks, knives, and spoons in small, clean terra-cotta flowerpots.
- Use miniature pepper or cherry tomato plants as centerpieces.
- Pour lemonade into old mason jars or retro soda-fountain glasses. To frost glasses, pop them in the freezer for a few hours.
- Arrange grilled meat on platters lined with banana leaves (sold fresh or frozen in Asian and Hispanic markets) or green-onion tops.
- Serve dips (try our Creamy Veggie Dip, page 96) in a hollowed-out cabbage or radicchio head or in a scooped-out crusty bread round. Cut top off to make level, then spoon out the insides, leaving a ¾-inch border all around so that the dip doesn't soak through. (Don't fill bread more than 1 hour ahead of time.)

■ Each serving: About 515 calories, 26 g protein, 39 g carbohydrate, 27 g total fat (10 g saturated), 1 g fiber, 65 mg cholesterol, 735 mg sodium.

* Star anise is available in Asian food markets or the spice section of some supermarkets. You can also order it from Adriana's Caravan, 800-316-0820.

Turkey Kabobs with Garden Tomato Jam

pictured on page 119

Cut lean turkey breast into cubes, then marinate in a savory spice mixture. After grilling, serve kabobs with a quickly cooked combination of tomato and onion, sweetened with raisins and orange juice.

PREP *30 minutes plus marinating*
GRILL *10 minutes*
MAKES *6 main-dish servings*

Turkey
- 1 large garlic clove, crushed with garlic press
- 1 tablespoon olive oil
- 1½ teaspoons chili powder
- ¾ teaspoon paprika
- ¾ teaspoon salt
- ¼ teaspoon ground red pepper (cayenne)
- ¼ teaspoon ground black pepper
- 2 pounds skinless, boneless turkey breast, cut into 1½-inch cubes

Garden Tomato Jam
- 1 navel orange
- 1 tablespoon olive oil
- 1 small onion, chopped
- 7 large plum tomatoes (about 1 pound), seeded and cut into ¼-inch dice
- ⅓ cup golden raisins
- ¼ teaspoon salt
  cilantro sprigs for garnish
- ¼ cup loosely packed fresh cilantro leaves, chopped

1. Prepare Turkey: In large self-sealing plastic bag, combine garlic, oil, chili powder, paprika, salt, ground red pepper, and black pepper. Add turkey to bag, tossing to coat with spice mixture. Seal bag, pressing out excess air. Place bag on plate; refrigerate at least 15 minutes or up to 1 hour.

2. Meanwhile, prepare Garden Tomato Jam: From orange, grate 1 teaspoon peel and squeeze ¼ cup juice. In 10-inch skillet, heat oil over medium-low heat. Add onion and cook until golden, about 5 minutes, stirring occasionally. Add tomatoes, raisins, salt, orange peel, and orange juice. Increase heat to medium-high; cook until tomato softens and liquid evaporates, about 6 minutes. Remove skillet from heat. Makes about 1½ cups.

3. Thread turkey on 4 skewers. Place skewers on grill over medium heat. Cook turkey 10 minutes or until juices run clear when turkey is pierced with tip of knife. Place skewers on platter; garnish with cilantro sprigs. Stir chopped cilantro into Garden Tomato Jam; serve with turkey.

■ Each serving turkey only: About 175 calories, 34 g protein, 1 g carbohydrate, 3 g total fat (1 g saturated), 0 g fiber, 94 mg cholesterol, 355 mg sodium.

■ Each ¼ cup jam: About 75 calories, 1 g protein, 13 g carbohydrate, 3 g total fat (0 g saturated), 2 g fiber, 0 mg cholesterol, 105 mg sodium.

Summer Vegetable & Salmon Grill Packet

Cooking salmon and vegetables in foil ensures that you don't lose any flavorful juices.

PREP *15 minutes*
GRILL *about 15 minutes*
MAKES *4 main-dish servings*

- 4 ears corn, husks and silk removed
- 1 red pepper, seeded and thinly sliced
- 2 green onions, sliced
- 1½ teaspoons salt
- ½ teaspoon grated fresh lime peel
- ¼ teaspoon coarsely ground black pepper
- 4 salmon steaks, ¾ inch thick (about 6 ounces each)
- 2 tablespoons thinly sliced fresh basil leaves
- 1 lime, cut into wedges

1. With knife, cut corn kernels from cobs. In large bowl, combine corn, red pepper, and onions. In cup, mix salt, lime peel, and black pepper. Sprinkle ½ teaspoon salt mixture over vegetables; toss to combine. Sprinkle remaining salt mixture on top side of steaks.

2. Spread vegetables in 14½" by 12½" extra heavy-duty foil cooking bag.* Arrange salmon steaks on top of vegetables, seasoned side up. Fold bag to seal as label directs.

3. Place foil packet on grill over medium heat. Cook salmon steaks 15 minutes, turning bag over once halfway through cooking.

4. Before serving, with kitchen shears, cut an X in top of foil packet to let steam escape, then carefully pull back foil to open. When packet is open, check that salmon is opaque throughout. Return packet to grill if longer cooking is necessary. Sprinkle with basil and serve with lime wedges.

■ Each serving: About 375 calories, 40 g protein, 23 g carbohydrate, 14 g total fat (3 g saturated), 4 g fiber, 87 mg cholesterol, 680 mg sodium.

* Look for foil cooking bags in your supermarket where foil and plastic wrap are sold. If you can't find them, make your own: Layer two 20" by 18" sheets of heavy-duty foil to make a double thickness. Place recipe ingredients on center of foil. Bring short ends up and over ingredients, and fold over 2 or 3 times to seal. Fold over remaining sides of foil 2 or 3 times to complete packet.

London Broil with Garlic & Herbs

Round steak, not the most tender of cuts, benefits from a quick marinade of vinegar, garlic, and oregano.

PREP *10 minutes plus marinating*
GRILL *15 minutes*
MAKES *6 main-dish servings*

- 2 tablespoons red wine vinegar
- 1 tablespoon olive oil
- 2 garlic cloves, crushed with garlic press
- ¾ teaspoon dried oregano
- ¾ teaspoon salt
- ½ teaspoon ground black pepper
- 1 beef top round steak, 1 inch thick (about 1½ pounds) fresh oregano sprigs for garnish

1. In large self-sealing plastic bag, mix vinegar, oil, garlic, dried oregano, salt, and ground black pepper. Add round steak, turning to coat. Seal bag, pressing out excess air. Place bag on plate and marinate 15 minutes at room temperature.

2. Remove steak from bag. Place steak on grill over medium heat; cook 15 minutes for medium-rare or until of desired doneness, turning steak over once.

3. Transfer steak to platter. Let stand 10 minutes to allow juices to set for easier slicing. To serve, thinly slice steak across the grain. Garnish platter with oregano sprigs.

■ Each serving: About 200 calories, 26 g protein, 1 g carbohydrate, 10 g total fat (3 g saturated), 0 g fiber, 72 mg cholesterol, 340 mg sodium.

Grilled Tomato & Basil Pizzas

Garden tomatoes and basil make a wonderful topping for pizza cooked over the coals. For the crust, use frozen bread dough or fresh dough from the supermarket or pizzeria. Serve the pizzas as a main course or cut into wedges for appetizers.

PREP *30 minutes*
GRILL *6 to 9 minutes per pizza*
MAKES *4 pizzas or 4 main-dish servings*

- 1 pound (1 piece) frozen bread dough, thawed (from 2- to 3-pound package)*
- 2 tablespoons olive oil
- 4 ripe medium tomatoes (about 1½ pounds), sliced
- 4 ounces fresh mozzarella cheese, sliced, or 1 cup shredded Fontina cheese
- ½ teaspoon salt
- ½ teaspoon ground black pepper
- 1 cup loosely packed fresh basil leaves, chopped, plus additional leaves for garnish

1. Cut thawed bread dough into 4 pieces. On oiled cookie sheet, spread and flatten 1 piece dough to about ⅛-inch thickness. Lightly brush dough with some oil. On same cookie sheet, repeat with another piece of dough. Repeat procedure with another oiled cookie sheet and remaining pieces of dough. For easiest handling, cover and refrigerate dough on cookie sheets until ready to use.

2. Place 1 piece of dough at a time, greased side down, on grill over medium-low heat. Grill 2 to 3 minutes or until grill marks appear on underside and dough stiffens (dough may puff slightly). Brush top with some oil. With tongs, turn crust over. Quickly arrange one-fourth of tomatoes and one-fourth of cheese on crust.

3. Cook pizza 4 to 6 minutes longer or until cheese melts and underside is evenly browned and cooked through. With tongs, transfer pizza to cutting board. Sprinkle with ⅛ teaspoon salt and ⅛ teaspoon pepper. Scatter one-fourth of chopped basil on pizza and garnish with basil leaves. Drizzle with some oil if you like. Serve immediately.

4. Repeat with remaining dough and topping ingredients.

■ Each serving: About 495 calories, 18 g protein, 63 g carbohydrate, 20 g total fat (7 g saturated), 4 g fiber, 34 mg cholesterol, 1,175 mg sodium.

* Instead of frozen bread dough, you can use 2 packages (10 ounces each) refrigerated pizza dough (found in the dairy case of your supermarket). In step 1, pat 1 package dough into 14" by 10" rectangle and cut crosswise in half for easier handling. Repeat with remaining dough.

all-american classic: the ultimate burger

Ever wonder why backyard burgers are great sometimes but not others? There's a knack to even a simple meal such as this.

SEVEN SECRETS

1. Buy only ground chuck, which is 81 to 85 percent lean—and be sure to get 1¼ pounds for 4 burgers, because 5 ounces raw cooks down to 4 ounces. Lean ground beef from sirloin or round (90 to 95 percent lean) won't give you a plump, juicy burger. If you must use lean meat, make it moister by mixing in 1 or 2 tablespoons of water, red or white wine, broth, or milk per pound.

2. If not using meat right away, refrigerate in its supermarket wrap up to 2 days. (And don't let the meat or its juice touch other foods; the spread of E. coli and other bacteria is a real risk.) For longer storage, rewrap in freezer wrap or foil and freeze; use within 3 months.

3. Handle the beef gently when shaping it so that you don't end up with a dense hockey puck. Start with a mound, flatten it slightly, and smooth edges all around.

4. Make sure the grill is hot before putting on the burgers. A heated grill sears the meat, so it won't stick. And a quick searing retains juices.

5. Don't flatten the patties with a spatula. Pressing squeezes out the flavorful juices and won't speed up cooking anyway.

6. Cook burgers to at least medium—160°F. on an instant-read thermometer inserted horizontally (centers should no longer be pink).

7. Cheese lovers: Don't get more cheese on the grill slats than on the burgers. Once patties are cooked to medium, blanket the top with Cheddar, Swiss, or another favorite, and cook with the grill lid down for about a minute.

GH's Best Burgers

PREP *5 minutes*
GRILL *10 to 12 minutes*
MAKES *4 burgers*

Shape *1¼ pounds ground beef chuck* into 4 patties, each ¾ inch thick.* Place patties on grill over medium heat; cook 10 to 12 minutes for medium or until of desired doneness, turning once.

■ Each burger: About 275 calories, 25 g protein, 0 g carbohydrate, 19 g total fat (7 g saturated), 0 g fiber, 87 mg cholesterol, 75 mg sodium.

* For child-size burgers, shape the meat into 8 patties, each ½ inch thick; cook 7 to 10 minutes for medium.

BURGERS DELUXE
• Mix chopped pickled jalapeño slices and shredded Monterey Jack cheese into the raw meat.
• Serve burgers open-faced on grilled lahvosh (soft Armenian flat bread, sold in supermarkets). Top with sliced red onion and tomato.
• Tuck into plain or whole wheat pitas with crumbled feta cheese and pitted olives.
• Where's the bread? Serve burgers on crisp salad greens with sliced avocado, diced tomato, cucumber chunks, and vinaigrette.
• Make a surprise cheeseburger: Bury a 1-ounce square of Gruyère or blue cheese in the center of each uncooked round.

Fast "Baked" Beans

Put authentic-tasting baked beans on the table in only 20 minutes! We used a variety of store-bought canned beans and added spices and molasses for homemade flavor.

PREP *10 minutes*
COOK *10 to 12 minutes*
MAKES *about 6 cups or*
    8 accompaniment servings

    2 teaspoons olive oil
    1 small onion, chopped
    1 cup ketchup
    3 tablespoons light molasses
    1 tablespoon Dijon mustard
    ½ teaspoon Worcestershire sauce
    ¼ teaspoon salt
       pinch ground cloves
    4 cans beans (15 to 19 ounces each),
       such as black, kidney, white, pink,
       and/or pinto, rinsed and drained

1. In 4-quart saucepan, heat oil over medium heat until hot. Add onion and cook 8 to 10 minutes or until tender and golden.
2. Stir in ketchup, molasses, mustard, Worcestershire, salt, cloves, and *½ cup water* until blended. Increase heat to high; add beans and heat to boiling. Reduce heat to medium-low; cover beans and simmer 5 minutes to blend flavors.

■ Each serving: About 320 calories, 19 g protein, 62 g carbohydrate, 2 g total fat (0 g saturated), 12 g fiber, 0 mg cholesterol, 1,085 mg sodium.

Summer Squash with Herbs

Fresh mint, oregano, and lemon accent tender summer squash in this easy summer side dish.

PREP **15 minutes**
COOK **15 minutes**
MAKES **6 accompaniment servings**

- 2 tablespoons olive oil
- 1 small onion, finely chopped
- 3 small zucchini (about 6 ounces each), cut lengthwise in half, then crosswise into ½-inch-thick pieces
- 3 small yellow summer squashes (about 6 ounces each), cut lengthwise in half, then crosswise into ½-inch-thick pieces
- 1 garlic clove, crushed with garlic press
- 1 teaspoon chopped fresh oregano
- ½ teaspoon salt
- ¼ teaspoon coarsely ground black pepper
- 2 tablespoons chopped fresh mint
- 1 teaspoon grated fresh lemon peel fresh oregano sprigs for garnish

1. In nonstick 12-inch skillet, heat olive oil over medium heat until hot. Add chopped onion and cook 5 to 7 minutes or until onion is golden, stirring frequently.
2. Increase heat to medium-high. Add zucchini, yellow squash, garlic, chopped oregano, salt, pepper, and 1 tablespoon mint; cook 10 minutes or until vegetables are tender and golden, stirring often.
3. Transfer vegetables to bowl and toss with lemon peel and remaining 1 tablespoon mint. Garnish with fresh oregano sprigs.

■ Each serving: About 75 calories, 2 g protein, 7 g carbohydrate, 5 g total fat (1 g saturated), 3 g fiber, 0 mg cholesterol, 200 mg sodium.

New Four-Bean Salad

pictured on pages 118-119

We've put a new spin on three-bean salad by tossing fresh green beans with green and black soybeans.

PREP **20 minutes plus standing**
COOK **5 minutes**
MAKES **about 8 cups or 16 accompaniment servings**

- 1 pound green beans, trimmed and cut into 1½-inch lengths
- ½ (16-ounce) bag (1½ cups) frozen shelled green soybeans (edamame)*
- 3 tablespoons extra virgin olive oil
- ¼ cup balsamic vinegar
- ¼ cup red wine vinegar
- 1 tablespoon sugar
- 1½ teaspoons salt
- ¼ teaspoon ground black pepper
- 1 can (15 ounces) black soybeans, rinsed and drained
- 1 can (15 ounces) pink beans, rinsed and drained
- 1 small red onion, finely chopped (½ cup)

1. In 12-inch skillet, heat *½ inch water* to boiling over high heat. Add green beans and cook 5 minutes or until tender-crisp. Place frozen soybeans in colander; drain green beans over soybeans. Rinse with *cold water* until cool; drain well.
2. In large bowl, with wire whisk, mix oil, vinegars, sugar, salt, and pepper until blended. Add green-bean mixture, black soybeans, pink beans, and onion; toss to combine. Let stand 1 hour to allow flavors to blend or refrigerate until ready to serve.

■ Each serving: About 100 calories, 6 g protein, 11 g carbohydrate, 4 g total fat (1 g saturated), 4 g fiber, 0 mg cholesterol, 295 mg sodium.

* One package (10 ounces) frozen baby lima beans may be substituted for edamame if desired.

Easy Tomato & Mozzarella Salad

Toss farm-stand tomatoes (we love to use red, yellow, and orange) with basil and extra virgin olive oil for one of summer's simple pleasures. For best flavor, don't refrigerate this salad.

PREP **20 minutes**
MAKES **about 8 cups or 8 accompaniment servings**

- 3 pounds tomatoes, cut into 1½-inch chunks
- 8 ounces lightly salted, small fresh mozzarella balls, each cut in half, or 1 package (8 ounces) mozzarella cheese, cut into ½-inch chunks
- 1 cup loosely packed fresh basil leaves, chopped
- 3 tablespoons extra virgin olive oil
- ¾ teaspoon salt
- ¼ teaspoon coarsely ground black pepper

In large bowl, toss tomatoes, mozzarella, basil, oil, salt, and pepper until evenly mixed.

■ Each serving: About 160 calories, 7 g protein, 9 g carbohydrate, 12 g total fat (5 g saturated), 2 g fiber, 22 mg cholesterol, 255 mg sodium.

Nothing updates a kitchen like a modish refrigerator with side-by-side doors. But why spend all that money if, when you entertain, the deli platter won't fit in the fridge and the ice cream cake is too big for the narrow freezer? Maytag's Wide-by-Side refrigerator ($1,679) offers a solution: It's not divided straight up and down, but zigzags, so the top refrigerator shelves are wider than the bottom ones and the bottom freezer baskets are larger than the top ones. That means you can slide large trays of cold cuts—or a watermelon from a roadside stand—into the fridge. You can even freeze a pan of lasagna. Other handy features: a cold-water and ice dispenser, a water filter, and a shelf that can be cranked up or down. In white, black, and bisque. 888-4-maytag or www.maytag.com

---

Ginger-Jalapeño Slaw

pictured on pages 118-119

Red and green cabbage costar in this Asian-accented slaw.

PREP **20 minutes plus chilling**
MAKES **about 8 cups or**
         8 accompaniment servings

⅓ cup seasoned rice vinegar
2 tablespoons olive oil
2 teaspoons grated, peeled fresh ginger
½ teaspoon salt
2 jalapeño chiles, seeded and minced
1 pound green cabbage, thinly sliced (about 6 cups)
½ pound red cabbage, thinly sliced (about 3 cups)
3 medium carrots, finely shredded (about 1½ cups)
2 green onions, thinly sliced
1 cup thinly sliced kale

1. In large bowl, whisk vinegar, oil, ginger, salt, and jalapeño chiles until blended. Add green cabbage, red cabbage, carrots, green onions, and kale; toss well to coat with dressing.
2. Cover and refrigerate slaw 1 hour before serving to allow flavors to blend.

■ Each serving: About 80 calories, 2 g protein, 12 g carbohydrate, 4 g total fat (1 g saturated), 3 g fiber, 0 mg cholesterol, 480 mg sodium.

All-American Potato Salad

pictured on pages 118-119

For quintessential potato-salad flavor, toss warm potatoes with vinaigrette, then, once they're cool, add mayonnaise dressing. (This salad tastes even better if you chill it overnight; do recheck the seasonings before serving to see if the salad needs more salt.)

PREP **45 minutes plus chilling**
COOK **about 10 minutes**
MAKES **about 8 cups or**
         16 accompaniment servings

3 pounds all-purpose potatoes (9 medium), peeled and cut into 1-inch chunks
¼ cup cider vinegar
2 tablespoons olive oil
1 tablespoon spicy brown mustard
½ teaspoon ground black pepper
1½ teaspoons salt
¾ cup mayonnaise
½ cup whole milk
2 medium celery stalks, chopped
½ small red onion, chopped
   chopped fresh parsley leaves and sliced radishes for garnish

1. In 4-quart saucepan, place potatoes and *enough water to cover;* heat to boiling over high heat. Reduce heat to low; cover and simmer 8 to 10 minutes or until potatoes are fork-tender.
2. Meanwhile, in large bowl, with wire whisk, mix vinegar, oil, mustard, pepper, and 1 teaspoon salt.
3. Drain potatoes. Add hot potatoes to bowl with vinaigrette; gently stir with rubber spatula to combine. Let stand until cool.
4. In small bowl, with wire whisk, mix mayonnaise, milk, and remaining ½ teaspoon salt until smooth. Add mayonnaise mixture, celery, and red onion to potatoes. Gently stir with rubber spatula to combine. Cover and refrigerate 4 hours or overnight. Garnish with parsley and radishes to serve.

■ Each serving: About 165 calories, 2 g protein, 17 g carbohydrate, 10 g total fat (2 g saturated), 2 g fiber, 7 mg cholesterol, 300 mg sodium.

---

desserts

Fresh Fruit Salad with Lime Syrup

We love to keep an extra batch of this syrup in the refrigerator. It's luscious tossed with peaches, cantaloupe, your favorite berries—or any mixture of fresh fruit.

PREP **30 minutes plus chilling**
COOK **5 minutes**
MAKES **about 20 cups or 20 servings**

2 limes
1 cup sugar
1 piece (7 pounds) watermelon (preferably seedless), cut into 1-inch chunks
1 medium pineapple, cut into 1-inch chunks
2 mangoes, peeled and cut into ¾-inch chunks
3 large bananas, sliced
3 kiwifruit, peeled and sliced

1. With vegetable peeler, remove 1-inch-wide strips of peel from limes. With knife, cut away any white pith.

2. In small saucepan, heat sugar and *½ cup water* to boiling over high heat; boil 3 minutes or until mixture becomes a light syrup (mixture will thicken upon chilling). Remove saucepan from heat; stir in peel from 1 lime. Cover and refrigerate syrup until well chilled, at least 3 hours or up to 1 week. (Cover remaining lime peel with plastic wrap and refrigerate until ready to assemble salad.

3. In large bowl, place watermelon, pineapple, and mangoes; cover and refrigerate. Up to 2 hours before serving, add banana and kiwifruit slices to bowl with other fruit; toss with lime syrup and reserved lime peel. Cover and refrigerate salad if not serving right away.

■ Each serving: About 120 calories, 1 g protein, 29 g carbohydrate, 1 g total fat (0 g saturated), 2 g fiber, 0 mg cholesterol, 3 mg sodium.

Peach Shortcakes with Ginger Cream

Brown-sugar biscuits are topped with a rosy fruit filling and ginger-spiked cream.

PREP *45 minutes plus chilling*
BAKE *about 15 minutes*
MAKES *10 servings*

Biscuits
2   cups all-purpose flour
⅓   cup packed dark brown sugar
2½ teaspoons baking powder
¾   teaspoon salt
1⅓ cups heavy or whipping cream

Fruit Topping
3   ripe plums (about ½ pound), pitted and coarsely chopped
⅓   cup granulated sugar
5   ripe medium peaches (about 2 pounds), peeled and sliced

Ginger Cream
1   cup heavy or whipping cream
3   tablespoons confectioners' sugar
3   tablespoons minced crystallized ginger

slivered crystallized ginger for garnish

1. Preheat oven to 425°F. Prepare Biscuits: In large bowl, combine flour and brown sugar, breaking up any lumps of brown sugar. Stir in baking powder and salt. Add cream and stir with fork until soft dough forms and leaves side of bowl.
2. Turn dough onto lightly floured surface; knead 4 times to mix thoroughly. Pat dough into a 10" by 6" rectangle. With floured knife, cut dough lengthwise in half; cut each half crosswise into 5 pieces to make 10 rectangles in all.
3. With large floured spatula, transfer rectangles to ungreased large cookie sheet. Bake Biscuits 15 minutes or until golden and transfer to wire rack to cool.
4. Meanwhile, prepare Fruit Topping: In 1-quart saucepan, combine plums and granulated sugar; heat to boiling over medium-high heat. Reduce heat to medium-low; cover and simmer 5 minutes or until plums soften and form a sauce. Uncover and simmer 5 minutes longer or until sauce thickens slightly. Pour sauce into large bowl; set aside to cool slightly.
5. Add peaches to bowl with plums; stir to combine. Let stand at least 30 minutes to allow flavors to develop.
6. Prepare Ginger Cream: In bowl, with mixer at medium speed, beat cream with confectioners' sugar and minced ginger until soft peaks form.
7. To serve, split Biscuits. Layer bottoms with peach mixture and whipped cream, then add tops. Garnish with slivered ginger.

■ Each serving: About 400 calories, 4 g protein, 50 g carbohydrate, 21 g total fat (13 g saturated), 2 g fiber, 77 mg cholesterol, 300 mg sodium.

Sugar & Spice Blueberry Crisp

You can put this together really fast. Try it warm, with a scoop of vanilla ice cream on top.

PREP *20 minutes plus cooling*
BAKE *about 35 minutes*
MAKES *8 servings*

½   cup granulated sugar
2   tablespoons cornstarch
3   pints blueberries
1   tablespoon fresh lemon juice
1   cup all-purpose flour
¾   cup quick-cooking or old-fashioned oats
½   cup packed light brown sugar
½   cup cold butter or margarine (1 stick), cut up
¾   teaspoon ground cinnamon

1. Preheat oven to 375°F. In large bowl, stir granulated sugar and cornstarch until blended. Add blueberries and lemon juice; stir to coat evenly. Spoon blueberry mixture into shallow 2-quart glass or ceramic baking dish; spread evenly.
2. In same bowl, combine flour, oats, brown sugar, butter, and cinnamon. With fingers, mix until coarse crumbs form. Crumble over blueberry mixture.
3. Place sheet of foil underneath baking dish; crimp foil edges to form a rim to catch any drips during baking. Bake crisp 35 to 40 minutes or until top is browned and fruit is bubbly at edges. Cool crisp on wire rack 1 hour to serve warm or cool completely to serve later. Reheat if desired.

■ Each serving: About 390 calories, 5 g protein, 64 g carbohydrate, 14 g total fat (8 g saturated), 5 g fiber, 33 mg cholesterol, 135 mg sodium.

Getting the pits out of cherries is such a tedious and messy task that most of us turn to cans for making a pie, even at the height of cherry season. To see if cherry pitters could ease the chore, our food appliances team tested 9 models. After going through pounds of cherries (hard work!), our pros found 2 gadgets that even make pitting kind of fun. They were simple to operate, removed the stones from every single cherry, and left the fruit plump, not squashed or mangled. Both handle ripe Bings as well as small, tart pie cherries, and they can be used on all but the largest olives, too. Look for them at kitchen stores.

The **Leifheit Pro Line Cherry Stoner,** $14, has 2 levers that you press together to force out a pit. When you're done, the gadget locks together so it can be stowed neatly in a drawer. If you bake often and find fresh cherry desserts irresistible, invest in the **Leifheit Cherrymat,** ($45). You load the hopper with about 15 cherries, then press the plunger; the pits fall into the attached container while the cherries fall into a bowl. Now you have no excuse not to try our Cherry-Berry Sauce (right).

Good Housekeeping
INSTITUTE REPORT

Country Peach Pie

Pour homemade sour-cream custard over fruit for a tender, one-crust pie.

PREP **45 minutes plus cooling**
BAKE **about 35 minutes**
MAKES **10 servings**

Piecrust
1¼ cups all-purpose flour
¼ teaspoon salt
4 tablespoons cold butter or margarine, cut up
2 tablespoons vegetable shortening

Custard Filling
1 container (8 ounces) sour cream
2 large eggs
¾ cup sugar
¼ cup all-purpose flour
1 teaspoon vanilla extract
4 ripe large peaches (about 1¾ pounds), peeled, pitted, and cut into ¼-inch-thick slices

1. Prepare Piecrust: In medium bowl, combine flour and salt. With pastry blender or 2 knives used scissor-fashion, cut in butter with shortening until mixture resembles coarse crumbs. Stir *4 to 6 tablespoons ice water,* 1 tablespoon at a time, into flour mixture, mixing after each addition until dough is just moist enough to hold together. With hands, shape dough into a disk. Wrap disk in plastic wrap and refrigerate 30 minutes or until firm enough to roll.

2. Meanwhile, preheat oven to 425°F. Prepare Custard Filling: In medium bowl, with wire whisk or fork, mix sour cream, eggs, sugar, flour, and vanilla until blended; set aside.

3. On lightly floured surface, with floured rolling pin, roll dough into a round about 1½ inches larger in diameter than inverted 9-inch pie plate. Ease dough into pie plate; trim edge, leaving 1-inch overhang. Fold overhang under; bring up over pie-plate rim and pinch to form high decorative edge.

4. Place peaches in crust. Pour custard over peaches.

5. Bake pie 35 to 40 minutes or until edge of custard is golden brown and knife inserted in center of pie comes out clean. Cool pie on wire rack 1 hour to serve warm or cool completely to serve later.

■ Each serving: About 280 calories, 4 g protein, 37 g carbohydrate, 13 g total fat (7 g saturated), 2 g fiber, 66 mg cholesterol, 135 mg sodium.

Cherry-Berry Sauce

This topping makes the most of cherry season; serve warm over ice cream, waffles, or pancakes.

PREP **20 minutes**
COOK **8 minutes**
MAKES **about 2¼ cups**

⅓ cup sugar
12 ounces dark sweet cherries (2 heaping cups), pitted and each cut in half
2 tablespoons butter or margarine
1 tablespoon fresh lime juice
½ pint raspberries (about 1 cup)

1. In 2-quart saucepan, combine sugar and *⅓ cup water;* heat to boiling over high heat. Reduce heat to medium and cook, uncovered, 5 minutes. Stir in cherries; cook 2 minutes or until mixture simmers. Remove saucepan from heat; stir in butter with lime juice until butter melts. Gently stir in raspberries. Pour into serving bowl and let stand 5 minutes.

2. Serve warm over ice cream, frozen yogurt, or toasted pound cake. Refrigerate sauce to serve cold.

■ Each ¼ cup: About 80 calories, 0 g protein, 14 g carbohydrate, 3 g total fat (0 g saturated), 2 g fiber, 0 mg cholesterol, 35 mg sodium.

July

spice up your barbecue

Shake it up, baby. New seasonings add snap to meat, fish, tofu, and veggies.

Coffee & Spice Steak with Cool Salsa

A dry rub of instant coffee, cinnamon, and allspice adds rich roasted, caramelized flavor. Our crisp watermelon and cucumber salsa is a refreshing go-along with any meat.

PREP *30 minutes*
GRILL *12 to 15 minutes*
MAKES *6 main-dish servings*

Cool Salsa
- 1 lime
- 2 cups diced (¼-inch) watermelon
- ½ English (seedless) cucumber, unpeeled and cut into ¼-inch dice
- 1 green onion, minced
- ¼ teaspoon salt
- ⅛ teaspoon coarsely ground black pepper

Coffee & Spice Steak
- 2 teaspoons instant-coffee granules
- 1 teaspoon sugar
- 1 teaspoon salt
- 1 teaspoon coarsely ground black pepper
- ½ teaspoon ground cinnamon
- ¼ teaspoon ground allspice
- 1 beef flank steak (about 1½ pounds)
- 2 teaspoons olive oil

1. Prepare Cool Salsa: From lime, grate 1 teaspoon peel and squeeze 2 tablespoons juice. In medium bowl, toss lime peel and juice with watermelon, cucumber, green onion, salt, and pepper. Cover and refrigerate salsa up to 2 hours if not serving right away. Makes about 3½ cups.
2. Prepare Coffee & Spice Steak: In cup, mix coffee granules, sugar, salt, pepper, cinnamon, and allspice. Coat both sides of steak with oil, then rub with coffee mixture.
3. Place steak on hot grill rack over medium heat. Cook steak 12 to 15 minutes for medium-rare or until desired doneness, turning once.
4. Transfer steak to cutting board; let stand 10 minutes to allow juices to set for easier slicing. Thinly slice steak and serve with salsa.

■ Each serving steak: About 215 calories, 27 g protein, 1 g carbohydrate, 11 g total fat (4 g saturated), 0 g fiber, 47 mg cholesterol, 445 mg sodium.

■ Each ½ cup salsa: About 20 calories, 0 g protein, 4 g carbohydrate, 0 g total fat, 0 g fiber, 0 mg cholesterol, 80 mg sodium.

Cajun Shrimp with Rémoulade Sauce

This takes only four minutes on the fire! We added fresh lemon peel to jarred Cajun seasoning (a blend of garlic, onion, chiles, peppers, and herbs). The creamy homemade sauce (made with light mayonnaise) pairs nicely with the Southern-style shrimp.

PREP *25 minutes*
GRILL *3 to 4 minutes*
MAKES *4 main-dish servings*

Rémoulade Sauce
- ½ cup light mayonnaise
- 2 tablespoons ketchup
- 2 tablespoons minced celery
- 1 tablespoon Dijon mustard with seeds
- 1 tablespoon minced fresh parsley leaves
- 2 teaspoons fresh lemon juice
- ½ teaspoon Cajun seasoning*
- 1 green onion, minced

Cajun Shrimp
- 1 tablespoon Cajun seasoning*
- 1 tablespoon olive oil
- 2 teaspoons grated fresh lemon peel
- 1¼ pounds large shrimp, shelled and deveined, with tail part of shell left on if you like green-onion and lemon-peel slivers for garnish lemon wedges (optional)

1. Prepare Rémoulade Sauce: In small bowl, mix all sauce ingredients. Cover and refrigerate up to 3 days if not serving right away. Makes about 1 cup.
2. Prepare Cajun Shrimp: In medium bowl, mix Cajun seasoning, oil, and grated lemon peel. Add shrimp to spice mixture and toss until evenly coated.
3. Place shrimp on hot grill rack (or hot flat grill topper) over medium-high heat and cook 3 to 4 minutes or just until shrimp are opaque throughout, turning shrimp over once.

4. Transfer shrimp to platter; garnish with green onion and lemon peel. Serve shrimp with lemon wedges if you like and Rémoulade Sauce.

■ Each serving shrimp: About 155 calories, 24 g protein, 2 g carbohydrate, 5 g total fat (1 g saturated), 0 g fiber, 175 mg cholesterol, 575 mg sodium.

■ Each 1 tablespoon sauce: About 30 calories, 0 g protein, 2 g carbohydrate, 3 g total fat (1 g saturated), 0 g fiber, 3 mg cholesterol, 95 mg sodium.

* Seasoning mixes vary among manufacturers, especially with regard to salt content. Add salt to taste if necessary.

Chile-Rubbed Ham with Peach Salsa

It's a quick grill—a fully cooked ham steak patted with paprika and smoky chiles before searing. Our soothing salsa, made with fresh peaches, cilantro, and fresh lime juice, tames the spice.

PREP *30 minutes*
GRILL *4 to 6 minutes*
MAKES *4 main-dish servings*

Peach Salsa
4 ripe peaches (about 1¼ pounds), pitted and cut into ¼-inch dice
1 cup loosely packed fresh cilantro leaves, chopped
1 jalapeño chile, seeded and minced
2 tablespoons peach jam
2 tablespoons fresh lime juice
¼ teaspoon salt

Chile-Rubbed Ham
1 tablespoon paprika
1 tablespoon olive oil
2 teaspoons minced canned chipotle chile in adobo or 2 teaspoons adobo sauce*
1 fully cooked center-cut ham steak, ½ inch thick (about 1¼ pounds)

1. Prepare Peach Salsa: In medium bowl, toss together all salsa ingredients. Cover and refrigerate salsa up to 1 day if not serving right away. Makes about 4 cups.
2. Prepare Chile-Rubbed Ham: In cup, mix paprika, oil, and chipotle. Spread mixture on both sides of ham.
3. Place ham on hot grill rack over medium-high heat. Cook 4 to 6 minutes, turning ham over once, until lightly browned and heated through. Serve ham with salsa.

■ Each serving ham: About 180 calories, 24 g protein, 1 g carbohydrate, 8 g total fat (2 g saturated), 0 g fiber, 72 mg cholesterol, 1,820 mg sodium.

■ Each ½ cup salsa: About 40 calories, 0 g protein, 10 g carbohydrate, 0 g total fat, 2 g fiber, 0 mg cholesterol, 80 mg sodium.

* Canned chipotle chiles are smoked jalapeño chiles packed in a thick vinegary sauce called adobo. Look for chipotle chiles in Hispanic markets and in some supermarkets.

food editor's Q&A

Q I'd like to make my own seasoning blends with whole spices. What is the easiest way?

a A coffee grinder blends dried spices quickly and evenly. Just be sure to clean it well before using it for coffee beans, or your morning cup will taste like cumin or coriander. (If you grind both coffee and spices often, it might be smart to invest in separate grinders.) Grind spices right before using them, so the flavor is really fresh. Experiment with fennel seeds, mustard seeds, and peppercorns—we used all three for Spicy Garlic Lamb with Cucumber Raita, page 110. You can also make your own blends of dried rosemary, thyme, oregano, and basil to coat chicken pieces or lamb chops.

Q Lately, I've seen ground cinnamon from Saigon at the store. How is it different from the regular cinnamon I always buy?

a Your bottle is from Indonesia, and it's still the most common form sold in this country. But about two years ago, U.S. importers began buying the spice from Vietnam. This Vietnamese, or Saigon, variety has a more intense flavor (think red-hot candies) and deep-brown color—and a higher price (about 85 cents more per ounce). If you would like to keep both on your shelf, use the Saigon cinnamon for bold spice rubs or deep, dark gingerbread, and shake the sweeter Indonesian variety onto toast or into crumb-cake toppings for a warm, homey appeal. (To grill with cinnamon, try our Coffee & Spice Steak with Cool Salsa, facing page.)

Q Is a freestone peach better than a cling peach?

a Almost all fresh peaches sold are freestone. They are generally softer and juicier, and because the pits pull away from the flesh so easily, they can be cut nicely into uniform pieces for tarts or pies. Cling (or clingstone) are used mostly for canned fruit and work best in recipes calling for diced or pureed peaches. Try cling peaches in milk shakes, salsas, and savory sauces, such as glazes for ribs, chicken, or pork.

Jerk Pork Chops with Grilled Pineapple

We love this shortcut Jamaican jerk—made with thick, juicy pork and succulent pineapple. Try our jerk rub on chicken pieces or salmon steaks, too.

PREP *15 minutes*
GRILL *about 12 minutes*
MAKES *4 main-dish servings*

1 baby pineapple or ½ regular pineapple
1 lime
2 tablespoons jerk seasoning*
1 tablespoon olive oil
4 pork loin chops, ¾ inch thick (about 8 ounces each with bone) lime wedges and cilantro sprigs for garnish

1. With sharp knife, cut pineapple lengthwise through crown to stem end in 4 wedges, leaving on leafy crown.
2. From lime, grate ½ teaspoon peel and squeeze 1 tablespoon juice. In small bowl, mix lime peel and juice with jerk seasoning and oil. Rub both sides of pork chops with jerk mixture.
3. Place pork chops on hot grill rack over medium heat; cook 10 to 12 minutes, turning chops over once, until browned on the outside and still slightly pink on the inside. While chops are cooking, add pineapple wedges, cut sides down, to same grill; cook 5 minutes, turning wedges over once. Transfer chops and pineapple to same platter. Garnish with lime wedges and cilantro sprigs.

■ Each serving: About 400 calories, 41 g protein, 8 g carbohydrate, 22 g total fat (7 g saturated), 1 g fiber, 116 mg cholesterol, 535 mg sodium.

* Seasoning mixes vary among manufacturers, especially with regard to salt content. Add salt to taste if necessary.

Nantucket Seafood Packets

Steam delicately seasoned scrod, plump mussels, and summer's best tomatoes in foil packets—cleanup is a cinch!

PREP *15 minutes*
GRILL *about 10 minutes*
MAKES *4 main-dish servings*

3 tablespoons margarine or butter, softened
1 teaspoon grated fresh lime peel
¾ teaspoon salt
½ teaspoon ground cumin
½ teaspoon ground coriander
⅛ teaspoon ground red pepper (cayenne)
4 pieces scrod fillet (about 6 ounces each)
12 large mussels
2 ripe medium tomatoes, cut into ½-inch dice
1 cup loosely packed fresh cilantro leaves, chopped

1. In small bowl, stir margarine, grated lime peel, salt, cumin, coriander, and ground red pepper until blended.
2. Arrange four 16" by 12" sheets of heavy-duty foil on work surface. Place 1 scrod fillet on half of each sheet of foil. Dot scrod fillets with margarine mixture. Top each scrod fillet with 3 mussels and one-fourth of tomatoes. Bring long sides of foil up and fold several times to seal well. Fold over ends to seal in juices.
3. Place foil packets on grill over medium heat and cook 10 minutes without turning packets over. Before serving, with kitchen shears, cut an X in top of each foil packet to let steam escape, then carefully pull back foil to open. After opening each packet, check that scrod flakes easily when tested with a fork and mussels are open. Return packets to grill if longer cooking is necessary. Sprinkle with cilantro to serve.

■ Each serving: About 265 calories, 36 g protein, 5 g carbohydrate, 11 g total fat (2 g saturated), 1 g fiber, 84 mg cholesterol, 760 mg sodium.

Spicy Garlic Lamb with Cucumber Raita

Leg of lamb isn't only for the oven; it's divine cooked on the grill. Cucumbers in a minted yogurt dressing balance the spicy meat.

PREP *30 minutes plus chilling*
GRILL *about 25 minutes*
MAKES *8 main-dish servings*

Cucumber Raita
6 Kirby cucumbers (about 1½ pounds)
1 teaspoon salt
2 cups plain low-fat yogurt
½ cup loosely packed fresh mint leaves, chopped
1½ teaspoons sugar

Spiced Lamb
1 tablespoon fennel seeds
1 tablespoon mustard seeds
1 tablespoon cumin seeds
2 teaspoons salt
1 teaspoon whole black peppercorns
1 teaspoon dried thyme leaves
3 whole cloves
3 garlic cloves, crushed with garlic press
2 tablespoons fresh lemon juice
3½ pounds boneless butterflied lamb leg, trimmed*
mint sprigs for garnish

1. Prepare Cucumber Raita: With vegetable peeler, remove several strips of peel from each cucumber. Cut each cucumber lengthwise in half; scoop out seeds. Cut each half lengthwise in half, then crosswise into ½-inch-thick pieces. In medium bowl, toss cucumbers with ¼ teaspoon salt; let stand 10 minutes. With hand, press cucumbers to remove as much liquid as possible; drain off liquid. Stir in yogurt, mint, sugar, and remaining ¾ teaspoon salt. Cover and refrigerate until ready to serve or up to 6 hours. Makes about 4 cups.

2. Prepare Spiced Lamb: In spice grinder or coffee grinder, blend fennel, mustard, cumin, salt, peppercorns, thyme, and cloves until finely ground.

3. In small bowl, mix garlic and lemon juice with ground spices until blended. Rub spice mixture over both sides of lamb.

4. Place lamb on hot grill rack over medium-low heat; cook 25 minutes for medium-rare or until desired doneness, turning lamb over once. Thickness of butterflied lamb will vary throughout; cut off sections of lamb as they are cooked and place on cutting board. Thinly slice lamb and arrange on platter; garnish with mint sprigs. Serve with Cucumber Raita.

■ Each serving lamb: About 275 calories, 39 g protein, 2 g carbohydrate, 11 g total fat (4 g saturated), 1 g fiber, 121 mg cholesterol, 675 mg sodium.

■ Each ½ cup raita: About 60 calories, 4 g protein, 10 g carbohydrate, 2 g total fat (0 g saturated), 2 g fiber, 4 mg cholesterol, 260 mg sodium.

* Ask butcher to debone a 4½-pound lamb leg shank half and slit the meat lengthwise to spread open like a thick steak.

grilling secret: the tastiest combos

A pinch of this, a brush of that—a spice rub, marinade, or glaze gives great flavor without piling on fat and calories. These can transform the blandest chicken breast into something that tastes decadent (but isn't). Four ways to leave boring barbecues behind:

PREMADE BLENDS

We sampled dozens of these in our test kitchens; some favorites are Thai, Cajun, jerk, and garam masala seasoning mixes, available in jars in the spice aisle. Use them as you like—we jazzed up store-bought jerk seasoning with lime juice and peel for Jerk Pork Chops with Grilled Pineapple (facing page). We also love a Caribbean-flavored marinade blend you mix with oil and vinegar.

HOMEMADE RUBS

Mix in a small bowl or cup; toss with shrimp or pat onto chops before grilling. (For these rubs and our marinades and glazes, adjust ingredients to taste.)
• Ground red pepper (cayenne), ground cumin, chili powder.
• Coarsely ground black pepper, ground coriander, ground cumin, crushed fennel seeds.
• Ground cinnamon, curry powder, brown sugar.
• Crumbled dried rosemary, dried thyme, dried oregano.

MARINADES

Whisk in a bowl; add steak or chicken quarters and let stand 15 minutes at room temperature before cooking.
• Grated fresh ginger, fresh lemon juice, soy sauce.
• Crumbled dried rosemary, minced garlic, red wine.
• Ground coriander, ground cumin, minced garlic, plain nonfat yogurt.
• Minced shallot, grainy mustard, red wine vinegar.

GLAZES

Whisk in a small bowl, then brush over beef, pork, or poultry during the last few minutes the meat is on the grill.
• Crushed red pepper flakes, ground ginger, balsamic vinegar, apricot or raspberry jam.
• Chinese five-spice powder, fresh lime juice, honey.
• Chopped fresh cilantro leaves, pureed mango chutney.
• Sliced green onion, hoisin sauce, seasoned rice vinegar.

Grilled Thai Chicken Salad

Add zest to boneless chicken with a spicy Thai blend, then grill it and slice for a delicious main-course salad.

PREP **30 minutes**
GRILL **about 12 minutes**
MAKES **4 main-dish servings**

Thai Dressing
- 2 tablespoons fresh lime juice
- 4 teaspoons Asian fish sauce
- 1 tablespoon reduced-sodium soy sauce
- 1 teaspoon sugar

Chicken Salad
- 4 large skinless, boneless chicken thighs (about 1½ pounds)
- 2 tablespoons Thai seasoning*
- 2 bags (10 ounces each) cut up romaine lettuce
- 2 cups loosely packed fresh mint leaves
- 2 papayas or mangoes or 1 of each, peeled, seeded, and sliced
- 2 green onions, sliced

1. Prepare Thai Dressing: In cup, combine lime juice, fish sauce, soy sauce, and sugar; set aside.

2. Prepare Chicken Salad: In medium bowl, toss chicken with Thai seasoning. Place chicken on hot grill rack over medium heat; cook 10 to 12 minutes or until juices run clear when thickest part of thigh is pierced with tip of knife, turning chicken over once.

3. In large bowl, toss lettuce, mint, papaya and/or mango, and green onions with dressing. Thinly slice chicken and arrange over salad.

■ Each serving: About 375 calories, 38 g protein, 24 g carbohydrate, 15 g total fat (4 g saturated), 7 g fiber, 121 mg cholesterol, 1,215 mg sodium.

* Seasoning mixes vary among manufacturers, especially with regard to salt content. Add salt to taste if necessary.

Hot Buttered Chili-Lime Corn

Serve sweet corn already buttered and seasoned hot off the grill. Chili powder and fresh lime peel add punch to this summer staple.

PREP **15 minutes**
GRILL **12 minutes**
MAKES **4 accompaniment servings**

- 4 ears corn, husks and silk removed, and each ear cut crosswise in half
- 2 tablespoons butter or margarine, softened
- 1 teaspoon chili powder
- ½ teaspoon salt
- ½ teaspoon fresh lime peel
  fresh lime wedges (optional)

1. Place corn in 14½" by 12½" extra heavy-duty foil cooking bag in a single layer.* In cup, stir butter, chili powder, salt, and lime peel until blended. Dot mixture on corn and fold bag to seal as label directs.

2. Place foil packet on grill over medium heat. Cook corn 12 minutes, turning foil packet over once halfway through cooking. Remove packet from grill.

3. Before serving, with kitchen shears, cut an X in top of foil packet to let steam escape, then carefully pull back foil to open. Serve corn with lime wedges if you like.

■ Each serving: About 115 calories, 3 g protein, 17 g carbohydrate, 5 g total fat (1 g saturated), 3 g fiber, 15 mg cholesterol, 260 mg sodium.

* Look for foil cooking bags in your supermarket where foil and plastic wrap are sold. If you can't find them, you can make your own: Layer two 20" by 18" sheets of heavy-duty foil to make a double thickness. Place recipe ingredients on center of foil. Bring short ends up and over ingredients and fold over 2 or 3 times to seal well. Fold over remaining sides of foil 2 or 3 times to seal in juices.

Southwestern Turkey Fajitas

pictured on facing page

Broiling the tomatillos adds a subtle smokiness to this luscious salsa. Serve any extra salsa with tortilla chips.

PREP **30 minutes**
GRILL **about 20 minutes**
MAKES **6 main-dish servings**

Tomatillo Salsa
- 1 pound tomatillos, husked and rinsed
- 1 small poblano chile, cut in half, stems and seeds discarded
- 1 small shallot, cut up
- 3 tablespoons fresh lime juice
- ¾ teaspoon salt
- ¾ teaspoon sugar
- ⅓ cup packed fresh cilantro leaves, chopped

Turkey & Onion Fajitas
- 2 whole turkey-breast tenderloins (about 1¾ pounds) or 6 medium skinless, boneless chicken-breast halves (about 1¾ pounds)
- 2 tablespoons fajita seasoning*
- 4 teaspoons olive oil
- 3 large onions, cut into ½-inch-thick slices
- 12 (6-inch) corn tortillas
  cilantro sprigs and red chiles for garnish

1. Prepare Tomatillo Salsa: Preheat broiler. Place tomatillos in broiling pan without rack. Place pan in broiler 5 to 6 inches from source of heat and broil tomatillos 10 minutes or until blackened in spots and blistering, turning tomatillos over once. When tomatillos are turned, add poblano, skin side up, to pan and broil 6 minutes or until charred.

2. In blender or food processor with knife blade attached, pulse tomatillos, poblano, shallot, lime juice, salt, and sugar until chopped. Stir in cilantro. Cover and refrigerate salsa up to 3

days if not serving right away. Makes about 2 cups.

3. Prepare Turkey & Onion Fajitas: In medium bowl, toss turkey tenderloins or chicken with fajita seasoning and 2 teaspoons oil. Brush onion slices with remaining 2 teaspoons oil.

4. Place turkey or chicken and onions on hot grill rack. Cook turkey 15 to 20 minutes (chicken 10 to 12 minutes) or until juices run clear when thickest part is pierced with tip of knife (internal temperature of turkey tenderloins should be 170°F. on meat thermometer), turning turkey or chicken over once. Cook onion slices 12 to 15 minutes or until tender and golden, turning them over once.

5. While turkey or chicken is cooking, place several tortillas on same grill and heat just until lightly browned, removing tortillas to a sheet of foil as they brown. Wrap tortillas in foil and keep warm.

6. To assemble fajitas: Transfer onions to bowl. Transfer turkey or chicken to cutting board and thinly slice. Top tortillas with equal amounts of turkey or chicken and onion; spoon some salsa on each and fold over to eat out of hand. Garnish with cilantro sprigs and red chiles. Serve with any remaining onions and salsa.

■ Each serving without salsa: About 350 calories, 36 g protein, 35 g carbohydrate, 7 g total fat (1 g saturated), 5 g fiber, 88 mg cholesterol, 440 mg sodium.

■ Each ¼ cup salsa: About 30 calories, 1 g protein, 6 g carbohydrate, 1 g total fat (0 g saturated), 1 g fiber, 0 mg cholesterol, 220 mg sodium.

* Seasoning mixes vary among manufacturers, especially with regard to salt content. Add salt to taste if necessary.

Southwestern
Turkey Fajitas,
facing page

Jeweled Fruit
Galettes, page 124

Plum Compote with
Ginger Syrup, page 127

Quick Blackberry
Sorbet, page 127

Raspberry-Peach
Tiramisu, page 128

Orange Pork &
Asparagus Stir-fry,
page 86

Pasta with
Asparagus Pesto,
page 87

Korean Steak
in Lettuce
Cups, page 89

Pork Chops with
Peppers & Onions,
page 85

Ginger-Jalapeño Slaw, page 104,
New Four-Bean Salad, page 103,
All-American Potato Salad, page 104

Plum-Glazed Ribs,
page 99

Turkey Kabobs with
Garden Tomato Jam,
page 100

Miso-Glazed Salmon
with Edamame Salad,
facing page

Miso-Glazed Salmon with Edamame Salad

pictured on facing page

Spread a mixture of miso, ginger, and cayenne pepper on a large salmon fillet. Enjoy with our healthy soybean salad for a Japanese-inspired meal.

PREP *30 minutes*
GRILL *about 12 minutes*
MAKES *4 main-dish servings*

Edamame Salad
1 bag (16 ounces) frozen shelled edamame (green soybeans) or frozen baby lima beans
¼ cup seasoned rice vinegar
1 tablespoon vegetable oil
1 teaspoon sugar
¾ teaspoon salt
⅛ teaspoon ground black pepper
1 bunch radishes (8 ounces), each cut in half and thinly sliced
1 cup loosely packed fresh cilantro leaves, chopped

Miso-Glazed Salmon
2 tablespoons red miso
1 green onion, minced
1 tablespoon grated, peeled fresh ginger
1 teaspoon brown sugar
⅛ teaspoon ground red pepper (cayenne)
1 salmon fillet with skin (1½ pounds)
baby greens for garnish

1. Prepare Edamame Salad: Cook edamame as label directs; drain. Rinse with cold running water to stop cooking, and drain again.
2. In medium bowl, whisk vinegar, oil, sugar, salt, and black pepper until blended. Add edamame, radishes, and cilantro, and toss until evenly coated. Cover and refrigerate salad up to 1 day if not serving right away. Makes about 4 cups.
3. Prepare Miso-Glazed Salmon: In small bowl, with spoon, mix miso, green onion, ginger, brown sugar, and ground red pepper. Rub miso mixture on flesh side of salmon.
4. Place salmon, skin side down, on hot greased grill rack over medium-low heat. Cook 10 to 12 minutes or just until salmon turns opaque throughout and flakes easily when tested with a fork. Serve salmon with Edamame Salad; garnish with baby greens.

■ Each serving salmon: About 280 calories, 29 g protein, 3 g carbohydrate, 16 g total fat (3 g saturated), 0 g fiber, 80 mg cholesterol, 450 mg sodium.

■ Each 1 cup salad: About 220 calories, 16 g protein, 23 g carbohydrate, 8 g total fat (0 g saturated), 3 g fiber, 0 mg cholesterol, 1,020 mg sodium.

Grilled Tofu & Veggies

Be sure to buy extra-firm tofu for this recipe; other varieties will fall apart while cooking.

PREP *25 minutes*
GRILL *about 12 minutes*
MAKES *4 main-dish servings*

Hoisin Glaze
⅓ cup hoisin sauce
2 garlic cloves, crushed with garlic press
1 tablespoon vegetable oil
1 tablespoon reduced-sodium soy sauce
1 tablespoon grated, peeled fresh ginger
1 tablespoon seasoned rice vinegar
⅛ teaspoon ground red pepper (cayenne)

Tofu & Veggies
1 package (15 ounces) extra-firm tofu
2 medium zucchini (about 10 ounces each), each cut lengthwise into quarters, then crosswise in half
1 large red pepper, cut lengthwise into quarters, stem and seeds discarded
1 bunch green onions, trimmed
1 teaspoon vegetable oil

1. Prepare Hoisin Glaze: In small bowl, with fork, mix all glaze ingredients until well blended.
2. Prepare Tofu & Veggies: Cut tofu horizontally into 4 pieces, then cut each piece crosswise in half. Place tofu on paper towels; pat dry with additional paper towels. Spoon half of Hoisin Glaze into medium bowl; add zucchini and red pepper. Gently toss vegetables to coat. Arrange tofu on large plate and brush both sides of tofu with remaining half of glaze. On another plate, rub green onions with oil.
3. Place tofu, zucchini, and red pepper on hot grill rack over medium heat. Cook tofu 6 minutes, gently turning over once with wide metal spatula. Transfer tofu to platter; keep warm. Continue cooking vegetables about 5 minutes longer or until tender and browned, removing them to platter with tofu as they are done. Add green onions to grill during last minute of cooking time; transfer to platter.

■ Each serving: About 245 calories, 15 g protein, 22 g carbohydrate, 11 g total fat (1 g saturated), 4 g fiber, 0 mg cholesterol, 615 mg sodium.

Cuban Pork & Plantains with Black-Bean Salsa

Make sure the plantains are very ripe; the skin should be black, and the fruit should yield to gentle pressure. (To speed ripening, place in a brown paper bag with a lime.)

PREP *45 minutes*
GRILL *about 18 minutes*
MAKES *6 main-dish servings*

Black-Bean Salsa
- 2 limes
- 1 orange
- 1 can (15 to 19 ounces) black beans, rinsed and drained
- ½ small sweet onion, diced
- ¼ cup loosely packed fresh cilantro leaves, chopped
- 1 medium jalapeño chile, seeded and minced
- ¾ teaspoon salt

Pork & Plantains
- 2 large garlic cloves, crushed with garlic press
- 1 teaspoon salt
- 1½ teaspoons coarsely ground black pepper
- 2 tablespoons olive oil
- 2 whole pork tenderloins (about 1½ pounds)
- 3 ripe medium plantains (about 1½ pounds), peeled and each cut lengthwise in half

  carambola (star fruit) slices for garnish

1. Prepare Black-Bean Salsa: From limes, grate ½ teaspoon peel and squeeze 3 tablespoons juice. From orange, grate ½ teaspoon peel. With knife, remove remaining peel and white pith from orange; cut sections into ½-inch dice. In medium bowl, combine lime peel and juice, orange peel, and diced orange with black beans and remaining salsa ingredients.

Cover and refrigerate salsa up to 2 days if not serving right away. Makes about 3 cups.

2. Prepare Pork & Plantains: In cup, mix garlic, salt, pepper, and 1 tablespoon oil until blended. Rub pork tenderloins all over with garlic mixture. Brush plantains with remaining 1 tablespoon oil.

3. Place tenderloins on hot grill rack over medium heat and cook 18 to 20 minutes or until browned on the outside and still slightly pink in the center, turning tenderloins over once (internal temperature of meat should be 155°F. on meat thermometer). On same grill with pork tenderloins, cook

plantains 7 to 8 minutes or until tender and browned, turning plantains over once.

4. Transfer plantains to a large platter. Transfer tenderloins to cutting board and thinly slice. Serve sliced pork and plantains with Black-Bean Salsa, and garnish with carambola slices.

■ Each serving pork & plantains: About 315 calories, 28 g protein, 29 g carbohydrate, 11 g total fat (3 g saturated), 2 g fiber, 78 mg cholesterol, 440 mg sodium.

■ Each ½ cup salsa: About 70 calories, 4 g protein, 17 g carbohydrate, 0 g total fat, 5 g fiber, 0 mg cholesterol, 475 mg sodium.

---

new for entertaining

Great grill gear

Better protection
The newest oven mitts claim to excel at shielding hands from heat and fire. But of the three brands we evaluated, only Kitchen Safe mitts from Wells Lamont resisted flaming and charring. The BBQ Mitts ($12.99 each) are comfortable and flexible. Trivets, pot holders, and oven mitts ($7.99 to $9.99) are also available. All come in red, blue, black, green, and natural. At specialty stores, including Linens 'n Things.

Retro egg holder
The Rubbermaid Servin' Saver Egg Keeper ($4.99) has been brought back by popular demand. The egg keeper has 20 wells for transporting deviled eggs without rolling. Other times of the year, use it for chocolate-dipped strawberries or Easter eggs. At mass merchandisers. www.rubbermaid.com

Flavor booster
Use BBQr's Delight wood pellets with gas, electric, or charcoal grills for

that smoky taste you get only from wood. Choose from 12 flavors in one-pound bags ($4.99) or single-use packets (99 cents). Try Jack Daniel's or Black Walnut with steaks, Orange with seafood. At Wal-Mart. www.bbqrsdelight.com or 877-275-9591

Fireside utensils
Like their namesake, **the new George Foreman barbecue tools** ($14.99 each) are oversize champs. The turner, fork, tongs, and basting brush are stainless steel with rubber handles for a good grip. The grill cleaning brush has a removable head so it can be replaced when it wears down. At department or specialty stores.

Well-adjusted accessory
Make the most of your grill and cut down on clutter with **Charcoal Companion's SpaceSaver Rib Rack** ($19.99). By holding the meat vertically, it cooks six pounds without taking up the entire surface. And it comes apart for storage. At specialty stores. 800-521-0505

summer
fruit finales

Your turn to bring the dessert?
Go bearing fruit with a jewel-toned cobbler,
cake, or compote.

Nectarine-Blackberry Cobbler

Homemade biscuits striped with jam bake over a panful of juicy fruit. You can substitute blueberries for the blackberries if you like.

PREP *45 minutes plus cooling*
BAKE *45 minutes*
MAKES *12 servings*

Fruit Filling
¾ cup sugar
2 tablespoons cornstarch
½ teaspoon ground cinnamon
10 medium nectarines (about 3½ pounds), unpeeled and cut into ¾-inch wedges
3 cups blackberries

Biscuits
1¾ cups all-purpose flour
1 tablespoon baking powder
¼ cup sugar
½ cup cold butter or margarine (1 stick), cut up
⅔ cup whole milk
¼ cup seedless red raspberry jam

1. Prepare Fruit Filling: Preheat oven to 425°F. In large bowl, combine sugar, cornstarch, and cinnamon. Add nectarines and blackberries; toss to coat. Place fruit in 13" by 9" glass or ceramic baking dish. Bake 15 minutes.

2. Meanwhile, prepare Biscuits: In large bowl, mix flour, baking powder, and 3 tablespoons sugar. With pastry blender or 2 knives used scissor-fashion, cut in 7 tablespoons butter until mixture resembles coarse crumbs. Add milk and stir with fork until mixture forms a dough that leaves side of bowl. Transfer dough onto a lightly floured surface and knead lightly 4 times to mix thoroughly.
3. Generously sprinkle 13-inch-long sheet of waxed paper with flour. With floured rolling pin, roll dough on waxed paper to 12" by 8" rectangle. Spread jam on dough to ½ inch from edges. Using waxed paper to help lift, roll dough, jelly-roll fashion, from a long side; discard waxed paper. With serrated knife, cut dough crosswise into 12 slices, wiping knife clean after each slice.
4. Arrange biscuits evenly over fruit in baking dish, cut side down. Melt remaining 1 tablespoon butter and brush over biscuits; sprinkle with remaining 1 tablespoon sugar. Bake 30 minutes or until biscuits are brown and fruit is hot and bubbly in center. Cool cobbler on wire rack 30 minutes to serve warm or cool completely to serve later.

■ Each serving: About 300 calories, 4 g protein, 53 g carbohydrate, 9 g total fat (5 g saturated), 4 g fiber, 24 mg cholesterol, 190 mg sodium.

Cherry Clafouti

Scatter handfuls of sweet cherries into a baking dish and pour on the traditional custardy batter that makes this country-French dessert. It's very easy but very impressive come dessert time. You can substitute kirsch, a cherry-flavor liqueur, for the amaretto.

PREP *20 minutes plus cooling*
BAKE *about 30 minutes*
MAKES *8 servings*

1 pint half-and-half or light cream
⅓ cup granulated sugar
2 tablespoons amaretto (almond-flavor liqueur)
⅛ teaspoon salt
4 large eggs
⅔ cup all-purpose flour
½ pound dark sweet cherries (stems removed), pitted
½ pound light sweet cherries, such as Rainier (stems removed), pitted
2 tablespoons sliced natural almonds confectioners' sugar

1. Preheat oven to 400°F. In medium bowl, with wire whisk, beat half-and-half, granulated sugar, liqueur, salt, and eggs until well blended. Gradually whisk in flour until smooth.
2. Place cherries in 10-inch round glass or ceramic baking dish (at least 1½ inches deep) or shallow 2-quart casserole. Pour batter over cherries. Sprinkle with almonds.
3. Bake 30 to 35 minutes or until custard is puffed and browned at edges. Cool clafouti on wire rack at least 15 minutes. Serve warm, sprinkled with confectioners' sugar.

■ Each serving: About 245 calories, 7 g protein, 30 g carbohydrate, 11 g total fat (5 g saturated), 2 g fiber, 128 mg cholesterol, 95 mg sodium.

Jeweled Fruit Galettes

pictured on page 114

Use a mix of whatever fruit you love—peaches, nectarines, plums, apricots, berries, or cherries—for these free-form individual tarts.

PREP *1 hour plus chilling and cooling*
BAKE *about 25 minutes*
MAKES *8 servings*

Crust

1¾ cups all-purpose flour
2 tablespoons sugar
¼ teaspoon baking powder
½ cup cold butter or margarine (1 stick), cut up
⅓ cup sour cream
1 large egg yolk

Fruit Topping

2 tablespoons all-purpose flour
½ teaspoon grated fresh lemon peel
pinch grated nutmeg
½ cup sugar
1½ pounds mixed fruit, such as nectarines, plums, peaches, apricots (thinly sliced), raspberries, blackberries, blueberries, grapes, or cherries (stems removed, pitted, and each cut in half)
2 tablespoons butter or margarine, cut into small pieces

1. Prepare Crust: In large bowl, mix flour, sugar, and baking powder. With pastry blender or 2 knives used scissor-fashion, cut in butter until mixture resembles coarse crumbs. In small bowl, with fork, beat sour cream, egg yolk, and *2 tablespoons water* until blended. Drizzle sour-cream mixture over flour mixture and stir with fork until dough begins to hold together. Gather dough into ball; divide in half and shape each half into a rectangle. Wrap each rectangle separately in plastic wrap and refrigerate 30 minutes or freeze 15 minutes until firm enough to roll.

2. On floured surface, with floured rolling pin, roll 1 rectangle into a 19" by 6½" strip. Using bowl or plate as a guide, cut out three 6-inch rounds, reserving trimmings. With wide spatula, transfer rounds to large cookie sheet, leaving room for a fourth round; refrigerate. Repeat with remaining dough and another cookie sheet. Gather trimmings; wrap and freeze 10 minutes. Reroll trimmings into a 12" by 6½" strip; cut out 2 more rounds; place one strip on each cookie sheet and refrigerate. (Discard remaining trimmings.)

3. Prepare Fruit Topping: Preheat oven to 400°F. In small bowl, mix flour, lemon peel, nutmeg, and ¼ cup sugar. Sprinkle about 2 teaspoons of the mixture on each dough round to ¾ inch from edges. Arrange fruit over sugar mixture. Fold uncovered dough edges up onto fruit, pleating edges and pressing them together to keep fruit in place. Sprinkle remaining ¼ cup sugar over fruit and dot with butter.

4. Place cookie sheets on 2 oven racks and bake 25 to 30 minutes or until crust is well browned and fruit is tender, rotating cookie sheets between upper and lower racks halfway through baking. With wide spatula, transfer galettes to wire racks to cool.

■ Each serving: About 365 calories, 5 g protein, 48 g carbohydrate, 18 g total fat (11 g saturated), 2 g fiber, 71 mg cholesterol, 175 mg sodium.

Summer Salsa with Sweet Tortilla Chips

This fruity salsa is best made just before serving, but the homemade chips can be baked up to one week ahead of time.

PREP *25 minutes plus cooling*
BAKE *about 10 minutes*
MAKES *8 servings*

Sweet Tortilla Chips

4 (about 8-inch) flour tortillas
1 tablespoon butter or margarine, melted
1 tablespoon sugar
pinch ground cinnamon

Summer Salsa

1 lime
1 tablespoon sugar
1 large ripe peach, unpeeled and chopped
1 large ripe red or purple plum, unpeeled and chopped
1 large ripe apricot, unpeeled and chopped
½ cup dark sweet cherries (stems removed), pitted and chopped
½ cup seedless green grapes, chopped

1. Prepare Sweet Tortilla Chips: Preheat oven to 375°F. Brush tortillas with butter. In cup, combine sugar and cinnamon. Sprinkle 1 side of each tortilla with cinnamon-sugar. Stack tortillas and cut into 6 wedges, making 24 wedges in total. Arrange tortilla wedges, sugar side up, in single layer on 2 large cookie sheets. Place cookie sheets on 2 oven racks and bake chips 10 to 12 minutes or until golden, rotating cookie sheets between upper and lower racks halfway through baking. Cool chips on cookie sheets on wire racks. Store chips in tightly covered container up to 1 week.

2. Just before serving, prepare Summer Salsa: From lime, grate ¼ teaspoon peel and squeeze 1 tablespoon juice. In medium bowl, stir lime peel, lime juice, sugar, and chopped fruit until combined. Makes about 3½ cups.

3. To serve, spoon salsa into serving bowl. Use chips to scoop up salsa.

■ Each serving: About 155 calories, 3 g protein, 28 g carbohydrate, 4 g total fat (2 g saturated), 2 g fiber, 4 mg cholesterol, 150 mg sodium.

To amuse your family or friends, or add interest to a fruit salad, try one of these recently introduced varieties. If you can't find them in your local market, check out Frieda's (www.friedas.com) and Melissa's (www.melissas.com) for stores near you or to order online.

GOLDEN KIWIFRUIT

This New Zealand sweetie is as big as the regular furry, green kiwi, but it has smooth brown skin and bright yellow flesh. Its tiny seeds are edible. Like the green kiwi, the golden variety has a flavor that suggests banana, strawberry, and papaya, but it is sweeter. Available mid-June through October.

• Select firm fruit and store at room temperature up to 7 days until slightly soft, or refrigerate up to 3 weeks, then ripen.

• Cut in half and scoop out fruit with a spoon, or eat out of hand, skin and all. Or use for our Jeweled Fruit Galettes (facing page).

GOLDEN SUNRISE PAPAYA

Available year-round, this South American import looks like a yellow pear when ripe.

• Choose fruit with firm, smooth, bright yellow skin. Papayas will ripen in 3 to 5 days at room temperature. Once ripe, eat immediately, or you can refrigerate for up to 1 week. Do not store unripe papayas below 45°F.

• Peel fruit, then remove small black inedible seeds from center. Enjoy as is, slice for salads, or dice for salsas.

MAMEY SAPOTE

Shaped like a football, this tropical wonder is uncommonly large (1 to 3 pounds) and has a rough brown skin. Its salmon-colored flesh is sweet and creamy, hinting of sweet potato. Inside, you'll find a giant pit. Available July through December.

• Select fruit that is firm or just slightly soft. Whole mamey sapotes should have a nick near the stem that exposes the interior. If you see green, the fruit is not yet ripe.

• To serve, cut in half and remove the pit. Enjoy the fruit right from the shell, cut into chunks for fruit salads, or whirl with yogurt or low-fat milk for a smoothie.

MONSTERA

Sometimes called Mexican breadfruit or ceriman, this unusual fruit from Florida looks like a cross between a long pinecone (9 to 12 inches) and a green banana with lizardlike scales. It weighs about 1 pound. The flesh is creamy and custardlike with tones of banana, pineapple, and mango. Available during summer months.

• The monstera ripens unevenly, usually starting from one end. As the scales pop off or loosen, pluck out the ripened fruit. Once the pulp is detached, a black- and gray-streaked central core will be visible. Wrap monstera in plastic wrap to encourage ripening, which it will continue to do even after cut. Keep at room temperature; don't refrigerate.

• Enjoy this fruit by the forkful.

PLUOT

A hybrid of plum and apricot, the pluot tastes like a very sweet plum. The skin ranges from light reddish-yellow to bright yellow. Look for varieties with descriptive names such as Dinosaur Egg (speckled) or Dapple Dandy (splashed with color). Available late May through September.

• Buy pluots when firm and allow to ripen at room temperature for 2 or 3 days. Do not refrigerate until fully ripe. Once soft, chill to keep longer.

• Eat out of hand, like a plum, cut into wedges for compotes, or halve and grill to serve with meat or poultry. Try a pluot instead of a plum for our Summer Salsa with Sweet Tortilla Chips (facing page).

SOUTH AFRICAN BABY PINEAPPLE

Sweeter than the Hawaiian Baby Pineapple, this tiny treat is grown in northern South Africa, where the climate is warm and humid year-round. Not including its leafy top, the Baby Pineapple is 5 inches high, with juicy yellow fruit and an edible crunchy core.

• Choose fruit that is golden and very fragrant. To prevent soft spots caused by temperature changes, keep the pineapple refrigerated if purchased chilled; leave on the counter if bought at room temperature.

• Serve it as you would regular pineapple. Cube or dice for fruit salads, or sprinkle slices with brown sugar and broil for a retro dessert. Use the shell as a fruit bowl. Or, cut the pineapple into wedges to grill. (See our Jerk Pork Chops with Grilled Pineapple, page 110)

SWEET YOUNG COCONUT

These coconuts are harvested early, then the thin, outer green shell is cut away, leaving a soft white husk that's trimmed into a point. Also known as a water coconut because of the amount of liquid swishing around inside, the young fruit has slightly sweet, mild white flesh that's soft enough to eat with a spoon. Available from Thailand year-round.

• Store up to 2 weeks in the refrigerator.

• Use a sharp knife to cut off the diamond-shaped point, then poke a hole in the exposed shell with a screwdriver and pry off the crown. Drain and reserve the water, or enjoy as a refreshing beverage. Scoop out the flesh with a spoon. For coconut milk, mix the flesh and coconut water in a blender and add to Thai-style soups.

Plum-Hazelnut Tart

Toasting hazelnuts brings out their rich flavor. (Toast in a shallow baking pan at 350°F. for 10 minutes, stirring occasionally.) While the nuts are warm, rub them with a clean kitchen towel to remove as much skin as possible, then cool before making the filling.

PREP *1 hour plus cooling*
BAKE *about 1 hour 40 minutes*
MAKES *12 servings*

Pastry
- 10 tablespoons butter or margarine (1¼ sticks), softened
- ¼ cup sugar
- 1 large egg yolk
- 1 teaspoon vanilla extract
- 1½ cups all-purpose flour

Hazelnut Filling
- 1 cup hazelnuts, toasted
- ¾ cup sugar
- 4 tablespoons butter or margarine, softened
- ¼ cup all-purpose flour
- 1 teaspoon vanilla extract
- ¼ teaspoon salt
- 1 large egg white
- 1 large egg

- 6 large firm, ripe plums (about 2 pounds), unpeeled and each cut into 12 wedges
- ¼ cup plum or currant jelly, melted and cooled

1. Prepare Pastry: Preheat oven to 375°F. In large bowl, with mixer at medium speed, beat butter and sugar until creamy, about 2 minutes. Reduce speed to low; beat in egg yolk and vanilla until blended. Gradually beat in flour; continue beating just until a crumbly dough forms.
2. Pat dough into 11-inch tart pan with removable bottom. For ease of handling, place sheet of plastic wrap over dough and smooth dough evenly over bottom and up side of pan. Refrigerate tart shell 15 minutes.
3. Remove plastic wrap. Line tart shell with foil and fill with pie weights, dried beans, or uncooked rice. Bake tart shell 20 minutes; remove foil with weights and bake 8 to 10 minutes longer or until golden brown. Cool tart shell in pan on wire rack.
4. Meanwhile, prepare Hazelnut Filling: In food processor with knife blade attached, pulse nuts and sugar until nuts are very finely ground. Add butter, flour, vanilla, salt, egg white, and whole egg. Process until blended.
5. Spoon filling into cooled tart shell and spread evenly. Arrange plums in concentric circles over filling, overlapping slightly. Bake tart about 1 hour and 10 minutes or until filling is browned and set. Cool on wire rack.
6. To serve, in small saucepan, heat jelly over low heat, stirring until melted; cool slightly. Brush jelly over plums.

■ Each serving: About 395 calories, 5 g protein, 46 g carbohydrate, 23 g total fat (10 g saturated), 3 g fiber, 74 mg cholesterol, 205 mg sodium.

plum crazy: our hit parade

Plums are ripe and ready in July, with the harvest of varieties such as the red-skinned, golden-fleshed globes called Santa Rosa, Laroda, Angeleno, and Red Beaut. These have small pits and slightly tart flesh. You can also find gorgeous black or reddish-black plums with sweeter, sunny-yellow flesh, such as the Black Beaut, Blackamber, and Queen Rosa.

Try the Kelsey or Wickson; their green skins turn gold when the fruit is ready to eat. Prune plums, or purple plums (better known as Italian, President, and Empress), are the sweetest and smallest variety and are available from the end of July through mid-September. They're just the right size for kids.

No matter which kind you buy, the best sign of a good plum is uniform color. If it's red, most of the plum should be red; if it's black, the surface should be almost entirely black. If you're buying plums to eat right away, look for plump fruit that yields to gentle pressure. But firm plums will ripen to juicy perfection at home: Simply place the fruit inside a paper bag (not plastic), close the top loosely, and keep at room temperature until the plums are slightly soft at the stem and tips. Don't overripen: Shriveled skin, mushy spots, or breaks in the skin are signs of plums past their prime.

Plums are great for busy cooks and bakers because they don't have to be peeled. (See the Plum Compote with Ginger Syrup, page 127, and Plum-Hazelnut Tart, this page.)

Quick Blackberry Sorbet

pictured on page 114

It takes just three ingredients (plus water) to make this cool dessert. Be sure to taste the berries first: If they are too tart, use a little more sugar.

PREP **15 minutes plus freezing**
COOK **5 minutes**
MAKES **about 4 cups or 8 servings**

- 6 cups blackberries
- ¾ cup sugar
- 1 tablespoon fresh lemon juice
  fresh mint leaves and blackberries for garnish

1. In food processor with knife blade attached, process blackberries until pureed. Pour puree into medium-mesh sieve set over medium bowl. With spoon, press puree through sieve into bowl; discard seeds.

2. In 2-quart saucepan, heat sugar and *¾ cup water* to boiling over medium-high heat. Reduce heat to low; simmer, uncovered, 5 minutes, stirring until sugar dissolves. Remove saucepan from heat; stir puree and lemon juice into hot sugar syrup until blended. Pour blackberry mixture into 9" by 9" metal baking pan; cover with foil or plastic wrap. Freeze until frozen solid, at least 5 hours or overnight.

3. With knife, cut blackberry mixture into 1-inch chunks. In food processor with knife blade attached, blend blackberry mixture, half at a time, until smooth but still frozen, stopping processor frequently to scrape down side. Serve immediately or spoon into freezer-safe container; freeze up to 1 month.

4. To serve, if too firm to scoop, let sorbet stand at room temperature 10 to 15 minutes to soften slightly for easier scooping. Garnish each serving with mint leaves and blackberries.

■ Each serving: About 125 calories, 1 g protein, 32 g carbohydrate, 0 g total fat, 6 g fiber, 0 mg cholesterol, 0 mg sodium.

Nectarine Upside-down Cake

It's the beloved upside-down cake—baked in a skillet with brown sugar and butter and served warm or cold—made with fresh summer fruit.

PREP **35 minutes plus cooling**
BAKE **about 50 minutes**
MAKES **12 servings**

- ¾ cup packed dark brown sugar
- ¾ cup butter or margarine (1½ sticks), softened
- 3 ripe medium nectarines (about 1 pound), unpeeled and cut into ½-inch wedges
- 1⅓ cups all-purpose flour
- ¼ cup cornmeal
- 2 teaspoons baking powder
- ½ teaspoon salt
- ¾ cup granulated sugar
- 2 large eggs
- 1 teaspoon vanilla extract
- 1 teaspoon grated fresh lemon peel
- ½ cup milk
- 1 cup blueberries

1. Preheat oven to 350°F. In 10-inch cast-iron or other heavy skillet with oven-safe handle (or handle wrapped in double thickness of foil), melt brown sugar with 4 tablespoons butter over low heat, stirring until sugar melts, about 2 minutes. Remove skillet from heat. Arrange nectarines in concentric circles in skillet.

2. On waxed paper, combine flour, cornmeal, baking powder, and salt.

3. In large bowl, with mixer at medium speed, beat granulated sugar and remaining ½ cup butter (1 stick) until creamy. Beat in eggs, 1 at a time, until blended. Beat in vanilla and lemon peel.

4. Reduce speed to low. Alternately add flour mixture and milk, beginning and ending with flour mixture; beat just until batter is smooth, occasionally scraping bowl with rubber spatula. Fold in blueberries.

5. Spoon batter over nectarines and spread evenly. Bake about 50 minutes or until toothpick inserted in center of cake comes out clean. Cool cake in pan on wire rack 10 minutes. Invert cake onto plate. Cool cake 30 minutes to serve warm, or cool completely to serve later.

■ Each serving: About 310 calories, 4 g protein, 45 g carbohydrate, 14 g total fat (8 g saturated), 2 g fiber, 70 mg cholesterol, 310 mg sodium.

Plum Compote with Ginger Syrup

pictured on page 114

Spoon this over vanilla ice cream for a special ending to a weeknight meal.

PREP **15 minutes plus chilling**
COOK **15 minutes**
MAKES **about 5 cups or 6 servings**

- ½ cup white zinfandel or rosé wine
- ½ cup sugar
- 3 strips orange peel (3" by ¾" each)
- 3 slices unpeeled fresh ginger (¼-inch-thick each)
- 4 whole black peppercorns
- 3 ripe medium plums (about 12 ounces), unpeeled and each cut into 8 wedges
- 3 ripe medium nectarines (about 1 pound), unpeeled and each cut into 8 wedges

1. In 3-quart saucepan, combine wine, sugar, orange peel, ginger, peppercorns, and *½ cup water*; heat to boiling over high heat. Reduce heat to low and simmer, uncovered, 10 minutes.

2. Add plums to syrup and simmer 5 minutes. Transfer fruit mixture to medium bowl; stir in nectarines. Cover and refrigerate at least 4 hours or overnight, stirring occasionally. Discard ginger before serving.

■ Each serving: About 120 calories, 1 g protein, 29 g carbohydrate, 1 g total fat (0 g saturated), 2 g fiber, 0 mg cholesterol, 2 mg sodium.

Raspberry-Peach Tiramisu

pictured on page 115

This delectable do-ahead treat is great when you need to feed a crowd; it's made with classic Peach Melba flavors (peaches and raspberries) and layered like traditional tiramisu.

PREP *1 hour plus chilling*
MAKES *16 servings*

- 3 cups red and/or golden raspberries
- ½ cup granulated sugar
- 1½ cups heavy or whipping cream
- 1 container (15 ounces) part-skim ricotta cheese
- 1 package (3 ounces) cream cheese, softened
- ½ cup confectioners' sugar
- 1 vanilla bean, split lengthwise
- 6 ripe medium peaches (about 2 pounds), peeled and cut into ¼-inch dice
- 1 tablespoon fresh lemon juice
- 2 tablespoons raspberry-flavor liqueur
- 2 packages (3 to 4½ ounces each) sponge-type ladyfingers

1. In food processor with knife blade attached, blend 2 cups raspberries with 3 tablespoons granulated sugar until pureed. Pour raspberry puree into medium-mesh sieve set over medium bowl. With spoon, press raspberry puree through sieve into bowl; discard seeds.

2. In clean food processor with knife blade attached, process 1¼ cups cream until soft peaks form. Transfer to large bowl. In same processor, combine ricotta, cream cheese, and confectioners' sugar. With tip of paring knife, scrape seeds from vanilla bean into food processor. Reserve vanilla-bean pod for another use. Blend cheese mixture until smooth; add remaining ¼ cup cream and blend until combined. Fold cheese mixture into cream in bowl.

3. In medium bowl, stir peaches, lemon juice, and ¼ cup granulated sugar until combined.

4. In cup, stir liqueur, remaining 1 tablespoon granulated sugar, and *1 tablespoon water* until mixed (sugar may not dissolve completely). Separate ladyfingers and brush flat sides with liqueur mixture.

5. In bottom of 4-quart trifle or straight-sided glass bowl, arrange one-third of ladyfingers. Spoon half of raspberry sauce over ladyfingers. Top with one-third of cheese mixture (about 1½ cups), spreading to cover. Spoon on half of peach mixture (about 2 cups). Repeat layering once. Top with remaining ladyfingers, then remaining cheese mixture. Cover and refrigerate overnight. Before serving, sprinkle with remaining raspberries.

■ Each serving: About 245 calories, 6 g protein, 27 g carbohydrate, 13 g total fat (8 g saturated), 3 g fiber, 84 mg cholesterol, 75 mg sodium.

size matters: a fruit lover's guide

A recipe calls for three cups of berries or one pound of plums. How much should you buy?

Fruit	Amount	Equivalent
Strawberries	1 pint	3¼ cups whole; 2¼ cups sliced
Raspberries & Blackberries	½ pint	1 cup
Blueberries	1 pint	2½ cups
Peaches & Nectarines	1 pound (3 medium)	2¼ cups peeled and sliced 2 cups peeled and diced
Plums	1 pound (4 to 5 medium)	3 cups sliced or diced
Cherries, Sweet	1 pound	3 cups; 2 cups pitted
Apricots	1 pound (6 medium)	1 cup sliced
Green Grapes	1 pound	3 cups

August

fast, fresh pasta dinners

Pull together a delicious topping—using herbs, veggies, seafood, and more—in the time it takes to cook the spaghetti.

Sesame Noodles
pictured on page 155

A peanut butter and sesame dressing spiked with orange juice makes this Chinese restaurant-style pasta a favorite with kids as well as adults.

PREP *15 minutes*
COOK *about 15 minutes*
MAKES *6 main-dish servings*

        salt
    1   package (16 ounces) spaghetti
    1   cup fresh orange juice
    ¼   cup seasoned rice vinegar
    ¼   cup soy sauce
    ¼   cup creamy peanut butter
    1   tablespoon Asian sesame oil
    1   tablespoon grated, peeled fresh
        ginger
    2   teaspoons sugar
    ¼   teaspoon crushed red pepper
    1   bag (10 ounces) shredded carrots
        (about 3½ cups)
    3   Kirby cucumbers (about 4 ounces
        each), unpeeled and cut into
        matchstick-thin strips
    2   green onions, thinly sliced
    2   tablespoons sesame seeds, toasted
        (optional)
        green onions for garnish

1. Heat large saucepot of *salted water* to boiling over high heat. Add pasta and cook as label directs.
2. Meanwhile, in medium bowl, with wire whisk or fork, mix orange juice, vinegar, soy sauce, peanut butter, oil, ginger, sugar, and crushed red pepper until blended; set sauce aside.
3. Place carrots in colander; drain pasta over carrots. In large serving bowl, toss pasta mixture, cucumbers, and sliced green onions with sauce in bowl. If you like, sprinkle pasta with sesame seeds. Garnish with green onions.

■ Each serving: About 445 calories, 15 g protein, 76 g carbohydrate, 9 g total fat (2 g saturated), 5 g fiber, 0 mg cholesterol, 1,135 mg sodium.

Rotelle with Ratatouille
pictured on page 154

Roasting the eggplant, pepper, and onion for this dish may take a little longer than top-of-the-range cooking, but the resulting rich flavor is worth it.

PREP *20 minutes*
ROAST *about 35 minutes*
MAKES *4 main-dish servings*

    1   medium eggplant (about 1½
        pounds), cut into 1-inch cubes
    1   medium red pepper, cut into 1-inch
        pieces
    1   large red onion, cut into 1-inch
        chunks
    2   garlic cloves, crushed with garlic
        press
    3   tablespoons olive oil
    ½   teaspoon ground black pepper
        salt
    1   pint red and/or yellow cherry
        tomatoes, each cut in half
    1   cup loosely packed fresh basil
        leaves, coarsely chopped
    1   tablespoon red wine vinegar
    1   package (16 ounces) rotelle or
        fusilli pasta
        fresh basil leaves for garnish

1. Preheat oven to 450°F. In large roasting pan (17" by 11½") or 15½" by 10½" jelly-roll pan, toss eggplant, red pepper, onion, garlic, oil, black pepper, and 1½ teaspoons salt until vegetables are well coated.
2. Roast vegetables 35 to 40 minutes or until tender and lightly browned, stirring occasionally.
3. In large bowl, toss tomatoes with chopped basil and vinegar; set aside to allow flavors to develop.
4. Meanwhile, heat large saucepot of *salted water* to boiling over high heat. Add pasta and cook as label directs.
5. When pasta has cooked to desired doneness, remove *¼ cup pasta cooking water* and reserve. Drain pasta. Add pasta, roasted vegetables, and reserved cooking water to tomatoes in bowl; toss well to distribute vegetables. Garnish each serving with basil leaves.

■ Each serving: About 595 calories, 18 g protein, 104 g carbohydrate, 13 g total fat (2 g saturated), 9 g fiber, 0 mg cholesterol, 1,040 mg sodium.

Pasta with Farm Stand Veggies

Gather the season's star veggies and combine with campanelle, a ruffled pasta that resembles a flower.

PREP *25 minutes*
COOK *about 15 minutes*
MAKES *4 main-dish servings*

  salt
1 package (16 ounces) campanelle or corkscrew pasta
2 tablespoons olive oil
2 garlic cloves, crushed with garlic press
1 teaspoon ground cumin
  pinch ground cinnamon
3 cups fresh corn kernels (from 5 to 6 ears)
2 small zucchini (about 8 ounces each), each cut lengthwise into quarters, then crosswise into ¼-inch-thick pieces
½ teaspoon ground black pepper
1 pint cherry tomatoes, each cut in half

1. Heat large saucepot of *salted water* to boiling over high heat. Add pasta and cook as label directs.
2. Meanwhile, in nonstick 12-inch skillet, heat oil over medium-high heat until hot. Add garlic, cumin, and cinnamon, and cook 30 seconds or until fragrant, stirring. Add corn and cook 4 minutes, stirring occasionally. Add zucchini, pepper, and 1½ teaspoons salt, and cook 6 minutes, stirring. Add tomatoes and cook about 2 minutes longer or until tomatoes are heated through and zucchini is tender.
3. When pasta has cooked to desired doneness, reserve *¼ cup pasta cooking water*. Drain pasta. In large serving bowl, toss pasta, corn mixture, and reserved cooking water until combined.

■ Each serving: About 620 calories, 20 g protein, 115 g carbohydrate, 11 g total fat (2 g saturated), 8 g fiber, 0 mg cholesterol, 1,055 mg sodium.

pound for pound: 12 secrets to perfect pasta

Whether you're creating one of our dinners from scratch or opening a jar of sauce, cooking the pasta correctly will make your dish taste better.

1. Make the right amount A pound of dry pasta usually serves 4; toss it with a lot of other ingredients (such as our Greek Pasta Bowl with Shrimp, page 135), and it will easily feed 6. For a first course or side dish, figure that 4 main-dish servings will equal 8 accompaniments.

2. Use enough water Fill a large (6- to 8-quart) saucepot with 4 to 6 quarts cold water for each pound of pasta. Too little water or a too small pot causes pasta to become gluey and stick together.

3. Wait for the boiling point You should see rolling bubbles; to get there quicker, cover and use high heat.

4. Salt the water Adding salt really improves the flavor; without it, the pasta tastes flat and bland. Most of the sodium is not absorbed, and we find that seasoning the pasta as it cooks means you won't have to over-salt it at the table.

5. Add and stir Stir the pasta into the rapidly boiling water to prevent it from sticking together or to the bottom of the pot. Don't break up long strands; as they begin to soften, gently push them down until they are completely submerged.

6. Keep it rolling Return water to a boil over high heat while stirring frequently to prevent clumping. Adjust the heat so the water continues to boil but won't boil over. Cook, uncovered, stirring every few minutes for uniform results.

7. Skip the oil You don't need it to keep pieces separate; stirring does that. And oil makes it harder for many sauces to cling.

8. Don't over- or undercook The cooking time depends on the size, shape, and brand. Use package directions as a guideline only—test a single piece. We like pasta best *al dente,* the Italian phrase for "to the tooth"— slightly resistant to the bite (but not soft), yet cooked through.

9. Save some water Before draining, reserve ½ to 1 cup cooking water, in case you need to extend or thin your sauce at the last minute, or in place of some of the oil in sautéed vegetables.

10. Drain quickly Pasta continues to cook in the hot water, so as soon as it's ready, pour it into a large colander and shake once to remove excess water.

11. Don't rinse The surface starch helps sauce adhere. The exception: If you want pasta to cool down quickly for summer salads or dishes served at room temperature, rinse it quickly under cold water.

12. Toss and serve pronto Add sauce or other ingredients as soon as possible to prevent sticking and for best flavor. Then serve immediately. The hotter the pasta, the more the flavor of the sauce will penetrate it. And if you wait too long before serving cream sauces, the pasta can soak up the sauce.

Bow Ties with Salmon & Peas

Sauté fresh salmon and toss with dill sauce for a spectacular main dish.

PREP **15 minutes**
COOK **about 15 minutes**
MAKES **6 main-dish servings**

    salt
  1 package (16 ounces) bow-tie or
      corkscrew pasta
  2 lemons
  2 tablespoons margarine or butter
  2 large shallots, thinly sliced (½ cup)
  1 pound skinless salmon fillet, cut
      into 1-inch chunks
  ¼ teaspoon ground black pepper
  1 package (10 ounces) frozen peas
  ½ cup loosely packed fresh dill,
      chopped
      fresh dill sprigs for garnish

1. Heat large saucepot of *salted water* to boiling over high heat. Add pasta and cook as label directs.

2. Meanwhile, from lemons, grate 2 teaspoons peel and squeeze 3 tablespoons juice; set aside.

3. In nonstick 12-inch skillet, melt margarine over medium heat. Add shallots and cook 2 minutes or until tender-crisp, stirring occasionally. Increase heat to medium-high. Add salmon, pepper, lemon peel, and 1 teaspoon salt, and cook 5 minutes or until salmon turns opaque throughout, gently stirring occasionally.

4. When pasta has cooked to desired doneness, remove *⅓ cup pasta cooking water*; add to salmon mixture, stirring gently to combine. Place frozen peas in colander, and drain pasta over peas. Return pasta and peas to saucepot. Add salmon mixture, chopped dill, and lemon juice; toss gently to combine. Garnish each serving with dill sprigs.

■ Each serving: About 470 calories, 28 g protein, 66 g carbohydrate, 10 g total fat (2 g saturated), 4 g fiber, 40 mg cholesterol, 680 mg sodium.

Orecchiette with Peppers

Tapenade—black-olive paste made with capers and anchovies—adds the perfect piquant flavoring to this colorful dish.

PREP **15 minutes**
COOK **about 15 minutes**
MAKES **4 main-dish servings**

    salt
  1 package (16 ounces) orecchiette
      or bow-tie pasta
  2 tablespoons olive oil
  1 large red pepper, cut into
      2" by ¼" strips
  1 large orange pepper, cut into
      2" by ¼" strips
  1 small red onion, thinly sliced
  2 garlic cloves, crushed with
      garlic press
  ½ teaspoon ground black
      pepper
  2 tablespoons store-bought
      tapenade
  1 cup loosely packed fresh basil
      leaves, cut into thin strips

1. Heat large saucepot of *salted water* to boiling over high heat. Add pasta and cook as label directs.

2. Meanwhile, in nonstick 12-inch skillet, heat oil over medium heat until hot. Add red and orange peppers and onion, and cook about 10 minutes or until tender-crisp and lightly browned, stirring occasionally. Add garlic, black pepper, and 1 teaspoon salt; cook 1 minute, stirring.

3. In large serving bowl, mix tapenade with *3 tablespoons pasta cooking water*; set aside.

4. Drain pasta. Add pasta and pepper mixture to tapenade in bowl and toss well. Add basil and toss gently to combine.

■ Each serving: About 520 calories, 16 g protein, 93 g carbohydrate, 9 g total fat (1 g saturated), 5 g fiber, 0 mg cholesterol, 830 mg sodium.

Pasta Niçoise

Combine elements of salade niçoise (potatoes, green beans, tuna, and garlic) with cavatappi, a short, spiral pasta. Serve hot or at room temperature.

PREP *15 minutes*
COOK *about 15 minutes*
MAKES *6 main-dish servings*

   salt
1 package (16 ounces) cavatappi or radiatore pasta
1 pound red potatoes, cut into ¾-inch chunks
1 pound green beans, trimmed and each cut crosswise in half
2 lemons
¾ cup chicken broth
¼ cup olive oil
2 teaspoons Dijon mustard
½ teaspoon ground black pepper
2 anchovies, minced
1 garlic clove, crushed with garlic press
1 can (12 ounces) solid white tuna packed in water, drained
1 cup loosely packed fresh parsley leaves, chopped
⅔ cup grated Parmesan cheese

1. Heat large saucepot of *salted water* to boiling over high heat. Add pasta and potatoes; heat to boiling. Cook 2 minutes; add green beans and cook 6 minutes longer or until pasta and vegetables are tender. Drain well.
2. Meanwhile, from lemons, grate 1 teaspoon peel and squeeze 3 tablespoons juice.
3. In small bowl, with wire whisk or fork, mix lemon peel, lemon juice, broth, oil, mustard, pepper, anchovies, and garlic.
4. Arrange pasta, potatoes, beans, and tuna on platter. Drizzle with dressing; sprinkle with parsley and Parmesan.

■ Each serving: About 570 calories, 31 g protein, 78 g carbohydrate, 15 g total fat (4 g saturated), 6 g fiber, 31 mg cholesterol, 745 mg sodium.

Fettuccine with Fresh Herbs & Tomatoes

Toss fettuccine with basil, mint, sage, rosemary, and tomatoes, and finish off the dish with crumbled ricotta salata cheese.

PREP *15 minutes*
COOK *about 15 minutes*
MAKES *4 main-dish servings*

   salt
1 package (16 ounces) fettuccine or linguine
1 cup loosely packed fresh basil leaves, chopped
¾ cup loosely packed fresh mint leaves, chopped
2 tablespoons fresh rosemary leaves, chopped
1 tablespoon fresh sage leaves, chopped
2 large tomatoes (about 8 ounces each), chopped
2 tablespoons extra virgin olive oil
¼ teaspoon ground black pepper
½ cup crumbled ricotta salata or ¼ cup grated Parmesan cheese

1. Heat large saucepot of *salted water* to boiling over high heat. Add fettuccine and cook as label directs.
2. Meanwhile, in large serving bowl, toss herbs with tomatoes, oil, pepper, and ¾ teaspoon salt; set aside.
3. When fettuccine has cooked to desired doneness, remove *½ cup pasta cooking water* and reserve. Drain fettuccine; add with reserved cooking water to herb mixture in bowl and toss well. Sprinkle with cheese to serve.

■ Each serving: About 565 calories, 19 g protein, 93 g carbohydrate, 13 g total fat (4 g saturated), 5 g fiber, 17 mg cholesterol, 920 mg sodium.

Fusilli with No-Cook Tomato Sauce

It's our quickest trick—combine ripe tomatoes with fragrant basil and zesty olives for a satisfying sauce that goes well with any pasta.

PREP *10 minutes*
COOK *about 15 minutes*
MAKES *4 main-dish servings*

   salt
1 package (16 ounces) long fusilli pasta
2 pounds ripe tomatoes (about 6 medium), cut into ½-inch chunks
1 cup packed fresh basil leaves, coarsely chopped
½ cup pimiento-stuffed olives, chopped, or salad olives
2 tablespoons olive oil
1 tablespoon red wine vinegar
¼ teaspoon ground black pepper

1. Heat large saucepot of *salted water* to boiling over high heat. Add pasta and cook as label directs.
2. Meanwhile, in large serving bowl, combine tomatoes (with their juice), basil, olives, oil, vinegar, pepper, and 1 teaspoon salt; stir gently to mix well.
3. Drain pasta; toss with tomato sauce in bowl.

■ Each serving: About 550 calories, 17 g protein, 96 g carbohydrate, 11 g total fat (2 g saturated), 6 g fiber, 0 mg cholesterol, 1,065 mg sodium.

Q I grow lots of basil in my garden, and I'd love to preserve some. What's the best way?

a You can dry it or freeze it, but freezing retains the fresh taste better. Before you start, wash basil in cold water and dry; a salad spinner works well for this step. To freeze your basil, pull leaves from stems. Then, in a food processor, with knife blade attached, puree 2 cups packed leaves with 2 tablespoons olive oil. Line a cookie sheet with waxed paper. Drop the mixture by teaspoonfuls onto the paper; freeze 1 hour or until firm. Transfer the dollops (you should have about 16) to a self-sealing, freezer-safe plastic bag; store up to 2 months. To use in a recipe, stir in a frozen dollop when you're almost finished cooking the soup, chicken or beef stew, or spaghetti sauce.

You can also freeze leaves whole, and keep them for up to a year. First, blanch leaves for 2 seconds in boiling water, then drain and rinse immediately with cold water. Pat leaves dry and store in a large, freezer-safe container, separating each layer with plastic wrap. Use in cooking as you would fresh basil leaves, but, cup for cup, frozen leaves are more compact than fresh ones, so use a little less than the recipe calls for.

Q Sometimes when I eat ice cream I get a sharp headache. Can this really be related to ice cream?

a Yes—in fact, experts call that intense pain an ice cream headache. It peaks after 30 to 60 seconds and passes in 1 to 5 minutes. Migraine sufferers are more likely to experience these headaches. No one is sure what causes the throbbing, but some theorize that when the frozen treat hits the back of the roof of your mouth, it stimulates a nerve that can hurt with intense cold and also can cause blood vessel dilation, producing a pulsing headache. (Robert Smith, M.D., founder of the Cincinnati Headache Center at the University of Cincinnati College of Medicine and an ice cream headache victim himself, confirmed that theory by putting crushed ice in different parts of his mouth.) But you don't need to pass on our great ice cream desserts this month; try keeping the cold stuff toward the front and sides of your mouth, and eat slowly. If a headache comes on, hold a little ice to your head; experts say that, ironically, the cold stops the throbbing.

Thin Spaghetti with Pesto & Tomatoes

pictured on page 155

Michael Chiarello, chef-owner of Tra Vigne restaurant in California's Napa Valley, cooked this up while visiting our test kitchen. We love the way the sweet tomato salad tastes on the spaghetti. Although there's nothing quite like Chiarello's fresh pesto, you can substitute a four-ounce container of store-bought refrigerated pesto if you're really pressed for time.

PREP **30 minutes**
COOK **about 6 minutes**
MAKES **4 main-dish servings**

Basil Pesto
2 cups packed fresh basil leaves
2 garlic cloves, cut in half
2 tablespoons pine nuts (pignoli), toasted
1 teaspoon salt
⅛ teaspoon ground black pepper
¼ cup olive oil
½ cup grated Parmesan cheese

Cherry Tomato Salad
1½ pints red and/or yellow cherry tomatoes, each cut in half (about 3½ cups)
½ small red onion, thinly sliced (about ½ cup)
⅓ cup packed fresh basil leaves, cut into strips
1 tablespoon extra virgin olive oil
1½ teaspoons red wine vinegar
½ teaspoon salt
¼ teaspoon ground black pepper

Pasta
salt
1 package (16 ounces) thin spaghetti

basil sprigs for garnish

1. Prepare Basil Pesto: In food processor with knife blade attached, blend basil, garlic, pine nuts, salt, and pepper until pureed. With processor running, gradually pour in oil until blended. Add Parmesan, pulsing to combine. Transfer pesto to small bowl. Place plastic wrap directly on pesto surface to prevent browning; set aside.

2. Prepare Cherry Tomato Salad: In medium bowl, mix tomatoes, onion, basil strips, oil, vinegar, salt, and pepper. Set aside.

3. Heat large saucepot of *salted water* to boiling over high heat. Add spaghetti and cook as label directs.

4. When spaghetti has cooked to desired doneness, remove ¼ *cup pasta cooking water* and reserve. Drain spaghetti and return to saucepot. Add pesto and reserved cooking water; toss well to distribute vegetables.

5. To serve, spoon spaghetti mixture into 4 serving bowls; top with tomato salad. Garnish with basil sprigs.

■ Each serving: About 680 calories, 22 g protein, 95 g carbohydrate, 24 g total fat (5 g saturated), 6 g fiber, 8 mg cholesterol, 1,225 mg sodium.

Gazpacho-Style Pasta

Classic gazpacho soup ingredients get pulsed in the food processor while the small seashell pasta cooks.

PREP *15 minutes*
COOK *about 15 minutes*
MAKES *4 main-dish servings*

    salt
1 package (16 ounces) small shell or orecchiette pasta
1 English (seedless) cucumber (about 1 pound), unpeeled and cut into 2-inch chunks
½ medium red pepper, cut up
½ medium yellow pepper, cut up
½ medium red onion, cut up
1 jalapeño chile, seeded and cut up
1 garlic clove, cut up
1½ pounds tomatoes (about 5 medium), cut into ½-inch chunks
2 tablespoons olive oil
2 tablespoons sherry vinegar or red wine vinegar
1 small bunch fresh parsley, tough stems discarded
    cucumber slices and cherry tomatoes for garnish

1. Heat large saucepot of *salted water* to boiling over high heat. Add pasta and cook as label directs.
2. Meanwhile, in food processor with knife blade attached, finely chop cucumber, peppers, onion, chile, and garlic, being careful not to puree them.
3. In large serving bowl, toss vegetable mixture with tomatoes, oil, vinegar, and 1½ teaspoons salt until well mixed. Set aside 4 parsley leaves for garnish; chop remaining parsley.
4. Drain pasta; add pasta and chopped parsley to vegetable mixture in bowl; toss well to combine. Garnish each serving with cucumber slices, cherry tomatoes, and reserved parsley leaves.

■ Each serving: About 555 calories, 18 g protein, 100 g carbohydrate, 9 g total fat (1 g saturated), 7 g fiber, 0 mg cholesterol, 1,045 mg sodium.

Greek Pasta Bowl with Shrimp

Fresh oregano and feta cheese flavor this easy dish. For an even speedier prep time, substitute frozen raw shelled and deveined shrimp for the fresh ones.

PREP *15 minutes*
COOK *about 15 minutes*
MAKES *6 main-dish servings*

    salt
1 package (16 ounces) gemelli or fusilli pasta
2 tablespoons olive oil
1 pound medium shrimp, shelled and deveined
2 garlic cloves, crushed with garlic press
1 tablespoon fresh oregano leaves, minced, or ½ teaspoon dried oregano
¼ teaspoon ground black pepper
2 bunches green onions, thinly sliced
3 medium tomatoes (about 1 pound), coarsely chopped
2 packages (4 ounces each) crumbled feta cheese
    fresh oregano sprigs for garnish

1. Heat large saucepot of *salted water* to boiling over high heat. Add pasta and cook as label directs.
2. Meanwhile, in nonstick 12-inch skillet, heat oil over medium-high heat until hot. Add shrimp, garlic, minced oregano, pepper, and ½ teaspoon salt, and cook 1 minute, stirring. Add green onions and cook 2 minutes or just until shrimp turn opaque throughout. Stir in tomatoes.
3. Drain pasta; return to saucepot. Add shrimp mixture and feta; toss well to combine. Garnish each serving with oregano sprigs.

■ Each serving: About 515 calories, 29 g protein, 65 g carbohydrate, 15 g total fat (7 g saturated), 4 g fiber, 127 mg cholesterol, 815 mg sodium.

Pasta Puttanesca with Arugula

For a refreshing summer meal, mix pasta with a perky caper and shallot dressing and lots of cut-up fresh tomatoes, chopped arugula, and basil.

PREP *15 minutes*
COOK *about 15 minutes*
MAKES *4 main-dish servings*

    salt
1 package (16 ounces) gemelli or corkscrew pasta
1½ pounds tomatoes (about 5 medium), cut into ½-inch chunks
1 medium shallot, minced (about ¼ cup)
1 garlic clove, crushed with garlic press
2 tablespoons olive oil
2 tablespoons capers, drained and chopped
1 tablespoon red wine vinegar
½ teaspoon grated fresh lemon peel
¼ teaspoon crushed red pepper
2 bunches arugula (about 4 ounces each), tough stems removed, leaves coarsely chopped
1 cup packed fresh basil leaves, chopped

1. Heat large saucepot of *salted water* to boiling over high heat. Add pasta and cook as label directs.
2. Meanwhile, in large serving bowl, toss tomatoes with shallot, garlic, olive oil, capers, vinegar, grated lemon peel, and crushed red pepper until well mixed.
3. Drain pasta; toss with tomato mixture in bowl. Just before serving, gently toss pasta mixture with arugula and basil until slightly wilted.

■ Each serving: About 540 calories, 18 g protein, 97 g carbohydrate, 10 g total fat (1 g saturated), 6 g fiber, 0 mg cholesterol, 310 mg sodium.

a little frozen heaven

Turn store-bought ice cream into a slice of something special with these frozen treats.

Raspberry-Peach Dome

pictured on page 156

It looks really impressive, but all you need is store-bought pound cake, ice cream, jam, and gelato to make this dome cake, which is layered in a deep bowl, frozen overnight, and then unmolded.

PREP *30 minutes plus freezing*
MAKES *16 servings*

Cake Dome
- 1 frozen pound cake loaf (10¾ to 12 ounces), thawed
- 2 tablespoons seedless red raspberry jam

Dome Filling
- 2 pints raspberry gelato, softened
- 1 quart peach ice cream, softened

   fresh raspberries for garnish

1. Prepare Cake Dome: With serrated knife, cut top crust from pound cake. Place cake on 1 long side; cut lengthwise into 3 equal slices. With small spatula, spread 1 tablespoon jam on cut side of 1 cake slice. Top with another cake slice and spread with remaining 1 tablespoon jam. Top with remaining cake slice. With knife, trim off remaining crusts along sides of cake. Slice jam-layered cake crosswise into ⅜-inch-thick slices.

2. Line a deep 2½-quart bowl with plastic wrap, leaving about a 2-inch overhang. Arrange cake rectangles along the bottom and up the side of bowl (slices will extend slightly above rim of bowl) to make a decorative design. If necessary, cut some rectangles into triangles to fill in any open areas, gently pushing cake pieces together to get a tight fit. With a knife or kitchen shears, trim off overhanging ends of cake to create an even rim

around bowl. (If you like, save cake trimmings to use as ice cream topping another day.) Place in freezer to firm cake dome slightly, about 20 minutes.

3. Prepare Dome Filling: With back of spoon, working quickly, gently spread gelato over cake layer to an even thickness. Place bowl in freezer 20 minutes to firm gelato slightly.

4. Spoon peach ice cream into center of bowl, and spread evenly. Cover bowl with plastic wrap and freeze overnight to ensure dome is frozen throughout. If not serving same day, wrap and freeze up to 2 weeks.

5. To serve, uncover bowl and invert onto platter. Wrap towel dampened with warm water around entire bowl for about 20 seconds to slightly soften dome. Remove bowl and plastic wrap. Let stand 10 to 15 minutes to soften for easier slicing. Garnish dome with raspberries.

■ Each serving: About 265 calories, 4 g protein, 39 g carbohydrate, 11 g total fat (6 g saturated), 0 g fiber, 75 mg cholesterol, 125 mg sodium.

THE ICE CREAM CONE WAS INVENTED IN 1896 BY ITALO MARCHIONY, AN ITALIAN IMMIGRANT.

---

make your own ice cream cones

Good Housekeeping INSTITUTE REPORT

GH Institute food appliance experts found the electric **Chef'sChoice WaffleCone Express 838 ($49.95)** almost fail-safe for turning out buttery vanilla-scented cones—a task that used to require fiddling with a stovetop device. The new machine works like a waffle iron, but has flat plates that bake batter into a thin, crisp disk in about 1 minute; then you roll the warm disk into a cone, using the wooden form that comes with the unit. Recipes are included or you can buy Chef'sChoice WaffleCone Mix (three 1-pound bags for $12.95), which makes about 14 cones per bag. Available from gourmet shops, catalogs, and Web sites. For the store nearest you, call 800-342-3255 or log on to www.chefschoice.com.

Banana-Caramel Tart

pictured on page 157

Dulce de leche is a sweet Latin dessert made by slowly cooking down milk (usually sweetened, condensed) until it's thick and almost caramelized. Traditionally, it's spread on bread or crackers or used in pastries and cakes. But now you can get it in luscious ice cream, which we layered with fresh bananas over a no-bake pecan cookie crust.

PREP *30 minutes plus freezing*
MAKES *12 servings*

Shortbread Cookie Crust
- 18 pecan shortbread cookies (about 14 ounces)
- 1 cup pecans, toasted
- 2 tablespoons butter or margarine, melted

Ice Cream Filling
- 2 pints dulce de leche ice cream, softened
- 4 ripe, medium bananas

1. Prepare Shortbread Cookie Crust: In food processor with knife blade attached, pulse cookies and ½ cup pecans until very finely ground. With food processor running, drizzle in butter until blended.
2. With hand, press cookie mixture evenly onto bottom and up side of 11" by 1" round tart pan with removable bottom. Place pan in freezer 15 minutes to firm crust. Meanwhile, coarsely chop remaining ½ cup pecans; set aside.
3. Prepare Ice Cream Filling: Spread 1 pint ice cream evenly over crust. Cut 3 bananas into ¼-inch-thick slices and arrange them in 1 layer over ice cream. Cover tart with plastic wrap and return to freezer for 30 minutes.
4. Spread second pint ice cream over banana layer. Slice remaining banana. Arrange banana slices, overlapping slightly, on ice cream in a ring 2 inches from edge of tart pan. Sprinkle top of tart with chopped pecans. Cover and freeze at least 6 hours or until firm. If not serving tart same day, wrap and freeze up to 2 weeks.
5. To serve, uncover tart and let stand at room temperature 10 minutes to soften slightly for easier slicing. Remove side of pan and place tart on platter.

■ Each serving: About 490 calories, 6 g protein, 47 g carbohydrate, 31 g total fat (12 g saturated), 3 g fiber, 75 mg cholesterol, 200 mg sodium.

quick licks: ice cream sandwiches

When the kids have eaten their broccoli, serve them one of these quick treats. They're easy to make with a package of cookies, ice cream, and a few little extras. They also freeze well—just wrap individually in plastic wrap, and store in a freezer-weight bag or container.

PB&J Layer peanut butter and jelly on a big, soft oatmeal-raisin cookie. Top with vanilla ice cream and another cookie.

S'more Spread marshmallow cream on a chocolate-covered or cinnamon graham cracker. Cover with chocolate ice cream, then another cracker.

Chocolate cherry Sandwich a scoop of cherry-vanilla ice cream between 2 large, soft chocolate cookies.

Pistachio shortbread Scoop some pistachio ice cream onto a small shortbread cookie. Top with another cookie, then dip side into toasted, finely chopped pistachio nuts.

Chocolate chipper Place a scoop of chocolate or vanilla ice cream between 2 chocolate-chip cookies. Roll side in toffee bits.

Tutti-frutti Scoop rainbow sherbet onto a crisp sugar cookie. Top with a second cookie. Roll in chopped candied cherries or oranges.

Caramel crunch Press a scoop of caramel-swirl ice cream between 2 amaretti cookies.

Raspberry white-chocolate wave Spread a scoop of raspberry gelato on a white-chocolate macadamia cookie. Top with another cookie.

Buried mint Place a scoop of mint chocolate-chip ice cream on a chocolate cookie. Push a soft, chocolate-covered mint candy into the middle of the ice cream. Top with another cookie.

Neapolitan Scoop strawberry ice cream onto a soft chocolate chocolate-chip cookie. Press a soft vanilla cookie on top.

Mini confetti treat Spread your favorite ice cream between 2 lemon cookies, then roll side in multicolored decors.

Ginger gem Fill 2 large, soft ginger-molasses cookies with lemon sherbet. Sprinkle side with a little finely grated fresh lemon peel.

And for the grown-ups . . .

Tiramisu treat Brush 1 side of a crisp Italian-style ladyfinger (also called Savoiardi) with coffee-flavor liqueur, then spread with coffee ice cream. Brush side of second ladyfinger with liqueur and place, liqueur-side down, over ice cream. Sprinkle top with ground cinnamon.

Cool Lime Pie

pictured on page 156

In this frosty version of Key lime pie, we swirled vanilla ice cream into the condensed-milk mixture. You'll need lots of fresh lime juice (zap limes for about ten seconds in the microwave so they're easier to squeeze) and a store-bought graham-cracker crust.

PREP *20 minutes plus freezing*
MAKES *10 servings*

4 to 5 limes
1 can (14 ounces) fat-free sweetened condensed milk
1 pint vanilla ice cream, softened
1 ready-to-use graham-cracker piecrust (6 ounces)
½ cup heavy or whipping cream
lime-peel slivers for garnish

1. From limes, finely grate 4 teaspoons peel and squeeze ⅔ cup juice. In large bowl, with wire whisk, stir undiluted condensed milk, lime peel, and lime juice until blended.
2. Whisk ice cream into condensed-milk mixture until evenly blended (mixture will be the consistency of sour cream).
3. Pour ice cream mixture into piecrust. Freeze at least 6 hours or until firm. If not serving pie same day, wrap and freeze up to 1 week.
4. To serve, uncover pie and let stand at room temperature 10 minutes to soften slightly for easier slicing. Meanwhile, in small bowl, with mixer at medium speed, beat cream until stiff peaks form. Top each serving of pie with a dollop of whipped cream and sprinkle with lime-peel slivers.

■ Each serving: About 300 calories, 5 g protein, 42 g carbohydrate, 12 g total fat (6 g saturated), 1 g fiber, 33 mg cholesterol, 160 mg sodium.

Tropical Sorbet Loaf

A slice of this looks like a summer sunset or pretty sand art made on a seaside boardwalk. The best part is, it's really easy; just scoop and freeze.

PREP *20 minutes plus freezing*
MAKES *16 servings*

1 pint raspberry or strawberry sorbet, softened
1 pint mango or passion fruit sorbet, softened
1 pint coconut sorbet, softened
1 pint orange or peach sorbet, softened
shaved coconut, fresh raspberries, and fresh mint leaves for garnish

1. Spray 9" by 5" loaf pan with non-stick cooking spray. Line pan with plastic wrap.
2. Using 2-inch (¼ cup) ice cream scoop, arrange 8 alternating scoops of sorbet (2 scoops of each sorbet) in 1 layer in pan. Place plastic wrap on sorbet scoops and press mixture down to flatten and eliminate air pockets; remove plastic wrap. Repeat to make 2 more layers, alternating sorbets within each layer and from layer to layer, and making sure to press mixture down each time. Cover and freeze until firm, at least 6 hours.
3. To serve, uncover pan and invert onto platter. Wrap towels dampened with warm water on bottom and sides of pan for about 20 seconds to slightly soften sorbet. Remove pan and plastic wrap. Garnish loaf with coconut, raspberries, and mint.

■ Each serving: About 125 calories, 0 g protein, 26 g carbohydrate, 1 g total fat (1 g saturated), 1 g fiber, 0 mg cholesterol, 15 mg sodium.

IN THE LATE 1890s, IN RESPONSE TO RELIGIOUS CRITICISM FOR SERVING RICH ICE CREAM SODAS ON SUNDAYS, SWEET SHOPS OMITTED THE CARBONATED WATER AND INVENTED THE "SUNDAY." THE SPELLING WAS LATER CHANGED TO "SUNDAE" TO AVOID ANY REFERENCE TO THE SABBATH.

keeping ice cream fresh

For every ice cream lover who has gone to sneak a spoonful of her favorite cherry-vanilla, only to find it covered with ice crystals, the **Tupperware Freez-N-Save Container ($9.50)** may be a gift from heaven. The Institute's food appliances department stored a half-gallon container (the old-fashioned rectangular cardboard carton that doesn't close tightly) of ice cream in the Tupperware container next to an identical half gallon left in its original package. The scoop: After 2 weeks, ice cream from the Tupperware looked, smelled, and tasted better. The Freez-N-Save can also hold 2 pint tubs. Call 888-919-8099 or visit www.tupperware.com.

Frozen Mochaccino Bars

Your favorite blended coffee-drink, frozen on a chocolate-cookie base and capped with whipped cream and a dusting of cinnamon. If you're a real java lover, seek out espresso or other rich coffee-flavored ice cream.

PREP *30 minutes plus freezing*
MAKES *16 servings*

Chocolate Cookie Crust
- 1 package (9 ounces) chocolate wafer cookies
- 1 tablespoon ground cinnamon
- 4 tablespoons butter or margarine, melted

Ice Cream Filling
- 1 quart coffee ice cream, softened
- 1 quart vanilla ice cream, softened

1. Prepare Chocolate Cookie Crust: In food processor with knife blade attached, pulse cookies and cinnamon until very finely ground. With food processor running, drizzle in butter until blended. With hand, pat 1 cup cookie-crumb mixture evenly onto bottom of 9" by 9" metal pan or glass baking dish. Place pan in freezer 15 minutes to firm crust.
2. Prepare Ice Cream Filling: Spoon coffee ice cream over cookie crust. Place plastic wrap on ice cream; press down to spread evenly and to eliminate any air pockets. Remove plastic wrap. Sprinkle remaining crumb mixture over ice cream. Return pan to freezer for 15 minutes.
3. Spoon vanilla ice cream over crumb layer. Place plastic wrap on ice cream and spread evenly; remove plastic wrap. Cover pan and freeze at least 6 hours or until firm. If not serving bars same day, wrap and freeze up to 2 weeks.
4. To serve, uncover and let stand at room temperature 10 minutes to soften slightly for easier slicing. Cut into 16 squares.

■ Each serving: About 365 calories, 6 g protein, 33 g carbohydrate, 23 g total fat (14 g saturated), 1 g fiber, 128 mg cholesterol, 210 mg sodium.

PRESIDENT GEORGE WASHINGTON AND HIS WIFE, MARTHA, SPENT $200 ON ICE CREAM DURING THE SUMMER OF 1790.

ice cream testing

Häagen-Dazs and Ben & Jerry's are the ultimate splurge—in terms of dollars, calories, and fat grams. But in a blind tasting, would they scoop lighter, lower-priced rivals? We conducted a 2-part test to find out. First, GH staffers compared 3 best-selling reduced-fat varieties—Breyers All Natural Light Vanilla, Edy's Grand Light Vanilla, and Healthy Choice Low-fat Vanilla. The spoons-down favorite was Breyers Light (130 calories and 4.5 fat grams per half cup), praised for its big dairy flavor and true vanilla notes.

In the next round, we slipped that skinny winner into the big league, pitting it against Häagen-Dazs Vanilla, Ben & Jerry's World's Best Vanilla, Dreyer's Grand Vanilla, and Breyers regular Natural Vanilla. The results? Häagen-Dazs (270 calories and 18 fat grams per half cup) took top honors, for its rich flavor and creamy texture (its first ingredient is cream). But beyond that, scores were close. To our surprise, Breyers Light held its own against the richer choices, which ranged from 150 to 250 calories and 9 to 18 fat grams per serving.

THE #1 ICE CREAM LICK NATIONWIDE IS VANILLA, FOLLOWED BY NUT FLAVORS, CHOCOLATE, AND FRUITY VARIETIES.

Rocky Road Ice Cream Cake

This ooey-gooey treat is like a big sundae in a springform pan. It's made with chocolate ice cream, our secret homemade Fudge Sauce (also delicious served hot over a bowl of plain ice cream), cookies, peanuts, and baby marshmallows. If you don't have time to make the sauce, a jar from the store will do just fine.

PREP *30 minutes plus chilling and freezing*
COOK *about 8 minutes*
MAKES *14 servings*

Fudge Sauce
- 1 cup heavy or whipping cream
- ¾ cup sugar
- 4 ounces unsweetened chocolate
- 2 tablespoons light corn syrup
- 2 tablespoons butter or margarine
- 2 teaspoons vanilla extract

Rocky Road Cake
- 2 pints chocolate ice cream, softened
- 14 chocolate sandwich cookies
- 2 cups miniature marshmallows
- 1 cup salted peanuts, coarsely chopped

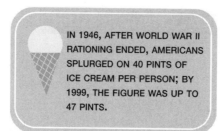

IN 1946, AFTER WORLD WAR II RATIONING ENDED, AMERICANS SPLURGED ON 40 PINTS OF ICE CREAM PER PERSON; BY 1999, THE FIGURE WAS UP TO 47 PINTS.

1. Prepare Fudge Sauce: In heavy 2-quart saucepan, heat cream, sugar, chocolate, and light corn syrup over medium heat until mixture boils, stirring occasionally. Cook 4 minutes longer or until sauce thickens slightly (mixture should be gently bubbling), stirring constantly. Remove saucepan from heat; stir in butter and vanilla until sauce is smooth and glossy. Cover surface of sauce with plastic wrap and refrigerate 2 hours or until cool. Makes about 1⅔ cups.

2. When sauce is cool, assemble Rocky Road Cake: Wrap bottom and side of 9" by 3" springform pan with foil. Spoon 1 pint chocolate ice cream into pan. Place plastic wrap on ice cream and press down to spread evenly and eliminate air pockets; remove plastic wrap. Insert cookies, standing upright, into ice cream to form a ring around side of pan, making sure to push cookie to pan bottom. Sprinkle 1 cup marshmallows and ½ cup peanuts over ice cream; press in gently with hand.

3. Spoon remaining ice cream over marshmallows and peanuts. Place plastic wrap on ice cream and spread evenly; remove plastic wrap. Spread ⅔ cup Fudge Sauce over ice cream (if sauce is too firm, microwave briefly to soften but not heat); reserve remaining sauce to serve later. Sprinkle remaining marshmallows and peanuts over sauce; press in gently with hand. Cover and freeze cake until firm, at least 6 hours.

4. To serve, uncover and remove foil from pan. Wrap towels dampened with warm water around side of pan for about 20 seconds to slightly soften ice cream. Remove side of pan and place cake on cake stand or plate. Let stand at room temperature about 10 minutes for easier slicing. Meanwhile, place remaining sauce in microwave-safe bowl; heat in microwave oven, uncovered, on High 30 to 40 seconds or until hot, stirring once. Serve hot fudge sauce to spoon over cake if you like.

■ Each serving: About 365 calories, 7 g protein, 36 g carbohydrate, 23 g total fat (11 g saturated), 2 g fiber, 77 mg cholesterol, 220 mg sodium.

■ Each tablespoon sauce: About 85 calories, 1 g protein, 8 g carbohydrate, 7 g total fat (4 g saturated), 0 g fiber, 15 mg cholesterol, 15 mg sodium.

September

SEASONAL SUPPERS

seasonal suppers

We sent three chefs to the store with the
same list and the same mission: a casual meal for six.
Their menus are good enough for company.

Nora Pouillon's Menu

Organic chef and restaurateur

Watermelon Gazpacho*
Greek Pasta Toss*
Raspberry Yogurt Brûlée*

Game plan

Drain a pint of yogurt for Raspberry
Yogurt Brûlée. Meanwhile, prepare
Watermelon Gazpacho and boil water
for pasta. While pasta cooks, arrange
ingredients for dessert in ramekins;
set aside. Prepare Greek Pasta Toss.
Broil dessert just before serving.

Watermelon Gazpacho

Made with pureed watermelon, this
new version of the classic cold soup is
a refreshing starter. To speed up prep
time, pulse pepper, zucchini, mint,
and onion in a food processor until
coarsely chopped. Transfer mixture to
a bowl, then puree the watermelon.

PREP *25 minutes*
MAKES *about 6 cups or 6 first-course
     servings*

- 4 pounds seedless watermelon,
rind removed, and melon cut
into large chunks
- 1 yellow or green pepper, cut into
¼-inch dice
- 1 small zucchini (about 6 ounces),
cut into ¼-inch dice
- ¼ cup packed fresh mint leaves,
finely chopped
- 3 tablespoons fresh lime juice
- 2 tablespoons minced red onion
- 1 garlic clove, crushed with
garlic press
- ¼ teaspoon salt
pinch crushed red pepper
mint sprigs and red onion strips
for garnish

1. In food processor with knife blade
attached or in blender at high speed,
puree watermelon in batches until
smooth. Pour each batch pureed watermelon into large bowl.
2. Stir yellow pepper and remaining
ingredients except garnish into watermelon puree. Cover soup and refrigerate until ready to serve. Garnish each
serving with a mint sprig and some
red onion strips.

■ Each serving: About 70 calories, 2 g
protein, 16 g carbohydrate, 1 g total fat
(0 g saturated), 2 g fiber, 0 mg cholesterol,
105 mg sodium.

* recipe given

Greek Pasta Toss

Here's a great Greek salad (minus the lettuce) with hot pasta and beans folded in.

PREP *25 minutes*
COOK *about 15 minutes*
MAKES *6 main-dish servings*

      salt
1   pound rotini or fusilli pasta
¼   cup olive oil
2   tablespoons balsamic vinegar
1   garlic clove, crushed with
       garlic press
¼   teaspoon coarsely ground
       black pepper
9   ripe medium tomatoes
       (about 3 pounds), cut into
       thin wedges
2   cans (15 to 19 ounces each)
       garbanzo beans, rinsed and
       drained
8   ounces feta cheese, coarsely
       crumbled
2   Kirby cucumbers (about 4 ounces
       each), unpeeled and cut into
       ¼-inch dice
½   cup kalamata olives, pitted and
       chopped
½   cup packed fresh parsley leaves,
       chopped
½   cup packed fresh dill, chopped

1. Heat large saucepot of *salted water* to boiling over high heat. Add pasta and cook as label directs.
2. Meanwhile, in large serving bowl, whisk oil, vinegar, garlic, ground pepper, and ½ teaspoon salt until blended. Add tomatoes, beans, feta, cucumbers, olives, parsley, and dill. Toss until evenly mixed and coated with dressing.
3. Drain pasta. Add pasta to tomato mixture in bowl; toss well.

■ Each serving: About 685 calories, 26 g protein, 97 g carbohydrate, 22 g total fat (8 g saturated), 12 g fiber, 34 mg cholesterol, 1,154 mg sodium.

nora
pouillon

Washington, D.C.
Pouillon's two restaurants, Asia Nora and Restaurant Nora, feature organic foods.

Natural origins I spent much of my childhood on a mountain farm in the Alps, where we grew our own vegetables. My mother brought me and my two sisters up to eat seasonal foods. In winter, we'd have cabbage soup, and in summer, tomato. Our family didn't live on heavy Austrian fare, but sometimes my mother would add little dumplings to the soup. I learned to cook by watching her.

Sweet memory On Sundays, my sisters and I made dessert. My mother was the first person on the street to have a Sunbeam electric mixer! We always made the same recipe, a basic pound cake, but in different shapes—round, rolled and filled with fresh berries and whipped cream, or baked in a sheet pan and cut into little squares that we ate with canned pineapple.

Why organic? When I came to this country in the sixties, I found that the most flavorful foods were those grown without chemicals. One reason people overeat, I think, is that they're not satisfied because food doesn't taste as good as it should.

Secret snacks Newman's Own Bavarian Pretzels and air-popped organic popcorn sprinkled with a little sea salt.

Favorite equipment My steamer and my blender, which I use to puree soups, vinaigrettes, dressings, and aioli.

Convenience foods Mustard and lots of spicy mix-ins, such as curry paste.

Her comforts Brown bread (sourdough or rye) from the Firehook Bakery in Washington, D.C., with fresh organic butter and a little salt on top—it's the best! I have it maybe once a week as an after-dinner snack, when my family and I (I have two daughters—Nina, 14, and Nadia, 11) are reading or watching TV.

Her green kids Children love vegetables if they're prepared right (serve a raw, cut-up plateful with mayonnaise or a favorite salad dressing). I make fresh fettuccine or spaghetti with steamed broccoli or sugar snaps for my girls. I have a bowl ready with olive oil, salt, pepper, and basil or Italian parsley, and I toss in the pasta and vegetables. Nadia likes to add butter and Parmesan cheese to hers.

—*Alice Garbarini Hurley*

"Watermelon isn't just for picnics or dessert: Here, it's pureed to make the base for a refreshing ice-cold soup"

Raspberry Yogurt Brûlée

pictured on page 158

For a supereasy sweet finish, broil raspberries under a topping of plain yogurt sprinkled with brown sugar. This dessert is so healthy and delicious, you'll want to make it again and again.

PREP *10 minutes plus standing*
BROIL *2 to 3 minutes*
MAKES *6 servings*

- 1 pint plain low-fat yogurt
- 3 half-pints raspberries
- ¼ cup packed brown sugar
  mint sprigs for garnish

1. Line medium-mesh sieve with single thickness of paper towel and place over bowl. Spoon yogurt over paper towel; let stand 30 minutes to drain liquid from yogurt. Discard liquid in bowl.
2. Preheat broiler. Divide raspberries evenly among six 6-ounce ramekins or custard cups. Spoon 2 heaping tablespoons drained yogurt on top of raspberries in each ramekin and sprinkle each with about 2 teaspoons sugar.
3. Place ramekins in 15½" by 10½" jelly-roll pan for easier handling. Place pan in broiler at position closest to source of heat and broil 2 to 3 minutes or until sugar melts and bubbles. Garnish with mint sprigs.

■ Each serving: About 115 calories, 5 g protein, 22 g carbohydrate, 2 g total fat (1 g saturated), 4 g fiber, 5 mg cholesterol, 60 mg sodium.

Joanne Weir's Menu

Host, "Weir Cooking in the Wine Country" (PBS)

Spaghetti with Tomato & Basil Pesto*
Green Bean, Cherry Tomato & Feta Salad*
Cinnamon Poached Plums*

Game plan

Start Cinnamon Poached Plums. While their juices cook down, heat a pot of water to boiling for Spaghetti with Tomato & Basil Pesto and prepare Green Bean, Cherry Tomato & Feta Salad. While pasta cooks, dice tomatoes and blend pesto.

Spaghetti with Tomato & Basil Pesto

pictured on page 158

A fresh and fragrant blender pesto and garden-fresh tomatoes make a quick and delicious no-cook sauce to toss with pasta. Whip up an extra batch of pesto and store it in the fridge for up to a week or freeze up to 3 months for a jump start on another meal.

PREP *20 minutes*
COOK *about 15 minutes*
MAKES *6 main-dish servings*

- salt
- 1 package (16 ounces) spaghetti or linguine
- 4 cups packed fresh basil leaves
- ¼ cup pine nuts (pignoli), toasted
- ¼ cup extra virgin olive oil
- ¼ teaspoon ground black pepper
- 1 garlic clove, cut in half
- 1 cup grated Parmesan cheese
- 3 ripe medium tomatoes (about 1 pound), cut into ½-inch dice

1. Heat large saucepot of *salted water* to boiling over high heat; add pasta and cook as label directs.
2. Meanwhile, in food processor with knife blade attached, place basil, pine nuts, oil, pepper, garlic, and 1 teaspoon salt; blend until pureed, occasionally scraping side with rubber spatula. Add ½ cup Parmesan and blend until mixed.
3. Place tomatoes in large serving bowl; stir in basil mixture.
4. When pasta has cooked to desired doneness, remove *¼ cup pasta cooking water* and reserve. Drain pasta. Add pasta and reserved cooking water to tomato mixture in bowl; toss until well coated. Sprinkle remaining ½ cup Parmesan on top to serve.

■ Each serving: About 490 calories, 19 g protein, 62 g carbohydrate, 19 g total fat (5 g saturated), 4 g fiber, 13 mg cholesterol, 805 mg sodium.

Green Bean, Cherry Tomato & Feta Salad

pictured on page 158

Summer simplicity: Steam some green beans, chop fresh mint, and cut cherry tomatoes in half. Toss it all together with a lemony dressing and top with crumbled feta cheese.

PREP **20 minutes**
COOK **about 10 minutes**
MAKES **6 accompaniment servings**

   salt
 1 pound green beans, stem ends
     trimmed
 3 tablespoons extra virgin
     olive oil
 2 tablespoons fresh lemon juice
 ¼ teaspoon ground black pepper
 1 can (15 to 19 ounces) white
     kidney beans (cannellini),
     rinsed and drained
 3 cups red and yellow cherry
     tomatoes, each cut in half
 ¼ cup loosely packed fresh mint
     leaves, coarsely chopped
 4 ounces feta cheese, crumbled
     (1 cup)

1. In 12-inch skillet, heat *½ inch water* and ½ teaspoon salt to boiling over high heat. Add green beans; heat to boiling. Reduce heat to medium-low; simmer, uncovered, 5 to 7 minutes or until beans are tender-crisp. Drain beans and rinse under cold running water to stop cooking. Drain again; set aside.
2. In large serving bowl, with wire whisk or fork, mix olive oil, lemon juice, pepper, and ½ teaspoon salt. Stir in kidney beans, tomatoes, mint leaves, and green beans, and toss gently to coat. Sprinkle crumbled feta on top to serve.

■ Each serving: About 220 calories, 8 g protein, 23 g carbohydrate, 11 g total fat (4 g saturated), 7 g fiber, 17 mg cholesterol, 575 mg sodium.

joanne weir

San Francisco
In addition to her television show, which is done on location in California's Napa Valley, Weir is the author of two companion cookbooks to the series.

Her legacy I come from a long line of chefs. At the turn of the last century, my great-grandmother ran a restaurant, Pilgrim's Pantry, in Boston. When I was a little girl, we had picnics at my grandfather's farm, in the Berkshire Mountains of Massachusetts. He made the bread and the mayonnaise, and he cooked chicken from the farm. He also made potato chips and served them hot. And he also gave us maple-walnut ice cream flavored with his own maple syrup. My mother is a fantastic gardener and cook, and she inspired me to do both.

Starting big—very big When I was about eight, I wanted to make oatmeal cookies all by myself. I followed the recipe carefully, as my mom had taught me. After I put the first batch in the oven, I called out to Mom that we would need to get more baking soda. "That's funny," she said. "I just bought a new box." We opened the oven door and found one huge cookie that covered the cookie sheet and was creeping over the sides. I had used 1½ cups of baking soda instead of 1½ teaspoons! Mom said the giant cookie still tasted good.

Salt craving I love potato chips, but they have to be great ones, like Tim's Cascade Chips. (I only indulge outdoors, on picnics!) And I love salsa with tortilla chips.

Can't live without My chef's knife. I use it to chop all my vegetables.

Help in a squeeze I always have lemons on hand. One of my favorite comfort dinners is roast chicken and a green salad with lemon and extra virgin olive oil.

Seasonal savvy In California wine country, something is always ripe. It's easy to eat fresh foods right out of the garden and orchard. I pay attention to what is ready to pick so that I can cook and eat seasonally.

—A.G.H.

"Plum simple dessert: let the fruit steep in a syrup of star anise, cinnamon sticks, and lemon while you get dinner together"

Cinnamon Poached Plums

PREP *10 minutes*
COOK *about 40 minutes*
MAKES *6 servings*

  1 lemon
  ¾ cup sugar
  8 whole cloves
  2 cinnamon sticks (each 3 inches long)
  2 whole star anise*
2½ pounds ripe but firm plums (about 10 plums)

1. With vegetable peeler, remove ¾-inch-wide strips of peel from lemon. Wrap and refrigerate lemon for use another day. With knife, cut away any white pith on peel.
2. In 3-quart saucepan, heat sugar, cloves, cinnamon, star anise, lemon-peel strips, and *3 cups water* to boiling over high heat. Reduce heat to low; simmer, uncovered, 5 minutes.
3. Meanwhile, cut each plum into quarters (halves if small); discard pits.
4. Add plums to poaching liquid in saucepan. Increase heat to high; cook 5 minutes or until plums are tender but still hold their shape.
5. With slotted spoon, transfer plums to medium bowl. Cook plum poaching liquid over high heat until reduced by half and slightly thickened, about 25 minutes; pour over plums.
6. Serve plums warm with some poaching liquid. Or, cover and refrigerate up to 2 days if not serving right away. Reheat if desired.

■ Each serving: About 170 calories, 1 g protein, 42 g carbohydrate, 1 g total fat (0 g saturated), 2 g fiber, 0 mg cholesterol, 0 mg sodium.

* Star anise, a star-shaped pod popular in various Asian cuisines for its distinctive licorice flavor, is available in Asian food markets or the spice section of some supermarkets. You can also order it from Adriana's Caravan; 800-316-0820.

Deborah Madison's Menu
vegetarian chef and cookbook author

Roasted Almonds
Marinated Olives
Gruyère Garden Frittata*
Toasted Garbanzos with Marjoram*
Tomato & Onion Salad*
Melon in Moscato d'Asti*

Game plan
Serve your guests roasted almonds and marinated olives while you prepare Toasted Garbanzos with Marjoram. Prep Gruyère Garden Frittata and put it in the oven. While it bakes, cut melon for dessert. Remove frittata from oven; let stand while you toss together Tomato & Onion Salad.

Gruyère Garden Frittata
pictured on page 159

This Italian-style omelette bursts with the flavors of basil, garlic, nutty cheese, and sautéed Swiss chard. It's delicious at any temperature, so there's no pressure to serve it straight from the oven. It's luscious for brunch, too.

PREP *40 minutes*
BAKE *about 10 minutes*
MAKES *6 main-dish servings*

  2 teaspoons extra virgin olive oil
  1 bunch green onions (about 4 ounces), thinly sliced
  1 small bunch Swiss chard (about 12 ounces), thick ribs and stems discarded, leaves coarsely chopped
  8 large eggs
  4 ounces Gruyère cheese, shredded (1 cup)
  ½ cup packed fresh basil leaves, chopped
  1 garlic clove, crushed with garlic press
  ½ teaspoon dried thyme
  ¼ teaspoon salt
  ¼ teaspoon ground black pepper
  2 tablespoons grated Parmesan cheese
  1 tablespoon margarine or butter

1. In nonstick 10-inch skillet with oven-safe handle (or with handle wrapped in double thickness of foil for baking in oven later), heat oil over medium heat until hot. Add green onions and cook 2 minutes or until wilted, stirring occasionally. Gradually add Swiss chard and cook, stirring, until excess moisture evaporates and chard is tender, about 10 minutes.
2. Meanwhile, preheat oven to 400°F. In large bowl, with wire whisk, mix eggs, Gruyère, basil, garlic, thyme, salt, pepper, and 1 tablespoon Parmesan until blended. Stir in Swiss chard mixture.
3. In same skillet, melt margarine over medium-high heat. Add egg mixture and stir once; cook 1 minute. Reduce heat to low; cook 5 minutes or until mixture begins to set around edge. Sprinkle remaining 1 tablespoon Parmesan over top of frittata. Place skillet in oven; bake 10 minutes or until frittata is set.
4. Loosen edge of frittata from skillet. Carefully slide frittata onto platter; cut into wedges to serve.

■ Each serving: About 230 calories, 16 g protein, 5 g carbohydrate, 17 g total fat (7 g saturated), 2 g fiber, 305 mg cholesterol, 410 mg sodium.

Toasted Garbanzos with Marjoram

pictured on page 159

Canned beans never tasted so yummy; all it takes is a quick turn in a skillet, fresh herbs, good olive oil, and balsamic vinegar. Serve warm or at room temperature.

PREP *10 minutes*
COOK *5 minutes*
MAKES *6 accompaniment servings*

- 2 cans (15 to 19 ounces each) garbanzo beans, rinsed and drained
- 1 tablespoon fresh marjoram or oregano leaves
- 1 garlic clove, peeled
- 1 tablespoon extra virgin olive oil
- 4 teaspoons balsamic vinegar
- 1 teaspoon salt
- ¼ teaspoon coarsely ground black pepper
- ⅛ teaspoon crushed red pepper marjoram sprigs for garnish

1. In 10-inch skillet, cook garbanzo beans over medium-high heat 5 minutes or until warm and dry. Remove skillet from heat.
2. Meanwhile, mince marjoram leaves with garlic. Add garlic mixture and remaining ingredients except garnish to beans in skillet; toss until evenly coated. Spoon garbanzo mixture into serving bowl, and garnish with marjoram sprigs.

■ Each serving: About 160 calories, 8 g protein, 23 g carbohydrate, 4 g total fat (0 g saturated), 6 g fiber, 0 mg cholesterol, 670 mg sodium.

deborah
madison

Santa Fe, New Mexico
Author of five books on healthy eating, including *Vegetarian Cooking for Everyone* and the upcoming *Saturday Market, Sunday Lunch* (Broadway Books, 2002)

Fruits of her family's labor My family had a great vegetable garden and a lot of fruit trees—apricot, fig, peach, quince, citrus, plum, and pomegranate. My father was a horticulture professor, and my mother an artist and writer—so there wasn't a big budget for eating out. And we just never had soft drinks, chips, or processed foods.

Solo debut The first thing I ever made on my own, when I was ten or so, was a cake from *The Joy of Cooking.* I think it was called One Bowl Silver White Cake. My brother and I loved it with poppy seeds in the batter. I got very good at making cakes and frostings because I liked them.

In her fridge Broccoli rabe, broccoli, sweet potatoes, carrots, herbs, beets, chard, and Napa cabbage. Fruits are harder because most of the supermarket ones seem lackluster. I buy local varieties in season and turn to dried fruits the rest of the year. I also usually have tofu in my refrigerator.

Fast food flavorings Coconut milk and chile pastes, to spice up that tofu for a quick meal.

Precious cargo Whenever I travel, I haul bags and bags of produce from farmers' markets. And when I go to California, I stock up on nuts, dried fruit, and olive oils. The only things I get in the supermarket (at least in summer) are cat food and tonic water.

Everyone has a weakness Mine is Reese's Peanut Butter Cups ... but only about once a year.

Best friend in the kitchen My microplane (a fine grater that resembles a carpenter's rasp). I love it for cheese—it makes such light shreds. And I sometimes use the microplane for lemon zest, too.

If you grow it, they will eat To get kids involved, if you have the space, consider planting really simple things—radishes, peas, or sprouts. Or take children to a farmers' market or a U-Pick, and let them talk to the farmer and choose the vegetables.

—A.G.H.

"Gently toasting the garbanzo beans brings out their nutty flavor—a spoonful of olive oil and fresh herbs finish the dish"

Tomato & Onion Salad

pictured on page 159

Savor summer's bumper crop in a simple side of tomato slices topped with onions, olive oil, and basil.

PREP **15 minutes**
MAKES **6 accompaniment servings**

- ½ cup thinly sliced red onion
- 3 tablespoons white wine vinegar or Champagne vinegar
- ¼ teaspoon plus pinch salt
- 5 medium tomatoes (about 1½ pounds), cut into ½-inch-thick slices
- 4 large basil leaves, thinly sliced
- ⅛ teaspoon coarsely ground black pepper
- 1 teaspoon extra virgin olive oil

1. In small bowl, toss onion with vinegar and a pinch of salt; set aside 10 minutes.
2. Place tomatoes on platter; top with onion mixture. Sprinkle with basil, pepper, and remaining ¼ teaspoon salt, and drizzle with oil.

■ Each serving: About 35 calories, 1 g protein, 6 g carbohydrate, 1 g total fat (0 g saturated), 1 g fiber, 0 mg cholesterol, 130 mg sodium.

Melon in Moscato d'Asti

A splash of Moscato d'Asti, a sparkling sweet white wine, turns plain melon chunks into a quick party dessert. Any variety of melon will work—use one kind or several.

PREP **10 minutes**
MAKES **6 servings**

- 6 cups (1½-inch) chunks ripe melon
- 1 cup chilled sparkling sweet white wine such as Moscato d'Asti or Asti Spumante

Place melon in medium bowl, and cover and refrigerate until ready to serve. Just before serving, toss melon with wine.

■ Each serving: About 110 calories, 1 g protein, 17 g carbohydrate, 0 g total fat, 1 g fiber, 0 mg cholesterol, 20 mg sodium.

food editor's Q&A

Q What is the point of draining yogurt for recipes? Don't you lose some nutrients?

a Draining yogurt results in a thick, custardy cheese that can be a low-fat alternative to cream cheese and sour cream. And it's easy to make; just line a fine-meshed sieve with cheesecloth or sturdy paper towels. Add yogurt and drain 8 to 24 hours. While most of the nutrients remain in the cheese, including the live, active cultures, a small amount of protein, calcium, and potassium do drain out into the whey (the liquid that collects under the sieve). Stir the whey into soups or smoothies for a nutritional boost. Check out Nora Pouillon's 30-minute version in her Raspberry Yogurt Brûlée, page 144.

Q I've never cooked Swiss chard. Are those long stems edible?

a Swiss chard is a quick-cooking green that is reminiscent of spinach, though sweeter. It comes with white, red, or golden stems and veins. Try it quickly stir-fried: Wash the greens and trim the stems (just cut an inch or so off the bottom); thinly slice the stems and coarsely chop the leaves. In a large skillet, heat a tablespoon of oil, a clove of garlic, chopped, and a pinch of red or black pepper and sauté just until garlic begins to color. Add the stems and cook over medium-high heat for 1 minute; stir in the leaves and cook 2 to 3 minutes longer or until tender. Sprinkle with salt. Added bonus: Swiss chard is rich in beta-carotene and supplies certain carotenoids that may lower the risk of macular degeneration. For a delicious main dish using Swiss chard, try Deborah Madison's frittata on page 146.

October

The All New Good Housekeeping Cookbook

recipes from
The All New Good Housekeeping Cookbook

Here's a sampling from our collection of recipes from dips to desserts, plus quick-fix dinners, yummy low-cal dishes, and tips from superstar chefs.

Roasted Red Pepper Dip

An unusual dip with Middle Eastern flavors. If you are not familiar with roasting peppers, this is the perfect time to learn how. Once you taste them, you'll wonder why you waited so long.

PREP **45 minutes**

MAKES **about 2 cups dip**

- 4 medium red peppers, roasted (see right)
- ½ teaspoon ground cumin
- ½ cup walnuts, toasted
- 2 slices firm white bread, torn into pieces
- 2 tablespoons vinegar, preferably raspberry
- 1 tablespoon olive oil
- ½ teaspoon salt
- ⅛ teaspoon ground red pepper (cayenne)
- toasted pita bread wedges

1. Cut roasted peppers into large pieces. In small skillet, toast cumin over low heat, stirring constantly, until very fragrant, 1 to 2 minutes.

2. In food processor with knife blade attached, process toasted walnuts until ground. Add peppers, cumin, bread, vinegar, oil, salt, and ground red pepper; puree until smooth. Transfer to bowl. If not serving right away, cover and refrigerate up to 4 hours. Serve with toasted pita bread wedges.

■ Each tablespoon: About 25 calories, 0 g protein, 2 g carbohydrate, 2 g total fat (0 g saturated), 0 mg cholesterol, 45 mg sodium.

roasted peppers master recipe

1. Preheat broiler. Line broiling pan with foil. Cut each pepper lengthwise in half; remove and discard stems and seeds. Arrange peppers, cut side down, in prepared broiling pan. Place pan in broiler, 5 to 6 inches from heat source. Broil, without turning, until skin is charred and blistered, 8 to 10 minutes.

2. Wrap peppers in foil and allow to steam at room temperature 15 minutes or until cool enough to handle.

3. Remove peppers from foil. Peel skin and discard.

Baked Artichokes with Parmesan Stuffing
pictured on facing page

This simple bread stuffing—seasoned with Parmesan cheese, anchovies, and pine nuts—is a classic match for artichokes. If serving as a first course, use six small artichokes.

PREP **1 hour**

BAKE **15 to 20 minutes**

MAKES **4 main-dish or 6 first-course servings**

- 4 large artichokes
- 1 large lemon, cut in half
- 2 tablespoons fresh lemon juice
- 4 slices firm white bread, coarsely grated
- 2 tablespoons olive oil
- 2 large garlic cloves, finely chopped
- 4 anchovy fillets, chopped
- ½ cup pine nuts (pignoli), lightly toasted (or walnuts, toasted and chopped)
- ⅓ cup freshly grated Parmesan cheese
- 2 tablespoons chopped fresh parsley
- ¼ teaspoon salt
- ¾ cup chicken broth

1. Trim artichokes: Bend back outer green leaves from around base of artichoke and snap off. With kitchen shears, trim thorny tops from remaining outer leaves, rubbing all cut surfaces with lemon half to prevent browning. Lay artichoke on its side and cut off stem so it's level with bottom of artichoke. Peel stem; place in bowl of cold water and juice of remaining lemon half. Cut 1 inch off top of artichoke; add artichoke to lemon water. Repeat with remaining artichokes.

2. In nonreactive 5-quart saucepot, heat *1 inch water* and 1 tablespoon lemon juice over high heat. Stand artichokes in boiling water; add stems and heat to boiling. Reduce heat; cover and simmer until knife inserted in bottom of artichokes goes in easily, 30 to 40 minutes. Drain. When cool enough to handle, pull out prickly center leaves from each artichoke and, with teaspoon, scrape out fuzzy choke (without cutting into heart) and discard. Finely chop stems.

3. Meanwhile, preheat oven to 400°F. Spread grated bread in jelly-roll pan. Place in oven and toast until golden, about 5 minutes.

4. In 1-quart saucepan, heat oil over medium heat. Add garlic and cook 1 minute. Add anchovies and cook until garlic is golden and anchovies have almost dissolved.

5. In medium bowl, combine toasted bread, pine nuts, Parmesan, fresh parsley, chopped artichoke stems, garlic mixture, salt, ¼ cup chicken broth, and remaining 1 tablespoon lemon juice.

6. Pour remaining ½ cup broth into 13" by 9" baking dish; stand artichokes in dish. Spoon bread mixture between artichoke leaves and into center cavities. Bake until stuffing is golden and artichokes are heated through, 15 to 20 minutes.

■ Each main-dish serving: About 360 calories, 17 g protein, 35 g carbohydrate, 20 g total fat (4 g saturated), 9 mg cholesterol, 935 mg sodium.

how to trim an artichoke

Baked Artichoke with Parmesan Stuffing

1. Bend back outer leaves from base of artichoke and snap off. With kitchen shears, trim thorny tops from remaining outer leaves.

2. Lay artichoke on its side; trim stem level with bottom of artichoke. Cut off one inch from top of artichoke.

3. After artichoke is cooked and cool enough to handle, pull out prickly center leaves.

4. With teaspoon, scrape out fuzzy choke (without cutting into heart).

Spicy Tangerine Beef

pictured on facing page

Here's a home-cooked version of the ever-popular take-out dish.

PREP *25 minutes*
COOK *25 minutes*
MAKES *4 main-dish servings*

- 4 tangerines or 3 medium navel oranges
- 1 large bunch broccoli (1½ pounds)
- 3 tablespoons vegetable oil
- 1 boneless beef top sirloin steak (12 ounces), thinly sliced crosswise
- 2 tablespoons plus ½ teaspoon cornstarch
- 2 tablespoons water
- 3 green onions, cut on diagonal into 2-inch pieces
- 1 red pepper, thinly sliced
- 3 garlic cloves, finely chopped
- 1 tablespoon minced, peeled fresh ginger
- 3 tablespoons soy sauce
- ¼ teaspoon crushed red pepper

1. Cut peel and white pith from 1 tangerine. Holding tangerine over small bowl to catch juice, cut on either side of membranes to release each section, allowing fruit and juice to drop into bowl. Remove eight strips peel (3" by ¾" each) from remaining tangerines. Cut off any remaining white pith from peel. Squeeze ¾ cup juice; set aside.

2. Cut broccoli into small flowerets. With vegetable peeler, peel broccoli stems; cut into ¼-inch-thick slices.

3. In 12-inch skillet, heat 2 tablespoons oil over high heat until very hot. Add strips of broccoli peel and cook until lightly browned, about 3 minutes. Transfer peel to large bowl.

4. On waxed paper, toss beef slices with 2 tablespoons cornstarch, coating evenly. Add half of beef to skillet and cook, stirring frequently (stir-frying),

until crisp and lightly browned on both sides, about 5 minutes, using slotted spoon to transfer beef to bowl with peel as it is browned. Repeat with remaining 1 tablespoon oil and remaining beef.

5. Add broccoli and water to skillet. Reduce heat to medium; cover and cook 2 minutes. Increase heat to high. Remove cover and add green onions and red pepper; cook, stirring occasionally, 2 minutes. Then add garlic and ginger; stir-fry for 1 minute.

6. Meanwhile, in cup, combine tangerine juice, soy sauce, crushed red pepper, and remaining ½ teaspoon cornstarch, and stir until blended. Add cornstarch mixture to skillet. Stir-fry until sauce thickens and boils.

7. Return beef mixture to skillet. Add citrus sections and juice in bowl; toss to combine.

■ Each serving: About 300 calories, 23 g protein, 21 g carbohydrate, 15 g total fat (3 g saturated), 52 mg cholesterol, 855 mg sodium.

Chinese Dumplings

pictured on facing page

Steamed dumplings are fun to make at home. Have them for brunch: It's the way the Chinese enjoy them.

PREP *45 minutes*
COOK *10 minutes*
MAKES *3 dozen dumplings*

- 2 cups packed, sliced Napa cabbage
- 8 ounces ground pork
- 1 green onion, finely chopped
- 1½ teaspoons minced, peeled fresh ginger
- 2 tablespoons soy sauce
- 1 tablespoon dry sherry
- 2 teaspoons cornstarch
- 36 (3½" by 3¼") wonton wrappers (9 ounces)
- 1 large egg white, beaten
  Soy Dipping Sauce (at right)

1. Prepare filling: In 2-quart saucepan, heat *1 inch water* to boiling over high heat. Add cabbage and heat to boiling. Cook 1 minute; drain. Immediately rinse with cold running water to stop cooking. With hands, squeeze out as much water as possible from cabbage. Finely chop cabbage. Squeeze out any remaining water from cabbage; place in medium bowl. Stir in pork, green onion, ginger, soy sauce, sherry, and cornstarch until well blended.

2. Arrange half of wonton wrappers on waxed paper. With pastry brush, brush each wrapper lightly with egg white. Spoon 1 rounded teaspoon filling onto center of each wrapper. Bring 2 opposite corners of each wrapper up over filling; pinch and pleat edges together to seal in filling. Repeat with remaining wrappers, egg white, and filling.

3. In deep, nonstick 12-inch skillet, heat ½ inch water to boiling over high heat. Place all dumplings, pleated edges up, in 1 layer in skillet. With spatula, move dumplings gently to prevent them from sticking to bottom of skillet. Heat to boiling. Reduce heat; cover skillet and simmer until dumplings are cooked through, about 5 minutes.

4. Meanwhile, prepare Soy Dipping Sauce.

5. With slotted spoon, transfer dumplings to platter. Serve with dipping sauce.

■ Each dumpling without sauce: About 40 calories, 2 g protein, 5 g carbohydrate, 1 g total fat (1 g saturated), 5 mg cholesterol, 105 mg sodium.

Soy Dipping Sauce

In small serving bowl, with spoon, mix together *¼ cup soy sauce, ¼ cup seasoned rice vinegar* or *white wine vinegar,* and *2 tablespoons peeled fresh ginger, cut into very thin slivers.* Makes about ½ cup sauce.

■ Each teaspoon sauce: About 5 calories, 0 g protein, 1 g carbohydrate, 0 g total fat, 0 mg cholesterol, 220 mg sodium.

Chinese Dumplings,
facing page

Spicy Tangerine Beef,
facing page

Rotelle with Ratatouille,
page 130

Thin Spaghetti with
Pesto & Tomatoes,
page 134

Sesame Noodles,
page 130

Cool Lime Pie,
page 138

Raspberry-Peach
Dome, page 136

156

Banana-Caramel Tart,
page 137

Green Bean, Cherry
Tomato & Feta Salad,
page 145

Spaghetti with
Tomato & Basil Pesto,
page 144

Raspberry Yogurt Brûlée,
page 144

Toasted Garbanzos with Marjoram, page 147

Tomato & Onion Salad, page 148

Gruyère Garden Frittata, page 146

Turkey Cutlet with Chopped
Salad, facing page

Turkey Cutlets with Chopped Salad

pictured on facing page

Turkey cutlets served over arugula and tomato salad warm the vegetables enough to bring out their flavor.

PREP *15 minutes*
COOK *12 minutes*
MAKES *4 main-dish servings*

1 green onion, thinly sliced
2 tablespoons freshly grated Parmesan cheese
4 tablespoons olive oil
1 tablespoon red wine vinegar
½ teaspoon Dijon mustard
¼ teaspoon salt
¼ teaspoon coarsely ground black pepper
1 pound turkey cutlets
⅓ cup seasoned dried bread crumbs
1 pound plum tomatoes (4 large), cut into ¾-inch pieces
2 small bunches arugula (6 to 8 ounces), coarsely chopped

1. Prepare dressing: In medium bowl, with fork, mix green onion, Parmesan, 2 tablespoons oil, vinegar, mustard, salt, and pepper; set aside.
2. With meat mallet, or between 2 sheets of plastic wrap with rolling pin, pound turkey cutlets to ¼-inch thickness. On waxed paper, coat cutlets with bread crumbs.
3. In nonstick 12-inch skillet, heat remaining 2 tablespoons olive oil over medium-high heat until very hot. Add turkey cutlets, a few at a time, and cook until cutlets are golden brown and lose their pink color throughout, about 2½ minutes per side. Transfer cutlets to warm dish as they are done.
4. Add tomatoes and arugula to reserved dressing; gently toss to mix. Pile salad on platter and top with cutlets.

■ Each serving: About 335 calories, 33 g protein, 15 g carbohydrate, 16 g total fat (3 g saturated), 73 mg cholesterol, 560 mg sodium.

things to add to oil-and-garlic sauce

Spaghetti with oil and garlic is just the starting point for many delicious sauces.
• Add 4 to 6 coarsely chopped anchovy fillets in oil, drained (or 1 to 1½ teaspoons anchovy paste) and 2 tablespoons capers, drained, to garlic-oil mixture; reduce heat and stir until anchovies break up, about 30 seconds.
• Add ½ cup Gaeta, kalamata, or green Sicilian olives, pitted and chopped, to cooked garlic and oil mixture; reduce heat and stir until heated.
• Add 2 to 3 ounces crumbled goat cheese (chèvre) to pasta; toss again.
• Add ⅓ cup chopped dried tomatoes to pasta with garlic-oil mixture and parsley; toss.
• Substitute 2 to 4 tablespoons chopped fresh basil, oregano, chives, or tarragon for parsley.

Maple-Glazed Pork Tenderloins

Plan on leftovers and look forward to a delicious sandwich treat.

PREP *10 minutes plus refrigerating*
GRILL *20 minutes*
MAKES *6 main-dish servings*

2 pork tenderloins (12 ounces each), trimmed
½ teaspoon salt
¼ teaspoon ground black pepper
8 wooden toothpicks
6 slices bacon
½ cup maple or maple-flavor syrup

1. Sprinkle pork tenderloins with salt and pepper. Place pork in bowl; cover and refrigerate 30 minutes.
2. Meanwhile, soak toothpicks in water for 30 minutes. Prepare grill.
3. Wrap 3 bacon slices around each tenderloin and secure with toothpicks. Place on grill and cook over medium heat, brushing frequently with syrup and turning over occasionally until meat thermometer inserted in center of pork reaches 155°F., 20 to 25 minutes. Internal temperature of pork will rise to 160°F. upon standing. Transfer pork to cutting board and let stand 5 minutes to set juices for easier slicing.

■ Each serving: About 265 calories, 28 g protein, 18 g carbohydrate, 9 g total fat (3 g saturated), 86 mg cholesterol, 350 mg sodium.

Spaghetti with Oil and Garlic

The classic combination of garlic and oil gives this pasta its heady flavor. Serve with grated Parmesan cheese.

PREP *5 minutes*
COOK *25 minutes*
MAKES *6 main-dish servings*

1 package (16 ounces) spaghetti or linguine
¼ cup olive oil
1 large garlic clove, finely chopped
⅛ teaspoon crushed red pepper (optional)
¾ teaspoon salt
¼ teaspoon coarsely ground black pepper
2 tablespoons chopped fresh parsley

1. In large saucepot, cook pasta as label directs. Drain.
2. Meanwhile, in 1-quart saucepan, heat oil over medium heat. Add garlic and cook just until golden, about 1 minute; add red pepper, if using, and cook 30 seconds longer. Remove saucepan from heat; stir in salt and black pepper. In warm serving bowl, toss pasta with sauce and parsley.

■ Each serving: About 360 calories, 10 g protein, 57 g carbohydrate, 10 g total fat (1 g saturated), 0 mg cholesterol, 360 mg sodium.

Herb-Crusted Rib Roast

You don't need a rack to roast this cut; the bones act as a natural rack, making clean-up easier.

PREP *15 minutes*
ROAST *2 hours 30 minutes*
MAKES *8 main-dish servings*

 1 (3-rib) beef rib roast from small end (5½ pounds), trimmed and chine bone removed
 1 teaspoon salt
 ½ teaspoon dried rosemary, crumbled
 ¼ teaspoon ground black pepper
 1 lemon
 1½ cups fresh bread crumbs (about 3 slices bread)
 ½ cup chopped fresh parsley
 2 garlic cloves, finely chopped
 1 tablespoon olive oil
 2 tablespoons Dijon mustard

1. Preheat oven to 325°F. In medium roasting pan (14" by 10"), place rib roast fat side up. In small bowl, combine salt, rosemary, and pepper. Use to rub on roast.
2. Roast beef until meat thermometer inserted in thickest part of meat (not touching bone) reaches 140°F., about 2 hours 30 minutes. Internal temperature of meat will rise to 145°F. (medium) upon standing. Or roast until desired degree of doneness.
3. About 1 hour before roast is done, prepare bread coating. From lemon, grate ½ teaspoon peel and squeeze 1 tablespoon juice. In small bowl, combine lemon peel and juice, fresh bread crumbs, parsley, garlic, and oil. Remove roast from oven; evenly spread mustard on top of roast. Press breadcrumb mixture onto mustard-coated roast. Roast 1 hour longer, or until crumb coating is golden and meat is desired degree of doneness.
4. When roast is done, transfer, rib side down, to warm large platter or cutting board and let stand 15 minutes to set juices for easier carving.

■ Each serving: About 350 calories, 39 g protein, 5 g carbohydrate, 18 g total fat (7 g saturated), 112 mg cholesterol, 510 mg sodium.

Snapper Livornese

Vibrant with olives, capers, and basil, this preparation works beautifully with any lean white fish.

PREP *10 minutes*
COOK *25 minutes*
MAKES *4 servings*

 1 tablespoon olive oil
 1 garlic clove, finely chopped
 1 can (14½ to 16 ounces) tomatoes
 ⅛ teaspoon salt
 ⅛ teaspoon ground black pepper
 4 red snapper fillets (6 ounces each)
 ¼ cup chopped fresh basil
 ¼ cup kalamata or Gaeta olives, pitted and chopped
 2 teaspoons capers, drained

1. In nonstick 10-inch skillet, heat oil over medium heat. Add garlic and cook just until very fragrant, about 30 seconds, stirring constantly. Stir in tomatoes with their juice, salt, and pepper, breaking up tomatoes with side of spoon. Heat sauce to boiling; reduce heat to low and simmer 10 minutes.
2. Meanwhile, with tweezers, remove any bones from snapper fillets.
3. Place snapper, skin side down, in sauce in skillet. Cover and simmer just until fish is opaque throughout, about 10 minutes.
4. With wide slotted spatula, transfer fish to warm platter. Stir basil, olives, and capers into tomato sauce.
5. To serve, spoon sauce over fish on platter.

■ Each serving: About 250 calories, 36 g protein, 6 g carbohydrate, 8 g total fat (1 g saturated), 63 mg cholesterol, 570 mg sodium.

Apple and Thyme Roast Chicken

Your kitchen will be filled with the fragrance of apples, herbs, and spices.

PREP *20 minutes*
ROAST *1 hour*
MAKES *4 main-dish servings*

 1 chicken (3½ pounds)
 2 sprigs plus 1 tablespoon chopped fresh thyme
 ¾ teaspoon salt
 ¼ teaspoon coarsely ground black pepper
 ⅛ teaspoon ground allspice
 1 jumbo onion (1 pound), cut into 12 wedges
 ¼ cup water
 2 teaspoons olive oil
 2 large Granny Smith apples, each cored and cut into quarters
 2 tablespoons applejack brandy or Calvados
 ½ cup chicken broth

1. Preheat oven to 450°F. Remove giblets and neck from chicken; reserve for another use. Rinse chicken inside and out with cold running water; drain. Pat chicken dry with paper towels.
2. With fingertips, gently separate skin from meat on chicken breast. Place 1 thyme sprig under skin of each breast half. In cup, combine chopped thyme, salt, pepper, and allspice.

expert tip

When roasting an unstuffed chicken or turkey, place some aromatics (carrots, onion, garlic, fresh herbs) in the cavity. The result is a wonderfully perfumed bird.

—Anne Rosenzweig
Chef/partner, Inside,
New York City

3. With chicken breast side up, lift wings up toward neck, then fold wing tips under back of chicken so wings stay in place. Tie legs together with string.

4. In medium roasting pan (14" by 10"), toss onion, chopped-thyme mixture, water, and olive oil. Push onion mixture to sides of pan. Place chicken, breast side up, on small rack in center of roasting pan.

5. Roast chicken and onion mixture 40 minutes. Add apples to pan; roast about 20 minutes longer. Chicken is done when temperature on meat thermometer inserted in thickest part of thigh, next to body, reaches 175° to 180°F. and juices run clear when thigh is pierced with tip of knife.

6. Transfer chicken to warm platter; let stand 10 minutes to set juices for easier carving.

7. Meanwhile, remove rack from roasting pan. With slotted spoon, transfer onion mixture to platter with chicken. Skim and discard fat from drippings in pan. Add applejack to pan drippings; cook 1 minute over medium heat, stirring constantly. Add chicken broth, and heat to boiling. Serve pan-juice mixture with chicken. Remove skin from chicken before eating, if desired.

how to roast a chicken

• Roast chicken on a rack in a roasting pan to allow heat to circulate under the bird. If you like, occasionally baste with the pan drippings. Basting doesn't make meat moister, but it does help to crisp and brown the skin.

• To be sure the whole bird is fully cooked, always use a meat thermometer. Insert the thermometer into thickest part of a thigh just under the drumstick, pointing toward the body. Do not let the thermometer touch any bone.

• To double-check doneness, insert a small knife into thickest part of thigh. The juices should run clear, with no trace of pink.

• Letting the bird rest after roasting results in firmer, juicier meat that is easier to carve. Chicken should stand at least ten minutes before carving so that the simmering juices can be absorbed into the meat.

■ Each serving with skin: About 590 calories, 49 g protein, 22 g carbohydrate, 33 g total fat (9 g saturated), 159 mg cholesterol, 710 mg sodium.

■ Each serving without skin: About 440 calories, 43 g protein, 22 g carbohydrate, 20 g total fat (5 g saturated), 132 mg cholesterol, 685 mg sodium.

carving a roast chicken

1. To remove the breast meat, using a thin knife, start along one side of the breastbone, cutting down along the rib cage (scraping against the bones as you go). Cut off the meat in one piece. Repeat on other side.

2. To carve the breast meat, hold the knife at a slight angle, and cut the meat crosswise into even slices.

3. To remove a leg, force it away from the body until it pops out of its socket. Separate the thigh from the body by cutting through the joint. Separate the drumstick from the thigh. Repeat on other side.

Ricotta Gnocchi with Browned Butter and Sage

PREP *1 hour*
COOK *about 17 minutes*
MAKES *8 first-course servings*

    3 tablespoons butter
    1 teaspoon chopped fresh sage
       leaves
  ¾ teaspoon salt, divided
  ¼ teaspoon ground black pepper
    1 container (15 ounces) ricotta
       cheese
  ⅓ cup freshly grated Parmesan cheese
  ¾ cup minced fresh parsley leaves
  ¾ cup all-purpose flour, or as needed

1. In 2-quart saucepan, melt butter over medium heat. Continue to cook, stirring, until butter turns golden brown (if butter gets too dark, it will be bitter). Remove from heat and add sage, ¼ teaspoon salt, and pepper; set aside.
2. In medium bowl, combine ricotta, Parmesan, parsley, and remaining ½ teaspoon salt. Sprinkle flour over ricotta mixture and, with your hands, work mixture into a soft, smooth dough. If dough is sticky, add flour as needed. Work dough just until flour is incorporated into cheese mixture; do not overwork.
3. Shape gnocchi (see box, *right*).
4. Repeat rolling, cutting, and shaping with remaining dough. (Gnocchi can be made up to 4 hours ahead. Arrange on floured jelly-roll pan; cover and refrigerate.)
5. In a 5-quart saucepot, bring *4 quarts water* to boiling over high heat. Add half of gnocchi and cook until they float to the surface, 2 to 3 minutes. Using a slotted spoon, transfer gnocchi to warm, shallow serving bowl. Repeat with remaining gnocchi. To serve, toss with sage butter.

■ Each serving: About 195 calories, 9 g protein, 11 g carbohydrate, 13 g total fat (8 g saturated), 42 mg cholesterol, 395 mg sodium.

how to shape gnocchi

1. Break off piece of the dough; on lightly floured surface, roll into ¾-inch-thick rope. (If rope doesn't hold together, return it to bowl and work in more flour.) Cut dough rope into ¾-inch lengths.

2. Place one piece of dough on inside curve of fork tines, gently pressing dough with thumb as you roll it along tines. Allow the dough to drop, slightly curling it off fork to form an oval.

Savory Tomato Tart

A dramatically beautiful main dish. For more color, include a yellow tomato, but it's equally delicious with all red.

PREP *45 minutes*
BAKE/BROIL *about 30 minutes*
MAKES *6 main-dish servings*

       Pastry for 11-Inch Tart
       (recipe follows on facing page)
    1 tablespoon olive oil
    3 medium onions, thinly sliced
  ½ teaspoon salt
    1 package (3½ ounces) goat
       cheese
    1 ripe medium yellow tomato
       (8 ounces), cut into ¼-inch-thick
       slices
    2 ripe medium red tomatoes
       (8 ounces each), cut into
       ¼-inch-thick slices
  ½ teaspoon coarsely ground black
       pepper
  ¼ cup kalamata olives, pitted and
       chopped

1. Preheat oven to 425°F. Prepare Pastry for 11-Inch Tart and use to line tart pan as directed. Line tart shell with foil; fill with pie weights or dry beans. Bake 15 minutes. Remove foil with weights. Bake until golden, 5 to 10 minutes longer. If shell puffs up during baking, gently press it down with back of spoon.
2. Meanwhile, in nonstick 12-inch skillet, heat oil over medium heat. Add onions and ¼ teaspoon salt; cook, stirring frequently, until very tender, about 20 minutes.
3. Turn oven control to broil. Spread onions over bottom of tart shell and crumble half of goat cheese on top. Arrange yellow and red tomatoes, alternating colors, in concentric circles over onion-cheese mixture. Sprinkle with remaining ¼ teaspoon salt and ground pepper. Crumble remaining goat cheese on top of tart.
4. Place tart on rack in broiling pan. Place pan in broiler about 7 inches from heat source. Broil until cheese has melted and tomatoes are heated through, 6 to 8 minutes. Sprinkle with olives.

■ Each serving: About 420 calories, 8 g protein, 33 g carbohydrate, 29 g total fat (15 g saturated), 54 mg cholesterol, 755 mg sodium.

Pastry for 11-Inch Tart

Tart pastry is a bit richer than pie pastry and bakes up crispier.

PREP *15 minutes plus chilling*
MAKES *enough pastry for one 11-inch tart shell*

1½ cups all-purpose flour
½ teaspoon salt
½ cup cold butter or margarine (1 stick), cut into pieces
2 tablespoons vegetable shortening
3 to 4 tablespoons ice water

1. In large bowl, combine flour and salt. With pastry blender or 2 knives used scissors-fashion, cut in butter and shortening until mixture resembles coarse crumbs.
2. Sprinkle in ice water, 1 tablespoon at a time, mixing lightly with fork after each addition, until dough is just moist enough to hold together.
3. Shape dough into disk; wrap in plastic wrap. Refrigerate 30 minutes or up to overnight. (If chilled overnight, let stand 30 minutes at room temperature before rolling.)
4. On lightly floured surface, with floured rolling pin, roll dough to 14-inch round. Ease dough into 11-inch tart pan with removable bottom. Fold overhang in and press dough against side of pan so it extends ⅛ inch above rim. Refrigerate or freeze until firm, 10 to 15 minutes. Fill and bake as directed in recipe.

Creamy Polenta with Sausage and Mushrooms

To keep this mixture creamy, prepare polenta just before serving.

PREP *25 minutes*
COOK *40 minutes*
MAKES *4 main-dish servings*

1 pound sweet Italian sausage links, casings removed
1 pound mushrooms, trimmed and sliced
1 medium onion, chopped
2 garlic cloves, finely chopped
¼ teaspoon coarsely ground black pepper
1 can (28 ounces) plum tomatoes in puree

Creamy Polenta
2 cups cold water
1 teaspoon salt
1½ cups yellow cornmeal
4½ cups boiling water
⅓ cup freshly grated Parmesan cheese
4 tablespoons butter or margarine, cut into pieces

2 tablespoons chopped fresh parsley leaves for garnish

1. Heat 12-inch skillet over medium-high heat until hot. Add sausage; cook, stirring frequently to break up sausage, until browned, about 10 minutes. With slotted spoon, transfer sausage to bowl.
2. Discard all but 1 tablespoon drippings from skillet. Add mushrooms, onion, garlic, and pepper; cook, stirring occasionally, until vegetables are golden and mushroom liquid has evaporated, about 10 minutes. Stir in tomatoes with their puree; heat to boiling over high heat, breaking up tomatoes with side of spoon. Return sausage to skillet. Reduce heat; cover and simmer 10 minutes.
3. Meanwhile, prepare Creamy Polenta: In 5-quart Dutch oven, combine cold water and salt. With wire whisk, gradually beat in cornmeal until smooth. Whisk in boiling water. Heat to boiling over high heat. Reduce heat to medium-low and cook, stirring frequently with wooden spoon, until mixture is very thick, 20 to 25 minutes. Stir Parmesan and butter into polenta until butter has melted.
4. Serve polenta topped with sausage mixture. Garnish with chopped fresh parsley.

■ Each serving: About 735 calories, 31 g protein, 64 g carbohydrate, 40 g total fat (18 g saturated), 108 mg cholesterol, 2,030 mg sodium.

expert tip

Even when there is nothing else in the house to eat, I always seem to have the ingredients to make Spaghetti with Walnuts. Cook 2 peeled and crushed garlic cloves in ¼ cup olive oil until golden. Remove the garlic and add 1 cup finely chopped walnuts and a pinch of salt. Cook until toasted, about 5 minutes. Toss the walnuts and oil with 1 pound cooked and drained spaghetti, ¼ cup grated Parmesan, and freshly ground black pepper. If available, add 2 tablespoons chopped fresh parsley or basil. Add a little of the cooking water if the pasta seems dry.

—Michele Scicolone
cookbook author

Grilled Chicken Breasts with Cumin, Coriander, and Lime

A Mexican-inspired blend of spices and fresh lime juice adds bold flavor to boneless chicken.

PREP **10 minutes**
GRILL **10 minutes**
MAKES **4 main-dish servings**

- 3 tablespoons fresh lime juice
- 2 tablespoons olive oil
- 1 teaspoon ground cumin
- 1 teaspoon ground coriander
- 1 teaspoon sugar
- 1 teaspoon salt
- ⅛ teaspoon ground red pepper (cayenne)
- 4 medium skinless, boneless chicken breast halves (1¼ pounds)
- 1 tablespoon chopped fresh cilantro leaves

1. Prepare grill. In large bowl, mix lime juice, oil, cumin, coriander, sugar, salt, and ground red pepper. Add chicken, turning to coat.
2. Arrange chicken on grill over medium heat and grill 5 to 6 minutes per side, brushing with any remaining cumin mixture halfway through cooking, until chicken loses its pink color throughout.
3. Transfer chicken to warm platter and sprinkle with cilantro.

■ Each serving: About 225 calories, 33 g protein, 2 g carbohydrate, 9 g total fat (1 g saturated), 82 mg cholesterol, 675 mg sodium.

✗ Sausage and Shrimp Gumbo

This gumbo gets full-bodied texture from okra and a flour-and-oil roux.

makes René choke

PREP **20 minutes**
COOK **40 minutes**
MAKES **6 main-dish servings**

- 1 pound hot Italian sausage links, pricked with fork
- 3 tablespoons vegetable oil
- ¼ cup all-purpose flour
- 2 stalks celery, chopped
- 1 green pepper, chopped
- 1 medium onion, chopped
- 1 can (14½ ounces) chicken broth
- ½ cup water
- 1 package (10 ounces) frozen whole okra
- 2 teaspoons hot pepper sauce
- ¼ teaspoon dried thyme
- ¼ teaspoon dried oregano
- 1 bay leaf
- 1 pound large shrimp, shelled and deveined (see box, right)
- 1 cup long-grain white rice, cooked as label directs

1. Heat 5-quart Dutch oven over medium-high heat until hot. Add sausages and cook, turning frequently, until well browned, about 10 minutes. Transfer sausages to plate to cool slightly. Cut each sausage into 3 pieces.
2. Discard all but 1 tablespoon drippings from Dutch oven. Add oil and heat over medium heat. With wooden spoon, gradually stir in flour until blended and cook, stirring constantly, until flour mixture (roux) is brown; do not let burn. Add celery, green pepper, and onion and cook, stirring occasionally, until vegetables are tender, 8 to 10 minutes. Return sausage to Dutch oven. Gradually stir in broth, water, frozen okra, hot pepper sauce, thyme, oregano, and bay leaf; heat mixture to boiling over high heat. Reduce heat; cover and simmer 15 minutes.
3. Add shrimp and cook, uncovered, until shrimp are opaque throughout,

shelling and deveining shrimp

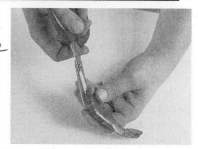

1. With kitchen shears or a small knife, cut the shrimp shell along the outer curve, just deep enough into flesh to expose the dark vein.

2. Peel back the shell from the cut and gently separate it from the shrimp. Discard the shell (or use to make fish stock).

3. Remove the vein with the tip of a small knife; discard. Rinse the shrimp under cold running water.

about 2 minutes. Discard bay leaf. Serve gumbo in large bowls with scoop of hot rice in center.

■ Each serving: About 490 calories, 28 g protein, 37 g carbohydrate, 25 g total fat (7 g saturated), 138 mg cholesterol, 955 mg sodium.

Niçoise Salad

As the story goes, the first niçoise salad was created in eighteenth-century France, and it's been a hit ever since.

PREP **35 minutes**
COOK **25 minutes**
MAKES **4 main-dish servings**

1 tablespoon white wine vinegar
1 tablespoon fresh lemon juice
1 tablespoon minced shallot
1 teaspoon Dijon mustard
1 teaspoon anchovy paste
¼ teaspoon sugar
¼ teaspoon coarsely ground black pepper
3 tablespoons extra virgin olive oil
1 pound medium red potatoes, cut into ¼-inch-thick slices
8 ounces French green beans (haricots verts) or regular green beans, trimmed
1 head Boston lettuce, leaves separated
12 cherry tomatoes, each cut in half
1 can (12 ounces) solid white tuna in water, drained and flaked
2 large hard-cooked eggs, shelled and each cut into quarters
½ cup niçoise olives

1. Prepare dressing: In small bowl, with wire whisk or fork, mix vinegar, lemon juice, shallot, mustard, anchovy paste, sugar, and black pepper until blended. In thin, steady stream, whisk in oil until blended.
2. In 3-quart saucepan, combine potatoes with enough water to cover; heat to boiling over high heat. Reduce heat; cover and simmer until tender, about 10 minutes. Drain.
3. Meanwhile, in 10-inch skillet, heat *1 inch water* to boiling over high heat. Add green beans; heat to boiling. Reduce heat to low and cook until tender-crisp, 6 to 8 minutes. Drain; rinse with cold running water. Drain again.
4. To serve, pour half of dressing into medium bowl. Add lettuce leaves; toss to coat. Line large platter with dressed lettuce leaves. Arrange potatoes, green beans, cherry tomatoes, tuna, eggs, and olives in separate piles on lettuce. Drizzle remaining dressing over salad.

■ Each serving: About 440 calories, 30 g protein, 30 g carbohydrate, 23 g total fat (4 g saturated), 140 mg cholesterol, 715 mg sodium.

Zucchini Ribbons with Mint

Making long, paper-thin strips of zucchini is an out-of-the-ordinary way to prepare it. If you don't have fresh mint, use parsley instead.

PREP **10 minutes**
COOK **4 minutes**
MAKES **4 accompaniment servings**

4 small zucchini (4 ounces each) or 2 medium zucchini (8 ounces each)
1 tablespoon olive oil
2 garlic cloves, crushed with side of chef's knife
½ teaspoon salt
2 tablespoons chopped fresh mint

1. Trim ends from zucchini. With vegetable peeler, peel long thin ribbons from each zucchini.
2. In 12-inch skillet, heat oil over medium heat. Add garlic and cook until garlic is golden; discard garlic. Increase heat to high. Add zucchini and salt and cook, stirring, just until zucchini wilts, about 2 minutes. Remove from heat and stir in mint.

■ Each serving: About 50 calories, 1 g protein, 4 g carbohydrate, 4 g total fat (0 g saturated), 0 mg cholesterol, 295 mg sodium.

Herbed Roasted Potatoes

Potato chunks tossed with parsley and butter cook into tender morsels when foil-wrapped.

PREP **15 minutes**
BAKE **30 minutes**
MAKES **6 accompaniment servings**

2 tablespoons butter or margarine
1 tablespoon chopped fresh parsley leaves
½ teaspoon freshly grated lemon peel
½ teaspoon salt
⅛ teaspoon coarsely ground black pepper
1½ pounds small red potatoes, cut in half

1. Preheat oven to 450°F. In 3-quart saucepan, melt butter with parsley, lemon peel, salt, and pepper over medium-low heat. Remove saucepan from heat; add potatoes and toss well to coat.
2. Place potato mixture in center of 24" by 18" sheet of heavy-duty foil. Fold edges over and pinch to seal tightly.
3. Place package in jelly-roll pan and bake until potatoes are tender when pierced with knife (through foil), about 30 minutes.

■ Each serving: About 125 calories, 2 g protein, 20 g carbohydrate, 4 g total fat (2 g saturated), 10 mg cholesterol, 240 mg sodium.

Vanilla Chiffon Cake

This tall, handsome cake doesn't need icing, just a dusting of confectioners' sugar and some fresh berries served on the side. The citrus variation is tart, so if you prefer your desserts on the sweet side, use ¾ cup orange juice and omit the lemon juice.

PREP **20 minutes**
BAKE **1 hour 15 minutes**
MAKES **16 servings**

2¼ cups cake flour (not self-rising)
1½ cups granulated sugar
  1 tablespoon baking powder
  1 teaspoon salt
  ¾ cup cold water
  ½ cup vegetable oil
  5 large eggs, separated, plus 2 large
    egg whites
  1 tablespoon vanilla extract
  ½ teaspoon cream of tartar
    confectioners' sugar

1. Preheat oven to 325°F. In large bowl, combine flour, 1 cup granulated sugar, baking powder, and salt. Make a well in center. Add cold water, oil, egg yolks, and vanilla; with wire whisk, stir until smooth.
2. In separate large bowl, with mixer at high speed, beat egg whites and cream of tartar until soft peaks form when beaters are lifted. Sprinkle in remaining ½ cup granulated sugar, 2 tablespoons at a time, beating until sugar has dissolved and egg whites stand in stiff, glossy peaks when beaters are lifted. With rubber spatula, gently fold one-third of beaten egg whites into egg yolk mixture, then fold in remaining egg whites until blended.
3. Scrape batter into ungreased 9- to 10-inch tube pan; spread evenly. Bake until cake springs back when lightly pressed with finger, about 1 hour 15 minutes. Invert cake in pan onto large metal funnel or bottle, and cool completely. Run thin knife around cake to loosen from side and center tube of pan. Remove from pan and place on serving plate. Dust with confectioners' sugar.

■ Each serving: About 215 calories, 4 g protein, 3 g carbohydrate, 9 g total fat (1 g saturated), 66 mg cholesterol, 265 mg sodium.

Citrus Chiffon Cake variation: Prepare as directed, but substitute *1 tablespoon freshly grated orange peel* and *1 teaspoon freshly grated lemon peel* for vanilla, and substitute *½ cup fresh orange juice* and *¼ cup fresh lemon juice* for cold water. In small bowl, combine *1 cup confectioners' sugar, 1 teaspoon freshly grated lemon peel, ¼ teaspoon vanilla extract,* and *about 5 teaspoons orange juice* to make a smooth glaze; spoon over cooled cake.

Tulipes

For an elegant presentation at a dinner party or other special occasion, serve your favorite ice cream in these delicate cookie shells.

PREP **30 minutes plus cooling**
BAKE **5 minutes per batch**
MAKES **about 1 dozen**

  3 large egg whites
  ¾ cup confectioners' sugar
  ½ cup all-purpose flour
  6 tablespoons butter, melted
    (do not use margarine)
  ½ teaspoon vanilla extract
  ¼ teaspoon salt
  1 quart ice cream or sorbet

1. Preheat oven to 350°F. Grease large cookie sheet. In large bowl, with wire whisk, beat egg whites, confectioners' sugar, and flour until blended and smooth. Beat in melted butter, vanilla, and salt.
2. Make 2 cookies at a time by dropping batter by heaping tablespoons, 4 inches apart, on prepared cookie sheet. With narrow metal spatula, spread batter to form 4-inch rounds. Bake cookies until they are golden around edges, 5 to 7 minutes.
3. Place two 2-inch diameter glasses upside down on surface. With spatula, quickly lift 1 hot cookie and gently shape over bottom of glass. Shape second cookie. When cookies are cool, transfer to wire rack. If cookies become too firm to shape, return cookie sheet to oven to soften cookies slightly.
4. Repeat Steps 2 and 3 with remaining batter. (Batter will become slightly thicker upon standing.) Store Tulipes in single layer in airtight container at room temperature. To serve, place on dessert plates and fill with ice cream.

■ Each serving with ice cream: About 190 calories, 3 g protein, 22 g carbohydrate, 11 g total fat (7 g saturated), 35 mg cholesterol, 155 mg sodium.

Chocolate Wows

After one bite of these decadent triple-chocolate, almost flourless cookies, you will understand why we call them "wows." They're elegant enough for a dinner party, sturdy enough for a child's lunch box.

PREP *20 minutes*
BAKE *15 minutes per batch*
MAKES *4 dozen cookies*

⅓ cup all-purpose flour
¼ cup unsweetened cocoa
1 teaspoon baking powder
¼ teaspoon salt
6 squares (6 ounces) semisweet chocolate, chopped
½ cup butter or margarine (1 stick)
2 large eggs
¾ cup sugar
1½ teaspoons vanilla extract
2 cups pecans, chopped
1 package (6 ounces) semisweet chocolate chips (1 cup)

1. Preheat oven to 325°F. Grease 2 large cookie sheets. In small bowl, combine flour, cocoa, baking powder, and salt.

2. In heavy 2-quart saucepan, melt semisweet chocolate squares and butter over low heat, stirring frequently, until smooth. Remove saucepan from heat and cool.

3. In large bowl, with mixer at medium speed, beat eggs and sugar until light and lemon-colored, about 2 minutes, frequently scraping bowl with rubber spatula. Reduce speed to low. Add cooled chocolate mixture, flour mixture, and vanilla; beat just until blended. Increase speed to medium and beat 2 minutes. With wooden spoon, stir in pecans and chocolate chips.

4. Drop cookie batter by rounded teaspoons, about 2 inches apart, on prepared cookie sheets. With small metal spatula, spread batter into 2-inch rounds.

5. Place cookie sheets on 2 oven racks and bake cookies 12 to 15 minutes, rotating cookie sheets between upper and lower racks halfway through baking, until tops are shiny and cracked. Let cookies remain on cookie sheets on wire racks 10 minutes to cool slightly. With wide spatula, transfer cookies to wire racks to cool completely.

6. Repeat with remaining batter. Store cookies in tightly covered container up to 1 week. Or, if you like, freeze cookies up to 2 months.

■ Each cookie: About 100 calories, 1 g protein, 9 g carbohydrate, 7 g total fat (3 g saturated), 14 mg cholesterol, 45 mg sodium.

chocolate and cocoa powder

We always use pure chocolate products and avoid artificially flavored compound (summer) coatings or premelted chocolate, which include large amounts of vegetable fats.

Unsweetened chocolate is simply ground cocoa beans. Professionals call it chocolate liquor. It's not very tasty on its own, so it is combined with sugar and other ingredients in recipes.

Bittersweet chocolate has been sweetened, but the amount of sugar varies greatly from brand to brand. Some bittersweet chocolates list the percentage of chocolate liquor on the label; a brand with 70 percent will be more bitter than one with 64 percent. Most European chocolate bars are bittersweet, and some bittersweet chocolate is now produced in the United States.

Semisweet chocolate is similar to bittersweet chocolate, although it is usually a bit sweeter. It is available in individually wrapped one-ounce squares and in bulk. It may be used instead of bittersweet chocolate.

Sweet chocolate, used to make German chocolate cake, is usually sold under a brand name and should not be confused with bitter- or semisweet chocolate.

Milk chocolate contains dried milk powder and a high proportion of sugar. It is essentially an eating chocolate—it's not usually used for baking.

White chocolate is not really a chocolate but rather a vanilla-flavored, sweetened cocoa butter (a by-product of chocolate processing), although some mid-priced brands substitute vegetable fat for the cocoa butter.

Unsweetened cocoa powder provides the rich chocolate flavor in many desserts. There are two kinds of cocoa powder: natural and Dutch-processed; check the label. In baking, the two are not interchangeable. They react differently when combined with baking soda or baking powder. However, for a cup of hot cocoa, you can use your favorite.

Natural cocoa powder, with its full, rich flavor, is the most common cocoa in American kitchens.

Dutch-processed cocoa powder (so named because the technique was developed in the Netherlands) has been treated with an alkali to mellow the cocoa's natural bitterness and to give baked goods a darker color.

Chocolate Cream Pie

Win friends and influence people with this indulgent pie. For pudding lovers, pour the hot filling into custard cups.

PREP **35 minutes plus cooling and chilling**
BAKE **10 minutes**
MAKES **10 servings**

    Chocolate Wafer Crumb Crust (recipe follows)
¾ cup sugar
⅓ cup cornstarch
½ teaspoon salt
3¾ cups whole milk
5 large egg yolks
3 squares (3 ounces) unsweetened chocolate, melted
2 tablespoons butter or margarine, cut into pieces
2 teaspoons vanilla extract
1 cup heavy or whipping cream chocolate curls, optional

1. Prepare Chocolate Wafer Crumb Crust as recipe directs.
2. Meanwhile, in heavy 3-quart saucepan, combine sugar, cornstarch, and salt; with wire whisk, stir in milk until smooth. Cook over medium heat, stirring constantly, until mixture has thickened and boils; boil 1 minute longer. In small bowl, with wire whisk, lightly beat egg yolks. Beat ½ cup hot-milk mixture into beaten egg yolks. Slowly pour yolk mixture back into milk mixture, stirring rapidly to prevent curdling. Cook over low heat, stirring constantly, until mixture is very thick or until temperature on thermometer reaches 160°F.
3. Remove pan from heat and stir in melted chocolate, butter, and vanilla until butter melts and mixture is smooth. Pour hot chocolate filling into cooled crust; press plastic wrap onto surface. Refrigerate until filling is set, about 4 hours.
4. To serve, in small bowl, with mixer at medium speed, beat cream until stiff peaks form; spoon over filling. Top with chocolate curls if desired.

■ Each serving: About 415 calories, 7 g protein, 38 g carbohydrate, 28 g total fat (16 g saturated), 171 mg cholesterol, 330 mg sodium.

toasting nuts

Toasting nuts brings out their flavor, and in the case of nuts such as hazelnuts, allows the skins to be removed.

To toast almonds, pecans, walnuts, or hazelnuts, preheat the oven to 350° F. Spread the shelled nuts in a single layer on a cookie sheet. Bake, stirring occasionally, until the nuts are lightly browned and fragrant, about 10 minutes. Toast hazelnuts until the skins begin to peel away. Let the nuts cool completely before chopping.

To skin hazelnuts, wrap the still-warm toasted nuts in a clean kitchen towel and let stand for about 10 minutes. Using the towel, rub off as much of the skin as possible (all of the skin may not come off).

Chocolate Wafer Crumb Crust

PREP **10 minutes**
BAKE **10 minutes**
MAKES **one 9-inch crust**

1¼ cups chocolate wafer crumbs (24 cookies)
4 tablespoons butter or margarine, melted
1 tablespoon sugar

1. Preheat oven to 375°F.
2. In 9-inch pie plate, with fork, mix wafer crumbs, melted butter, and sugar until crumbs are evenly moistened. Press mixture firmly onto bottom and up side of pie plate, making small rim.
3. Bake 10 minutes; cool on wire rack. Fill as recipe directs.

November

Thanksgiving, Your Way

In the GH Kitchen with Jean-Georges

Thanksgiving, your way

Three menus: Whether you go fancy with a traditional feast, choose healthy fare, or want a fast, last-minute holiday meal, we have the recipes to make it all easy.

Oyster-Corn Chowder

Oysters are traditionally included in the stuffing, but we made them the star of this delicious creamy chowder chock-full of corn and potatoes.

PREP **20 minutes**
COOK **about 40 minutes**
MAKES **about 10 cups or 12 first-course servings**

- 2 slices bacon, each cut crosswise in half
- 1 medium onion, finely chopped
- 1 pint shucked oysters (2 dozen), with their liquid
- 1 pound all-purpose potatoes (about 3 medium), peeled and cut into ¼-inch pieces
- 2 bottles (8 ounces each) clam juice
- 1 cup half-and-half or light cream
- 1 can (15 to 16 ounces) whole-kernel corn, drained
- 2 cups whole milk
- ¾ teaspoon salt
- ¼ teaspoon ground black pepper
- ¼ cup snipped fresh chives fresh chives for garnish

1. In 4-quart saucepan, cook bacon over medium-low heat until it's browned. Transfer bacon to paper towels to drain; coarsely crumble. Discard all but 1 teaspoon bacon fat from saucepan.

1 Traditional

MENU

Oyster-Corn Chowder
Sunchoke Relish
Holiday Roast Turkey
Succotash-Corn Bread Stuffing
Sautéed Brussels Sprouts & Shallots or Creamed Onions & Peas
Yukon Gold Mashed Potatoes
Sweet Potato & Pear Brûlée
Cranberry-Orange Sauce
Apple Pie
Pumpkin-Pecan Pie
Chocolate Truffle Tart with Hazelnut Crust

2. Add onion to bacon fat in saucepan and cook over medium heat 10 minutes or until tender and golden, stirring occasionally.
3. Meanwhile, drain oysters, reserving oyster liquid. If necessary, add enough *water* to equal ⅔ cup.
4. Add potatoes, clam juice, and oyster liquid to onion in saucepan; heat mixture to boiling over high heat. Reduce heat to medium-low; cover and simmer 10 minutes or until potatoes are tender. Remove saucepan from heat.
5. With slotted spoon, remove 1 cup solids from saucepan. In blender, puree solids with half-and-half until smooth.

6. Return puree to saucepan; stir in corn, milk, salt, and pepper. Heat mixture just to boiling over medium-high heat. Add oysters and cook 3 to 5 minutes or until oyster edges curl and oyster centers are firm, stirring frequently. Stir in crumbled bacon and snipped chives. Garnish each serving with chives.

■ Each serving: About 125 calories, 5 g protein, 16 g carbohydrate, 5 g total fat (3 g saturated), 1 g fiber, 23 mg cholesterol, 300 mg sodium.

Sunchoke Relish

Serve this as the centerpiece to your harvest relish tray: Arrange assorted olives, baby carrots, celery sticks, radishes, and cottage cheese on a platter and place it on the dinner table for guests to help themselves throughout the meal.

PREP *30 minutes plus chilling*
COOK *about 45 minutes*
MAKES *about 5½ cups*

1 pound sunchokes, well scrubbed and cut into ¼-inch dice
3 large celery stalks, cut into ¼-inch dice
1 large onion, cut into ¼-inch dice
1 small red pepper, cut into ¼-inch dice
1 cup cider vinegar
½ cup sugar
1 tablespoon dry mustard
1 teaspoon salt
⅛ teaspoon ground cloves

1. In 4-quart saucepan, combine all ingredients; heat to boiling over high heat. Reduce heat to medium-low and simmer, covered, 15 minutes, stirring occasionally. Uncover and simmer 25 minutes longer or until most of liquid evaporates, stirring occasionally.

2. Spoon into serving bowl; cover and refrigerate until well chilled, about 3 hours or up to 2 weeks.

■ Each ¼ cup: About 40 calories, 1 g protein, 9 g carbohydrate, 0 g total fat, 1 g fiber, 0 mg cholesterol, 110 mg sodium.

talking turkey

1 How do I figure out what size bird I need?

The rule is 1 pound of uncooked turkey per person. That gives you enough for everyone to have a generous serving, with leftovers for the weekend.

2 Should I buy a fresh or frozen turkey?

Truthfully, most people can't tell the difference. Fresh birds usually cost more per pound but are a boon for last-minute shoppers—defrosting a frozen turkey can take up to 4 days in the refrigerator. If you choose a fresh bird from the butcher, buy it no more than 2 days ahead. (Fresh turkeys in the supermarket are vacuum sealed and often carry expiration dates.)

3 How do I thaw a frozen turkey?

Place it, in its original wrapping, in a shallow pan on the bottom shelf of the refrigerator. Allow 24 hours per 5 pounds of turkey (a 20-pound turkey will take 4 days). If you don't have enough refrigerator space, place the frozen bird, in its original wrapping, in a large cooler or basin; fill the container with cold water, completely submerging the turkey. Change the water every half hour to maintain the cold temperature. Figure it will take at least 30 minutes per pound.

4 What's the deal on cooking stuffing in a turkey—is it safe or not?

A few years ago, consumers were advised to bake stuffing separately to be sure it cooked completely and didn't retain undercooked turkey juices. Now, experts agree that it is safe to stuff a turkey, as long as you test the stuffing temperature (it should be 165°F. in the center). You can make stuffing ahead of time, but refrigerate wet and dry ingredients separately and combine them right before adding to the bird. Don't pack the mixture tightly or it will take longer to cook; use ¾ cup per pound of turkey. Roast the turkey immediately after stuffing it. But if you really prize moist meat, bake your stuffing separately. New breeding practices produce turkeys with a higher percentage of white meat. Because it is leaner, it cooks faster than dark meat. With a stuffed turkey, you might end up overcooking the bird before your stuffing is ready.

5 What's the best roasting method?

Place turkey, breast side up, on a rack in a large roasting pan. To keep the meat tender, cover the turkey with a loose tent of foil for the first 2 to 3½ hours, depending on size; roast turkey in 325°F. oven until thigh temperature on meat thermometer reaches 175°F. and breast temperature reaches 165°F. (internal temperature will rise 5° to 10°F. upon standing). Remove foil during the last 1¼ hours of roasting time to brown turkey.

6 Do I need to baste?

We've found that it's not necessary; it doesn't make the meat juicier because most of the liquid runs off into the pan instead of going into the meat. But basting will produce a rich golden bird—and help crisp the skin.

7 How many hours should I cook a turkey?

	HOURS FOR UNSTUFFED	HOURS FOR STUFFED
8-12 pounds	2¾-3	3-3½
12-14 pounds	3-3¾	3½-4
14-18 pounds	3¾-4¼	4-4¼
18-20 pounds	4¼-4½	4¼-4¾
20-24 pounds	4½-5	4¾-5¼

8 How do I test the temperature of a bird?

Insert the tip of a meat thermometer into the thickest part of the thigh. Make sure that the pointed end of the thermometer is angled toward the turkey body but not touching any bone.

Holiday Roast Turkey

pictured on pages 194-195

If you want to stuff your turkey, make sure that the final stuffing temperature reaches a safe 165°F. Also, you will need to roast the bird about 30 minutes longer than called for in this recipe. As usual, we have decided not to stuff the turkey. We find that baking the stuffing separately yields a juicier bird because the total roasting time is reduced.

PREP **45 minutes**
ROAST **about 3¾ hours**
MAKES **14 main-dish servings**

```
1   fresh or frozen (thawed) turkey
     (about 14 pounds)
1½  teaspoons salt
½   teaspoon ground black pepper
½   teaspoon dried thyme
     Giblet Gravy or Port Gravy (at right)
     fresh herbs, fresh fruit, and
     grape leaves for garnish
```

1. Preheat oven to 325°F. Remove giblets and neck from turkey; reserve for making gravy.
2. Fasten neck skin to back with 1 or 2 skewers. With turkey breast side up, fold wings under back of turkey so they stay in place. If drumsticks are not held by band of skin or stuffing clamps, tie legs and tail together with string.
3. Place turkey, breast side up, on rack in large roasting pan (17" by 11½"). Rub turkey all over with salt, pepper, and thyme. Insert meat thermometer into thickest part of thigh next to body, being careful that pointed end of thermometer does not touch bone. Cover turkey with a loose tent of foil, letting top of thermometer poke through foil. Roast turkey about 3¾ hours; start checking for doneness during last hour of roasting.
4. While turkey is roasting, prepare giblet broth for either Giblet Gravy or Port Gravy.
5. To brown turkey, remove foil during last 1¼ hours of roasting time and baste with pan drippings occasionally if you like. Turkey is done when thigh temperature on meat thermometer reaches 175° to 180°F., drumstick feels soft when pressed with fingers (protected by paper towels), and breast temperature reaches 165°F. (Internal temperature of turkey will rise 5° to 10°F. upon standing.)
6. When turkey is done, place on large platter; cover with foil to keep warm. Complete Giblet Gravy or Port Gravy.
7. To serve, garnish platter with fresh herbs, fruit, and grape leaves. Serve with gravy. Remove skin from turkey before eating if you like.

■ Each serving turkey without skin or gravy: About 330 calories, 57 g protein, 0 g carbohydrate, 10 g total fat (3 g saturated), 0 g fiber, 150 mg cholesterol, 330 mg sodium.

■ Each serving turkey with skin: About 445 calories, 60 g protein, 0 g carbohydrate, 21 g total fat (6 g saturated), 0 g fiber, 174 mg cholesterol, 375 mg sodium.

Giblet Gravy

In 3-quart saucepan, heat *giblets* (do not add liver; broth may taste bitter), *neck, 1 medium onion,* cut in half, *1 celery stalk,* cut into 3-inch pieces, *1 carrot,* cut into 3-inch pieces, *1 bay leaf, 2 parsley sprigs,* and *4 cups water* to boiling over high heat. Reduce heat to low and simmer 45 minutes. Strain giblet broth into large bowl, reserving meat and broth. Pull meat from neck; discard bones. Coarsely chop neck meat and giblets. Cover and refrigerate meat and broth separately.

To make gravy, remove rack from roasting pan. Strain pan drippings into 4-cup glass measure or medium bowl. Add *1 cup giblet broth* to roasting pan. Place pan over medium-high heat and stir until brown bits are loosened and liquid boils; boil 1 minute. Strain liquid into drippings in measuring cup. Let stand 1 minute, until fat separates from drippings. Spoon

2 tablespoons fat from drippings into 2-quart saucepan; skim and discard any remaining fat from drippings. Add remaining giblet broth and enough *water* to drippings in cup to equal 3 cups total. (If you have any leftover giblet broth, save for use another day.)

Stir *¼ cup all-purpose flour* and *½ teaspoon salt* into fat in saucepan; cook over medium heat, stirring, until flour turns golden brown. Gradually stir in drippings mixture and cook, stirring, until gravy boils and thickens slightly. Stir in reserved giblets and neck meat; heat through. Pour gravy into gravy boat. Makes about 3½ cups.

■ Each ¼ cup gravy: About 55 calories, 5 g protein, 2 g carbohydrate, 3 g total fat (1 g saturated), 0 g fiber, 63 mg cholesterol, 130 mg sodium.

Port Gravy

Prepare Giblet Gravy as above but substitute *¾ cup tawny port wine* for giblet broth to deglaze roasting pan. Don't stir in reserved giblets and neck meat. Makes about 3 cups.

■ Each ¼ cup gravy: About 45 calories, 7 g protein, 1 g carbohydrate, 3 g total fat (1 g saturated), 0 g fiber, 3 mg cholesterol, 130 mg sodium.

Succotash-Corn Bread Stuffing

pictured on pages 194-195

We make our corn bread already bursting with succotash ingredients such as bacon, lima beans, and corn. To convert it into a delicious stuffing, just crumble and drizzle with chicken broth. If you like, bake up to two days ahead, then reheat in the oven with the turkey before serving.

PREP *about 55 minutes*
BAKE *about 40 minutes*
MAKES *about 12 cups*

- 4 slices bacon
- 7 tablespoons margarine or butter, melted
- 3 celery stalks, cut into ¼-inch dice
- 2 medium carrots, cut into ¼-inch dice
- 2 medium onions, cut into ¼-inch dice
- 1 package (10 ounces) frozen Fordhook lima beans, cooked
- ½ teaspoon dried thyme
- ⅛ teaspoon ground red pepper (cayenne)
- 1¼ teaspoons salt
- 2 cups yellow cornmeal
- 2 teaspoons baking powder
- 1 teaspoon baking soda
- 2 cups buttermilk
- 1 can (14¾ ounces) cream-style corn
- 4 large eggs, lightly beaten
- ½ cup chicken broth, warmed
  fresh thyme sprigs for garnish

1. In 12-inch skillet, cook bacon over medium-low heat until browned. Transfer bacon to paper towels to drain; coarsely crumble. Discard all but 1 tablespoon bacon fat from skillet.
2. Add 1 tablespoon margarine to bacon fat in skillet. Add diced celery, carrots, and onions, and cook over medium heat 20 to 25 minutes or until vegetables are tender and golden, stirring occasionally. Remove skillet from heat; stir in bacon, lima beans, dried thyme, ground red pepper, and ¼ teaspoon salt; set aside.
3. Preheat oven to 350°F. Grease 13" by 9" glass or ceramic baking dish or shallow 3½-quart casserole.
4. In large bowl, mix cornmeal, baking powder, baking soda, and remaining 1 teaspoon salt. Stir in vegetable mixture, buttermilk, corn, eggs, and remaining 6 tablespoons margarine until thoroughly blended. Pour batter into baking dish; spread evenly.
5. Bake corn bread 40 to 45 minutes or until toothpick inserted in center comes out clean.
6. Transfer dish to wire rack. With fork, break corn bread into large chunks; drizzle with broth. Garnish with thyme sprigs and serve. (If not serving right away, cool corn-bread chunks completely in dish on wire rack; cover and refrigerate up to 2 days. About 50 minutes before serving, preheat oven to 325°F. Cover dish with foil and bake 20 minutes. Remove cover and bake 20 minutes longer or until heated through and slightly crisp on top. Drizzle corn-bread chunks with broth as above.)

■ Each ½ cup: About 135 calories, 4 g protein, 17 g carbohydrate, 6 g total fat (1 g saturated), 2 g fiber, 38 mg cholesterol, 390 mg sodium.

Sautéed Brussels Sprouts & Shallots

pictured on page 195

To put a new spin on this holiday classic, we tossed the sprouts with luscious caramelized shallots. You can trim and quarter the Brussels sprouts a day ahead; then store in an airtight container in the refrigerator.

PREP *20 minutes*
COOK *about 25 minutes*
MAKES *about 7½ cups or 12 accompaniment servings*

- 1 tablespoon margarine or butter
- 3 large shallots, thinly sliced
- 3 containers (10 ounces each) Brussels sprouts, trimmed and each cut into quarters
- ¾ teaspoon salt
- ⅛ teaspoon coarsely ground black pepper

1. In nonstick 12-inch skillet, melt margarine over medium heat. Add shallots and cook, covered, until tender and golden, about 8 minutes, stirring occasionally. Reserve 1 tablespoon sautéed shallots for garnish.
2. Add Brussels sprouts, salt, pepper, and ¼ cup water to shallots remaining in skillet, and cook, covered, until Brussels sprouts are tender, 12 to 15 minutes, stirring occasionally. Top with reserved shallots to serve.

■ Each serving: About 55 calories, 2 g protein, 7 g carbohydrate, 2 g total fat (0 g saturated), 2 g fiber, 0 mg cholesterol, 180 mg sodium.

Creamed Onions & Peas

A comforting, old-fashioned side dish with a new twist—we call for lots of peas and just a few onions. If you want to get a head start on this, cook and peel onions and prepare the sauce the day before. Cover and refrigerate separately.

PREP *30 minutes*
COOK *about 25 minutes*
MAKES *about 6 cups or*
 12 accompaniment servings

1 container or bag (10 ounces) pearl onions
2 tablespoons margarine or butter
2 tablespoons all-purpose flour
½ teaspoon salt
¼ teaspoon dried thyme
⅛ teaspoon ground nutmeg
⅛ teaspoon ground black pepper
2¼ cups whole milk
2 bags (16 ounces each) frozen peas, thawed

1. In 12-inch skillet, heat *1 inch water* to boiling over high heat. Add onions; heat to boiling. Reduce heat to low; cover and simmer 10 to 15 minutes or until tender. Drain onions.

2. When cool enough to handle, peel onions, leaving base of root ends in place to help onions hold their shape.

3. Meanwhile, in 2-quart saucepan, melt margarine over medium heat. Stir in flour, salt, thyme, nutmeg, and pepper until blended, and cook 1 minute, stirring constantly. Gradually stir in milk and cook, stirring frequently, until sauce thickens slightly and boils.

4. Return onions to skillet. Add sauce and peas, and cook over medium-high heat, covered, until sauce boils and peas are heated through, stirring often.

■ Each serving: About 120 calories, 6 g protein, 15 g carbohydrate, 4 g total fat (1 g saturated), 4 g fiber, 6 mg cholesterol, 235 mg sodium.

Yukon Gold Mashed Potatoes

pictured on page 195

A simple and delicious dish flavored with the tang of buttermilk and fresh chives. Potatoes can be peeled and cut up to 2 hours ahead of time without discoloring if you keep them submerged in a bowl of cold water.

PREP *20 minutes*
COOK *about 25 minutes*
MAKES *about 10 cups or*
 12 accompaniment servings

5 pounds Yukon Gold potatoes (about 15 medium), peeled and cut into 1-inch chunks
4 tablespoons margarine or butter
1½ teaspoons salt
¼ teaspoon ground black pepper
1½ cups buttermilk
½ cup snipped fresh chives
 fresh chives for garnish

1. In 5- to 6-quart saucepot, place potatoes and enough *water* to cover; heat water to boiling over high heat. Reduce heat to low; cover and simmer 15 minutes or until potatoes are fork-tender. Reserve *½ cup potato cooking water*; drain potatoes.

2. Return potatoes to saucepot. Cook potatoes over low heat 1 to 2 minutes or until potatoes are dry, stirring constantly. Remove potatoes from heat. With potato masher, mash potatoes with margarine, salt, and pepper. Add buttermilk, reserved cooking water, and snipped chives. Mash until mixture is well blended; heat through over low heat. Garnish with chives.

■ Each serving: About 195 calories, 4 g protein, 36 g carbohydrate, 4 g total fat (1 g saturated), 3 g fiber, 1 mg cholesterol, 380 mg sodium.

best scrubbers for turkey day

Good Housekeeping INSTITUTE REPORT

Cleanup duty is no one's favorite part of Thanksgiving, but the right scrubber can make the chore a little easier. We put 12 pads to the metal, first baking sweet potatoes in a sticky glaze, removing them, and letting the glaze cook on for 10 more minutes. Then a trio of home-care staffers stepped up to the sinks and washed, noting each pad's cleaning speed, ease of use, and the number of pans it cleaned before disintegrating. **The winner:** Scotch-Brite Heavy Duty Scour Pad from 3M (75 cents). This flat, nonsoapy pad was the thickest and held up best; it could easily have gone on after our three-pan test. **Our second favorite:** soap-filled scrub pads, which are a bargain and work well but do fizzle faster than the nonsoap types. Most averaged roughly 1 pan per pad, though Scotch-Brite Never Rust Heavy Duty Wool Soap Pads from 3M (8 for 99 cents) were still going strong after 3 uses.

Third choice: plain copper mesh pads, although they required more muscle and were harder to grip. Our least favorite were scrub sponges (scrubber on top, sponge on the bottom). They weren't strong enough to handle our sticky mess (the abrasive side wore down quickly). Caution: These tough-stuff pads will scratch, so if your cookware is nonstick, choose a gentler version.

Sweet Potato & Pear Brûlée

pictured on page 194

This delectably different approach to sweet potato casserole is easy to prepare. If you don't have a food processor with a slicing disk, you can use a sharp chef's knife to thinly slice the main ingredients in no time.

PREP **20 minutes**
BAKE/BROIL **about 50 minutes**
MAKES **8 accompaniment servings**

½ cup packed dark brown
    sugar
½ teaspoon salt
¼ teaspoon ground cinnamon
2½ pounds sweet potatoes (about 3
    large), peeled and cut to fit your
    food processor feed tube
1½ pounds Bosc or Bartlett pears
    (about 3 medium), peeled, cored,
    and cut to fit your food processor
    feed tube
3 tablespoons margarine or butter,
    cut up

1. Preheat oven to 425°F. In small bowl, mix sugar, salt, and cinnamon.
2. In food processor with slicing disk attached, slice sweet potatoes and pears; transfer to large bowl. Toss potatoes and pears with margarine and 2 tablespoons sugar mixture.
3. In shallow 2½-quart glass or ceramic baking dish, place sweet potato mixture (don't worry if dish is filled to capacity). Cover dish with foil and bake 45 minutes or until potatoes and pears are fork-tender. Remove from oven and turn oven control to broil.
4. Remove foil and sprinkle remaining brown-sugar mixture on top. Broil, uncovered, 5 minutes or until sugar mixture is hot and bubbly.

■ Each serving: About 150 calories, 1 g protein, 31 g carbohydrate, 3 g total fat (0 g saturated), 3 g fiber, 0 mg cholesterol, 145 mg sodium.

food editor's Q&A

Q What's the difference between a turkey breast labeled hotel-style and one that isn't?

a Hotel-style breasts have whole wings attached and usually include portions of the back, neck skin, ribs, giblets, and neck. They're mainly sold in the Northeast. In our recipes we call for traditional breasts, which are available nationwide and come with no extra parts. The hotel-style breasts generally cost less per pound, are bigger (7 to 9 pounds compared to 4 to 8 pounds), and contain some dark meat. You can use the giblets to make gravy (as we did in our Holiday Roast Turkey, page 174).

Q What's wrong with my mashed potatoes? I made them in my food processor, but they were so gluey nobody would eat them.

a When potatoes cook, the starch granules inside them swell. Vigorous motion after cooking—such as the rapid spinning of a food processor blade—ruptures the delicate granules, resulting in a gummy mess. The best way to make mashed potatoes is to simmer the potatoes (never boil) with just enough water to cover until fork-tender, and then to mash them by hand with a potato masher, press them through a ricer, or beat on low speed with an electric mixer. For a step-by-step guide, check out our Yukon Gold Mashed Potatoes (facing page).

Q Which pears are best for cooking?

a Bosc and Anjou varieties are tops at holding their shape and texture; we love Boscs in Sweet Potato & Pear Brûlée (at left) and Spice-Roasted Pears (page 182). In a pinch, Bartletts and other varieties work fine, too. Avoid Comice pears for cooking. Their tender, juicy flesh tends to fall apart when baked whole or used in pies. Smaller pears such as Seckel and Forelle are fine for cooking but take longer to peel and core because of their size.

Cranberry-Orange Sauce

pictured on pages 194-195

This year, instead of reaching for the canned cranberry sauce, try this easy homemade version that's flavored with a touch of orange!

PREP **10 minutes plus chilling**
COOK **about 10 minutes**
MAKES **about 2½ cups**

2 large oranges
1 bag (12 ounces) cranberries
    (3 cups)
1 cup sugar
¼ teaspoon ground cinnamon
    orange-peel slivers for garnish

1. From oranges, grate ½ teaspoon peel and squeeze juice (add enough *water* to juice to equal 1 cup).
2. In 2-quart saucepan, heat cranberries, sugar, cinnamon, grated orange peel, and orange juice to boiling over high heat, stirring occasionally. Reduce heat to medium and cook, uncovered, 5 to 8 minutes or until most cranberries pop, stirring occasionally. (Mixture will thicken as it chills.) Spoon sauce into serving bowl; cover and refrigerate until well chilled, about 3 hours or up to 4 days. Garnish with orange-peel slivers.

■ Each ¼ cup: About 100 calories, 0 g protein, 26 g carbohydrate, 0 g total fat, 2 g fiber, 0 mg cholesterol, 1 mg sodium.

Apple Pie

Two varieties of apples instead of just one combine for a unique blending of flavors in this holiday favorite. Pop the apples into our favorite GH crust, made with a combination of butter for taste and shortening for flakiness.

PREP **1 hour plus chilling and cooling**
BAKE **1 hour 20 minutes**
MAKES **10 servings**

Piecrust
- 2¼ cups all-purpose flour
- ½ teaspoon salt
- ½ cup cold butter or margarine (1 stick), cut up
- ¼ cup vegetable shortening

Apple Filling
- ⅓ cup granulated sugar
- ⅓ cup packed brown sugar
- ¼ cup all-purpose flour
- ½ teaspoon ground cinnamon
- ⅛ teaspoon salt
- 1½ pounds Granny Smith or other tart cooking apples (4 medium), peeled, cored, and thinly sliced
- 1½ pounds Golden Delicious or Gala apples (4 medium), peeled, cored, and thinly sliced
- 1 tablespoon fresh lemon juice
- 1 tablespoon butter or margarine, cut up

Glaze
- 1 tablespoon milk or water
- 1 teaspoon granulated sugar

1. Prepare Piecrust: In large bowl, mix flour and salt. With pastry blender or 2 knives used scissors-fashion, cut in butter with shortening until mixture resembles coarse crumbs. Sprinkle *6 to 7 tablespoons ice water*, 1 tablespoon at a time, into flour mixture, mixing lightly with fork after each addition, until dough is just moist enough to hold together.

2. Shape dough into 2 disks. Wrap each disk in plastic wrap and refrigerate 30 minutes or until firm enough to roll.

3. Meanwhile, preheat oven to 425°F. and prepare Apple Filling: In large bowl, mix sugars, flour, cinnamon, and salt. Add apples and lemon juice; toss to combine.

4. On lightly floured surface, with floured rolling pin, roll 1 disk of dough into a 12-inch round. Ease dough into 9-inch pie plate; trim edge, leaving 1-inch overhang. Reserve trimmings. Spoon Apple Filling into crust; dot with butter.

5. Roll dough for top crust into 12-inch round. Using 2½-inch apple-shaped cookie cutter, cut out apple shape in middle of round. Center round over filling. Fold overhang under; bring up over pie-plate rim and pinch to make high decorative edge. From dough trimmings, with sharp knife, cut out two 1-inch leaves. Brush underside of leaves with water and arrange decoratively next to apple stem on top of pie. Cut several short slashes in top crust to allow steam to escape during baking.

6. Prepare Glaze: Brush crust with milk; sprinkle with sugar.

7. Place sheet of foil under pie plate; crimp foil edges to form a rim to catch any drips during baking. Bake pie 20 minutes. Turn oven control to 375°F.; bake 1 hour longer or until apples are tender when pierced with knife. If necessary, cover pie loosely with foil during last 30 minutes of baking to prevent overbrowning. Cool pie on wire rack 1 hour to serve warm, or cool completely to serve later.

■ Each serving: About 370 calories, 4 g protein, 53 g carbohydrate, 17 g total fat (8 g saturated), 3 g fiber, 30 mg cholesterol, 260 mg sodium.

Pumpkin-Pecan Pie

We added a crunchy sugared-pecan topping to this smooth and creamy holiday pie.

PREP **1 hour plus chilling and cooling**
BAKE **about 1¼ hours**
MAKES **10 servings**

Piecrust
- 1¼ cups all-purpose flour
- ¼ teaspoon salt
- 4 tablespoons cold butter or margarine, cut up
- 2 tablespoons vegetable shortening

Pumpkin Filling
- 1 can (15 ounces) pure pumpkin (not pumpkin-pie mix)
- 1 cup half-and-half
- ¾ cup packed dark brown sugar
- 2 tablespoons bourbon (optional)
- 1 teaspoon ground cinnamon
- ½ teaspoon ground ginger
- ¼ teaspoon ground nutmeg
- ¼ teaspoon salt
- 2 large eggs

Sugared Pecans
- ¾ cup pecan halves
- 2 tablespoons dark brown sugar
- 1 tablespoon butter (no substitutions)

1. Prepare Piecrust: In medium bowl, mix flour and salt. With pastry blender or 2 knives used scissors-fashion, cut in butter with shortening until mixture resembles coarse crumbs. Sprinkle about *4 tablespoons ice water*, 1 tablespoon at a time, into flour mixture, mixing lightly with fork after each addition until dough is just moist enough to hold together. Shape dough into a disk.

2. Preheat oven to 425°F. On lightly floured surface, with floured rolling pin, roll dough into 12-inch round. Ease dough into 9-inch pie plate; trim edge, leaving 1-inch overhang. Fold overhang under; pinch to form high fluted edge. With fork, prick bottom and side of pie shell at 1-inch intervals to prevent puffing and shrinking during baking. Refrigerate pie shell 30 minutes or freeze 10 minutes to firm pastry slightly before baking.

3. Line pie shell with foil and fill with pie weights, dried beans, or uncooked rice. Bake 20 minutes; remove foil with weights and bake 10 minutes longer or until lightly browned. Cool on wire rack at least 15 minutes. Turn oven control to 350°F.

4. Prepare Pumpkin Filling: In large bowl, with wire whisk, mix together all ingredients.

5. Pour filling into pie shell. Bake pie 45 to 50 minutes or until knife inserted 1 inch from edge of pie comes out almost clean (filling in center of pie will be slightly jiggly). Cool on wire rack. Do not turn oven off.

6. While pie is cooling, prepare Sugared Pecans: Place pecans on cookie sheet and bake 10 minutes or until lightly toasted.

7. In 1-quart saucepan, heat sugar with butter to boiling over medium heat, stirring occasionally. Add pecans to saucepan and stir to coat. Return pecans to same cookie sheet; arrange in single layer. Cool completely on cookie sheet on wire rack.

8. Refrigerate pie up to 1 day. To serve, coarsely chop pecans and sprinkle on top of cooled pie.

■ Each serving: About 245 calories, 4 g protein, 33 g carbohydrate, 12 g total fat (6 g saturated), 2 g fiber, 65 mg cholesterol, 195 mg sodium.

Chocolate Truffle Tart with Hazelnut Crust

This luscious dessert combines a fragrant hazelnut crust with a rich and silky chocolate ganache filling.

PREP *about 45 minutes plus chilling and cooling*
BAKE *about 1 hour*
MAKES *12 servings*

Hazelnut Crust
½ cup hazelnuts
2 tablespoons sugar
1¼ cups all-purpose flour
½ teaspoon salt
½ cup cold butter (no substitutions)

Chocolate Filling
7 ounces semisweet chocolate
1 ounce unsweetened chocolate
4 tablespoons butter (no substitutions)
⅓ cup sugar
1 teaspoon vanilla extract
pinch salt
⅔ cup plus ½ cup heavy or whipping cream
3 large eggs

1. Prepare Hazelnut Crust: Preheat oven to 375°F. Place hazelnuts in 9" by 9" metal baking pan. Bake 10 to 15 minutes or until lightly toasted. To remove skins, wrap hot hazelnuts in clean cloth towel and let stand 10 minutes. With hands, roll hazelnuts back and forth until most of skins come off. Discard skins and cool nuts completely.

2. Turn oven control to 425°F. Reserve 8 whole hazelnuts for garnish. In food processor with knife blade attached, blend remaining hazelnuts with sugar until finely ground. Add flour and salt to nut mixture and pulse to blend. Add butter and pulse just until mixture resembles coarse crumbs. With processor running, add about *4 tablespoons ice water,* 1 tablespoon at a time, stopping just before dough forms a ball. Shape dough into

a disk; wrap in plastic wrap and refrigerate 30 minutes.

3. On lightly floured surface, with floured rolling pin, roll dough into 14-inch round. Ease dough round into 11" by 1" round tart pan with removable bottom. Fold overhang in and press against side of tart pan to form a rim ⅛ inch above edge of pan. Refrigerate tart shell 30 minutes or freeze 10 minutes to firm pastry slightly before baking.

4. Line tart shell with foil and fill with pie weights, dried beans, or uncooked rice. Bake tart shell 20 minutes; remove foil with weights and bake 8 to 10 minutes longer or until golden. Cool on wire rack. Turn oven control to 350°F.

5. Meanwhile, prepare Chocolate Filling: In heavy 3-quart saucepan, melt chocolates and butter over low heat, stirring frequently. Stir in sugar, vanilla, and salt until well blended; remove pan from heat. In small bowl, with fork or wire whisk, lightly beat ⅔ cup cream with eggs. Gradually whisk cream mixture into chocolate mixture.

6. Pour chocolate mixture into tart shell. Bake 15 to 17 minutes or until custard is just set (center will appear jiggly). Cool on wire rack. Serve at room temperature or refrigerate up to 1 day.

7. If refrigerated, let tart stand at room temperature 1 hour to soften before serving. In small bowl, with mixer at medium speed, beat remaining ½ cup cream until stiff peaks form. Spoon 8 dollops of whipped cream around edge of tart; top each with a reserved hazelnut.

■ Each serving: About 415 calories, 6 g protein, 29 g carbohydrate, 32 g total fat (17 g saturated), 2 g fiber, 118 mg cholesterol, 260 mg sodium.

2 Lighter Fare

Vegetable Soup with Bow Ties & Dill

Chicken broth brimming with vegetables and tiny pasta is seasoned with a hint of lemon and fresh dill—a perfect beginning to a light feast!

PREP **25 minutes**
COOK **about 30 minutes**
MAKES **about 9 cups or**
8 first-course servings

- 1 lemon
- 1 tablespoon olive oil
- 1 large shallot, finely chopped
- 4 medium carrots, each cut lengthwise into quarters, then thinly sliced crosswise
- 2 medium celery stalks, thinly sliced
- 1 can (48 ounces) fat-free chicken broth (6 cups)
- 1 package (10 ounces) frozen peas
- ¾ cup small bow-tie pasta, cooked
- 3 tablespoons chopped fresh dill
- ⅛ teaspoon ground black pepper

1. With vegetable peeler or small knife, remove 3" by 1" strip of peel from lemon; squeeze 1 tablespoon juice.
2. In nonstick 5- to 6-quart saucepot, heat oil over medium-high heat. Add shallot and cook 2 minutes or until golden, stirring frequently. Add carrots and celery, and cook 5 minutes or until tender-crisp, stirring occasionally.
3. Add broth, lemon peel, and *1 cup water* to saucepot; heat to boiling over medium-high heat. Reduce heat to low; cover and simmer 10 minutes or until vegetables are tender.
4. Remove cover; stir in frozen peas and cook 1 minute longer. Stir in cooked pasta, dill, pepper, and lemon juice; heat through.

■ Each serving: About 120 calories, 5 g protein, 17 g carbohydrate, 2 g total fat (1 g saturated), 3 g fiber, 0 mg cholesterol, 770 mg sodium.

Turkey Breast with Roasted Vegetable Gravy

pictured on page 196

We slimmed down this Thanksgiving centerpiece by serving a skinless turkey breast, degreasing the drippings, and thickening the gravy with vegetables.

PREP **40 minutes**
ROAST **about 2 hours**
MAKES **8 main-dish servings**

- 1 fresh or frozen (thawed) bone-in turkey breast (about 6 pounds)
- ½ teaspoon salt
- ¼ teaspoon ground black pepper
- 2 medium onions, each cut into quarters
- 2 celery stalks, cut into 3-inch pieces
- 2 carrots, peeled and cut into 3-inch pieces
- 3 garlic cloves, peeled
- ½ teaspoon dried thyme
- 1 can (14½ ounces) chicken broth
  fresh herbs for garnish

1. Preheat oven to 350°F. Place turkey breast, skin side up, on rack in small roasting pan (14" by 10"). Rub turkey with salt and pepper. Insert meat thermometer into center of breast, being careful that pointed end of thermometer does not touch bone.
2. Scatter onions, celery, carrots, garlic, and thyme around turkey in roasting pan. Cover turkey with a loose tent of foil, letting top of thermometer poke through. Roast turkey 1 hour. Remove foil and roast 1 hour to 1 hour and 15 minutes longer, or until temperature on meat thermometer reaches 165°F. (Internal temperature of turkey breast will rise 5° to 10°F. upon standing.) When turkey is done, place on large platter; cover with foil to keep warm.
3. Meanwhile, prepare gravy: Remove rack from roasting pan. Pour vegetables and drippings into sieve set over 4-cup liquid measure or medium bowl; transfer solids to blender. Let juices stand until fat separates from drippings. Skim and discard fat from turkey drippings.
4. Add broth to roasting pan. Stir until browned bits are loosened. Pour broth mixture through sieve into drippings in measuring cup.
5. In blender at low speed, blend reserved solids with drippings mixture and *1 cup water* until pureed. Pour pureed mixture into 2-quart saucepan; heat to boiling over high heat. Makes about 4 cups gravy.
6. To serve, remove skin from turkey. Serve sliced turkey with gravy. Garnish with herbs.

■ Each serving turkey without skin: About 285 calories, 63 g protein, 0 g carbohydrate, 2 g total fat (1 g saturated), 0 g fiber, 174 mg cholesterol, 255 mg sodium.

■ Each ¼ cup gravy: About 20 calories, 1 g protein, 3 g carbohydrate, 0 g total fat, 1 g fiber, 0 mg cholesterol, 125 mg sodium.

Rutabaga Mash

pictured on page 196

The mild turniplike flavor of rutabaga makes a nice addition to mashed potatoes and sweet carrots. If rutabaga is unavailable, you can substitute celery root, which will lend a pleasant celery overtone to the dish (see box at right).

PREP *30 minutes*
COOK *about 25 minutes*
MAKES *about 8 cups or
8 accompaniment servings*

2 rutabagas or celery roots (about 1¼ pounds each), peeled and cut into 1-inch chunks
1½ pounds all-purpose potatoes (about 5 medium), peeled and cut into 1-inch chunks
1 pound carrots, peeled and cut into 1½-inch pieces
¼ cup nonfat (skim) milk, warmed
2 tablespoons margarine or butter
2 tablespoons brown sugar
1¼ teaspoons salt
¼ teaspoon coarsely ground black pepper

1. In 5- to 6-quart saucepot, place rutabagas or celery roots, potato chunks, carrots, and enough *water* to cover; heat to boiling over high heat. Reduce heat to low; cover and simmer 20 to 25 minutes or until vegetables are fork-tender. Drain vegetables and return to saucepot. Cook over low heat 1 to 2 minutes or until any remaining liquid evaporates and vegetables are dry, stirring constantly.

2. With potato masher, mash vegetables in saucepot with milk, margarine, brown sugar, salt, and pepper until almost smooth (mixture will be slightly lumpy).

■ Each serving: About 170 calories, 4 g protein, 34 g carbohydrate, 3 g total fat (1 g saturated), 6 g fiber, 0 mg cholesterol, 450 mg sodium.

rooting for new vegetables

This holiday, go beyond sweet potatoes. These root vegetables will add color, flavor, texture, and nutrients to your spread and are at their peak season in November. Try rutabagas or celery root in Rutabaga Mash (at left) and sunchokes for our Sunchoke Relish (page 173).

RUTABAGAS

Buying tips Also called yellow turnip, wax turnip, and swede. Rutabagas should be large (1¼ to 1½ pounds) but not huge or heavy and without any decay or soft spots.

Store At cool room temperature (below 68°F.) or in the crisper drawer of the refrigerator up to 1 month.

To prepare Cut the rutabagas into quarters, then peel using a sharp knife. They are delicious mashed with milk and butter.

SUNCHOKES

Buying tips Also called Jerusalem artichokes. Buy firm sunchokes that are free from mold (an irregular shape is no problem).

Store In a plastic bag with a few holes poked in it. Keep in the crisper drawer of the refrigerator up to 2 weeks.

To prepare Scrub under cold running water. Peel and drop into cold water to prevent discoloration. Enjoy sunchokes raw in salad or tossed with olive oil and roasted at 425°F. for about an hour.

CELERY ROOT (CELERIAC)

Buying tips Choose firm, small (less than 4 inches in diameter) celery root knobs that are well shaped (the smoother the knob, the easier it is to peel). Avoid those with soft spots. If only large celery root is available, remove the center—it may be soft and woody.

Store In the crisper drawer of the refrigerator up to 5 days.

To prepare Scrub under cold running water. Use a small knife to cut away the peel and root end. If preparing ahead, place the cut celery root in a bowl containing 4 cups cold water and 2 tablespoons lemon juice or vinegar; set aside until ready to cook. Drain well. Serve raw (as a salad), boiled, or mashed (alone or with potatoes).

Creamy Green Bean & Golden Onion Bake

pictured on page 196

We were inspired by the popular green-bean casserole, but to keep it on the healthy side, we caramelized fresh onions and mixed up our own low-fat creamy mushroom sauce. We think you'll enjoy our version just as much as the original!

PREP *about 1 hour*
BAKE *30 minutes*
MAKES *10 cups or*
        8 accompaniment servings

2½ pounds green beans, trimmed and each cut diagonally in thirds
 1 tablespoon olive oil
 2 medium onions, each cut into quarters and thinly sliced
 1 tablespoon margarine or butter
 2 medium celery stalks, finely chopped
 1 package (12 ounces) sliced mushrooms
 1 can (14½ ounces) chicken broth (1¾ cups)
 1 cup nonfat (skim) milk
 2 tablespoons cornstarch
¾ teaspoon salt
¼ teaspoon dried thyme
⅛ teaspoon ground black pepper

1. In 5- to 6-quart saucepot, heat *3 quarts water* to boiling. Add green beans and cook 10 minutes or until tender. Drain beans and return to saucepot.
2. Meanwhile, in nonstick 12-inch skillet, heat oil over medium heat until hot. Add onions and cook, covered, 20 minutes or until tender and golden, stirring occasionally. Transfer onions to small bowl; set aside.
3. In same skillet, melt margarine over medium-high heat. Add celery and cook 5 minutes, stirring occasionally.

Add mushrooms and cook 13 to 15 minutes or until tender and golden, stirring occasionally.
4. In medium bowl, whisk broth, milk, cornstarch, salt, thyme, and black pepper until blended. Stir cornstarch mixture into vegetables in skillet and heat to boiling. Boil 1 minute, stirring.
5. Add mushroom sauce and half of caramelized onions to green beans in saucepot and toss until evenly mixed. Transfer mixture to shallow 2½-quart glass or ceramic baking dish; scatter remaining onions on top. If not baking right away, cover and refrigerate up to 1 day.
6. To serve, preheat oven to 400°F. Bake bean casserole, covered, 30 to 40 minutes or until hot.

■ Each serving: About 120 calories, 6 g protein, 18 g carbohydrate, 4 g total fat (1 g saturated), 6 g fiber, 1 mg cholesterol, 485 mg sodium.

Acorn Squash with Maple Glaze

pictured on page 196

For a low-fat side dish, we flavor baked winter squash with a simple glaze of pure maple syrup and a dash of cinnamon. Do-ahead tip: Bake squash in the morning, then reheat in the microwave or regular oven just before serving.

PREP *15 minutes*
BAKE *about 30 minutes*
MAKES *8 accompaniment servings*

 2 large acorn squashes (about 1½ pounds each)
½ cup pure maple syrup
½ teaspoon salt
¼ teaspoon ground cinnamon

1. Preheat oven to 450°F. Cut each squash lengthwise in half; discard seeds. Cut each half lengthwise into 2 wedges. In liquid measuring cup,

combine maple syrup, salt, cinnamon, and *2 tablespoons water.*
2. Place squash wedges, flesh side down, in 15½" by 10½" jelly-roll pan. Pour maple-syrup mixture over wedges. Cover pan with foil and bake 30 to 40 minutes or until tender, turning wedges over once halfway through baking.
3. To serve, place squash on platter; drizzle with any maple glaze remaining in jelly-roll pan.

■ Each serving: About 105 calories, 1 g protein, 28 g carbohydrate, 0 g total fat, 3 g fiber, 0 mg cholesterol, 150 mg sodium.

Spice-Roasted Pears

pictured on page 197

An unexpectedly delicious finale to your holiday menu that's as easy to make as it is good for you. Make it a day ahead and reheat it to serve, if you'd like.

PREP *30 minutes*
BAKE *about 40 minutes*
MAKES *8 servings*

 1 large lemon
 8 firm Bosc pears
 2 teaspoons plus ⅓ cup sugar
 1 cup apple cider
 2 cinnamon sticks (each 3 inches long)
 6 whole cloves
 2 tablespoons butter or margarine, melted

1. Preheat oven to 450°F. With vegetable peeler or small knife, remove peel from lemon in 3" by ¾" strips; discard white pith and squeeze juice from lemon.
2. With melon baller or knife, remove cores from bottom of unpeeled pears but do not remove stems. With pastry brush, brush insides of pears with lemon juice, then sprinkle insides with a total of 2 teaspoons sugar.

3. In shallow 2-quart ceramic or glass baking dish, mix lemon peel, cider, cinnamon, and cloves. Place remaining ⅓ cup sugar on waxed paper.
4. With pastry brush, brush pears with butter, then roll in sugar to coat. Place pears, cored ends down, in baking dish. Spoon any leftover butter and any remaining sugar from waxed paper around pears in dish.
5. Bake pears 40 to 50 minutes or until fork-tender, occasionally basting with any syrup that forms in dish. Cool slightly to serve warm. Or, cool pears completely, cover baking dish, and refrigerate up to 1 day. Reheat in microwave to serve.

■ Each serving: About 165 calories, 1 g protein, 34 g carbohydrate, 4 g total fat (2 g saturated), 4 g fiber, 8 mg cholesterol, 30 mg sodium.

3 Last Minute

MENU
Harvest Salad
No-Cook Cranberry-Ginger Relish
Roasted Turkey Breast with Winter Vegetables
Bourbon-Glazed Baby Carrots
Steamed Broccoli with Buttery Herb Crumbs
Gingered Pear & Dried Fruit Crisp

Harvest Salad
pictured on page 199

A quick and easy first course of mixed greens tossed with a raspberry vinaigrette and dried cherries, then topped with blue cheese and roasted pumpkin seeds.

PREP *15 minutes*
MAKES *8 first-course servings*

- 3 tablespoons raspberry or balsamic vinegar
- 2 tablespoons olive oil
- ¼ teaspoon salt
- ¼ teaspoon ground black pepper
- 2 bags (10 ounces each) European-style salad greens
- ½ cup dried tart cherries
- 4 ounces blue cheese, crumbled (½ cup)
- ⅓ cup roasted, salted pumpkin seeds red and yellow cherry tomatoes for garnish

1. In large bowl, with wire whisk or fork, mix vinegar, oil, salt, and pepper until blended. Add salad greens and cherries; toss until evenly coated.
2. Arrange tossed greens on 8 salad plates; sprinkle each with cheese and pumpkin seeds. Garnish with cherry tomatoes.

■ Each serving: About 170 calories, 7 g protein, 11 g carbohydrate, 11 g total fat (4 g saturated), 3 g fiber, 11 mg cholesterol, 335 mg sodium.

No-Cook Cranberry-Ginger Relish
pictured on page 1

This easy, no-cook, no-fuss relish is sure to be a winner. You can prepare it up to four days ahead.

PREP *10 minutes plus chilling*
MAKES *about 3 cups*

- 1 bag (12 ounces) cranberries (3 cups)
- 1 medium Granny Smith apple, peeled, cored, and cut up
- 1 jar (12 ounces) seedless raspberry jam
- 2 tablespoons crystallized ginger, minced
- 1 tablespoon sugar
- ⅛ teaspoon salt

In food processor with knife blade attached, pulse all ingredients until cranberries are coarsely chopped. Spoon into serving bowl; cover and refrigerate until well chilled, about 3 hours or up to 4 days.

■ Each ¼ cup: About 110 calories, 0 g protein, 27 g carbohydrate, 0 g total fat, 2 g fiber, 0 mg cholesterol, 35 mg sodium.

Roasted Turkey Breast with Winter Vegetables

pictured on page 1

We've significantly streamlined the holiday meal by roasting the potatoes, parsnips, and onion alongside the turkey to make it a one-pan, low-maintenance process. If you are really pressed for time, buy a cooked turkey from the supermarket and roast the vegetables in an oven at 450°F. for about 40 minutes.

PREP **50 minutes**
ROAST **about 2 hours**
MAKES **8 main-dish servings**

Winter Vegetables

- 1 bag (28 ounces) baby red potatoes
- 1½ pounds parsnips, peeled and cut into 2" by 1" pieces
- 1 large onion, cut into 8 wedges
- 2 tablespoons olive oil
- 1 teaspoon salt
- ¼ teaspoon ground black pepper

Turkey Breast

- 2 garlic cloves, crushed with garlic press
- 1 tablespoon margarine or butter, softened
- 1 teaspoon grated fresh lemon peel
- ½ teaspoon dried thyme
- ½ teaspoon dried rosemary
- ½ teaspoon salt
- ¼ teaspoon ground black pepper
- 1 fresh or frozen (thawed) bone-in turkey breast (about 6 pounds)

Pan Gravy

- ⅓ cup all-purpose flour
- 2 tablespoons margarine or butter
- 1 can (14½ ounces) fat-free chicken broth (1¾ cups)
- ¼ teaspoon salt
- ⅛ teaspoon ground black pepper

fresh herbs for garnish

1. Prepare Winter Vegetables: If potatoes are large, cut each in half. Toss all vegetable ingredients together in large bowl to coat evenly.

2. Prepare Turkey Breast: In cup, mix garlic, margarine, lemon peel, thyme, rosemary, salt, and pepper.

3. Preheat oven to 350°F. With fingertips, gently separate skin from meat on turkey breast. Spread herb mixture on meat under skin.

4. Place turkey breast, skin side up, on small rack in large (17" by 11½") roasting pan; scatter vegetable mixture around turkey. Insert meat thermometer into center of turkey breast, being careful that pointed end of thermometer does not touch bone. Cover turkey with a loose tent of foil, letting top of thermometer poke through. Roast turkey 1 hour. Remove foil and roast 1 hour to 1 hour and 15 minutes longer or until temperature on meat thermometer reaches 165°F. (Internal temperature of turkey breast will rise 5° to 10°F. upon standing.)

5. When turkey is done, transfer vegetables to bowl and turkey to large platter; cover with foil to keep warm.

6. Meanwhile, prepare Pan Gravy: Remove rack from roasting pan. Skim and discard fat from drippings in roasting pan. Add *1 cup water* to roasting pan. Stir until browned bits are loosened; strain drippings through sieve into small bowl and set aside. In 2-quart saucepan, cook flour over medium heat until golden, stirring often, 8 to 10 minutes. Stir in margarine until it melts and flour is evenly moistened. Gradually whisk in broth, pan drippings, salt, and pepper until blended; heat to boiling over high heat, stirring frequently. Cook 1 minute or until sauce thickens slightly. Makes about 3 cups gravy.

7. To serve, pour any turkey juices from platter into gravy. Remove skin from turkey if you like, then carve. Serve vegetables and sliced turkey with Pan Gravy. Garnish with fresh herbs.

■ Each serving vegetables and turkey with skin: About 600 calories, 68 g protein, 28 g carbohydrate, 23 g total fat (6 g saturated), 6 g fiber, 169 mg cholesterol, 610 mg sodium.

■ Each serving vegetables and turkey without skin: About 455 calories, 66 g protein, 28 g carbohydrate, 8 g total fat (2 g saturated), 6 g fiber, 175 mg cholesterol, 575 mg sodium.

■ Each ¼ cup gravy: About 35 calories, 1 g protein, 3 g carbohydrate, 1 g total fat (0 g saturated), 0 g fiber, 0 mg cholesterol, 230 mg sodium.

what's my wine?

Whether you're serving the meal or bringing a bottle, you may choose red or white wine. "Both go well with turkey," says Leslie Brenner, wine expert and author of *The Art of the Cocktail Party* and *Fear of Wine*.

Best white wine choices are Chardonnay (for its rich flavor and supple texture) or Sauvignon Blanc (an elegant white). Warm, welcoming reds like Pinot Noir and Beaujolais are also excellent matches. And Brenner suggests giving Beaujolais Nouveau a whirl, but notes, "It's impossible to recommend particular ones until we taste them, and they're not released until later this month." Her suggestions, all between $8 and $15:

WHITE WINES
Sauvignon Blanc Markham; Simi; Kendall-Jackson Vintner's Reserve; Robert Mondavi Coastal
Chardonnay St. Francis; Fetzer Sundial; Chateau Ste. Michelle; Columbia Crest

RED WINES
Pinot Noir Robert Mondavi Coastal; Beringer Founder's Estate; Meridian; Louis Jadot
Beaujolais Georges Duboeuf Morgon; Louis Jadot Brouilly; Joseph Drouhin Beaujolais Villages; Jaffelin Beaujolais Villages; Beaujolais Nouveau from above producers.

Bourbon-Glazed Baby Carrots

pictured on page 1

You can whip up this tasty side dish in no time with packaged peeled and washed baby carrots.

PREP *5 minutes*
COOK *about 20 minutes*
MAKES *8 accompaniment servings*

  2 bags (16 ounces each) peeled baby carrots
  ¼ cup sugar
  2 tablespoons margarine or butter
  ½ teaspoon salt
  1 tablespoon bourbon

1. In 12-inch skillet, heat carrots and *1 cup water* to boiling over high heat. Reduce heat to low; cover and simmer 10 minutes or until carrots are tender-crisp. Drain; return to skillet.
2. Meanwhile, in 1-quart saucepan, cook sugar, margarine, and salt over medium-high heat 4 to 5 minutes or until sugar and margarine melt and turn golden, stirring frequently.
3. Add mixture to carrots in skillet; stir in bourbon (sugar mixture will harden). Cook over medium-high heat 7 to 10 minutes or until sugar mixture melts, carrots are tender and glazed, and liquid evaporates, stirring.

■ Each serving: About 95 calories, 1 g protein, 15 g carbohydrate, 3 g total fat (1 g saturated), 2 g fiber, 0 mg cholesterol, 225 mg sodium.

Steamed Broccoli with Buttery Herb Crumbs

pictured on page 1

Bags of broccoli flowerets make prep time a snap for this tasty side dish.

PREP *10 minutes*
COOK *about 15 minutes*
MAKES *8 accompaniment servings*

  1 lemon
  3 tablespoons margarine or butter
  4 slices bread, torn into ⅜-inch pieces
  1 garlic clove, crushed with garlic press
  ¼ cup packed fresh parsley leaves, chopped
  2 bags (12 ounces each) fresh broccoli flowerets
  ¼ teaspoon salt
  ⅛ teaspoon ground black pepper

1. From lemon, grate 1 teaspoon peel and squeeze 2 tablespoons juice.
2. In 12-inch skillet, melt 2 tablespoons margarine over medium heat. Add bread and cook until golden, about 8 minutes, stirring often. Stir in garlic, parsley, and lemon peel; cook 30 seconds. Remove skillet from heat.
3. Meanwhile, add about *¾ inch water* to wide-bottomed 5- to 6-quart saucepot. Place collapsible steamer basket (about 11 inches in diameter) in saucepot; heat water to boiling over high heat. Add broccoli to steamer basket; cover and steam 5 to 6 minutes or until tender-crisp.
4. Transfer broccoli to serving bowl; toss with salt, pepper, lemon juice, and remaining 1 tablespoon margarine. Sprinkle crumbs on top.

■ Each serving: About 95 calories, 4 g protein, 11 g carbohydrate, 5 g total fat (1 g saturated), 3 g fiber, 0 mg cholesterol, 220 mg sodium.

Gingered Pear & Dried Fruit Crisp

pictured on page 198

Dessert doesn't get much easier than this! Canned pears are mixed with chunks of dried fruit and a sprinkling of cinnamon, then topped with crumbled gingersnap cookies.

PREP *15 minutes*
BAKE *about 30 minutes*
MAKES *8 servings*

  2 cans (28 to 29 ounces each) pear halves in light syrup
  1 tablespoon cornstarch
  1 cup mixed dried fruit, cut into large pieces
  ¼ teaspoon ground cinnamon
  1½ cups gingersnap cookies (about 20 cookies)
  3 tablespoons butter or margarine
  2 tablespoons brown sugar
     fresh mint sprigs for garnish

1. Preheat oven to 400°F. Drain pears, reserving 1 cup syrup. With wire whisk, mix cornstarch into reserved pear syrup until blended. In shallow 2½-quart glass or ceramic baking dish, toss pears with reserved syrup mixture, dried fruit, and cinnamon until evenly mixed. Bake filling, covered, 15 minutes.
2. Meanwhile, in food processor with knife blade attached, blend gingersnap cookies, butter, and brown sugar until finely ground and evenly mixed. With fingertips, press cookie mixture into small chunks and scatter over pear filling.
3. Bake crisp, uncovered, 10 to 12 minutes longer or until filling is hot and bubbling and cookie topping is crisp. Spoon into dessert bowls; garnish with mint sprigs.

■ Each serving: About 270 calories, 2 g protein, 54 g carbohydrate, 6 g total fat (1 g saturated), 4 g fiber, 0 mg cholesterol, 185 mg sodium.

In the GH Kitchen with
Jean-Georges

Cookbook author and award-winning chef, Jean-Georges Vongerichten dazzles us with a (mostly) make-ahead dinner party.

Butternut Squash Ravioli
pictured on page 198

Jumbo ravioli are filled with a garlicky mixture of roasted butternut squash and creamy mascarpone cheese, then tossed with a brown-butter sauce just before serving.

PREP **40 minutes**
ROAST **45 to 50 minutes**
MAKES **8 first-course servings**

> 1 butternut squash (about 2 pounds)
> 2 garlic cloves, unpeeled
> 1 tablespoon olive oil
> 2 teaspoons fresh thyme leaves
> ½ teaspoon salt
> ¼ teaspoon crushed red pepper
> ¼ cup mascarpone cheese or sour cream
> 2 tablespoons grated Parmesan cheese
> ⅛ teaspoon ground nutmeg
> 1 large egg yolk
> 16 (3½" by 3½" each) wonton-skin wrappers*
> cornmeal for dusting
> 4 tablespoons butter (no substitutions)
> 1 tablespoon balsamic vinegar
> 1 tablespoon sherry vinegar
> pinch ground black pepper
> marjoram or thyme leaves for garnish

1. Preheat oven to 375°F. Cut ends from butternut squash; halve squash lengthwise. Remove and discard seeds; cut each half crosswise into 1-inch-thick slices; do not peel.

2. Toss squash, garlic, oil, thyme, salt, and crushed red pepper in 15½" by 10½" jelly-roll pan until evenly mixed. Arrange squash slices in single layer; roast 45 to 50 minutes or until squash is fork-tender. Set squash aside until cool enough to handle.

3. With spoon, scrape squash flesh from skins into medium bowl; discard skins. Squeeze garlic pulp into bowl with squash; discard skins. Add mascarpone, Parmesan, nutmeg, and seasonings remaining in jelly-roll pan to bowl. With potato masher or fork, mash mixture until blended and almost smooth.

4. In small bowl, beat egg yolk with *1 tablespoon water*. Place 1 wonton wrapper on work surface and brush with some egg mixture. Place 1 heaping

Instead of turning to heavy-on-the-cheese ravioli filling, Vongerichten loves to stuff tender pasta pillows with vegetables, from beets to mushrooms. For us, he whipped up a special mixture of golden squash, fragrant thyme, and a little scoop of mascarpone, the soft Italian cheese.

1. To start, roast the squash with a sprinkle of hot pepper and garlic.
2. Then mash in the cheeses and nutmeg.
3. Spoon fillings onto pasta sheets or wonton wrappers.
4. Use pastry wheel to cut pasta sheets into ravioli.
5. Serve with brown-butter sauce.

tablespoon squash filling in center of wrapper. Top with another wrapper; press edges together to seal in filling, pressing out any air pockets. Sprinkle ravioli lightly with cornmeal to prevent sticking, and place ravioli in waxed-paper–lined jelly-roll pan. Repeat with remaining wonton wrappers, egg mixture, and filling to make a total of 16 ravioli, placing waxed paper between layers. Cover and refrigerate up to 4 hours.

5. In 8-quart saucepot, heat *6 quarts water* to boiling over high heat. Add ravioli and cook 8 minutes or until cooked through.

6. While ravioli are cooking, in 1-quart saucepan, melt butter over medium heat and cook until butter is golden brown, about 4 to 5 minutes, stirring constantly. Remove saucepan from heat; stir in vinegars and black pepper.

7. With slotted spoon, remove ravioli, 1 at a time, from water and drain well. Place 2 ravioli on each of 8 plates; drizzle with brown-butter sauce. Garnish with marjoram or thyme leaves.

■ Each serving: About 195 calories, 4 g protein, 20 g carbohydrate, 12 g total fat (6 g saturated), 3 g fiber, 54 mg cholesterol, 330 mg sodium.

*Jean-Georges prepared his own ravioli dough. If you like, you can make your own or purchase fresh pasta sheets at some supermarkets or an Italian market. Depending on the size of pasta sheets, you may be able to make multiple ravioli from each sheet. Cut pasta sheets into 3½-inch squares, using sharp knife or fluted pastry cutter, then follow the recipe as above through step 4, substituting the pasta squares for the wonton wrappers. In step 5, cook ravioli 10 minutes or until cooked through.

Steak with Shiitake Mushrooms & Soy-Shallot Sauce

For full flavor, make the sauce base for these steaks a day ahead.

PREP *1 hour plus chilling overnight*
COOK *about 45 minutes*
MAKES *8 main-dish servings*

Soy-Shallot Sauce
1 bottle (10 ounces) reduced-sodium soy sauce (1⅓ cups)
4 garlic cloves, sliced
2 large shallots, thinly sliced
½ cup rice vinegar
2 teaspoons whole black peppercorns
1 tablespoon plus 1 teaspoon honey
½ cup cold unsalted butter (no substitutions), cut up
¼ cup fresh lime juice
¼ teaspoon ground black pepper

Shiitake Topping
2 tablespoons unsalted butter (no substitutions)
½ pound shiitake mushrooms, stems removed and discarded and caps cut into ¼-inch dice
2 tablespoons minced, peeled fresh ginger
3 packages (3.5 ounces each) enoki mushrooms, about 1 inch of tough ends cut off and discarded, caps and remaining stems cut into ¼-inch pieces
¼ teaspoon salt
⅛ teaspoon ground black pepper
1 bunch fresh chives, minced

Steaks
4 boneless beef top loin steaks, 1¼ inches thick (12 ounces each), each cut crosswise in half, or 8 beef tenderloin steaks (filet mignon), 1 inch thick (6 ounces each)
½ teaspoon salt
½ teaspoon ground black pepper
1 tablespoon unsalted butter

cooked baby beets, baby beet tops or watercress sprigs for garnish

1. Prepare Soy-Shallot Sauce: In 1-quart saucepan, heat soy sauce, garlic, shallots, vinegar, peppercorns, and honey to boiling over high heat. Reduce heat to medium; cook until mixture is reduced to 1½ cups, about 20 minutes. Cover and refrigerate sauce base overnight or up to 1 week. (Reserve cold butter, fresh lime juice, and ground pepper to complete sauce in step 4.)

2. Prepare Shiitake Topping: In nonstick 12-inch skillet, melt butter over medium-high heat. Add shiitake mushrooms and ginger, and cook about 8 minutes or until shiitakes are lightly browned, stirring frequently. Add enoki mushrooms, salt, and pepper, and cook 3 minutes or until enoki soften slightly. Stir in chives; transfer mushroom mixture to bowl.

3. Prepare Steaks: Sprinkle steaks with salt and pepper. In same skillet used to cook mushrooms, melt butter over medium-high heat. Add steaks and cook about 15 minutes for medium-rare, turning over once.

4. While steaks are cooking, strain sauce base through sieve into medium bowl; discard solids. Return sauce base to 1-quart saucepan and heat to boiling over high heat. Remove pan from heat. Whisk cold butter into hot mixture, 1 tablespoon at a time, until well blended; whisk in fresh lime juice and pepper.

5. To serve, place each steak in the middle of a dinner plate; spread steak with about ¼ cup Shiitake Topping. Pour about 3 tablespoons Soy-Shallot Sauce around each steak. Garnish with baby beets and baby beet tops or watercress sprigs.

■ Each serving: About 590 calories, 38 g protein, 13 g carbohydrate, 42 g total fat (20 g saturated), 1 g fiber, 146 mg cholesterol, 1,745 mg sodium.

Pavlova with Passion Fruit Sorbet

Jean-Georges used custom-made silicone molds to make his meringue spheres. We used a piping bag to form the meringue into similar-shaped shells. You can prepare the dessert through step 5 up to 2 days ahead.

PREP *1 hour*
BAKE *2 hours plus 1 hour drying*
MAKES *8 servings*

Meringues

    3 large egg whites
  ⅛ teaspoon cream of tartar
  ½ cup granulated sugar
  ½ cup confectioners' sugar

Filling and Topping

1½ cups heavy or whipping
      cream
    1 pint passion fruit sorbet
    4 ripe passion fruits, each
        cut in half, with seeds and
        pulp scooped out and
        reserved

1. Prepare Meringues: Preheat oven to 200°F. Line large cookie sheet with foil.
2. In small bowl, with mixer at high speed, beat egg whites with cream of tartar until foamy. Gradually sprinkle in granulated sugar, 2 tablespoons at a time, beating after each addition until sugar dissolves and whites stand in stiff, glossy peaks when beaters are lifted. Beat in confectioners' sugar just until blended.
3. Spoon meringue into large decorating bag fitted with large (about ⅜-inch) writing tip. Onto cookie sheet, pipe meringue into sixteen 2½-inch rounds, about 1 inch apart. Pipe remaining meringue on each round to make 1-inch-high rim.
4. Bake meringues 2 hours or until crisp but not brown. Turn off oven; dry meringues in oven 1 hour. Gently peel meringues off foil; cool completely on wire rack.

5. Prepare Filling and Topping: In small bowl, with mixer at high speed, beat cream until stiff peaks form. Place 8 meringue shells on cookie sheet. Scoop ¼ cup sorbet into each meringue; top with remaining meringues, rim side down. Spread whipped cream over desserts to cover completely, shaping each one into a sphere. Freeze desserts at least 30 minutes to firm or up to 2 days.
6. To serve, transfer pavlovas to dessert plates. Let stand 10 minutes to soften slightly. Drizzle with passion fruit pulp and seeds. Let guests crack top of meringues with spoon before eating.

■ Each serving: About 315 calories, 2 g protein, 34 g carbohydrate, 17 g total fat (10 g saturated), 1 g fiber, 62 mg cholesterol, 55 mg sodium.

Named for the Russian ballerina Anna Pavlova, this light-as-air dessert seals a dinner party with a kiss.
1. Scoop sorbet into baked meringue shell.
2. Top with another meringue shell.
3. Drizzle with passion fruit pulp and wow your guests.

a stoveside chat with jean-georges

He may be on the shortlist of top chefs, presiding over nine restaurants including New York City's hot Jean Georges (dinner, $85 to $115), but Vongerichten is surprisingly candid about his own less-than-haute tastes.

Earthy origins I grew up on fresh "peasant food" in Alsace, France. My family had a coal business. My grandmother, Mathilde, and my mother, Jeannine, cooked lunch for about 50 of the workers every day, and I would wake up to the smells of typical country fare such as choucroute, a savory sauerkraut dish.

Sweet triumph I learned to make my own kugelhopf—which is a sweet, light dessert bread—when I was eight, under the watchful eyes of my mom and grandmother.

Advice for home chefs The secret is to use whatever produce is in its peak season. Everything else is pure passion. You have to season with your senses.

What powers the pro My breakfast is usually granola with fresh fruit—berries, bananas, mango, whatever is in season. And a café latte (Grande) from Starbucks. And maybe once or twice a week, I stop at Krispy Kreme on my way to work. I like their original doughnuts.

Secret stash Chocolate. I like dark and milk—and little bars of Valhrona. For quick comfort, I love those packs of instant flavored Asian noodles.

That's toasty! I have 32 vintage toasters! I just love the smell of toast in the morning and started collecting them about 15 years ago. Now I receive at least one a year for my birthday.

Proudest moment When my peers voted me best chef of the year in 1998.

Steal his style In my latest cookbook, *Simple to Spectacular* ($45, Broadway Books), written with Mark Bittman, most of the ingredients I call for can be found in any supermarket. I don't like to fuss.

December

we gather together

One of the great comforts of the season is sharing with those we love. Whether you're inviting over a large group or just a few close friends, our menus—and tricks—make it all the breeze.

Open House

This year, set aside some time to enjoy your friends and family. Plan a trim-the-tree evening, a New Year's Day gathering, or a neighborhood get-together. Here's a menu that will appeal to both kids and adults. All the dishes may be made ahead, so you can visit with your guests.

Menu for 24

- ❖ Triple-Onion Dip
- ❖ Baked Brie with Lemon & Herbs
- ❖ Caraway-Brined Pork Loin
- ❖ Cranberry & Apricot Chutney
- ❖ Green Beans with Fennel, Mint & Oranges
- ❖ Roasted Vegetables
- ❖ Cabbage Salad Duo
- ❖ Toasted Barley Pilaf
- ❖ Baked Penne & Peas
- ❖ Kiddie Tea Sandwiches
- ❖ Caramel-Pecan Bars
- ❖ Cranberry-Cheesecake Fingers

GAME PLAN

Up to 1 month before party
Bake Caramel-Pecan Bars; wrap well and freeze.

Up to 4 days before party
Prepare Cranberry & Apricot Chutney and spoon into storage containers.

Up to 3 days before party
Make Triple-Onion Dip.

Up to 2 days before party
Trim and cook the beans for Green Beans with Fennel, Mint & Oranges. Toss beans with oranges, fennel, and dressing. (On party day, bring to room temperature to serve.)

Up to 1 day before party
1. Prepare Caraway-Brined Pork Loin through step 2 and refrigerate.
2. Assemble Baked Penne & Peas and refrigerate.
3. Cut red onions, carrots, parsnips, and red or yellow peppers for Roasted Vegetables; refrigerate vegetables in individual plastic bags. Separate and peel the garlic cloves; wrap and refrigerate.
4. Shred and mix the slaws for the Cabbage Salad Duo and place each in a self-sealing plastic bag, turning the bags occasionally to make sure dressings are well distributed.
5. Put together Toasted Barley Pilaf; refrigerate.
6. Prepare Baked Brie with Lemon & Herbs and wrap in foil to bake the next day.
7. Assemble Kiddie Tea Sandwiches. Layer with damp paper towels, wrap with plastic wrap, and refrigerate.
8. Last but not least, bake our irresistible Cranberry-Cheesecake Fingers—they should be refrigerated overnight for proper cutting and ease of serving.

Day of party, 3 hours before guests arrive
1. Roast vegetables; arrange on serving platter.
2. Roast pork loin; slice and arrange on platter.
3. Bake penne.
4. Bake Brie; arrange with fruit and crackers on platter.
5. Set out salads and sandwiches.

Triple-Onion Dip

Yellow and green onions and shallots are cooked until tender and sweet for this better-than-store-bought creamy dip. Serve with baby carrots and potato chips.

PREP *25 minutes*
COOK *about 12 minutes*
MAKES *about 3 cups*

- 1 tablespoon olive oil
- 1 large yellow onion, finely chopped
- 2 medium shallots, finely chopped (about ½ cup)
- 2 green onions, thinly sliced
- 1 teaspoon salt
- ½ teaspoon ground black pepper
- ½ cup (about half 8-ounce container) whipped cream cheese
- ¾ cup reduced-fat sour cream
- ¾ cup light mayonnaise
- 1½ teaspoons cayenne pepper sauce

1. In nonstick 12-inch skillet, heat oil over medium heat until hot. Add yellow onion and shallots, and cook, covered, 10 to 12 minutes or until tender and golden, stirring occasionally.

2. Wrap and refrigerate 1 tablespoon green onion for garnish. Add salt, pepper, and remaining green onions to skillet, and cook 2 minutes, uncovered, or until tender, stirring occasionally. Transfer mixture to bowl or plate; refrigerate until cool.

3. In medium bowl, whisk cream cheese, sour cream, and mayonnaise until blended. Add cooled onion mixture and cayenne pepper sauce; stir to blend. Cover and refrigerate up to 2 days if not serving right away.

4. To serve, spoon dip into decorative bowl. Sprinkle with reserved green onion.

■ Each tablespoon: About 30 calories, 0 g protein, 1 g carbohydrate, 3 g total fat (1 g saturated), 0 g fiber, 6 mg cholesterol, 90 mg sodium.

Baked Brie with Lemon & Herbs
pictured on page 236

Brie cheese is split and filled with parsley, thyme, lemon, and pepper, then baked until slightly runny and fragrant. Choose a whole medium-size wheel or a wedge from a larger one. The Brie can be assembled ahead through step 2 and refrigerated up to one day. When ready to serve, continue from step 3.

PREP *15 minutes plus cooling*
BAKE *15 minutes*
MAKES *24 appetizer servings*

- 1 cup loosely packed fresh parsley leaves, chopped
- 1 tablespoon fresh thyme leaves, minced
- 1 teaspoon grated fresh lemon peel
- ½ teaspoon coarsely ground black pepper
- 1 wheel (2.2 pounds) cold ripe Brie cheese (about 7½-inch diameter) or one 2-pound wedge
  apple wedges, grapes, assorted crackers

1. In small bowl, mix parsley, thyme, lemon peel, and pepper; set aside.

2. With long slicing knife, cut Brie horizontally in half. Remove top layer; sprinkle parsley mixture over bottom layer. Replace top layer, rind side up. Wrap Brie in foil.

3. Let wrapped Brie stand at room temperature 1 hour. Meanwhile, preheat oven to 350°F.

4. Place wrapped Brie on small cookie sheet and bake 15 minutes. Cool Brie on cookie sheet on wire rack 20 minutes. (If served hot, cheese will be too soft and runny.) Unwrap Brie and carefully transfer to serving plate. Serve with apple wedges, grapes, and crackers.

■ Each serving: About 140 calories, 9 g protein, 0 g carbohydrate, 12 g total fat (7 g saturated), 0 g fiber, 42 mg cholesterol, 265 mg sodium.

Caraway-Brined Pork Loin
pictured on page 193

Brining meat in an aromatic mixture of spices, sugar, and salt ensures succulence. For best flavor, allow pork to soak in brine up to 24 hours.

PREP *20 minutes plus chilling and marinating 18 to 24 hours*
ROAST *about 1 hour*
MAKES *24 main-dish servings*

- ½ cup packed light brown sugar
- ½ cup kosher salt
- ¼ cup caraway seeds, crushed
- ¼ cup coriander seeds, cracked
- 3 tablespoons cracked black pepper strips of peel from 2 lemons, pith removed
- 4 garlic cloves, crushed with side of chef's knife
- 2 boneless pork loin roasts (about 3 pounds each)

1. In 1-quart saucepan, heat *1 cup water* with sugar, salt, caraway, coriander, pepper, and lemon peel to boiling over high heat. Reduce heat to low; simmer 2 minutes. Transfer mixture to large bowl; stir in garlic and *7 cups cold water*. Refrigerate 1 hour or freeze 30 minutes until brine is cool.

2. Place roasts with brine in jumbo self-sealing plastic bag. Seal bag, pressing out excess air. Place bag in large bowl or roasting pan and refrigerate pork 18 to 24 hours.

3. When ready to cook pork, preheat oven to 400°F. Remove pork from bag; discard brine (it's OK if some seeds stick to pork). Place pork on rack in large roasting pan (17" by 11½"). Roast pork roasts 1 hour to 1 hour and 15 minutes or until an instant-read thermometer inserted into thickest part of pork reaches 150°F. (temperature will rise 5° to 10°F. upon standing). Transfer pork to cutting board and let stand 10 minutes to set juices for easier slicing.

4. Meanwhile, remove rack from roasting pan. Add *½ cup water* to pan; place pan over medium-high heat and cook 2 minutes, stirring to loosen browned bits. Pour pan drippings through sieve into small bowl. Let stand until fat separates from meat juice; discard fat. Spoon drippings over sliced meat.

■ Each serving: About 205 calories, 22 g protein, 1 g carbohydrate, 12 g total fat (4 g saturated), 0 g fiber, 68 mg cholesterol, 345 mg sodium.

Cranberry & Apricot Chutney

pictured on facing page

This wonderful alternative to cranberry sauce tastes like Christmas. Enjoy it, as we did, with the pork loin, or try it with roast turkey or baked ham. It's also great on sandwiches!

PREP *20 minutes plus chilling*
COOK *25 minutes*
MAKES *about 5 cups*

- 1 bag (12 ounces) cranberries (3 cups)
- 1 small yellow or red pepper, chopped
- ½ small red onion, finely chopped
- 2 cups apple juice or apple cider
- 1 cup packed light brown sugar
- ½ cup cider vinegar
- ½ cup dried apricots (4 ounces), cut into thin strips
- ⅓ cup golden raisins
- ⅓ cup crystallized ginger, chopped
- ½ cinnamon stick
- ½ teaspoon salt
- ¼ teaspoon crushed red pepper
  pinch ground cloves

In 4-quart saucepan, heat all ingredients to boiling over high heat. Reduce heat to medium and cook, uncovered, about 25 minutes or until mixture thickens slightly, stirring occasionally. Discard cinnamon. Spoon chutney into serving bowl; cover and refrigerate until well chilled, at least 3 hours or up to 4 days.

■ Each ¼ cup serving: About 100 calories, 1 g protein, 25 g carbohydrate, 0 g total fat, 2 g fiber, 0 mg cholesterol, 65 mg sodium.

Green Beans with Fennel, Mint & Oranges

pictured on facing page

Green beans and oranges combine for a colorful addition to your holiday table. Lemon and herbs highlight this crisp salad that serves as a refreshing counterpoint to the rich pork.

PREP *1 hour*
COOK *about 10 minutes*
MAKES *about 20 cups or
24 accompaniment servings*

- 2 lemons
  salt
- 2 pounds green beans, trimmed
- 1 cup packed Italian parsley leaves, chopped
- ½ cup packed fresh mint leaves, chopped
- ¼ cup olive oil
- ¾ teaspoon coarsely ground black pepper
- 4 navel oranges
- 2 large fennel bulbs (about 1¼ pounds each), trimmed and thinly sliced

1. From lemons, grate 2 teaspoons peel and squeeze ¼ cup juice; set aside.
2. In 5- to 6-quart Dutch oven, heat *2 inches water* and 1 teaspoon salt to boiling over high heat. Add green beans; heat to boiling. Reduce heat to low; simmer, uncovered, 5 to 7 minutes or until beans are tender-crisp. Drain beans; rinse under cold running water to stop cooking. Drain again and pat dry on paper towels.
3. Meanwhile, in small bowl, stir lemon peel and juice, parsley, mint, oil, pepper, and 2 teaspoons salt. Set dressing aside.
4. With knife, cut peel and white pith from oranges and discard. Holding 1 orange over a medium bowl to catch juice, cut out segments between membranes. Drop segments into bowl. Squeeze membranes to release any juice into bowl. Repeat with remaining oranges.

5. In large serving bowl, toss together green beans, dressing, fennel, orange segments, and orange juice. Serve at room temperature.

■ Each ¾ cup serving: About 60 calories, 2 g protein, 9 g carbohydrate, 3 g total fat (0 g saturated), 3 g fiber, 0 mg cholesterol, 240 mg sodium.

Roasted Vegetables

pictured on facing page

A savory medley of buttery parsnips, sweet peppers, and mellow onions roasted together for optimum flavor.

PREP *30 minutes*
ROAST *about 45 minutes*
MAKES *about 13 cups or
24 accompaniment servings*

- 3 large red onions, each cut into 12 wedges
- 2 pounds carrots, peeled and cut into 2" by 1" pieces
- 2 pounds parsnips, peeled and cut into 2" by 1" pieces
- 2 medium red or yellow peppers, cut into 1½-inch pieces
- 1 whole head garlic, separated into cloves and peeled
- 3 tablespoons olive oil
- 2 teaspoons salt
- ¼ teaspoon ground black pepper

1. Preheat oven to 475°F. In large bowl, toss vegetables with oil, salt, and pepper until evenly coated.
2. Divide vegetable mixture between two 15½" by 10½" jelly-roll pans or 2 shallow large roasting pans. Place pans on 2 oven racks and roast vegetables 45 minutes or until vegetables are tender and golden, rotating pans between upper and lower racks halfway through cooking time and tossing once.

■ Each ½ cup serving: About 65 calories, 1 g protein, 12 g carbohydrate, 2 g total fat (0 g saturated), 2 g fiber, 0 mg cholesterol, 210 mg sodium.

Clockwise, Caraway-Brined Pork
Loin, page 191; Green Beans with
Fennel, Mint & Oranges, facing page;
Baked Penne & Peas, page 202;
Toasted Barley Pilaf, page 202;
Cabbage Salad Duo, page 201;
Roasted Vegetables, facing page;
and Cranberry & Apricot Chutney,
facing page

Holiday Roast Turkey, page 174; Sautéed Brussels Sprouts & Shallots, page 175; Succotash-Corn Bread Stuffing, page 175; Sweet Potato & Pear Brûlée, page 177; Giblet Gravy, page 174; Cranberry-Orange Sauce, page 177; and Yukon Gold Mashed Potatoes, page 176

Turkey Breast with Roasted Vegetable Gravy, page 180; Acorn Squash with Maple Glaze, page 182; Rutabaga Mash, page 181; and Creamy Green Bean & Golden Onion Bake, page 182

Spice-Roasted Pears, page 182

Gingered Pear &
Dried Fruit Crisp,
page 185

Butternut Squash Ravioli,
page 186

Harvest Salad, page 183

Toasted Barley Pilaf, page 202

Baked Penne & Peas, page 202

Cabbage Salad Duo, facing page

Cabbage Salad Duo

pictured on facing page and page 193

A creamy green cabbage slaw is served alongside vibrant red cabbage tossed with a flavorful vinaigrette. Eaten together or separately, they're delicious and add a festive look to your holiday menu. You can make both salads ahead of time, but remember to refrigerate them separately. When it's party time, pull them out and serve them side by side.

PREP *50 minutes*

MAKES *about 28 cups or 24 accompaniment servings*

Red Cabbage Salad

½ cup cider vinegar
⅓ cup loosely packed fresh dill, chopped
¼ cup olive oil
2 teaspoons sugar
1 teaspoon salt
¼ teaspoon ground black pepper
1 medium head red cabbage (about 2½ pounds), thinly sliced, tough ribs discarded

Green Cabbage Salad

½ cup light mayonnaise
¼ cup reduced-fat sour cream
¼ cup cider vinegar
¼ cup loosely packed fresh dill, chopped
2 teaspoons sugar
½ teaspoon salt
¼ teaspoon ground black pepper
1 large head green cabbage (about 4½ pounds), thinly sliced, tough ribs discarded

1. Prepare Red Cabbage Salad: In large bowl, whisk vinegar, dill, olive oil, sugar, salt, and black pepper until blended. Add red cabbage and toss until evenly coated.

2. Prepare Green Cabbage Salad: In another large bowl, whisk mayonnaise, sour cream, vinegar, dill, sugar, salt, and black pepper until blended. Add green cabbage and toss until evenly coated.

3. If not serving right away, cover and refrigerate salads separately. To serve, arrange red and green cabbage mixtures side by side on large platter.

■ Each ¾ cup serving: About 70 calories, 2 g protein, 8 g carbohydrate, 5 g total fat (1 g saturated), 2 g fiber, 3 mg cholesterol, 195 mg sodium.

instant appetizers

When guests drop in, uncork the wine and serve a snack you can whip up in minutes. These are great for cocktail parties, too.

White Christmas Place an 8-ounce block of cream cheese or Neufchâtel cheese on a platter and top with a few spoonfuls of hot-pepper jelly, mango chutney, olive paste (olivada), or salsa. Surround it with olive oil, potato chips, crackers, and/or toasted raisin-nut or pumpernickel bread cut into triangles.

Little latkes Heat frozen mini potato pancakes; top with dollops of sour cream and sliced green onion.

Toasted almonds Spread whole natural nuts in a single layer on a cookie sheet; sprinkle with salt if you like. Bake at 350°F. for about 10 minutes or until lightly browned and fragrant, stirring occasionally. Serve almonds in a pretty bowl.

Greek platter Arrange baby carrots, celery sticks, toasted pita wedges, and assorted olives around store-bought hummus.

Gourmet grilled cheese In a skillet, prepare grilled Cheddar cheese sandwiches on raisin-nut or thick country bread. Cut each sandwich into eighths and serve with jarred chutney.

Dunking potatoes Stir minced garlic, capers, and lemon juice into light mayonnaise. Serve as a dip with oven-browned shoestring potatoes (sold frozen in bags).

Winter's-night goat cheese Coat a log of plain goat cheese with cracked black pepper and sprinkle with chopped roasted red peppers from a jar. Drizzle with extra virgin olive oil and serve with toasted, sliced French bread or water crackers.

Stuffed celery Toast chopped walnuts in a skillet for 2 minutes, until fragrant, shaking skillet often. Mix crumbled blue cheese and cream cheese until smooth. Spoon into celery sticks and sprinkle with nuts.

Hot popcorn Toss microwaved popcorn with Cajun seasoning mix or grated Parmesan cheese and ground red pepper (cayenne).

Mexican dip In a glass pie plate, layer store-bought bean dip, jarred salsa, sour cream, shredded Cheddar cheese, and sliced green onion. Serve with tortilla chips at room temperature or warm (microwave, lightly covered, on High for 1 minute).

Quick pinwheels Spread large plain or flavored flour tortillas with cream cheese and sprinkle with chopped pimiento-stuffed olives or sundried tomatoes. Roll up and slice crosswise into rounds.

Emergency pizza Spread an unsplit large pita bread with spaghetti sauce and top with shredded mozzarella or a sprinkle of Parmesan or Romano. Bake at 450°F. about 5 minutes, until cheese melts and pita is crisp. Cut into wedges.

Toasted Barley Pilaf

pictured on pages 193 and 200

Nutty whole-grain flavor is heightened by tangy dried cherries and rich toasted pecans for a wonderful wintertime accompaniment that holds up nicely on a buffet table.

PREP *25 minutes*
COOK *about 30 minutes*
MAKES *about 16 cups or*
     24 accompaniment servings

- 2 bags (1 pound each) pearl barley
  salt
- 2 cups pecans, toasted and chopped
- 2 cups dried tart cherries
- 2 bunches fresh parsley leaves,
  chopped (about 2 cups)
- 1 cup seasoned rice vinegar
- ⅓ cup olive oil
- ½ teaspoon ground black pepper
  fresh parsley sprigs for garnish

1. Preheat oven to 400°F.
2. In two 15½" by 10½" jelly-roll pans, toast barley 20 minutes or until fragrant and lightly browned, shaking pans occasionally.
3. In 5- to 6-quart Dutch oven, heat barley, *8 cups water,* and 2 teaspoons salt to boiling over high heat. Reduce heat to low; cover and simmer 30 minutes or until barley is tender and all liquid is absorbed.
4. Spoon barley into large serving bowl; stir in pecans and remaining ingredients except parsley. Serve warm or at room temperature. Garnish with parsley sprigs.

■ Each ⅔ cup serving: About 275 calories, 5 g protein, 43 g carbohydrate, 10 g total fat (1 g saturated), 8 g fiber, 0 mg cholesterol, 510 mg sodium.

Baked Penne & Peas

pictured on pages 193 and 200

This satisfying pasta dish is split between two pans—keep one on the table and the other, ready to serve, in the oven. If you want, prepare a day ahead, cover, and refrigerate. When ready to bake, cook for 35 to 40 minutes or until hot and bubbly, covering with foil if the top browns too quickly.

PREP *45 minutes*
BAKE *about 20 minutes*
MAKES *24 main-dish servings*

-   salt
- 2 packages (16 ounces each) penne
  or ziti pasta
- 4 tablespoons margarine or butter
- 1 large onion, chopped
- 2 garlic cloves, crushed with garlic
  press
- 2 cans (14½ ounces each) diced
  tomatoes
- 1 cup packed fresh basil leaves,
  chopped
- ½ teaspoon ground black pepper
- 3 tablespoons cornstarch
- 5 cups whole milk
- 1 cup heavy or whipping cream
- 2 cups grated Parmesan cheese
  (6 ounces)
- 1 bag (20 ounces) frozen peas

1. In 12-quart saucepot, heat *salted water* to boiling over high heat. Add pasta and cook as label directs, but just until al dente.
2. Meanwhile, in 5- to 6-quart saucepot, melt margarine over medium heat. Add onion and cook 10 to 12 minutes or until tender and golden, stirring occasionally. Add garlic and cook 1 minute, stirring. Add tomatoes, basil, pepper, and 2 teaspoons salt; heat to boiling. Reduce heat to medium-low and simmer 5 minutes, stirring occasionally.
3. In cup, with wire whisk or fork, mix cornstarch and ½ cup milk until blended. Pour cornstarch mixture,

cream, 1 cup Parmesan, and remaining milk into tomato mixture; heat to boiling over medium-high heat. Boil 1 minute or until sauce thickens, stirring often; set aside.
4. Preheat oven to 400°F. Place frozen peas in large colander and drain pasta over peas. Return pasta and pea mixture to 12-quart saucepot. Stir sauce into pasta mixture until combined.
5. Spoon pasta mixture into 2 shallow 3½- to 4-quart glass or ceramic casseroles or two 13" by 9" glass baking dishes. Sprinkle ½ cup Parmesan cheese on top of each casserole. Bake casseroles, uncovered, about 20 minutes or until hot and bubbly.

■ Each serving: About 300 calories, 12 g protein, 39 g carbohydrate, 11 g total fat (5 g saturated), 3 g fiber, 27 mg cholesterol, 615 mg sodium.

Kiddie Tea Sandwiches

Ideal finger food for the youngsters—crustless peanut butter and jelly, ham and cheese, and egg-salad sandwiches. We cut ours into rectangles, squares, and triangles for easy serving, but if you like, use cookie cutters to make fun shapes.

PREP *45 minutes*
MAKES *20 peanut butter and jelly,*
     20 ham and cheese, and
     16 egg-salad mini sandwiches

- 1 loaf (1 pound) very thinly sliced
  white or whole wheat bread
  (about 28 slices)
- 5 tablespoons creamy peanut butter
- 4 tablespoons grape jelly
- 8 tablespoons mayonnaise
- 5 slices ham (about 5 ounces)
- 5 slices American cheese
  (about 5 ounces)
- 2 large eggs, hard-cooked
- 1 teaspoon spicy brown mustard

1. Prepare peanut butter and jelly sandwiches: On 1 side of 5 bread slices, spread 1 tablespoon peanut butter. On 1 side of 5 more bread slices, spread 2 teaspoons jelly. Place peanut butter-topped slices facedown on top of jelly-topped slices. Cut off crusts from each sandwich, then cut each into 4 triangular mini sandwiches.

2. Prepare ham and cheese sandwiches: On 10 bread slices, spread about 1½ teaspoons mayonnaise. Top 5 mayonnaise-coated bread slices with 1 slice of ham and 1 slice of cheese. Top with remaining 5 mayonnaise-coated bread slices. Cut off crusts and cut each sandwich into 4 square mini sandwiches.

3. Prepare egg-salad sandwiches: In small bowl, with fork, mash eggs with mustard and remaining 3 tablespoons mayonnaise. Spread 2 tablespoons egg salad on 4 bread slices. Top with remaining 4 bread slices. Cut off crusts and cut each sandwich into 4 rectangular mini sandwiches.

4. Line tray with damp paper towels. Arrange sandwiches on top; cover with damp paper towels. Cover tray tightly with plastic wrap and refrigerate until ready to serve or overnight.

5. Just before serving, arrange on decorative platter.

■ Each peanut butter and jelly sandwich: About 60 calories, 2 g protein, 8 g carbohydrate, 2 g total fat (1 g saturated), 1 g fiber, 0 mg cholesterol, 65 mg sodium.

■ Each ham and cheese sandwich: About 85 calories, 4 g protein, 5 g carbohydrate, 6 g total fat (2 g saturated), 0 g fiber, 13 mg cholesterol, 260 mg sodium.

■ Each egg-salad sandwich: About 55 calories, 2 g protein, 5 g carbohydrate, 3 g total fat (1 g saturated), 0 g fiber, 28 mg cholesterol, 75 mg sodium.

the steak is in the mail

Is it worth splurging on mail-order steaks for a gift or a special holiday dinner? To find out, eight GH food experts sat down to a blind tasting of filet mignon. Without any bias from steak sauce or even a shake of salt or pepper, they sliced into the samples, purchased from seven mail-order companies. The results: Only two (the most expensive and—surprise!—the least costly of our seven) earned the tasters' kudos.

For an ultimate splurge, try Lobel's of New York. Tasters were unanimous in their praise for the prime steaks from this butcher on Manhattan's Upper East Side, where Jackie Kennedy Onassis bought her meat. Noting that the filets were so tender they could be cut with a fork, the panel gave them a perfect score for texture and high marks for beefy flavor. These were the only steaks shipped fresh, not frozen; the butcher house claims that in their vacuum-sealed plastic wrappers the filets will keep for a week in the refrigerator. But perfection costs a whopping $45 per pound, plus a hefty charge for mandatory overnight delivery. Lobel's of New York, eight 6-ounce filets, $134.95, plus $29.95 shipping; 1-877-783-4512 or www.lobels.com

For near perfection, tasters singled out the Kansas City Steak Company. The steaks had the requisite melt-in-your-mouth texture characteristic of good filet mignon. They also scored well on taste, with experts deeming them "delicious" and "buttery." Another plus: no fat around the edge. At $20 per pound, these are "an incredible bargain," the panelists concurred. Kansas City Steak Company, eight 6-ounce filets, $59, plus $12.75 shipping; 800-524-1844 or www.kcsteak.com

How to Cook a Perfect Steak

For a slab brown and crusty outside yet juicy inside, and tasting like it was grilled outdoors:

1. Preheat a seasoned cast-iron skillet over medium heat for 5 minutes until it's white hot.

2. Place steaks in skillet and cook about 6 minutes on each side for rare (135° F.), 8 minutes per side for medium (145° F.), and 10 minutes per side for well done (160° F.). Check temperature with an instant-read thermometer.

Caramel-Pecan Bars

pictured on page 4

We created these easy-to-make pan cookies—a delicious combination of caramel, melted chocolate, and pecans baked on a shortbread crust—based on the popular bite-size candies that resemble little turtles.

PREP *about 1 hour plus cooling and chilling*
BAKE *25 to 30 minutes*
MAKES *48 bars*

Cookie Crust
- ¾ cup butter (1½ sticks), softened (no substitutions)
- ¾ cup confectioners' sugar
- 1½ teaspoons vanilla extract
- 2¼ cups all-purpose flour

Caramel-Pecan Filling
- 1 cup packed light or dark brown sugar
- ½ cup honey
- ½ cup butter (1 stick), cut up (no substitutions)
- ⅓ cup granulated sugar
- ¼ cup heavy or whipping cream
- 2 teaspoons vanilla extract
- 1½ cups pecans, toasted and coarsely chopped

- 2 ounces semisweet chocolate, melted

1. Preheat oven to 350°F. Grease 13" by 9" metal baking pan and line pan with foil.
2. Prepare Cookie Crust: In large bowl, with mixer at medium speed, beat butter, confectioners' sugar, and vanilla until creamy, about 2 minutes. At low speed, gradually beat in flour until evenly moistened (mixture will resemble fine crumbs).
3. Sprinkle crumbs in prepared pan. With hand, firmly pat crumbs evenly onto bottom of pan. Bake crust 25 to 30 minutes or until lightly browned. Place on wire rack.

4. Prepare Caramel-Pecan Filling: In 2-quart saucepan, heat all filling ingredients except pecans to full rolling boil over high heat, stirring frequently. Reduce heat to medium-high; set candy thermometer in place and continue cooking, without stirring, until temperature reaches 248°F. or firm-ball stage (when small amount of mixture dropped into very cold water forms a firm ball that does not flatten upon removal from water).
5. Sprinkle pecans evenly over warm crust. Pour hot caramel over nuts. Cool in pan on wire rack 1 hour or until caramel is room temperature and has formed a skin on top.
6. With fork, drizzle melted chocolate over caramel layer. Cover and refrigerate until cold and chocolate is set, at least 1 hour.
7. When cold, transfer with foil to cutting board. Cut lengthwise into 6 strips, then cut each strip crosswise into 8 bars. Store bars in tightly covered container, with waxed paper between layers, in refrigerator up to 2 weeks or in freezer up to 3 months. Let bars stand at room temperature to soften slightly before serving.

■ Each bar: About 140 calories, 1 g protein, 16 g carbohydrate, 8 g total fat (4 g saturated), 1 g fiber, 15 mg cholesterol, 55 mg sodium.

Cranberry-Cheesecake Fingers

pictured on page 4

Save yourself some baking time the day of your party with these luscious make-ahead treats. After they chill at least 6 hours, they'll be ready to slice and serve. They are baked in a 13" by 9" baking pan—a great way to serve cheesecake to a crowd!

PREP *30 minutes plus cooling and chilling*
BAKE *about 50 minutes*
MAKES *48 fingers*

Crumb Crust
- 2¼ cups graham-cracker crumbs
- ½ cup butter or margarine (1 stick), melted
- 3 tablespoons sugar

Cranberry-Cheese Filling
- 2 packages (8 ounces each) light cream cheese (Neufchâtel), softened
- ¾ cup sugar
- 2 teaspoons grated fresh lemon peel
- 2 teaspoons vanilla extract
- 3 large eggs
- 1 can (16 ounces) whole-berry cranberry sauce

1. Preheat oven to 350°F. Grease 13" by 9" metal baking pan.
2. Prepare Crumb Crust: In bowl, with fork, stir graham-cracker crumbs, melted butter, and sugar until blended. With hand, press mixture evenly onto bottom of prepared pan. Bake crust 10 minutes. Cool crust completely in pan on wire rack.
3. Prepare Cranberry-Cheese Filling: In small bowl, with mixer at medium speed, beat softened cream cheese until smooth; gradually beat in sugar. Beat in lemon peel, vanilla, and eggs just until blended.
4. Pour cream-cheese mixture evenly over cooled crust. In small bowl, mix cranberry sauce with spoon to loosen. Spoon dollops of sauce over cheese mixture. With tip of knife, cut and twist through mixture to create marble design.
5. Bake 40 to 45 minutes or until toothpick inserted in center comes out almost clean. Cool completely in pan on wire rack. Cover and refrigerate at least 6 hours or overnight until firm enough to slice.
6. To serve, cut lengthwise into 4 strips, then cut each strip crosswise into 12 fingers.

■ Each finger: About 100 calories, 2 g protein, 11 g carbohydrate, 6 g total fat (3 g saturated), 0 g fiber, 26 mg cholesterol, 85 mg sodium.

An Elegant Dinner

Planning a dinner party for eight shouldn't be a frenzied experience for the host. For this festive menu, we've built in do-ahead tips so that anyone can breeze through it without a hitch.

Menu for 8

- ❖ Boston-Watercress Salad with Crab Cakes
- ❖ Cranberry-Port Wine Mold
- ❖ Black-Pepper Beef Roast with Shallot Sauce
- ❖ Horseradish Cream
- ❖ Potato & Gruyère Gratin
- ❖ Cauliflower & Brussels Sprouts with Tarragon Butter
- ❖ Baked Chocolate-Hazelnut Puddings

GAME PLAN

Up to 3 days before party

1. Make Cranberry-Port Wine Mold. Cover and refrigerate in the container. About 2 hours before dinner, unmold onto a platter (see box, page 206); return to fridge to firm up.

2. Mix the ingredients for Horseradish Cream; spoon into a tightly covered container.

Up to 1 day before party

1. Wash and spin-dry the greens for Boston-Watercress Salad with Crab Cakes. Store with a damp paper towel in loosely closed plastic bag. On the morning of the party, shape the crab cakes; keep chilled until ready to pan-fry.

2. Cut and trim the vegetables for Cauliflower & Brussels Sprouts with Tarragon Butter. Store each vegetable in separate plastic bags overnight in the refrigerator. If you like, premix the butter with the salt, pepper, and tarragon in a custard cup and refrigerate.

Night before party

Make Baked Chocolate-Hazelnut Puddings through step 5. Refrigerate the filled ramekins. Whip the cream and vanilla, and refrigerate.

Day of party

1. A few hours before guests arrive, assemble Potato & Gruyère Gratin; cover and set aside.

2. Prepare the roast, but don't bake.

3. Set up the vegetable steamer in a pot.

When guests arrive

1. Pop Black-Pepper Beef Roast into the oven once guests arrive. You won't need to check on it until just before it's ready to come out, in about 1 hour and 15 minutes.

2. Ten minutes after the roast goes in, put the gratin in the oven, so it's ready at the same time the meat is.

3. While the roast rests and gratin cools, steam vegetables and prepare the shallot sauce.

About half an hour before dessert

Put Baked Chocolate-Hazelnut Puddings into the oven. After dinner, serve them warm with dollops of chilled whipped cream, cups of steaming coffee, and an after-dinner liqueur.

Boston-Watercress Salad with Crab Cakes

pictured on page 237

With light and dark greens and tangy mustard vinaigrette, this lovely salad pairs perfectly with warm crab cakes.

PREP *20 minutes*
COOK *15 minutes*
MAKES *8 first-course servings*

Boston-Watercress Salad

- 2 heads Boston lettuce (about 8 ounces each), torn into bite-size pieces
- 1 bunch watercress, tough stems discarded
- 3 tablespoons olive oil
- 1 tablespoon seasoned rice vinegar
- 1 tablespoon Dijon mustard with seeds
- ¼ teaspoon salt
- ¼ teaspoon ground black pepper

Crab Cakes

- ½ cup light mayonnaise
- ¼ teaspoon salt
- ¼ teaspoon ground black pepper
- 1 large egg
- 1 pound lump crabmeat, picked over to remove any cartilage
- 3 tablespoons plus ⅓ cup plain dried bread crumbs
- 1 tablespoon olive oil

  lemon wedges

1. Prepare Boston-Watercress Salad: Toss lettuce and watercress in large bowl; cover and refrigerate until ready to serve.

2. In small bowl, whisk oil, vinegar, mustard, salt, and pepper until mixed.

3. Prepare Crab Cakes: In medium bowl, whisk mayonnaise, salt, pepper, and egg until blended. With rubber spatula, gently fold in crabmeat and 3 tablespoons bread crumbs just until combined. With hands, gently shape mixture into eight 1-inch-thick cakes.

4. Place remaining ⅓ cup bread crumbs on waxed paper. One at a time, coat crab cakes with bread crumbs. Cover and refrigerate crab cakes if not serving right away.

5. When ready to assemble, in nonstick 12-inch skillet, heat oil over medium heat until hot. Add crab cakes and cook 10 minutes or until cakes are golden brown on both sides and heated through, turning cakes over once.

6. Toss greens with dressing; divide among 8 plates. Place 1 crab cake next to salad on each plate. Serve with lemon wedges.

■ Each serving: About 220 calories, 14 g protein, 10 g carbohydrate, 14 g total fat (2 g saturated), 1 g fiber, 88 mg cholesterol, 535 mg sodium.

Cranberry-Port Wine Mold

pictured on page 234

A side dish for grown-ups, this jewel-like mold is beautiful and luscious. Garnish with kumquats, lemon leaves, and frosted cranberries for an eye-catching holiday favorite.

PREP *20 minutes plus chilling*
COOK *about 15 minutes*
MAKES *8 accompaniment servings*

- 1 lemon
- 3 cups cranberry-juice cocktail
- 1¼ cups sugar
- 4 whole allspice
- 1 cinnamon stick (about 3 inches long), broken in half
- 2 envelopes (¼ ounce each) unflavored gelatin
- 1 cup port wine
  pinch salt
  kumquats, lemon leaves, and frosted cranberries for garnish

1. From lemon, with vegetable peeler, remove 4 strips peel, about 3" by ¾" each; squeeze 3 tablespoons juice.
2. In 2-quart saucepan, heat cranberry juice, sugar, allspice, cinnamon stick, and lemon peel to boiling over high heat; boil 10 minutes.
3. Meanwhile, in small bowl, evenly sprinkle gelatin over port. Let stand 2 minutes to soften gelatin.

4. With slotted spoon, remove lemon peel and spices from cranberry juice and discard. Stir in gelatin mixture and cook over low heat 1 to 2 minutes until gelatin completely dissolves, stirring frequently. Stir in lemon juice and salt.
5. Pour gelatin mixture into 5- to 6-cup decorative mold. Cover mold and refrigerate 6 hours or overnight until gelatin is firm.
6. Unmold gelatin onto large round platter (see box, below). Garnish with kumquats, lemon leaves, and frosted cranberries. Cover and refrigerate up to 2 hours.

■ Each serving: About 225 calories, 2 g protein, 48 g carbohydrate, 0 g total fat, 0 g fiber, 0 mg cholesterol, 25 mg sodium.

Black-Pepper Beef Roast with Shallot Sauce

pictured on page 235

This no-fuss boneless roast just about cooks itself while you ready the rest of the menu. Serve the roast with the shallot sauce made with pan drippings, and a dollop of our Horseradish Cream (facing page).

PREP *25 minutes*
ROAST *1 hour 15 minutes*
MAKES *10 main-dish servings*

- 1 boneless beef rib-eye roast (about 3 pounds), tied
- 1 tablespoon plus 1 teaspoon cracked black pepper
- 1 tablespoon olive oil
- 1 teaspoon salt
- 1 medium shallot, minced (¼ cup)
- 1 can (14½ ounces) beef broth (about 1¾ cups)

1. Preheat oven to 350°F. Place beef on rack in small roasting pan (14" by 10").
2. In small bowl, stir pepper, oil, and salt until blended. Rub pepper mixture on all sides of beef.
3. Roast beef 1 hour and 15 minutes or until instant-read thermometer inserted into thickest part of beef reaches 135°F. Internal temperature of meat will rise 5° to 10°F. (medium-rare) upon standing. Or, roast to desired doneness. Transfer beef to large platter; let stand 10 minutes for easier slicing.
4. Meanwhile, prepare shallot sauce: Spoon 2 tablespoons fat from roasting pan into 10-inch skillet; discard any remaining fat. Cook minced shallot with fat in skillet over medium heat 3 to 5 minutes or until tender and lightly browned, stirring frequently.
5. Add broth to drippings remaining in roasting pan; place pan over medium-high heat and heat 2 minutes, stirring to loosen brown bits. Add broth mixture to skillet; increase heat to high and heat to boiling. Boil 3 minutes or until sauce is slightly reduced. Pour into sauceboat and keep warm. Makes about 1⅔ cups sauce.
6. To serve, remove string from beef. Cut into slices; serve with shallot sauce.

■ Each serving beef only: About 330 calories, 26 g protein, 1 g carbohydrate, 24 g total fat (9 g saturated), 0 g fiber, 85 mg cholesterol, 300 mg sodium.

■ Each tablespoon sauce: About 10 calories, 0 g protein, 0 g carbohydrate, 1 g total fat (1 g saturated), 0 g fiber, 1 mg cholesterol, 55 mg sodium.

---

how to unmold a gelatin salad

Four steps to help slide a shimmery gelatin salad out of a mold in one piece:
1. Fill a large bowl with warm—not hot—water. Dip the mold into the water for 10 seconds (no longer, or the gelatin will begin to melt).
2. Carefully insert a small metal spatula around the inside edge of the mold to release the gelatin. Dry the outside of the mold.
3. Sprinkle a chilled serving platter with a little cold water (a moistened platter will help you easily slide the mold into place if it comes out off-center). Place platter over the mold, then, holding the two together tightly, invert them quickly, and give the mold a firm shake or tap to release the gelatin.
4. Not budging? Hold the mold on its side and tap it several times until the gelatin begins to loosen. Then invert again.

Q I like to buy fresh bread from a local bakery, but it gets stale practically overnight. Is there any way to revive it?

a The easiest way is to generously sprinkle the crust of the bread with water. Place the loaf, uncovered, directly on the rack in a preheated 400°F. oven for 5 to 8 minutes or until it is slightly crisp and hot. Remove and let stand for a couple minutes, then slice and serve warm.

Q Can I substitute Swiss cheese for Gruyère in recipes? It's easier to find in my store.

a Both are delicious on a fruit plate, but Gruyère melts more easily, and its assertive flavor holds up better when cooked. (Try it layered in Potato & Gruyère Gratin, below.) Readily identified by its large holes, Swiss (sometimes called Emmentaler) is made from partially skimmed milk, so it's not as hearty.

Q Just what is gelato? I've been seeing more and more of it next to the ice cream in the supermarket freezer.

a Gelato is a soft, rich Italian-style ice cream that contains less air than classic American scoops, making it supercreamy and dense. But, surprisingly, for all its luxe flavor, packaged gelato is often not as much of a heavyweight: A half-cup serving of Häagen-Dazs chocolate gelato—the first ingredient is skim milk—contains 240 calories and 8 grams of fat (4.5 grams saturated). The same brand's chocolate ice cream—the first ingredient is cream—has 270 calories and 18 grams of fat (11 grams saturated) per half cup. Gelato and ice cream are interchangeable in recipes; but we love the true, intense flavor of coconut or hazelnut gelato for our easy hot fudge-drenched dessert (page 210).

Horseradish Cream

pictured on page 235

This simple condiment pairs well with mouthwatering roast beef. Save any leftovers for sandwiches another day.

PREP **10 minutes plus chilling**
MAKES **about 1¾ cups**

1½ cups sour cream
¼ cup prepared white horseradish
¼ teaspoon salt
¼ teaspoon coarsely ground black pepper
¼ cup snipped fresh chives

1. In small bowl, stir sour cream, horseradish, salt, and pepper until blended. Cover and refrigerate mixture until chilled or up to 3 days.
2. To serve, stir in chives.

■ Each tablespoon: About 25 calories, 0 g protein, 1 g carbohydrate, 2 g total fat (1 g saturated), 0 g fiber, 5 mg cholesterol, 30 mg sodium.

Potato & Gruyère Gratin

pictured on page 235

Try our simplified version of a classic French recipe of sliced potatoes baked in a creamy sauce with layers of cheese.

PREP **40 minutes**
BAKE **about 1 hour 5 minutes**
MAKES **8 accompaniment servings**

1 tablespoon margarine or butter
1 medium onion, chopped
½ cup heavy or whipping cream
1 tablespoon cornstarch
1 cup chicken broth
¼ teaspoon salt
¼ teaspoon ground black pepper
2 pounds red-skin potatoes (about 5 medium), cut into ¼-inch-thick slices
3 ounces Gruyère cheese, shredded (¾ cup)

1. In 2-quart saucepan, melt margarine over medium heat. Add chopped onion and cook 10 minutes or until tender and golden, stirring occasionally.
2. In small bowl, with wire whisk, mix cream and cornstarch until blended. Stir cream mixture, chicken broth, salt, and pepper into onion in saucepan; heat to boiling over medium-high heat, stirring frequently. Boil 1 minute, stirring.
3. Preheat oven to 350°F. In large bowl, toss potatoes with onion mixture until evenly mixed. Spread half of potato mixture evenly in shallow 2-quart ceramic or glass baking dish; sprinkle with half of Gruyère cheese. Arrange remaining potato mixture on top, spreading evenly. Top with remaining cheese.
4. Cover with foil and bake 35 minutes. Remove foil and bake 30 minutes longer or until potatoes are fork-tender and top of gratin is lightly browned. Let gratin cool 10 minutes before serving.

■ Each serving: About 220 calories, 6 g protein, 25 g carbohydrate, 11 g total fat (6 g saturated), 2 g fiber, 32 mg cholesterol, 265 mg sodium.

Cauliflower & Brussels Sprouts with Tarragon Butter

pictured on page 235

A little flavored butter goes a long way in this easy steamed winter vegetable combo.

PREP **25 minutes**
STEAM **about 10 minutes**
MAKES **8 accompaniment servings**

1 container (10 ounces) Brussels sprouts, trimmed and each cut into quarters
1 large head cauliflower (about 2 pounds), trimmed and cut into flowerets
2 tablespoons butter or margarine
½ teaspoon salt
¼ teaspoon dried tarragon
¼ teaspoon ground black pepper

1. Add about ¾ *inch water* to wide-bottomed 5- to 6-quart saucepot. Place collapsible steamer basket (about 11 inches in diameter) in saucepot; heat water to boiling over high heat. Add Brussels sprouts to steamer basket; cover and steam 3 minutes. Add cauliflower and steam 5 minutes longer or until vegetables are tender-crisp.

2. In large serving bowl, toss vegetables with butter, salt, tarragon, and pepper.

■ Each serving: About 50 calories, 2 g protein, 6 g carbohydrate, 3 g total fat (1 g saturated), 3 g fiber, 0 mg cholesterol, 205 mg sodium.

Baked Chocolate-Hazelnut Puddings

pictured on page 237

Bake this rich, soufflelike dessert in individual ramekins. If you like, substitute toasted blanched almonds for the hazelnuts.

PREP **30 minutes plus chilling**
BAKE **25 minutes**
MAKES **8 servings**

¾ cup hazelnuts
4 tablespoons butter or margarine, softened, plus extra for greasing
¾ cup sugar
7 large eggs, separated
8 ounces semisweet chocolate, melted and cooled
¼ teaspoon salt
¾ cup heavy or whipping cream
1 teaspoon vanilla extract

1. Preheat oven to 350°F. Place hazelnuts in 15½" by 10½" jelly-roll pan. Bake 10 to 15 minutes or until toasted. To remove skins, wrap hot hazelnuts in clean cloth towel; let stand 10 minutes. With hands, roll hazelnuts back and forth until most of skins come off.

2. Meanwhile, generously butter eight 6-ounce ramekins; set aside.

3. In food processor with knife blade attached, pulse hazelnuts with ¼ cup sugar until very finely ground.

4. In large bowl, with mixer at medium speed, beat 4 tablespoons butter until smooth. Add ¼ cup sugar; beat until creamy. Add egg yolks, 1 at a time, beating after each addition. Beat in hazelnut mixture and chocolate until blended.

5. In another large bowl, with mixer at high speed, beat egg whites, salt, and remaining ¼ cup sugar until stiff peaks form when beaters are lifted. Stir one-fourth of beaten whites into chocolate mixture until well combined. Gently fold remaining whites into chocolate mixture. Spoon batter into prepared ramekins. Cover and refrigerate 4 hours or overnight.

6. Preheat oven to 350°F. Place ramekins in large roasting pan (17" by 11½"); place pan in oven. Pour *boiling water* into roasting pan to come halfway up sides of ramekins. Bake 25 minutes or until knife inserted in center comes out with some fudgy batter stuck to it. Cool ramekins on wire rack 5 minutes.

7. Meanwhile, in small bowl, with mixer at medium speed, beat cream with vanilla until soft peaks form.

8. To serve, scoop out small amount of pudding mixture from top of each dessert; fill with some whipped cream. Replace scooped-out pudding over cream. Serve puddings with remaining whipped cream.

■ Each serving: About 500 calories, 10 g protein, 37 g carbohydrate, 37 g total fat (17 g saturated), 3 g fiber, 235 mg cholesterol, 215 mg sodium.

Supersimple Supper

Guests coming on short notice? With a quick trip to the supermarket (for bagged broccoli and salad, precooked polenta, a couple of pints of gelato, and a few other time-savers), you can pull together a delightful meal in less than an hour. Follow our kitchen steps to dovetail the tasks.

Menu for 6

- ❖ Mesclun Salad with Parmesan Polenta Rounds
- ❖ Roast Salmon with Capers & Tarragon
- ❖ Lemon Broccoli
- ❖ Crusty bread
- ❖ Gelato with Hot Fudge Sauce

GAME PLAN

1. Prepare Hot Fudge Sauce on the stovetop and set aside.

2. Set up the makings for Mesclun Salad: Slice the polenta and arrange on a cookie sheet with Parmesan topping; whisk the salad dressing in a serving bowl; rinse and spin-dry the mesclun; preheat broiler.

3. Set up Lemon Broccoli: Make the topping and put the steamer basket in the saucepot.

4. Mix the crumb topping for the Roast Salmon with Capers & Tarragon and pat onto the salmon fillet in foil-lined jelly-roll pan. Cut lemon into wedges for garnish.

5. When ready to sit down to dinner, broil the polenta rounds, toss the salad, and arrange on plates. Reduce oven temperature to 450°F. During the salad course, let the salmon roast and the broccoli steam.

6. After dinner, while the coffee brews, reheat the hot fudge and spoon over servings of gelato.

Mesclun Salad with Parmesan Polenta Rounds

Serve slices of polenta, broiled with Parmesan cheese and seasonings, over baby salad greens tossed with a creamy balsamic vinaigrette.

PREP **20 minutes**
BROIL **about 6 minutes**
MAKES **6 first-course servings**

1 log (16 ounces) precooked polenta, cut into 18 slices
2 ounces Parmesan cheese, coarsely grated (½ cup)
¼ teaspoon dried thyme
½ teaspoon salt
½ teaspoon coarsely ground black pepper
1 tablespoon white wine vinegar
1 tablespoon balsamic vinegar
1 tablespoon olive oil
1 tablespoon light mayonnaise
½ teaspoon Dijon mustard
¼ teaspoon sugar
2 bags (about 5 ounces each) mesclun salad greens

1. Preheat broiler. Arrange polenta slices on nonstick cookie sheet. In small bowl, mix Parmesan, thyme, ¼ teaspoon salt, and ¼ teaspoon pepper. Sprinkle 1 teaspoon cheese mixture on top of each slice. Place cookie sheet in broiler at closest position to source of heat; broil polenta 6 to 8 minutes or until cheese melts and top is golden.

2. Meanwhile, in large bowl, whisk vinegars, oil, mayonnaise, mustard, sugar, and remaining ¼ teaspoon salt and ¼ teaspoon pepper until blended. Add salad greens and toss until coated.

3. To serve, divide salad greens among 6 salad plates. Top each salad with 3 warm polenta rounds.

■ Each serving: About 135 calories, 6 g protein, 14 g carbohydrate, 6 g total fat (2 g saturated), 2 g fiber, 8 mg cholesterol, 630 mg sodium.

Roast Salmon with Capers & Tarragon

pictured on page 238

A whole salmon fillet with a crusty crumb-and-herb topping looks festive, tastes fabulous, and is surprisingly quick and easy to prepare.

PREP **10 minutes**
ROAST **about 30 minutes**
MAKES **6 main-dish servings**

3 tablespoons margarine or butter
⅓ cup plain dried bread crumbs
¼ cup loosely packed fresh parsley leaves, minced
3 tablespoons drained capers, minced
1 teaspoon dried tarragon, crumbled
2 teaspoons grated fresh lemon peel
¼ teaspoon salt
¼ teaspoon coarsely ground black pepper
1 whole salmon fillet (about 2 pounds)
lemon wedges
fresh tarragon sprigs for garnish

1. Preheat oven to 450°F.

2. In 1-quart saucepan, melt margarine over low heat. Remove saucepan from heat; stir in bread crumbs, parsley, capers, dried tarragon, lemon peel, salt, and pepper.

3. Line 15½" by 10½" jelly-roll pan with foil; grease foil. Place salmon, skin side down, in pan and pat crumb mixture on top.

4. Roast 30 minutes or until salmon turns opaque throughout and topping is lightly browned. With 2 large spatulas, carefully transfer salmon to platter (it's OK if salmon skin sticks to foil). Serve with lemon wedges. Garnish with fresh tarragon.

■ Each serving: About 325 calories, 28 g protein, 5 g carbohydrate, 21 g total fat (4 g saturated), 0 g fiber, 76 mg cholesterol, 425 mg sodium.

Lemon Broccoli

pictured on page 238

Ready-to-cook, precut broccoli flowerets are quickly steamed and then tossed with a savory lemon butter.

PREP *10 minutes*
STEAM *about 5 minutes*
MAKES *6 accompaniment servings*

    1 lemon
    2 bags (12 ounces each) fresh
       broccoli flowerets
    1 tablespoon butter or
       margarine
    ¼ teaspoon salt
    ⅛ teaspoon ground black
       pepper

1. From lemon, grate 1 teaspoon peel and squeeze 1 tablespoon juice; set aside.

2. Add about *¾ inch water* to wide-bottomed 5- to 6-quart saucepot. Place collapsible steamer basket (about 11 inches in diameter) in saucepot; heat water to boiling over high heat. Add broccoli to steamer basket; cover and steam 5 to 6 minutes or until broccoli is tender-crisp.

3. In large serving bowl, toss broccoli with lemon peel and juice, butter, salt, and pepper.

■ Each serving: About 40 calories, 3 g protein, 5 g carbohydrate, 2 g total fat (0 g saturated), 3 g fiber, 0 mg cholesterol, 145 mg sodium.

cooking with steam

Steaming is a great way to cook veggies fast and lock in their flavor, color, and nutrients. Try it with asparagus, artichokes, cauliflower, green beans, carrots, or our simple Lemon Broccoli, above.

• Bring a small amount of water (about ¾ inch) to a rapid boil in a saucepan over high heat. If you like, add a sprig or two of a fresh herb, such as basil, tarragon, oregano, or thyme.

• Place the vegetables in the perforated steamer basket, or use a collapsible steamer insert, bamboo steamer, or even a rack (as long as it elevates the food above the water).

• Cover the steamer and reduce heat to medium. Start your timer. Cook over constantly simmering water, checking to be sure it doesn't boil away; add more if needed. Vegetables taste and look best when just tender-crisp, so don't overcook. (A cut-up bunch of broccoli usually takes about 3 to 5 minutes; a pound of green beans, about 8 to 10 minutes.)

• Be careful when removing the lid—angle it away from you after cooking, so the hot steam doesn't scald you.

Gelato with Hot Fudge Sauce

pictured on page 239

You can make the world's best fudge sauce right on your stove. Ladle it over coconut or hazelnut gelato for a fabulous finale. The sauce will keep in the refrigerator up to one week. To reheat, zap the amount you need in the microwave on Medium, or warm over low heat in a saucepan on the stovetop.

PREP *10 minutes*
COOK *about 8 minutes*
MAKES *6 servings*

    1   cup heavy or whipping cream
    ¾   cup sugar
    4   ounces unsweetened chocolate
    2   tablespoons light corn syrup
    2   tablespoons butter or
        margarine
    2   teaspoons vanilla extract
    1½ pints coconut and/or hazelnut
        gelato

1. In heavy 2-quart saucepan, heat cream, sugar, chocolate, and corn syrup over medium heat until mixture comes to a boil, stirring occasionally. Cook 4 minutes longer or until sauce thickens slightly (mixture should be gently boiling), stirring constantly.

2. Remove saucepan from heat; stir in butter and vanilla until smooth and glossy. Serve immediately, or cover surface with plastic wrap and refrigerate. Makes about 1⅔ cups sauce.

3. To serve, scoop gelato into 6 dessert bowls. Pass sauce separately to spoon over gelato.

■ Each tablespoon sauce: About 85 calories, 1 g protein, 8 g carbohydrate, 6 g total fat (3 g saturated), 0 g fiber, 12 mg cholesterol, 15 mg sodium.

■ Each ½ cup serving gelato: About 250 calories, 5 g protein, 36 g carbohydrate, 10 g total fat (4 g saturated), 0 g fiber, 75 mg cholesterol, 65 mg sodium.

cookies from
Christmas Past

Our GH staff raided the recipe files of our moms, grandmas, and aunts for their most treasured holiday confections. Now they're yours to have and to share.

Cookie Jigsaw

Associate Food Director Debby Goldsmith has fond memories of making an adorable holiday cookie puzzle with her mother every year. The original recipe came from a December 1965 issue of *Good Housekeeping*. Goldsmith updated the recipe and continued the tradition with her son, Brandon, now 13. To make the puzzle ahead of time, wrap and freeze undecorated pieces; then unwrap, thaw completely, and follow decorating directions.*

PREP *1 hour 15 minutes plus cooling and decorating*
BAKE *about 30 minutes*
MAKES *about 3½ dozen cookies*

      lightweight cardboard or sturdy paper for pattern template
¾   cup butter or margarine (1½ sticks), softened
¾   cup sugar
1   large egg
1   tablespoon milk
2   teaspoons vanilla extract
2½ cups all-purpose flour
1½ teaspoons baking powder
¼   teaspoon salt
¾   cup light corn syrup
      assorted decorations: green, red, white, yellow, and blue sugar crystals; chocolate sprinkles; multicolor, white, and star-shaped candy decors; and small round yellow candies

* Recipe is suitable for packing and shipping.

1. On cardboard or paper, draw a Christmas-tree template 10 inches high (from tip of tree to top of trunk) and 10½ inches wide (at base of tree above trunk), with a 1-inch high by 2-inch wide trunk. Cut out template and set aside.

2. In large bowl, with mixer at medium speed, beat butter and sugar until creamy. Beat in egg, milk, and vanilla until well blended (mixture may look curdled). On waxed paper, combine flour, baking powder, and salt. At low speed, beat in flour mixture just until blended. Pat dough into a small rectangle.

3. Preheat oven to 325°F. Grease and flour large cookie sheet. Place dough in center of cookie sheet. With floured rolling pin, roll dough into 13" by 11" rectangle. Bake 15 minutes.

4. Place cookie sheet on wire rack; center tree template lengthwise on warm cookie. With knife, cut around template into cookie; remove template, leaving tree outline. Press floured 1½-inch star-shaped cookie cutter into cookie at top of tree; remove cutter, leaving star outline. Press floured 1-inch round cookie cutters into tree in several places, leaving ornament outlines. Press 2½-inch star cutter into remaining cookie around tree, leaving star outlines.

5. Cut Christmas tree into various geometric-shaped puzzle pieces, being careful not to cut into ornament outlines. Cut remaining cookie around tree into puzzle pieces, being careful not to cut into star outlines.

6. Return cookie sheet to oven and bake 12 to 14 minutes longer or until cookie is light brown. Set cookie sheet on wire rack; cut through all designs and pieces. Cool cookie puzzle on cookie sheet 10 minutes. Carefully slide puzzle, in 1 piece, onto wire rack; cool completely.

7. To decorate: In 1-quart saucepan, heat light corn syrup to boiling over medium heat, stirring frequently. Boil 1 minute, stirring. Remove round ornament pieces from tree; brush tree and trunk with corn syrup. Sprinkle tree with green sugar crystals to coat, then attach small round yellow candies as desired. Sprinkle or dip trunk into chocolate sprinkles. Brush ornament pieces with corn syrup; sprinkle or dip into choice of colored sugar crystals or decors. Remove star decorations from around tree; brush with corn syrup and sprinkle or dip into yellow sugar crystals. Brush puzzle pieces around tree with corn syrup; sprinkle with blue sugar crystals to coat, then sprinkle lightly with white decors and stars. Reheat corn syrup if it becomes too thick.

8. Allow puzzle pieces to dry completely, about 1 hour. When puzzle pieces are dry, reassemble puzzle on large tray to serve, or store in tightly covered container at room temperature up to 1 week.

■ Each cookie: About 95 calories, 1 g protein, 15 g carbohydrate, 4 g total fat (2 g saturated), 0 g fiber, 15 mg cholesterol, 80 mg sodium.

Chocolate Brownie Biscotti

Editorial Assistant Patricia Ambrosini's aunt baked enough biscotti for the entire family to enjoy throughout the holidays. Beyond dessert, these crunchy cookies would pop up in the morning alongside a cup of her Irish mother's coffee or in the afternoon atop her Italian father's cappuccino.*

PREP *45 minutes plus cooling*
BAKE *50 minutes*
MAKES *about 3 dozen cookies*

2½ cups all-purpose flour
1⅓ cups sugar
¾ cup unsweetened cocoa
2 teaspoons baking powder
½ teaspoon baking soda
½ teaspoon salt
½ cup butter or margarine
   (1 stick), melted
3 large eggs
2 teaspoons vanilla extract
1 cup almonds, toasted and
   coarsely chopped
4 ounces semisweet chocolate,
   coarsely chopped

1. Preheat oven to 325°F. In medium bowl, mix flour, sugar, cocoa, baking powder, baking soda, and salt.
2. In large bowl, with mixer at medium speed, beat butter, eggs, and vanilla until mixed. Reduce speed to low; gradually add flour mixture and beat just until blended. With hand, knead in almonds and chocolate until combined.
3. Divide dough in half. On ungreased large cookie sheet, shape each half into 12" by 3" log, about 3 inches apart. Bake logs 30 minutes. Cool logs on cookie sheet on wire rack 15 minutes.
4. Place logs on cutting board. With serrated knife, cut each log crosswise into ½-inch-thick diagonal slices. With long metal spatula, place slices, top side up, ¼ inch apart, on same cookie sheet. Bake slices 20 minutes to allow biscotti to dry out. Cool biscotti completely on cookie sheet on wire rack. (Biscotti will harden as they cool.) Store biscotti in tightly covered container at room temperature up to 2 weeks, or in freezer up to 6 months.

■ Each cookie: About 135 calories, 3 g protein, 17 g carbohydrate, 7 g total fat (3 g saturated), 2 g fiber, 25 mg cholesterol, 105 mg sodium.

Anise Slices

Features Editor Mary Kate Hogan shares the secrets of her aunt Anne, 90, a wonderful baker. This family favorite is delicious and simple to make, and the cookies keep well—if they aren't devoured right away! Freeze the dough up to a month ahead, then slice and bake when hungry.*

PREP *30 minutes plus chilling*
BAKE *about 12 minutes per batch*
MAKES *about 6 dozen cookies*

¾ cup sugar
½ cup butter (1 stick), softened
   (no substitutions)
1 large egg
½ teaspoon vanilla extract
1¾ cups all-purpose flour
1 tablespoon anise seeds, crushed
½ teaspoon baking powder
¼ teaspoon salt

1. In large bowl, with mixer at medium speed, beat sugar and butter until creamy, about 1 minute, occasionally scraping bowl with rubber spatula. Reduce speed to low; beat in egg and vanilla until blended. Beat in flour, anise seeds, baking powder, and salt until well combined, occasionally scraping bowl.
2. Divide dough in half. Shape each half into 5½" by 2" rectangle. Wrap each rectangle in plastic wrap and refrigerate 2 hours or until dough is firm enough to slice. (Or place dough in freezer about 1 hour.)

3. Preheat oven to 350°F. Grease large cookie sheet. With knife, cut rectangle crosswise into scant ⅛-inch-thick slices. Place cookies, 1 inch apart, on cookie sheet.
4. Bake cookies 12 to 14 minutes or until lightly browned. Transfer cookies to wire rack to cool. Repeat with remaining dough. Store cookies in tightly covered container at room temperature up to 2 weeks, or in freezer up to 3 months.

■ Each cookie: About 30 calories, 0 g protein, 4 g carbohydrate, 2 g total fat (1 g saturated), 0 g fiber, 7 mg cholesterol, 25 mg sodium.

Cinnamon Spirals

Research Editor Sally Dorst remembers these simple, not-too-sweet cookies as one of her favorites. Her mother originally made them for her from scraps of leftover pie dough. Dorst loved them best warm, just minutes out of the oven. If you want them sweeter, add two more tablespoons sugar to the dough mixture.*

PREP *40 minutes plus chilling and
   cooling*
BAKE *about 12 minutes per batch*
MAKES *about 4 dozen cookies*

½ cup butter or margarine (1 stick),
   softened
4 ounces cream cheese, softened
1¼ cups all-purpose flour
¼ teaspoon salt
⅓ cup sugar
1 teaspoon ground cinnamon

1. In large bowl, with mixer at medium speed, beat butter and cream cheese until creamy, about 2 minutes. Reduce speed to low; gradually beat in flour and salt until well mixed, occasionally scraping bowl with rubber spatula.
2. On sheet of plastic wrap, pat dough into small rectangle. Wrap in plastic wrap and refrigerate 1 hour or until

dough is firm enough to roll. (Or freeze dough for 30 minutes.)

3. Meanwhile, in small bowl, mix sugar and cinnamon; set aside.

4. On lightly floured surface, with floured rolling pin, roll cookie dough into 15" by 12" rectangle. Sprinkle cinnamon-sugar mixture evenly over dough.

5. Starting from a long side, tightly roll rectangle jelly-roll fashion. Brush last ½ inch of dough with *water* to help seal edge. Cut log crosswise in half. Slide logs onto cookie sheet; cover with plastic wrap and refrigerate 2 hours or until dough is firm enough to slice. (Or freeze dough for 45 minutes.)

6. Preheat oven to 400°F. Remove 1 log from freezer; with serrated knife, cut log crosswise into ¼-inch-thick slices. Place cookies, ½ inch apart, on ungreased large cookie sheet.

7. Bake cookies 12 to 14 minutes or until lightly browned. Transfer cookies to wire rack to cool. Repeat with remaining log. Store cookies in tightly covered container at room temperature up to 3 days, or in freezer up to 3 months.

■ Each cookie: About 45 calories, 1 g protein, 4 g carbohydrate, 3 g total fat (2 g saturated), 0 g fiber, 8 mg cholesterol, 40 mg sodium.

Lebkuchen

GH News Director Toni Gerber Hope loves her family's chewy spice bars. Her grandmother, Sophie Katz Guinzburg, met weekly with friends to play cards, which apparently was a kind of cooking competition, too. One of the women, known as Birdie Vogel Dear, was very secretive about her recipes. But sly Sophie was able to "guess" the ingredients by saying, "These are so delicious, they must have a cup of sugar in them," and unsuspecting Birdie would reply, "Cup and a half." This recipe is one of Birdie's "secrets."*

PREP *15 minutes plus cooling*
BAKE *30 minutes*
MAKES *64 bars*

1	box (16 ounces) dark brown sugar (2¼ cups packed)
4	large eggs
1½	cups all-purpose flour
1½	teaspoons ground cinnamon
1	teaspoon baking powder
¾	teaspoon ground cloves
1	cup walnuts, coarsely chopped
1	cup dark seedless raisins or ¾ cup diced mixed candied fruit
½	cup confectioners' sugar
1	tablespoon fresh lemon juice

1. Preheat oven to 350°F. Grease 13" by 9" metal baking pan. Line pan with foil; grease foil.

2. In large bowl, with mixer at medium speed, beat brown sugar and eggs until well mixed, about 1 minute, occasionally scraping bowl with rubber spatula. Reduce speed to low; gradually beat in flour, cinnamon, baking powder, and cloves until blended, occasionally scraping bowl. Stir in walnuts and raisins.

3. Spoon mixture into pan and spread evenly. Bake 30 minutes. Cool completely in pan on wire rack.

4. In medium bowl, mix confectioners' sugar and lemon juice. Drizzle sugar icing over Lebkuchen. Let stand 10 minutes to allow icing to set. Transfer with foil to cutting board. Cut lengthwise into 8 strips, then cut each strip crosswise into 8 bars. Store bars in tightly covered container, with waxed paper between layers, at room temperature up to 2 weeks, or in freezer up to 3 months.

■ Each bar: About 65 calories, 1 g protein, 12 g carbohydrate, 2 g total fat (0 g saturated), 0 g fiber, 13 mg cholesterol, 15 mg sodium.

decorating: a short and sweet guide

Cutout cookies with bright trimmings, like cheerfully wrapped packages, are always inviting. But let's face it, most of us don't have time to pipe on frostings or paint on intricate designs (as our talented cookie stylist Karen Tack did; see page 240 for examples). These methods work their magic in minutes and are fun to do with kids.

BEFORE-BAKING BRUSHES
Egg-yolk wash Beat 1 large egg yolk with ¼ teaspoon water. Divide beaten egg among a few small cups and tint each with food coloring.

Milk paint Tint a couple of tablespoons of evaporated milk with food coloring for an old-fashioned glazed look.

AFTER-BAKING FLOURISHES
Sugar coating Boil 1 cup light corn syrup for 1 minute, stirring. Brush syrup on cookie; dust with colored sugar crystals, sprinkles, or candy decors. Or, fill small bowls with trimmings and dip in cookies to decorate.

Fast frosting Whisk 1½ cups confectioners' sugar with 1 to 2 tablespoons milk until blended; tint with desired food coloring and brush on.

Marbling Brush on a thin coat of Ornamental Frosting (page 217). With tip of small paintbrush, drop dots of another frosting on top. Using a toothpick, drag edges of colored dots through base frosting in a swirling motion to create designs.

Candy land Frost cookies with store-bought frosting, then press on chocolate chips, miniature marshmallows, gumdrops, etc., to create tempting treats.

Hot chocolate Melt white or dark chocolate; pour into small self-sealing plastic bag. Snip ⅛ inch off a bottom corner of bag (this is your writing tip). Drizzle over baked cookies. Variations: Write names, draw simple shapes such as hearts and stars, or use the chocolate as a glue to anchor decors or candies. Allow 2 hours or more to dry.

After cookies have dried, store in a tightly covered container with waxed paper between layers.

Angeletti

Freelance home economist Marjorie Cubisino says her mother-in-law, Carmel, is "the best cook I ever met!" She would cook fabulous meals and bake up a storm out of a tiny apartment oven and stove. Carmel made these Italian cookies every December for the holidays—they have been Marjorie's husband's favorite since he was a child.*

PREP *40 minutes plus cooling*
BAKE *about 7 minutes per batch*
MAKES *about 5 dozen cookies*

½ cup butter or margarine
    (1 stick), melted
¾ cup granulated sugar
¼ cup whole milk
1½ teaspoons vanilla extract
3 large eggs
3 cups all-purpose flour
1 tablespoon baking powder
¼ teaspoon salt
2 cups confectioners' sugar
½ cup multicolor candy decors

1. Preheat oven to 375°F. Grease large cookie sheet.
2. In large bowl, whisk butter, granulated sugar, milk, vanilla, and eggs until blended. In medium bowl, mix flour, baking powder, and salt. Stir flour mixture into egg mixture until evenly blended. Cover surface of dough with plastic wrap or waxed paper; let stand 5 minutes.
3. With floured hands, shape dough by level tablespoons into 1-inch balls. Place balls, 2 inches apart, on cookie sheet. Bake cookies 7 to 8 minutes or until puffed and light brown on bottoms. Transfer cookies to wire rack to cool. Repeat with remaining dough.
4. When cookies are cool, in small bowl, whisk confectioners' sugar and *3 tablespoons plus 1½ teaspoons water* until blended. Dip top of each cookie into glaze. Place cookies on wire rack set over waxed paper to catch any drips. Immediately sprinkle cookies with decors. Allow glaze to set, about 20 minutes. Store cookies, with waxed paper between layers, in tightly covered container at room temperature up to 3 days, or in freezer up to 3 months.

■ Each cookie: About 75 calories, 1 g protein, 13 g carbohydrate, 2 g total fat (1 g saturated), 0 g fiber, 15 mg cholesterol, 55 mg sodium.

Linzer Cookies

Freelance writer Delia Blackler's mother-in-law, Helgard Perretta, has been baking wonderful treats for family and friends for years. As a child, Blackler's husband, Stephen, would hand deliver his mom's cookies to eagerly awaiting neighbors and friends. The only problem with these thin almond cookies sandwiched with jam, says Blackler: "It's a challenge to eat just one."*

PREP *1 hour plus chilling and cooling*
BAKE *about 12 minutes per batch*
MAKES *about 2 dozen cookies*

½ cup blanched almonds
1 cup granulated sugar
2¾ cups all-purpose flour
1 tablespoon grated fresh lemon
    peel
½ teaspoon baking powder
¼ teaspoon salt
1 cup butter or margarine (2 sticks),
    softened
1 package (3 ounces) cream cheese,
    softened
1 large egg
    confectioners' sugar
½ cup seedless red raspberry or
    other favorite jam

1. In food processor with knife blade attached, blend almonds with ½ cup granulated sugar until almonds are finely ground. Add flour, lemon peel, baking powder, salt, and remaining ½ cup granulated sugar; pulse until evenly mixed. Add butter, cream cheese, and egg, and process just until dough forms, occasionally stopping processor and scraping side with spatula.
2. Divide dough in half; flatten each half into a disk. Wrap each disk in plastic wrap and refrigerate 2 hours or until dough is firm enough to roll. (Or place dough in freezer for 30 minutes.)
3. Preheat oven to 350°F. On lightly floured surface, with floured rolling pin, roll 1 piece of dough ⅛ inch thick. With floured 3-inch fluted round cookie cutter, cut dough into as many rounds as possible. With floured 1-inch star or fluted round cookie cutter, cut out and remove centers from half of rounds. Reserve centers and trimmings to reroll. With lightly floured wide spatula, carefully place rounds, about 1 inch apart, on ungreased large cookie sheet.
4. Bake cookies 12 to 14 minutes or until edges are lightly browned. Transfer cookies to wire rack to cool completely. Repeat with remaining dough and reserved centers and trimmings.
5. When cookies are cool, sprinkle confectioners' sugar through sieve over cookies with cutout centers. In small saucepan, melt jam over low heat, stirring frequently. Brush whole cookies with melted jam; place cutout cookies on top of jam. Store cookies, with waxed paper between layers, in tightly covered container at room temperature up to 1 week, or in freezer up to 2 months. (If cookies are stored in freezer, you may need to sprinkle with confectioners' sugar again before serving.)

■ Each cookie: About 210 calories, 3 g protein, 25 g carbohydrate, 11 g total fat (6 g saturated), 1 g fiber, 35 mg cholesterol, 130 mg sodium.

Pizzelles

With her mom and aunt, Editorial Assistant Jill Sieracki carries on the holiday tradition of her Italian grandmother, who always baked up stacks of pizzelles. The three women still mix the batter in Grandma's large turquoise bowl and cook these paper-thin treats with her antique pizzelle iron.

PREP *30 minutes plus cooling*
BAKE *about 1 minute per batch*
MAKES *about 2½ dozen cookies*

- ¾ cup sugar
- ½ cup butter or margarine (1 stick), softened
- 3 large eggs
- 2 teaspoons vanilla extract
- 1¾ cups all-purpose flour
- 1 teaspoon baking powder

1. Preheat pizzelle iron† as manufacturer directs. In large bowl, with mixer at medium speed, beat sugar and butter until creamy. Reduce speed to low; beat in eggs and vanilla until blended. Beat in flour and baking powder just until well mixed, occasionally scraping bowl with rubber spatula.
2. Pour 1 rounded tablespoon batter at a time onto center of each pizzelle mold. Cover; bake as manufacturer directs (do not lift cover during baking).
3. When done, lift cover and loosen pizzelle with fork. Transfer to wire rack to cool completely. Trim cookie edges with scissors if necessary. Store cookies in tightly covered container at room temperature up to 2 weeks, or in freezer up to 3 months.

■ Each cookie: About 80 calories, 1 g protein, 11 g carbohydrate, 4 g total fat (2 g saturated), 0 g fiber, 30 mg cholesterol, 55 mg sodium.

†Pizzelle irons are available in electric and stovetop models in various sizes. Be sure to follow manufacturer's directions for using the correct amount of batter in your iron.

best baker for prized pizzelles

Pizzelles, traditionally anise-flavored cookies and an Italian specialty, were baked in the old country over an open flame in long-handled irons that imprinted the wafers with fancy patterns, family crests, and initials. Today's convenient electric models lack heritage, but they bake two pizzelles on both sides at once, in under a minute, without sacrificing the cookie's delicate beauty. Our pick: the VillaWare Prego Pizzelle Baker, Model 3600-NS ($49.95), lights up when the nonstick surface is ready. 800-822-1335

Aunt Martha's Nutmeg Bells

Textiles Director Kathleen Huddy Sperduto loved her great-aunt Martha's repertoire of cookies, but Sperduto's favorite was this crisp, spiced, sugar one. Now every holiday Sperduto's children, William and John, look forward to them, too. As a special treat, Sperduto sometimes hangs these cookies on her Christmas tree as ornaments. To hang them, she makes a hole with a drinking straw in the top of each cookie before baking. After the frosting has dried on the baked cookies, she threads nylon fishing line through the holes.*

PREP *1 hour plus chilling, cooling, and decorating*
BAKE *about 10 minutes*
MAKES *about 5½ dozen cookies*

- 2 cups sugar
- 1 cup butter (2 sticks), softened (no substitutions)
- 2 large eggs
- 2 teaspoons vanilla extract
- 3½ cups all-purpose flour
- 4 teaspoons baking powder
- 1 teaspoon salt
- 1 teaspoon ground nutmeg
  Ornamental Frosting (page 217), optional

1. In large bowl, with mixer at medium speed, beat sugar and butter until creamy, about 2 minutes. Reduce speed to low; beat in eggs and vanilla until blended. Gradually beat in flour, baking powder, salt, and nutmeg until well blended, occasionally scraping bowl with rubber spatula.
2. Divide dough in thirds; flatten each into a disk. Wrap each disk in plastic wrap and refrigerate 2 hours or until dough is firm enough to roll. (Or freeze for 30 minutes.)
3. Preheat oven to 350°F. On lightly floured surface, with floured rolling pin, roll 1 piece of dough ⅛ inch thick. With floured 3½-inch bell-shaped cookie cutter, cut dough into as many cookies as possible; wrap and refrigerate trimmings. Place cookies, 1 inch apart, on ungreased large cookie sheet.
4. Bake cookies 10 to 12 minutes or until lightly browned. Transfer cookies to wire rack to cool. Repeat with remaining dough and trimmings.
5. When cookies are cool, prepare Ornamental Frosting if you like; use to decorate cookies as desired (see box, page 213). Set cookies aside to allow frosting to dry completely, about 1 hour. Store cookies in tightly covered container (with waxed paper between layers if decorated) at room temperature up to 2 weeks, or in freezer up to 3 months.

■ Each cookie without frosting: About 75 calories, 1 g protein, 11 g carbohydrate, 3 g total fat (2 g saturated), 0 g fiber, 14 mg cholesterol, 90 mg sodium.

Flapjacks

Associate Research Editor Clare Ellis remembers baking these treats with her sister as a small child. "I loved them because they're quick, easy, and delicious—a perfect recipe for a young baker!" Ellis says. Flapjacks, nothing like an American pancake, are a British treat made from oats and baked in a flat tin. Traditionally, they're thick and biscuitlike, but this version is more like a crisp, crumbly cookie.

PREP **15 minutes plus cooling**
BAKE **about 16 minutes**
MAKES **16 cookies**

> 5 tablespoons butter or margarine
> ⅓ cup packed brown sugar
> 1⅓ cups old-fashioned oats, uncooked
>   pinch salt

1. Preheat oven to 350°F. Grease 8-inch round cake pan. Line pan with foil; grease foil.
2. In 2-quart saucepan, melt butter over low heat. Add sugar and cook 1 minute or until well blended, stirring. Remove saucepan from heat; stir in oats and salt until evenly mixed.
3. Sprinkle oat mixture into cake pan; with spatula, firmly pat down mixture.
4. Bake 16 to 18 minutes or until golden. Let cool in pan on wire rack 10 minutes. Lift cookies out of pan with foil and place on cutting board. While still warm, cut into 16 wedges. Transfer Flapjacks with foil to wire rack to cool completely. Store cookies in single layer in tightly covered container up to 1 week, or in freezer up to 3 months.

■ Each cookie: About 100 calories, 2 g protein, 13 g carbohydrate, 5 g total fat (3 g saturated), 1 g fiber, 10 mg cholesterol, 50 mg sodium.

Ginger Cutouts

pictured on page 240

As a young girl growing up in Chappaqua, New York, freelance research editor Hannah McCouch was consistently lured to her friend Pixi Ladd's house by the intoxicating aromas wafting from the kitchen. "Pixi's mom baked cookies a lot, so her house was the best place to be after school." At Christmas, these crisp, gingery cutouts were Mrs. Ladd's specialty.*

PREP **1 hour plus cooling and decorating**
BAKE **about 8 minutes per batch**
MAKES **about 6 dozen cookies**

> 1 teaspoon baking soda
> 1 cup light (mild) molasses
> 1 cup butter or margarine
>   (2 sticks), softened
> 1 cup sugar
> 1 tablespoon ground ginger
> 1 teaspoon ground cinnamon
> ½ teaspoon ground allspice
> ½ teaspoon salt
> 1 large egg
>   about 5 cups all-purpose flour
>   Ornamental Frosting (facing page)

1. Preheat oven to 375°F. In cup, stir baking soda into molasses; set aside until pale brown and frothy.
2. Meanwhile, in large bowl, with mixer at medium speed, beat butter with sugar, ginger, cinnamon, allspice, and salt until creamy, occasionally scraping bowl with rubber spatula. At low speed, beat in molasses mixture and egg (mixture may look curdled). Gradually add 4¾ cups flour; beat just until blended, occasionally scraping bowl.
3. On lightly floured surface, knead dough until thoroughly mixed, adding in remaining ¼ cup flour if necessary. Divide dough in half; wrap half of dough with plastic wrap and refrigerate until ready to roll out.
4. On floured surface, with floured rolling pin, roll remaining half of dough slightly thinner than ¼ inch. With floured 4-inch assorted cookie cutters, cut dough into as many cookies as possible; reserve trimmings. Place cookies, ½ inch apart, on ungreased large cookie sheet. Reroll trimmings and cut out more cookies.
5. Bake cookies 8 to 10 minutes or until edges begin to brown. Transfer cookies to wire racks to cool. Repeat with remaining dough.
6. When cookies are cool, prepare Ornamental Frosting; use to decorate cookies as desired (see box, page 213). Set cookies aside to allow frosting to dry completely, about 1 hour. Store cookies, with waxed paper between layers, in tightly covered container at room temperature up to 1 week, or in freezer up to 3 months.

■ Each cookie without frosting: About 80 calories, 1 g protein, 13 g carbohydrate, 3 g total fat (2 g saturated), 0 g fiber, 10 mg cholesterol, 65 mg sodium.

spell out the joy of hanukkah

Use the Jewish Aleph Bet Cookie Cutters from the Kosher Cook (27 pieces; $36 includes shipping and handling) to start a new tradition: cookies shaped like the letters on a dreidel. The letters stand for "A great miracle happened there." Or charm children by spelling out their Hebrew names. We found that these tin cutters work best if you roll the dough to no less than ¼ inch thick. To order a set, call 1-866-883-6235.

Sour Cream Nut Rolls

Former Features Editor Kathleen Renda's mom, Rose, has been making cookies for decades. She normally bakes with the "little bit of this and a little bit of that" method. But we got her to write down the exact measurements for these scrumptious walnut rolls.*

PREP *50 minutes plus standing and cooling*
BAKE *about 40 minutes*
MAKES *about 4 dozen cookies*

Walnut Filling
2½ cups walnuts, toasted and cooled
¾ cup sugar
2 tablespoons butter or margarine, melted
1 tablespoon vanilla extract
2 teaspoons grated fresh orange peel
¼ teaspoon salt

Sour Cream Dough
1 package active dry yeast
1 teaspoon plus ¼ cup sugar
3 cups all-purpose flour
¾ teaspoon salt
½ cup butter or margarine (1 stick), melted
½ cup sour cream
2 large eggs

1. Prepare Walnut Filling: In food processor with knife blade attached, pulse all filling ingredients until walnuts are finely ground; set aside.
2. Prepare Sour Cream Dough: In small bowl, combine yeast, 1 teaspoon sugar, and *¼ cup warm water* (105° to 115°F.). Let stand until yeast mixture foams, about 5 minutes.
3. In large bowl, stir together flour, salt, and remaining ¼ cup sugar. Stir in butter, sour cream, 1 egg, 1 egg yolk, and yeast mixture until evenly moistened. With floured hands, knead dough in bowl a few times until

dough comes together (dough will be sticky). Cover bowl with plastic wrap; let dough stand 10 minutes.
4. Divide dough in half. On lightly floured surface, with floured rolling pin, roll half of dough into 14" by 12" rectangle. Sprinkle half of Walnut Filling evenly over dough. Gently press down on filling so it sticks to dough.
5. Starting from a long side of dough rectangle, tightly roll dough jelly-roll fashion. Place roll, seam side down, on 1 side of ungreased large cookie sheet. Repeat with remaining half of dough and filling. Place second roll, 4 inches from first roll, on same cookie sheet. Cover rolls with plastic wrap and let rise in warm place (80° to 85°F.) 1 hour. If you like, instead of rising 1 hour, refrigerate rolls, on cookie sheet, overnight. When ready to bake, let stand at room temperature 30 minutes before completing steps 6 and 7.
6. Preheat oven to 325°F. Bake nut rolls 35 minutes. Meanwhile, in cup, lightly beat remaining egg white. Brush rolls with egg white. Bake 5 minutes longer or until golden. Transfer rolls to wire rack to cool.
7. When rolls are cool, with serrated knife, cut crosswise into ½-inch-thick slices. Store cookies in tightly covered container at room temperature up to 3 days, or in freezer up to 3 months.

■ Each cookie: About 115 calories, 2 g protein, 11 g carbohydrate, 7 g total fat (2 g saturated), 1 g fiber, 17 mg cholesterol, 80 mg sodium.

Ornamental Frosting

Use this hard-drying frosting tinted with food coloring to decorate Ginger Cutouts (facing page), Aunt Martha's Nutmeg Bells (page 215), and the Christmas Barn (page 222).

PREP *about 5 minutes*
MAKES *about 3 cups*

1 package (16 ounces) confectioners' sugar
3 tablespoons meringue powder††
assorted food colorings (optional)

1. In bowl, with mixer at medium speed, beat confectioners' sugar, meringue powder, and *⅓ cup warm water* until mixture is blended and so stiff that knife drawn through it leaves a clean-cut path, about 5 minutes.
2. If you like, tint frosting with food colorings as desired; keep covered with plastic wrap to prevent drying out. With small metal spatula, artists' paintbrushes, or decorating bags with small writing tips, decorate cookies with frosting. (You may need to thin frosting with a little *warm water* to obtain the right spreading or piping consistency.)

■ Each tablespoon: About 40 calories, 0 g protein, 10 g carbohydrate, 0 g total fat, 0 g fiber, 0 mg cholesterol, 3 mg sodium.

†† Available in stores where cake-decorating supplies are sold, or from Wilton Industries, 800-794-5866.

Lemon-Glazed Flowers

Associate Food Editor Lori Conforti would anxiously await the arrival of these tasty cookies every Christmas. Her mother's German nanny, Irmgard Kersten, used to send Conforti's family an assortment of holiday cookies. Although they were all great, the lemon-glazed cookies were Conforti's favorite. The full recipe makes nine dozen cookies—if you like, freeze half of the dough up to three months and bake another time. (For each half of dough you use, prepare half of Lemon Glaze.)*

PREP *45 minutes plus chilling and cooling*
BAKE *about 10 minutes per batch*
MAKES *about 9 dozen cookies*

Butter Cookies
1½ cups butter or margarine (3 sticks), softened
1⅓ cups granulated sugar
½ teaspoon salt
3 large eggs
4½ cups all-purpose flour

Lemon Glaze
1½ cups confectioners' sugar
¼ cup plus 1 teaspoon fresh lemon juice (from 1 to 2 lemons)

1. Prepare Butter Cookies: In large bowl, with mixer at low speed, beat butter, granulated sugar, and salt until blended. Increase speed to high; beat until creamy. At low speed, beat in eggs, 1 at a time, beating well after each addition. Gradually beat in flour just until blended.
2. Divide dough into 4 equal pieces; flatten each into a disk. Wrap each disk with plastic wrap and refrigerate 2 hours or until dough is firm enough to roll. (Or, place dough in freezer for 30 minutes if using butter, 45 minutes if using margarine.)
3. Meanwhile, prepare Lemon Glaze:

In small bowl, whisk confectioners' sugar and lemon juice until smooth; cover and set aside.
4. Preheat oven to 350°F. On lightly floured surface, with floured rolling pin, roll 1 piece of dough ⅛ inch thick. With floured 2½-inch round scalloped cookie cutter, cut dough into as many cookies as possible; wrap and refrigerate dough trimmings. With floured wide spatula, carefully place cookies, 1 inch apart, on ungreased large cookie sheet.
5. Bake cookies 10 to 12 minutes or until cookies are lightly browned. Transfer cookies to wire rack. Brush tops of warm cookies generously with Lemon Glaze; cool on wire rack. Repeat with remaining dough, trimmings, and glaze.
6. Store cookies, with waxed paper between layers, in tightly covered container at room temperature up to 1 week, or in freezer up to 3 months.

■ Each cookie: About 60 calories, 1 g protein, 8 g carbohydrate, 3 g total fat (2 g saturated), 0 g fiber, 13 mg cholesterol, 40 mg sodium.

Toffee-Peanut Butter Rounds

Freelance copywriter Alice Garbarini Hurley spotted these cookies a few years ago at a Christmas fair on Cape Cod. All the dry ingredients were layered in a decorative jar. Hanging from the jar was a recipe card listing the quantity of eggs and butter to add, along with mixing and baking instructions. Hurley bought the jar for a friend, but changed her mind and baked them for her daughter, Annie. They both loved them so much that she figured out the recipe and has been giving gift jars of Toffee–Peanut Butter Round mix ever since.*

PREP *30 minutes plus cooling*
BAKE *about 10 minutes per batch*
MAKES *about 4½ dozen cookies*

1 cup butter or margarine (2 sticks), melted and cooled
2 large eggs
2¼ cups all-purpose flour
1 cup peanut-butter chips
¾ cup old-fashioned oats, uncooked
½ cup granulated sugar
½ cup packed light brown sugar
½ cup packed dark brown sugar
½ teaspoon baking soda
½ teaspoon salt
4 chocolate-covered toffee candy bars (1.4 ounces each), coarsely chopped (about 1 cup)

1. Preheat oven to 375°F. In large bowl, with mixer at medium speed, beat butter and eggs until blended. Add remaining ingredients and beat until well mixed, occasionally scraping bowl with rubber spatula.
2. Drop dough by rounded tablespoons, 2 inches apart, onto ungreased large cookie sheet.
3. Bake cookies 10 minutes or until lightly browned. Transfer cookies to wire rack to cool. Repeat with remaining dough. Store cookies in tightly covered container at room temperature up to 1 week, or in freezer up to 3 months.

■ Each cookie: About 125 calories, 2 g protein, 15 g carbohydrate, 6 g total fat (4 g saturated), 1 g fiber, 19 mg cholesterol, 90 mg sodium.

Editor's note: To give the mix as a gift, layer all dry ingredients in a 1½-quart jar with a tight-fitting lid. Store at room temperature up to 3 months. Include recipe with gift jar.

Mostaccioli

Food Director Susan Westmoreland happily recalls a "sea of cookies" spread atop a clean white sheet on her grandparents' bed—the only place large enough to cool the hundreds of mostaccioli Grandma Elsie baked for friends and family.*

PREP *45 minutes plus cooling*
BAKE *about 7 minutes per batch*
MAKES *about 5 dozen cookies*

Cookies
   2 cups all-purpose flour
 ½ cup unsweetened cocoa
1 ½ teaspoons baking powder
   1 teaspoon ground cinnamon
 ¼ teaspoon ground cloves
 ¼ teaspoon salt
 ¾ cup granulated sugar
 ½ cup butter or margarine (1 stick), softened
   1 large egg
 ½ cup whole milk

Chocolate Glaze
   3 tablespoons unsweetened cocoa
1 ¼ cups confectioners' sugar

   white candy decors for garnish

1. Prepare Cookies: Preheat oven to 400°F. In medium bowl, combine flour, cocoa, baking powder, cinnamon, cloves, and salt. In large bowl, with mixer at low speed, beat granulated sugar with softened butter until blended, occasionally scraping bowl with rubber spatula. Increase speed to high; beat until light and creamy. At low speed, beat in egg. Alternately beat in flour mixture and milk, beginning and ending with flour mixture, just until combined, occasionally scraping bowl.
2. With cocoa-dusted hands, shape dough by level tablespoons into 1-inch balls. Place balls, 2 inches apart, on ungreased large cookie sheet. Bake cookies 7 to 9 minutes or until puffed (they will look dry and slightly cracked). Transfer cookies to wire rack to cool. Repeat with remaining dough.
3. When cookies are cool, prepare Chocolate Glaze: In medium bowl, with wire whisk or fork, gradually mix cocoa with *¼ cup boiling water* until smooth. Gradually stir in confectioners' sugar and blend well. Dip top of each cookie into glaze. Place cookies on wire rack set over waxed paper to catch any drips. Immediately sprinkle cookies with decors. Allow glaze to set, about 20 minutes. Store cookies, with waxed paper between layers, in tightly covered container at room temperature up to 3 days, or in freezer up to 3 months.

■ Each cookie: About 55 calories, 1 g protein, 9 g carbohydrate, 2 g total fat (1 g saturated), 8 mg cholesterol, 40 mg sodium.

new goodies for bakers

TALKATIVE TIMER No more watching the clock while cookies bake. The Digital Talking Timer ($19.95) speaks up at regular intervals, telling you how many minutes or seconds are left, then announces when time's up with the sound of a car horn, teapot whistle, cuckoo clock, or three other built-in choices. Stand the timer on the counter, attach it to the fridge, or clip it on your clothing. 1-888-442-6256 or www.digitalcookwareinc.com

BUDGET BEATER If you bake only during the holidays, why buy an expensive mixer? The Hamilton Beach Clean-Mix Stand Mixer costs an affordable $39.99, but it has enough muscle to stir a double batch of cookies. And it comes with conveniences usually found just on pricier models, such as a glass bowl and splatter shield. The model even converts to a hand mixer. At mass merchandisers; 800-851-8900 or www.hamiltonbeach.com

SELF SERVER Stop searching for a scoop when you need to measure out dry ingredients. The lid of Rubbermaid's Pour'n Saver Canister detaches for scooping and holds exactly 1 cup. The canisters come in a 2-quart ($5.49) or 3-quart ($6.99) size—perfect for storing a 5-pound bag of flour or sugar. At mass merchandisers; www.rubbermaid.com

BUTTER CUTTER Bakers can get frustrated when they need to measure butter (or margarine) if the markings on the wrapper aren't aligned with the stick. Next time, pop the naked stick into the Professional ButterMate from KitchenArt ($14.95). The gadget slices off the exact amount of butter you need, whether it's 5 tablespoons for brownies or the merest sliver to top a biscuit. The holder fits in the dairy compartment of your refrigerator and is dishwasher-safe. At gourmet and department stores; 1-888-999-2806 or www.kitchenart.com

HIDEAWAY CORD Push a button on the Oster EasyStore Hand Mixer with Retractable Cord ($24.99), and the cord slides into the mixer for tangle-free storage. This model easily handles everything from delicate whipped cream to heavy bread dough. Available in black or white at department and specialty stores. 800-334-0759; www.oster.com

Italian Tricolors

During the holidays, Food Appliances Director Sharon Franke and her sister, Nancy Lehrer, would purchase an assortment of cookies at their neighborhood bakery. These multicolored Italian treats were always the first to go. Franke thought only a bakery could make them, but we created a version that any home cook can whip up.*

PREP *1 hour plus cooling and chilling*
BAKE *about 10 minutes*
MAKES *3 dozen cookies*

  1 tube or can (7 to 8 ounces) almond paste, broken into small pieces
  ¾ cup butter or margarine (1½ sticks), softened
  ¾ cup sugar
  ½ teaspoon almond extract
  3 large eggs
  1 cup all-purpose flour
  ¼ teaspoon salt
 15 drops red food coloring
 15 drops green food coloring
  ⅔ cup apricot preserves
  3 ounces semisweet chocolate
  1 teaspoon vegetable shortening

1. Preheat oven to 350°F. Grease three 8" by 8" disposable or metal baking pans. Line bottom of pans with waxed paper; grease and flour waxed paper.
2. In large bowl, with mixer at medium-high speed, beat almond paste with softened butter, sugar, and almond extract until well blended (there will be some small lumps of almond paste remaining). Reduce speed to medium; beat in eggs, 1 at a time, until blended. Reduce speed to low; beat in flour and salt just until combined.
3. Transfer one-third of batter (about 1 rounded cup) to small bowl. Transfer half of remaining batter to another small bowl. (You should have equal amounts of batter in each bowl.) Stir red food coloring into 1 bowl of batter until evenly blended. Repeat with green food coloring and another bowl

of batter, leaving 1 bowl untinted. (Batters may still have small lumps of almond paste remaining.)
4. Spoon untinted batter into 1 pan. With metal spatula (offset if possible), spread batter evenly (layer will be about ¼ inch thick). Repeat with red batter in second pan. Repeat with green batter in remaining pan.
5. Bake cookie layers on 2 oven racks 10 to 12 minutes, rotating pans between upper and lower racks halfway through baking time, until layers are set and toothpick inserted in center of layers comes out clean.
6. Cool in pans on wire racks 5 minutes. Run knife around sides of pans to loosen layers. Invert layers onto racks, leaving waxed paper attached; cool completely.
7. When layers are cool, press apricot preserves through coarse sieve into small bowl to remove any large pieces of fruit. Remove waxed paper from green layer. Invert green layer onto flat plate or small cutting board; spread with half of apricot preserves. Remove waxed paper from untinted layer; invert onto green layer. Spread with remaining apricot preserves. Remove waxed paper from red layer; invert onto untinted layer.
8. In 1-quart saucepan, heat chocolate with shortening over low heat until melted, stirring frequently. Spread melted chocolate mixture on top of red layer (not on sides); refrigerate until chocolate is firm, at least 1 hour. If you like, after chocolate has set, cover and refrigerate stacked layers up to 3 days before cutting and serving.
9. To serve, with serrated knife, trim edges (about ¼ inch from each side). Cut stacked layers into 6 strips. Cut each strip crosswise into 6 pieces. Store cookies, in single layer, in tightly covered container in refrigerator up to 1 week, or in freezer up to 3 months.

■ Each cookie: About 125 calories, 2 g protein, 15 g carbohydrate, 7 g total fat (3 g saturated), 1 g fiber, 29 mg cholesterol, 65 mg sodium.

Meltaway Pecan Balls

Associate Production Director Luke Braun's mom, Michael Carman, entitled her version of these treats the "Best Cookies in the World." After one bite of these melt-in-your-mouth pecan balls, you'll know why! Carman says the cookies' flavor improves over time, but her family usually gobbles them up in a day or so.*

PREP *40 minutes plus cooling*
BAKE *about 16 minutes per batch*
MAKES *about 6 dozen cookies*

  1 cup pecans
 1½ cups confectioners' sugar
  1 cup butter (2 sticks), cut up (no substitutions)
  1 teaspoon vanilla extract
  2 cups all-purpose flour

1. Preheat oven to 325°F. In food processor with knife blade attached, pulse pecans with ¼ cup confectioners' sugar until nuts are very finely ground. Add butter and vanilla, and process until smooth, occasionally stopping processor and scraping side with rubber spatula. Add flour; process until evenly mixed and dough forms.
2. With floured hands, shape dough by rounded teaspoons into ¾-inch balls. Place balls, 1 inch apart, on ungreased large cookie sheet. Bake 16 to 18 minutes, or until bottoms are lightly browned and cookies are light golden. Transfer cookies to wire rack; cool slightly, about 3 minutes.
3. Meanwhile, place remaining 1¼ cups sugar in small bowl. While still warm, gently roll cookies, 1 at a time, in sugar to coat. Place cookies on rack to cool completely. When cool, gently roll cookies in sugar again.
4. Repeat with remaining cookie dough and sugar. Store cookies in tightly covered container at room temperature up to 2 weeks, or in freezer up to 3 months. (If cookies are stored

in freezer, you may need to roll them in confectioners' sugar again before serving.)

■ Each cookie: About 55 calories, 1 g protein, 5 g carbohydrate, 4 g total fat (2 g saturated), 0 g fiber, 7 mg cholesterol, 30 mg sodium.

White Chocolate-Macadamia Jumbos

Samantha Buckanoff, former assistant in the nutrition department, got this recipe from her aunt, Joanne Steinback, who made these cookies every year for their family holiday get-togethers. Buckanoff loved them because "they were huge, packed with chocolate, and soft and chewy—just the way I like my cookies!"*

PREP *30 minutes plus cooling*
BAKE *about 15 minutes per batch*
MAKES *about 2 dozen cookies*

2½ cups all-purpose flour
¾   cup butter or margarine
     (1½ sticks), softened
¾   cup granulated sugar
½   cup packed dark brown
     sugar
3   tablespoons corn syrup
2   teaspoons vanilla extract
1   teaspoon baking soda
1   teaspoon salt
2   large eggs
12 ounces white chocolate,
     Swiss confectionery bar,
     or white baking bar, coarsely
     chopped
1   jar (6½ ounces) macadamia nuts,
     chopped (about 1⅓ cups)
1½ cups dried tart cherries

1. Preheat oven to 325°F. In large bowl, with mixer at medium speed, beat flour, butter, sugars, corn syrup, vanilla, baking soda, salt, and eggs until blended, occasionally scraping bowl with rubber spatula. With spoon, stir in white chocolate, nuts, and dried cherries.

2. Drop dough by slightly rounded ¼ cups, 3 inches apart, onto ungreased large cookie sheet. Bake cookies 15 to 17 minutes or until lightly browned. Transfer cookies to wire rack to cool. Repeat with remaining dough. Store cookies in tightly covered container at room temperature up to 3 days, or in freezer up to 3 months.

■ Each cookie: About 310 calories, 4 g protein, 37 g carbohydrate, 16 g total fat (7 g saturated), 2 g fiber, 37 mg cholesterol, 275 mg sodium.

Sugar Hearts

Rachel Long Mattox, a friend of Copy Editor Michele Tomasik, contributed this delicious cookie recipe that has been cherished by family and friends for years. Mattox's father is a Protestant minister; her mother would bake these cookies on Christmas Eve, before the candlelight church service, and then deliver them to parishioners—sometimes until past midnight. The recipients always waited up, knowing Mattox's mom's cookies would eventually arrive. If you're making these treats way ahead, it's best to freeze them before decorating. Thaw completely, then follow directions in step 5.*

PREP *1 hour plus chilling and cooling*
BAKE *about 12 minutes per batch*
MAKES *about 6½ dozen cookies*

1   cup butter (2 sticks), softened
     (no substitutions)
1½ cups confectioners' sugar
1   large egg
1   teaspoon vanilla extract
2½ cups all-purpose flour
1   teaspoon baking soda
1   teaspoon cream of tartar
     about ¾ cup light corn syrup
     (optional)
     green, red, and white sugar
     crystals (optional)

1. In large bowl, with mixer at medium speed, beat butter and confectioners' sugar until creamy. Reduce speed to low; beat in egg and vanilla until blended. Beat in flour, baking soda, and cream of tartar until well combined, occasionally scraping bowl with rubber spatula.

2. Divide dough in half; flatten each half into a disk. Wrap each disk in plastic wrap and refrigerate 2 hours or until dough is firm enough to roll. (Or place dough in freezer for 15 minutes.)

3. Preheat oven to 350°F. On floured surface, with floured rolling pin, roll 1 piece of dough ¼ inch thick. With floured heart-shaped cookie cutters in various sizes, cut dough into as many cookies as possible; wrap and refrigerate trimmings. Place cookies, 1 inch apart, on ungreased large cookie sheet.

4. Bake cookies 12 to 14 minutes or until lightly browned. Transfer cookies to wire rack to cool. Repeat with remaining dough and trimmings.

5. When cookies are cool, decorate with sugar crystals if you like: In 1-quart saucepan, heat corn syrup to boiling over medium heat, stirring frequently. Boil 1 minute, stirring. Brush cookie with corn syrup, then sprinkle or dip into colored sugar crystals. Repeat with remaining cookies. Reheat syrup if it becomes too thick. Allow decoration to dry completely, about 1 hour. Store cookies in tightly covered container (with waxed paper between layers if decorated) at room temperature up to 1 week, or in freezer up to 3 months.

■ Each cookie without sugar crystals: About 45 calories, 1 g protein, 5 g carbohydrate, 3 g total fat (2 g saturated), 0 g fiber, 10 mg cholesterol, 45 mg sodium.

bake our little red barn

Start a new tradition this holiday season and make this adorable gingerbread barn with your kids. See it on page 233.

See it on page 233.

YOU WILL NEED

cardboard or posterboard, for patterns
1 batch Gingerbread Dough (recipe at right)
3 batches Ornamental Frosting (page 217)
red, blue, black, and green food-color pastes
#2 (1/32-inch opening) writing tip
#4 (1/16-inch opening) writing tip
#7 (1/8-inch opening) writing tip
#10 (1/4-inch opening) writing tip
#60 (1/3-inch opening) leaf tip couplers
disposable decorating bags
2 small artist's paint brushes
14 packages (5 sticks each) Wrigley's Spearmint chewing gum
4 packages (5 sticks each) Wrigley's Big Red chewing gum
1 roll strawberry-flavor fruit leather
1 package (7 ounces) marzipan
1 large (1/8 inch) silver dragée
nontoxic felt-tip marker (sold in crafts stores)
2 lollipop sticks (6 inches long each)
1 piece (8" by 6") foam core, at least 3/16 inch thick, for base
toy Christmas trees for decoration

Gingerbread Dough

Recipe makes enough dough for one barn; use leftover dough to make decorative pieces, such as gingerbread ornaments to hang on your tree.

2½ cups packed brown sugar
1½ cups heavy or whipping cream
1¼ cups light (mild) molasses
9½ cups all-purpose flour
2 tablespoons baking soda
1 tablespoon ground ginger

1. In very large bowl, with wire whisk, beat sugar, cream, and molasses until mixture is smooth. In medium bowl, combine flour, baking soda, and ginger. With spoon, stir flour mixture into cream mixture in 3 additions until dough is too stiff to stir, then knead with hands until flour is incorporated and dough is smooth.
2. Divide dough into 4 equal portions; flatten each into a disk to speed chilling. Wrap each disk well with plastic wrap and refrigerate at least 4 hours or overnight until dough is firm enough to roll.

MAKE PATTERNS

Copy diagrams (facing page) at 200% and cut patterns from cardboard. In addition to patterns given, you will need to cut the following: 2 Barn Sides (8" by 4"), 2 Lower Roof Panels (9" by 2¼"), 2 Upper Roof Panels (9" by 3").

ROLL DOUGH

1. Grease and flour 4 large cookie sheets (17" by 14"). Roll out dough, 1 disk at a time, on each cookie sheet to 3/16-inch thickness. (Put damp paper towels under cookie sheets to keep them from shifting while you roll dough. Placing 3/16-inch dowels or rulers on either side of dough to use as a guide will help you roll dough to uniform thickness.)
2. Chill rolled dough on cookie sheets in refrigerator or freezer at least 10 minutes or until firm enough to cut easily.
3. Use chilled dough, floured cardboard patterns, and sharp paring knife to cut all barn, cupola, and flag pieces on cookie sheets, leaving at least 1¼ inches between pieces, as dough will expand slightly during baking. Wrap and reserve trimmings in refrigerator. (For the back of the barn, it is not necessary to cut out a window.)

BAKE DOUGH

1. Preheat oven to 300°F.
2. Brush pieces lightly with *water* before baking. Bake 25 to 35 minutes until pieces are firm to the touch. (Do not overbake or else pieces will be very crisp and difficult to trim to proper size. Smaller pieces will bake faster than larger pieces on same sheet; remove them as they are done.) Remove cookie sheets from oven.
3. While gingerbread is still warm, place patterns on top again and retrim if necessary. Let pieces cool completely on cookie sheets before removing.

PAINT FRONT, BACK, AND SIDES OF BARN, CUPOLA, AND FLAG

1. Prepare first batch Ornamental Frosting; tint ½ batch red. Remove ½ cup and fill decorating bag fitted with a #2 writing tip. Add about *1 tablespoon water* to remaining frosting.

2. Use unthinned frosting to outline red sections of flag. Paint front, back, and sides of barn and cupola with thinned frosting; let dry. Fill in red sections of flag with thinned frosting; let dry. Reserve remaining red frosting in bag.

DECORATE FRONT, BACK, AND SIDES OF BARN AND CUPOLA

1. Add *1 to 2 tablespoons water* to remaining ½ batch untinted white frosting; cover and set aside.

2. Make second batch Ornamental Frosting. Place 1½ cups frosting in bag fitted with #4 writing tip.

3. Using nontoxic marker, mark door frame (3¼" by 3"), Z-shaped design, and window frame (2½" by 2¼") on front of barn. With white frosting in bag, pipe outline of door frame, Z, and window; let dry.

4. Beginning at bottom, pipe 6 horizontal lines ½ inch apart on sides of barn. Also from bottom, pipe 13 horizontal lines ½ inch apart on front and back of barn. For sides of cupola, pipe 2 parallel lines down sides; pipe 2 parallel lines down 2 sides of front and back pieces; pipe vertical lines on door frame; let dry.

5. Fill in window and door frames and Z with thinned white frosting; let dry. With frosting in bag, pipe parallel lines over top of each frame and Z; let dry.

(continued on next page)

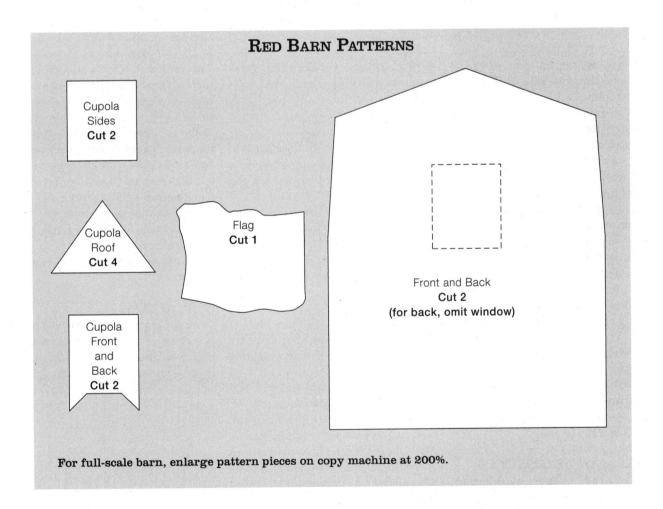

RED BARN PATTERNS

Cupola Sides
Cut 2

Cupola Roof
Cut 4

Flag
Cut 1

Cupola Front and Back
Cut 2

Front and Back
Cut 2
(for back, omit window)

For full-scale barn, enlarge pattern pieces on copy machine at 200%.

DECORATE FLAG

1. Tint ½ cup frosting blue. Add *1 to 2 teaspoons water* until spreadable. Paint blue section of flag; let dry.

2. Refit bag of white frosting with #7 writing tip. Pipe 6 stripes. Refit bag with #2 tip and pipe 5 rows of 6 dots and 4 rows of 5 dots for 50 stars. With white frosting, attach 1 lollipop stick to flag for flagpole; attach dragée to top of pole; let dry.

ASSEMBLE BARN

1. Prepare third batch Ornamental Frosting to use as glue when ready to assemble barn. Cover with damp paper towel and plastic wrap to prevent frosting from drying out.

2. Place ½ batch frosting in bag fitted with #10 writing tip; pipe along cut edge of foam-core base. Attach bottom of front, back, and side pieces of barn to foam-core base. Use extra frosting along inside seams to reinforce corners. Place some full soup cans or other heavy objects next to barn walls, both inside and outside, to support pieces while drying.

3. Assemble front, back, and sides of cupola on counter or other work surface, gluing pieces together along seams with a generous amount of reserved unthinned red frosting.

4. Assemble roof of cupola with a generous amount of unthinned white frosting, attaching pieces together along 1¾-inch sides and leaving a ⅛-inch-wide hole in center top to attach flagpole.

5. Let barn dry overnight. Store unused frosting on counter, covered with several layers of damp paper towels and plastic wrap.

MAKE AND DECORATE COW

1. For head, shape a tablespoon marzipan into a 1½-inch oval, tapering slightly at one end. Shape ⅛ teaspoon marzipan into a ½-inch oval; flatten slightly for nose. Use toothpick to make nostrils. Press nose onto tapered end of oval. Use a small knife to make a slit for mouth. Roll 2 tiny balls marzipan for eyes; press to attach. Pinch area behind eyes to form ears. Insert lollipop stick into base of head, shaping excess marzipan onto stick to attach. Roll 2 tiny balls marzipan to form horns; attach to head in front of ears. Roll 1 rounded teaspoon marzipan into a 2-inch rope; attach around neck to form a yoke; let dry.

2. Paint cow head and neck with thinned white frosting; let dry.

3. Tint 1 tablespoon unthinned frosting pink and tint another tablespoon black. Thin pink and black frosting with *water* to painting consistency. Tint ¼ cup unthinned frosting green and place in decorating bag with #60 leaf tip.

4. With small artist's brushes, paint features on cow face, eyes, ears, nose, and mouth as shown on page 233. With green frosting, pipe wreath around yoke and let dry.

5. To make bow: Cut fruit leather into an 8" by ¼" strip. Tie into a bow. Cut two 3" by ¼" strips; press to back side of bow for streamers.

6. To attach cow to barn: Pipe a line of thick white frosting along base and inside of window. Insert cow into window and attach; let dry. With small dab of frosting attach bow to wreath; let dry.

THATCH ROOF

1. Unwrap packages of spearmint gum. Cut each stick crosswise into thirds.

2. Using white frosting and #10 tip, pipe a thick horizontal line about ½ inch from base of each panel of barn roof. Attach gum pieces side by side in a row along the line. Pipe another line of frosting about ½ inch higher, and add another row of gum slightly overlapping top of row below. Repeat to cover all roof pieces; let dry.

3. Unwrap 2 packages of cinnamon gum. Using white frosting, pipe a thick horizontal line about ½ inch from base of one side of cupola roof. Cut one stick gum crosswise into thirds, then trim pieces at an angle to fit the base of roof. Attach pieces side by side in a row along line at base of cupola roof. Make 3 more rows with remaining gum, cutting pieces at an angle to fit and leaving hole in top for flagpole. Repeat process on remaining 3 sides of roof; let dry.

4. Insert flagpole into cupola roof; attach from underside with frosting and let dry.

5. Attach 2 lower roof panels to base of barn with ample frosting to secure them. Support with cans; let dry. Attach upper roof panels to lower roof panels as above. Add remaining spearmint gum to peak of roof, overlapping slightly.

6. Unwrap remaining cinnamon gum. Cut each piece crosswise into six ½-inch-wide pieces. Pipe a thick vertical line of frosting along one edge of barn side. Starting about ½ inch from base of the line, glue 1 piece gum. Add another piece gum about ½ inch higher; add more pieces slightly overlapping to reach top of edge. Repeat process along remaining 3 edges of barn.

7. Pipe frosting along front and back edges of roof. Attach remaining gum, overlapping pieces; let dry.

8. Frost bottom edge of cupola; attach to roof.

DISPLAY TIPS

Display barn in a cool, dry area away from heat. To transport barn, place it in a box and cushion with bubble wrap to protect it while in transit.

Bonus

Bonus Recipes

breads

Buttermilk Biscuits Three Ways

Try this trio of biscuits for a new spin on a family favorite. Serve warm Monterey Jack and Parmesan-pepper biscuits with dinner and reheat the maple-glazed walnut variety for breakfast the next morning.

PREP *30 minutes*
BAKE *12 to 15 minutes per batch*
MAKES *about 1½ dozen biscuits*

6 cups all-purpose flour
⅓ cup sugar
2 tablespoons cream of tartar
1 tablespoon baking soda
1½ teaspoons salt
1 cup shortening or butter-flavor shortening
2¼ cups buttermilk
¼ pound Monterey Jack cheese with jalapeño chiles, shredded (1 cup)
1 cup walnuts, coarsely chopped
2 tablespoons maple syrup
½ cup grated Parmesan cheese
½ teaspoon coarsely ground black pepper

1. In large bowl, mix flour, sugar, cream of tartar, baking soda, and salt. With pastry blender or 2 knives used scissor-fashion, cut in shortening until mixture resembles coarse crumbs. Stir in buttermilk; quickly mix just until dough forms and leaves side of bowl. Turn dough onto lightly floured surface. Divide dough into thirds and cover lightly with plastic wrap.
2. Preheat oven to 425°F. With floured hands, knead Monterey Jack into one-third of dough, kneading about 8 strokes to mix thoroughly. With floured rolling pin, roll dough ¾ inch thick. With floured 3-inch round biscuit cutter, cut out biscuits. With wide metal spatula, place biscuits, about 1 inch apart, on ungreased large cookie sheet. Press trimmings together; roll and cut to make more biscuits (you will have about 6 biscuits). Bake 12 to 15 minutes or until golden. Transfer to wire rack.
3. Knead walnuts into second one-third of dough, kneading and cutting dough as above. Brush biscuits with maple syrup. Place biscuits on ungreased cookie sheet; bake as above.
4. Meanwhile, knead Parmesan and pepper into remaining dough, kneading and cutting as above. Sprinkle top of biscuits with additional pepper if you like. Place on ungreased cookie sheet; bake as above.
5. Serve biscuits warm or cool on wire rack to serve later. Reheat biscuits if desired.

■ Each Monterey Jack Biscuit: About 350 calories, 10 g protein, 37 g carbohydrate, 18 g total fat (7 g saturated), 1 g fiber, 18 mg cholesterol, 535 mg sodium.

■ Each Maple-Walnut Biscuit: About 425 calories, 8 g protein, 44 g carbohydrate, 25 g total fat (4 g saturated), 3 g fiber, 1 mg cholesterol, 435 mg sodium.

■ Each Parmesan Biscuit: About 310 calories, 8 g protein, 37 g carbohydrate, 14 g total fat (4 g saturated), 1 g fiber, 6 mg cholesterol, 555 mg sodium.

main dishes

Pasta with Chicken & Vegetables

This simple skillet supper delivers a hearty one-dish meal packed with flavor. Artichoke hearts, red and yellow peppers, and mushrooms add something extra to everyday chicken and pasta.

PREP *20 minutes*
COOK *about 35 minutes*
MAKES *8 main-dish servings*

2 jars (6 ounces each) marinated artichoke hearts
3 tablespoons balsamic vinegar
½ teaspoon coarsely ground black pepper
½ teaspoon dried basil
½ teaspoon sugar
salt
2 tablespoons olive oil
4 large red and/or yellow peppers, cut into ½-inch slices
1 pound mushrooms, each cut in half
1 medium onion, chopped
1 package (1 pound) penne or rigatoni pasta
1¼ pounds skinless, boneless chicken-breast halves, cut crosswise into ¾-inch-thick slices

1. Drain artichoke hearts, reserving marinade from 1 jar. In small bowl, mix marinade, vinegar, pepper, basil, sugar, and ½ teaspoon salt; set aside.
2. In nonstick 12-inch skillet, heat 1 tablespoon oil over medium-high heat until hot. Add peppers and ¼ teaspoon salt, and cook until tender and golden, stirring frequently. With slotted spoon, transfer peppers to large bowl. Add mushrooms, onion, and ¼ teaspoon salt to skillet, and cook until tender and golden, stirring frequently. Transfer mushroom mixture to bowl with peppers.
3. In large saucepot, cook pasta in *boiling salted water* as label directs.
4. Meanwhile, in same skillet, heat remaining 1 tablespoon olive oil over medium-high heat. Add chicken to skillet; sprinkle with ¼ teaspoon salt and cook until it loses its pink color throughout, stirring occasionally.
5. Return cooked vegetables to skillet with chicken. Add artichoke hearts and marinade mixture, tossing to coat well; heat through.
6. Drain pasta; return to saucepot. Add chicken mixture and toss well.

■ Each serving: About 395 calories, 26 g protein, 56 g carbohydrate, 8 g total fat (1 g saturated), 6 g fiber, 41 mg cholesterol, 590 mg sodium.

Braised Chicken & Lentils

Curry powder enhances chicken and lentils in this Indian-inspired meal for two.

PREP **15 minutes**
COOK **about 1 hour**
MAKES **2 main-dish servings**

- 1 tablespoon olive oil
- 2 large chicken leg quarters, skin removed
- 1 teaspoon salt
- 1 large carrot, chopped
- 1 small celery stalk, chopped
- 1 small onion, chopped
- 1 small garlic clove, minced
- 1 teaspoon curry powder
- ½ cup dry lentils, rinsed and picked over
- 1 can (14½ ounces) stewed tomatoes
- 2 tablespoons chopped fresh parsley leaves

1. In nonstick 10-inch skillet, heat oil over medium-high heat until hot. Add chicken legs; sprinkle with ¼ teaspoon salt and cook until browned on both sides. Transfer chicken to plate.
2. Reduce heat to medium. To drippings remaining in skillet, add carrot, celery, and onion, and cook 10 minutes, stirring occasionally. Add garlic and curry powder, and cook 1 minute, stirring. Add lentils, remaining ¾ teaspoon salt, and *1½ cups water;* heat to boiling over medium-high heat. Reduce heat to low; cover and simmer 15 minutes or until lentils are almost tender.
3. Add tomatoes and chicken to skillet; heat to boiling over medium-high heat. Reduce heat to low; cover and simmer 20 minutes or until lentils are tender and juices run clear when chicken is pierced with tip of knife. Stir in chopped parsley.

■ Each serving: About 545 calories, 53 g protein, 51 g carbohydrate, 16 g total fat (3 g saturated), 19 g fiber, 145 mg cholesterol, 1,805 mg sodium.

Chicken, Rice & Bean Casserole

Two kinds of beans and several veggies pump up this hearty one-dish meal.

PREP **30 minutes**
BAKE **40 minutes**
MAKES **4 main-dish servings**

- 4 large skinless chicken-leg quarters (about 3 pounds with bones)
- ½ teaspoon paprika
- ½ teaspoon salt
- ½ teaspoon coarsely ground black pepper
- 1 tablespoon vegetable oil
- 1 medium onion, chopped
- 1 medium green pepper, chopped
- 1 cup long-grain white rice
- 1 can (8 ounces) tomato sauce
- ½ cup pimiento-stuffed olives, each cut in half
- 1 can (15 to 19 ounces) garbanzo beans, rinsed and drained
- 1 can (15 to 19 ounces) red kidney beans, rinsed and drained

1. Sprinkle chicken with paprika, salt, and pepper.
2. Preheat oven to 375°F. In 12-inch skillet, heat oil over medium-high heat until hot. Add chicken and cook until golden on all sides; transfer to plate.
3. Reduce heat to medium; add onion and green pepper to skillet, and cook until tender-crisp. Add rice, stirring until opaque. Stir in tomato sauce and *1¼ cups water;* boil over high heat.
4. Spoon rice mixture into 13" by 9" glass baking dish. Tuck chicken into rice. Cover baking dish and bake 30 minutes. Gently stir olives and beans into rice mixture. Cover and bake 10 minutes longer or until beans and olives are heated through, rice is tender, and juices run clear when thickest part of chicken leg is pierced with tip of knife.

■ Each serving: About 740 calories, 57 g protein, 90 g carbohydrate, 17 g total fat (4 g saturated), 16 g fiber, 155 mg cholesterol, 2,085 mg sodium.

Balsamic Chicken

Potatoes and chicken get a flavor boost from brown sugar, vinegar, and soy sauce.

PREP **20 minutes**
COOK **about 25 minutes**
MAKES **4 main-dish servings**

- 1 pound red potatoes, cut into 1-inch pieces
- 6 large skinless, boneless chicken thighs (about 1¼ pounds), each cut in half
- 2 tablespoons all-purpose flour
- ½ teaspoon salt
- 2 teaspoons olive oil
- 3 garlic cloves, each cut lengthwise in half
- 2 tablespoons brown sugar
- 2 tablespoons balsamic vinegar
- 2 tablespoons soy sauce
- 2 bunches arugula, tough stems discarded

1. In 2-quart saucepan, place potatoes and *enough water to cover;* heat to boiling over high heat. Reduce heat to low; cover and simmer 7 to 10 minutes or until potatoes are fork-tender; drain and set aside.
2. Meanwhile, in medium bowl, toss chicken with flour and salt.
3. In nonstick 12-inch skillet, heat oil over medium heat until hot. Add chicken and garlic, and cook, covered, 20 minutes or until chicken is browned and loses its pink color throughout, turning chicken over once.
4. In cup, stir brown sugar, vinegar, and soy sauce. Add brown-sugar mixture to skillet, tossing to coat chicken well. Remove skillet from heat; add potatoes and half of arugula, tossing to mix well. Arrange remaining arugula on platter. Top with chicken mixture.

■ Each serving: About 355 calories, 33 g protein, 37 g carbohydrate, 8 g total fat (2 g saturated), 3 g fiber, 118 mg cholesterol, 925 mg sodium.

Spicy Shrimp Stir-fry

Red potatoes and snow peas serve as mellow accompaniments to spicy-hot shrimp.

PREP *30 minutes*
COOK *about 25 minutes*
MAKES *2 main-dish servings*

    6 small red potatoes (about 12
         ounces)
    ½ cup loosely packed fresh parsley
         leaves, chopped
    3 teaspoons plus 1 tablespoon
         vegetable oil
    ¼ teaspoon salt
    1 lemon
    ¾ pound large shrimp, shelled and
         deveined
    2 tablespoons soy sauce
    1 tablespoon peeled, grated fresh
         ginger
    1 garlic clove, crushed with garlic
         press
    ⅛ to ¼ teaspoon ground red pepper
         (cayenne)
    6 ounces snow peas or snap peas,
         strings removed

1. In 3-quart saucepan, place potatoes and *enough water to cover;* heat to boiling over high heat. Reduce heat to low; cover and simmer 15 minutes or until potatoes are fork-tender. Drain; return potatoes to saucepan. Stir in parsley, 2 teaspoons oil, and ⅛ teaspoon salt; cover to keep warm.
2. From lemon, grate 2 teaspoons peel and squeeze 1 tablespoon juice. In medium bowl, mix lemon peel, lemon juice, shrimp, soy sauce, ginger, garlic, and ground red pepper until blended.
3. In nonstick 10-inch skillet, heat 1 teaspoon oil over medium-high heat until hot. Add snow peas and remaining ⅛ teaspoon salt, and cook about 5 minutes or until tender-crisp, stirring frequently. Transfer to 2 dinner plates.
4. In same skillet, heat remaining 1 tablespoon oil over medium-high heat until hot but not smoking. Add shrimp mixture and cook until shrimp

turn opaque throughout, about 3 minutes, stirring constantly. Serve shrimp mixture with potatoes and snow peas.

■ Each serving: About 475 calories, 36 g protein, 46 g carbohydrate, 17 g total fat (1 g saturated), 6 g fiber, 216 mg cholesterol, 1,500 mg sodium.

Beef-Stew Casserole

This oven version of beef stew bakes up extra thick and chunky.

PREP *1 hour*
BAKE *2 hours*
MAKES *8 main-dish servings*

    1 pound small white onions
    1 tablespoon vegetable oil
    2 pounds beef for stew, cut into
         2-inch chunks
    1 can (14½ ounces) beef broth
         (1¾ cups)
    2 tablespoons Worcestershire sauce
    1 teaspoon salt
    1 container (10 ounces) mushrooms
    6 medium all-purpose potatoes
         (2 pounds), peeled and each
         cut into quarters
    1 pound carrots, cut into 2-inch
         chunks
    2 tablespoons all-purpose flour
    1 container (10 ounces) Brussels
         sprouts, each cut in half

1. Preheat oven to 375°F. Peel onions, leaving a little of the root ends to help onions hold their shape during cooking. In 8-quart Dutch oven, heat oil over medium-high heat until hot. Add onions and cook until golden brown; with slotted spoon, transfer onions to large bowl.
2. Add half of beef to Dutch oven and cook until lightly browned; transfer to bowl with onions. Repeat with remaining beef.
3. Return beef and onions to Dutch oven; stir in broth, Worcestershire sauce, salt, mushrooms, and *½ cup*

water. Heat to boiling over high heat, scraping to loosen brown bits from bottom of Dutch oven. Cover and bake 1 hour, stirring occasionally.
4. Stir in potatoes and carrots; cover and bake 30 minutes.
5. In cup, mix flour and *¼ cup water;* stir into stew in Dutch oven. Add Brussels sprouts; cover and bake 30 minutes longer or until meat and vegetables are fork-tender, stirring occasionally.
6. Before serving, skim fat from liquid in Dutch oven.

■ Each serving: About 360 calories, 34 g protein, 34 g carbohydrate, 10 g total fat (3 g saturated), 6 g fiber, 70 mg cholesterol, 550 mg sodium.

Chinese "Pepper Steak"

You'll never miss the steak in this delicious stir-fry. Tofu is quickly marinated in a soy-ginger mixture, cooked with colorful vegetables, and served over rice.

PREP *30 minutes*
COOK *about 20 minutes*
MAKES *4 main-dish servings*

    1 package (16 ounces) firm tofu,
         drained and cut into ½-inch
         cubes
    2 tablespoons soy sauce
    1 tablespoon Asian sesame oil
    2 teaspoons peeled, grated fresh
         ginger
    1 cup long-grain white rice
    1 tablespoon vegetable oil
    ¼ pound mushrooms, each cut into
         quarters
    1 red pepper, cut into ½-inch-wide
         strips
    1 yellow pepper, cut into ½-inch-
         wide strips
    ¼ pound snow peas or snap peas,
         strings removed
    1 green onion, thinly sliced
    ⅛ teaspoon salt

1. In medium bowl, with rubber spatula, gently stir tofu, soy sauce, sesame oil, and ginger until blended; set aside.
2. Prepare rice as label directs; cover to keep warm.
3. In nonstick 12-inch skillet, heat vegetable oil over medium-high heat until hot. Add mushrooms, red and yellow peppers, snow peas, green onion, and salt, and cook until vegetables are tender-crisp and lightly browned, stirring frequently. Gently stir in tofu mixture; heat through. Serve with cooked rice.

■ Each serving: About 365 calories, 16 g protein, 50 g carbohydrate, 13 g total fat (2 g saturated), 4 g fiber, 0 mg cholesterol, 580 mg sodium.

Red Beans & Rice

A premixed seasoning blend guarantees you can have this dish on the table in no time! Serve with a mixed green salad to round out the meal.

PREP **15 minutes**
COOK **20 minutes**
MAKES **4 main-dish servings**

1½ cups long-grain white rice
¾ teaspoon salt
 2 tablespoons olive oil
 1 large onion, cut into ¼-inch dice
 1 large green pepper, cut into ¼-inch dice
¾ teaspoon Cajun seasoning
 2 cans (15 to 16 ounces each) red or pink beans, rinsed and drained

1. Prepare rice as label directs but use only ¾ teaspoon salt.
2. Meanwhile, in 3-quart saucepan, heat oil over medium heat until hot. Add onion and green pepper, and cook 15 minutes or until vegetables are tender and lightly browned. Stir in Cajun seasoning; cook 1 minute longer.

3. Add beans and *1 cup water* to onion mixture; heat to boiling over high heat. Reduce heat to low and cover and simmer 5 minutes to blend flavors.
4. Spoon red-bean mixture over rice to serve.

■ Each serving: About 515 calories, 17 g protein, 95 g carbohydrate, 8 g total fat (1 g saturated), 13 g fiber, 0 mg cholesterol, 815 mg sodium.

Vegetable-Barley Paella

This medley of beans, vegetables, and barley provides a comforting meal on a cold winter night.

PREP **25 minutes**
COOK **about 1¼ hours**
MAKES **6 main-dish servings**

 2 cans (14½ ounces each) vegetable broth or chicken broth (3½ cups)
¾ cup pearl barley
 2 tablespoons olive oil
 1 medium onion, cut into ¼-inch dice
 2 small zucchini (8 ounces each), cut into 1-inch chunks
10 ounces mushrooms, each cut in half
 1 teaspoon salt
 1 teaspoon dried oregano
 1 medium head cauliflower, separated into 1-inch flowerets
 2 medium carrots, cut into ¼-inch-thick slices
 1 package (9 ounces) frozen artichoke hearts, thawed
 1 package (9 ounces) frozen whole green beans, thawed
 1 can (15 to 19 ounces) black beans, rinsed and drained
½ cup pimiento-stuffed olives, drained and chopped

1. In 4-quart saucepan, heat broth, barley, and *2 cups water* to boiling

over high heat. Reduce heat to low; cover and simmer 1 hour.
2. Meanwhile, in 12-inch skillet, heat olive oil over medium heat until hot. Add onion and cook 10 minutes or until tender, stirring occasionally. Add zucchini, mushrooms, salt, and oregano, and cook 10 minutes longer or until zucchini is lightly browned and tender-crisp, stirring occasionally. Remove skillet from heat.
3. In 5-quart Dutch oven or saucepot, heat *1 inch water* to boiling over high heat. Add cauliflower and carrots; heat to boiling. Reduce heat to low; cover and simmer 5 minutes. Add artichokes and green beans; heat to boiling. Reduce heat to low; cover and simmer 5 minutes longer or until all vegetables are tender. Drain cauliflower mixture; return to Dutch oven.
4. After barley has cooked 1 hour, remove cover and cook over high heat until most of liquid is absorbed. Stir barley, zucchini mixture, and black beans into cauliflower mixture; heat through. Sprinkle with olives to serve.

■ Each serving: About 290 calories, 13 g protein, 52 g carbohydrate, 8 g total fat (1 g saturated), 16 g fiber, 0 mg cholesterol, 1,455 mg sodium.

Chicken-Salad Olé

Lime and medium-hot salsa add a Mexican kick to this chicken salad.

PREP *15 minutes*
COOK *15 minutes*
MAKES *4 main-dish servings*

    1   large lime
    1   bag (10 ounces) spinach, tough
        stems discarded
    1   small head Boston lettuce
    2   teaspoons plus 3 tablespoons
        olive oil
    4   small skinless, boneless chicken-
        breast halves (about 1 pound)
    ½   teaspoon salt
    1   teaspoon Dijon mustard
    ½   teaspoon sugar
    ¾   cup medium-hot salsa
    ¼   cup pitted ripe olives, finely chopped

1. From lime, grate 1 teaspoon peel and squeeze 1 tablespoon juice. Reserve peel for garnish.
2. Into bowl, tear spinach and lettuce leaves into bite-size pieces; refrigerate.
3. In nonstick 12-inch skillet, heat 2 teaspoons oil over medium-high heat until hot. Add chicken breasts and cook 5 minutes or until golden brown. Turn chicken and sprinkle with ¼ teaspoon salt; reduce heat to medium. Cook chicken until juices run clear when pierced with tip of knife, about 5 minutes longer. Transfer chicken to plate; discard drippings.
4. While chicken is cooking, prepare dressing: In small bowl, with wire whisk or fork, mix mustard, sugar, lime juice, remaining 3 tablespoons oil, and remaining ¼ teaspoon salt. Add dressing to spinach and lettuce in bowl; toss to coat. Place salad on large platter.
5. In same skillet over medium heat, mix salsa, olives, and *¼ cup water;* heat through.
6. Cut each chicken-breast half diagonally into 3 slices, keeping slices together. Arrange chicken on salad.

Spoon salsa mixture over chicken; sprinkle chicken with lime peel.

■ Each serving: About 295 calories, 29 g protein, 6 g carbohydrate, 18 g total fat (3 g saturated), 3 g fiber, 73 mg cholesterol, 660 mg sodium.

Deli Roast Beef & Bean Salad

Caper sauce adds zest to this tasty main-dish salad.

PREP *30 minutes*
MAKES *6 main-dish servings*

Bean Salad
    1   can (15 to 19 ounces) garbanzo
        beans, rinsed and drained
    1   jar (6 ounces) marinated artichoke
        hearts, drained
    1   jar (4 ounces) marinated
        mushrooms, drained
    2   medium tomatoes, each cut into
        8 wedges
    ½   small red onion, thinly sliced
    ¼   cup niçoise or small pitted ripe
        olives
    2   tablespoons chopped fresh parsley
        leaves
    2   tablespoons red wine vinegar
    1   tablespoon olive oil
    ¼   teaspoon salt
    ¼   teaspoon ground black pepper

Caper Sauce
    ¼   cup olive oil
    2   tablespoons Dijon mustard
    1   tablespoon fresh lemon juice
    1   tablespoon capers, drained
    1   teaspoon sugar
    ¼   teaspoon salt
    ¼   teaspoon ground black pepper

    1   head romaine lettuce
    1   pound thinly sliced deli roast beef

1. Prepare Bean Salad: In large bowl, with rubber spatula, stir all salad ingredients until combined. Let stand 15 minutes to blend flavors.

2. Meanwhile, prepare Caper Sauce: In small bowl, with wire whisk or fork, mix all sauce ingredients with *2 tablespoons water* until blended.
3. Arrange romaine leaves, roast-beef slices, and garbanzo-bean mixture on large platter. Spoon Caper Sauce over romaine and roast beef.

■ Each serving: About 430 calories, 31 g protein, 23 g carbohydrate, 24 g total fat (5 g saturated), 7 g fiber, 73 mg cholesterol, 890 mg sodium.

Hearty Italian Bean Soup

Beans and vegetables combine for a flavorful low-fat soup.

PREP *20 minutes*
COOK *about 35 minutes*
MAKES *4 main-dish servings*

    2   cans (15 to 19 ounces each) white
        kidney beans (cannellini), rinsed
        and drained
    1   tablespoon olive oil
    2   medium celery stalks, cut into
        ¼-inch dice
    2   medium carrots, thinly sliced
    1   medium onion, chopped
    1   small zucchini (about 8 ounces),
        cut into ½-inch dice
    ½   teaspoon dried basil
    ½   teaspoon salt
    ¼   teaspoon coarsely ground black
        pepper
    1   can (14½ ounces) stewed
        tomatoes
    1   can (14½ ounces) vegetable or
        chicken broth (1¾ cups)
    1   package (10 ounces) frozen
        chopped spinach, thawed and
        squeezed dry
        grated Parmesan cheese (optional)

1. Place 1½ cups beans in medium bowl; with potato masher or fork, mash beans until almost smooth.
2. In 5-quart Dutch oven, heat oil over medium-high heat until hot. Add celery, carrots, onion, zucchini, basil,

salt, and pepper; cook until vegetables are tender and begin to brown, about 15 minutes, stirring occasionally.

3. Stir in tomatoes, broth, spinach, mashed beans, and *2 cups water,* breaking up tomatoes with side of spoon; heat to boiling. Reduce heat to low; cover and simmer soup 15 minutes to blend flavors. Stir in remaining beans; heat through. Serve with grated Parmesan if you like.

■ Each serving: About 330 calories, 16 g protein, 58 g carbohydrate, 5 g total fat (1 g saturated), 16 g fiber, 0 mg cholesterol, 1,375 mg sodium.

sides

Sautéed Zucchini & Mushrooms

Balsamic vinegar and a dash of sugar make this side dish tangy sweet.

PREP *10 minutes*
COOK *about 15 minutes*
MAKES *4 accompaniment servings*

2 tablespoons olive oil
2 zucchini (about 8 ounces each), cut into ½-inch-thick slices
10 ounces mushrooms, each cut in half
½ teaspoon salt
¼ teaspoon ground black pepper
1 tablespoon balsamic vinegar
½ teaspoon sugar

1. In 10-inch skillet, heat oil over medium-high heat. Add zucchini, mushrooms, salt, and pepper, and cook 15 minutes or until vegetables are browned and tender-crisp.
2. Stir in vinegar, sugar, and *1 tablespoon water;* heat through.

■ Each serving: About 100 calories, 3 g protein, 7 g carbohydrate, 7 g total fat (1 g saturated), 2 g fiber, 0 mg cholesterol, 295 mg sodium.

Peas, Onions & Radishes

This simple trio of vegetables can be on the table in just 30 minutes.

PREP *10 minutes*
COOK *about 20 minutes*
MAKES *6 accompaniment servings*

2 tablespoons margarine or butter
1 large onion, cut into 1-inch pieces
2 large bunches radishes, each radish sliced lengthwise in half
½ teaspoon salt
¼ teaspoon ground black pepper
½ teaspoon sugar
1 package (10 ounces) frozen peas, thawed

1. In 3-quart saucepan, melt margarine over medium heat. Add onion and cook 10 minutes or until onion is tender and golden, stirring occasionally.
2. Add radishes, salt, and pepper, and cook 5 minutes or until golden, stirring frequently. Stir in sugar and *2 tablespoons water;* cover and cook 5 minutes or until radishes are tender-crisp.
3. Stir in peas and cook 2 minutes or until heated through.

■ Each serving: About 95 calories, 4 g protein, 12 g carbohydrate, 4 g total fat (1 g saturated), 3 g fiber, 0 mg cholesterol, 305 mg sodium.

Broccoli Rabe with Garlic

Sauté broccoli rabe, a slightly bitter green, with garlic for a perfect pairing.

PREP *10 minutes*
COOK *about 10 minutes*
MAKES *4 accompaniment servings*

2 tablespoons olive oil
1 large garlic clove, sliced
1 large bunch broccoli rabe (1½ pounds), ends trimmed
½ teaspoon salt

In 4-quart saucepan, heat oil over medium-high heat until hot. Add garlic; cook 1 minute. Add broccoli rabe and salt; cook 10 to 12 minutes or until broccoli rabe is tender-crisp, stirring often.

■ Each serving: About 95 calories, 3 g protein, 6 g carbohydrate, 7 g total fat (1 g saturated), 3 g fiber, 0 mg cholesterol, 320 mg sodium.

desserts

Mocha Truffles

Make these truffles up to two weeks ahead—they're perfect for holiday gift-giving.

PREP *30 minutes plus chilling*
COOK *about 5 minutes*
MAKES *about 4 dozen truffles*

12 ounces semisweet chocolate, coarsely chopped
¾ cup sweetened condensed milk
1 tablespoon instant-coffee powder or granules
2 tablespoons coffee-flavor liqueur
⅛ teaspoon salt
    unsweetened cocoa

1. In heavy 2-quart saucepan, melt chocolate over low heat, stirring occasionally. Stir in undiluted sweetened condensed milk, instant-coffee powder, liqueur, and salt until well mixed.
2. Refrigerate mixture about 30 minutes or until easy to shape.
3. Place cocoa in small bowl. Dust hands with cocoa, then shape 1 rounded teaspoon chocolate mixture into a ball. Dip ball in cocoa. Repeat with remaining chocolate mixture. Store in tightly covered container, with waxed paper between layers, in refrigerator up to 2 weeks.

■ Each truffle: About 55 calories, 1 g protein, 7 g carbohydrate, 3 g total fat (2 g saturated), 1 g fiber, 2 mg cholesterol, 10 mg sodium.

Fruit Bundles

Impress your guests with these elegant packages of fruit-filled puff pastry. Sprinkle confectioners' sugar over the top for a finishing touch.

PREP *30 minutes plus cooling*
BAKE *about 20 minutes*
MAKES *8 servings*

¾ cup pitted dried plums (prunes)
¾ cup dried apricot halves
¾ cup apple juice
1 medium Golden Delicious apple, peeled, cored, and cut into ½-inch pieces
1 tablespoon all-purpose flour
½ teaspoon ground cinnamon
¼ cup plus 1 tablespoon granulated sugar
1 package (17¼ ounces) frozen puff-pastry sheets, slightly thawed
confectioners' sugar

1. With scissors, coarsely chop dried plums and apricots. In 1-quart saucepan, heat dried plums, apricots, and apple juice to boiling over high heat. Reduce heat to low; simmer 8 to 10 minutes or until fruit is soft and liquid is absorbed. Remove saucepan from heat; cool completely.
2. In large bowl, combine apple pieces, flour, cinnamon, cooled fruit mixture, and ¼ cup granulated sugar.
3. Unfold 1 sheet of pastry on lightly floured surface. With floured rolling pin, roll pastry to 12-inch square. Cut into four 6-inch squares. Spoon one-eighth of fruit mixture onto center of each square.
4. Brush *water* on edges of 1 pastry square. Bring corners of pastry square together over fruit mixture; gently squeeze and twist pastry together to seal in fruit filling, forming a bundle. Fan out corners of pastry. Repeat to make 3 more bundles.
5. Preheat oven to 425°F. Repeat steps 3 and 4 with second sheet of pastry to make 4 more bundles.

6. Place bundles, 2 inches apart, on ungreased large cookie sheet. Brush tops of bundles with *water,* then sprinkle with remaining 1 tablespoon granulated sugar. Bake 20 to 25 minutes or until bundles are puffed and golden. Sprinkle with confectioners' sugar. Serve bundles warm or transfer to wire rack to cool.

■ Each serving: About 455 calories, 6 g protein, 59 g carbohydrate, 24 g total fat (6 g saturated), 4 g fiber, 0 mg cholesterol, 155 mg sodium.

Peanut-Chocolate Balls

Finely chopped peanuts add a crunchy coating to these rich candies.

PREP *about 45 minutes plus chilling*
COOK *about 5 minutes*
MAKES *about 6 dozen candies*

1 cup creamy peanut butter
1 cup confectioners' sugar
1 tablespoon honey
6 ounces semisweet chocolate, coarsely chopped
1 tablespoon vegetable shortening
2 cups dry-roasted peanuts, finely chopped

1. In medium bowl, mix peanut butter, confectioners' sugar, and honey until evenly blended, kneading with hands if necessary. Line 15½" by 10½" jelly-roll pan with waxed paper. Shape peanut butter mixture into ¾-inch balls; place in jelly-roll pan. Cover and refrigerate 2 hours or until firm.
2. When peanut butter balls are firm, in 1-quart saucepan, heat chocolate and shortening over low heat until melted and smooth, stirring frequently. Remove saucepan from heat; cool slightly.
3. Place chopped peanuts in small bowl. With fork, carefully dip peanut butter balls into chocolate mixture. Then, using fork, roll balls in peanuts to coat. Return coated balls to jelly-roll pan. Loosely cover pan, and refrigerate

1 hour or until coating is set. Store in tightly covered container in refrigerator up to 2 weeks.

■ Each candy: About 65 calories, 2 g protein, 5 g carbohydrate, 5 g total fat (1 g saturated), 1 g fiber, 0 mg cholesterol, 50 mg sodium.

Rice-Pudding Surprise

A layer of pureed strawberries rests beneath creamy pudding in this fat-free dessert.

PREP *20 minutes plus chilling*
COOK *about 1 hour*
MAKES *6 servings*

3½ cups fat-free (skim) milk
½ cup long-grain white rice
4 teaspoons sugar
½ teaspoon salt
1 package (10 ounces) frozen sliced strawberries with syrup, thawed
1¼ cups vanilla low-fat frozen yogurt, slightly softened

1. In 3-quart saucepan, heat milk, rice, sugar, and salt to boiling over medium-high heat. Reduce heat to low; cover and simmer 50 to 55 minutes, stirring occasionally, until rice is very tender and mixture is creamy. Pour rice mixture into large bowl; refrigerate until well chilled.
2. Meanwhile, drain syrup from strawberries; reserve for use another day. In blender at medium speed or in food processor with knife blade attached, blend strawberries until pureed; pour into small bowl.
3. Into pureed strawberries, stir 2 tablespoons frozen yogurt. Stir remaining yogurt into rice-pudding mixture.
4. Into six 8-ounce dessert bowls or goblets, spoon strawberry mixture; top with rice-pudding mixture. Refrigerate if not serving right away.

■ Each serving: About 190 calories, 7 g protein, 39 g carbohydrate, 0 g total fat, 1 g fiber, 2 mg cholesterol, 275 mg sodium.

Little Red Barn, page 222

Cranberry-Port Wine Mold,
page 206

Black-Pepper Beef Roast with Shallot Sauce, page 206; Horseradish Cream, page 207; Potato & Gruyère Gratin, page 207; and Cauliflower & Brussels Sprouts with Tarragon Butter, page 208

Baked Brie with Lemon & Herbs,
page 191

Boston-Watercress Salad with
Crab Cake, page 205

Baked Chocolate-Hazelnut
Pudding, page 208

Roast Salmon with Capers &
Tarragon, page 209, and
Lemon Broccoli, page 210

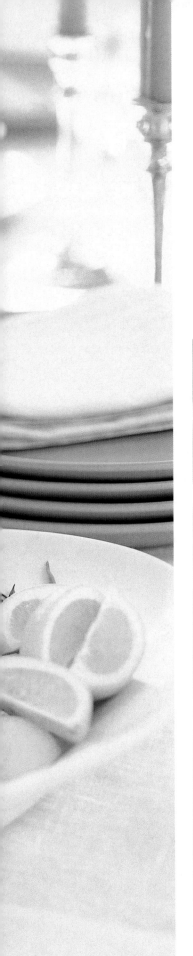

Gelato with Hot Fudge Sauce,
page 210

Ginger Cutouts, page 216

Cantaloupe Sherbet

Fill cantaloupe shells with creamy sherbet for a fun and refreshing summertime dessert.

PREP *30 minutes plus freezing*
MAKES *8 cantaloupe sherbet wedges plus 1½ cups sherbet*

- 1 small ripe cantaloupe (2 pounds), cut in half and seeds discarded
- 2 cups whole milk
- ⅓ cup sugar
- 1 envelope unflavored gelatin
- ¼ cup light corn syrup
- ½ teaspoon salt

1. Scoop out cantaloupe pulp, leaving ⅛-inch shell; refrigerate shell. In food processor with knife blade attached, puree pulp and 1 cup milk.
2. In 2-quart saucepan, mix sugar and gelatin; stir in remaining 1 cup milk and cook over low heat until gelatin dissolves. Remove saucepan from heat; stir in corn syrup, salt, and cantaloupe mixture. Pour into 13" by 9" metal baking pan. Cover and freeze until partially frozen, about 3 hours, stirring occasionally.
3. In food processor, blend cantaloupe mixture until smooth but still frozen; return to pan. Cover and freeze until almost firm, about 1 hour.
4. Spoon as much cantaloupe sherbet as possible into cantaloupe shells; smooth top. Cover with plastic wrap and freeze until firm, about 4 hours. Freeze any remaining sherbet.
5. To serve, let cantaloupe halves stand at room temperature 15 minutes to soften slightly.
6. Cut each cantaloupe half into 4 wedges.

■ Each wedge (or ½ cup sherbet): About 100 calories, 3 g protein, 18 g carbohydrate, 2 g total fat (1 g saturated), 1 g fiber, 6 mg cholesterol, 140 mg sodium.

Sugar 'n' Spice Angel Food Cake

We've added cinnamon, ginger, and allspice for a new twist on angel food cake. You'll enjoy every bite of this fat-free, light-as-air treat.

PREP *25 minutes plus cooling*
BAKE *30 to 35 minutes*
MAKES *16 servings*

- 1 cup cake flour (not self-rising)
- 1 teaspoon ground cinnamon
- 1 teaspoon ground ginger
- ¼ teaspoon ground allspice
- 1 cup plus 1 tablespoon confectioners' sugar
- ¾ teaspoon salt
- ¾ cup granulated sugar
- ¼ cup packed dark brown sugar
- 1⅔ cups egg whites (12 to 14 large whites)
- 1 teaspoon cream of tartar
- 1½ teaspoons vanilla extract

1. Preheat oven to 375°F. In medium bowl, with fork, mix flour, cinnamon, ginger, allspice, 1 cup confectioners' sugar, and ¼ teaspoon salt; set aside. In small bowl, combine granulated sugar and brown sugar.
2. In large bowl, with mixer at high speed, beat egg whites, cream of tartar, and remaining ½ teaspoon salt until soft peaks form; beat in vanilla. Beating at high speed, sprinkle in sugar mixture, 2 tablespoons at a time, beating until sugar completely dissolves and whites stand in stiff peaks.
3. Sift flour mixture over egg whites, one-third at a time, folding in with rubber spatula after each addition, just until flour mixture disappears. (Be careful not to overmix or else cake won't rise properly.)
4. Spoon batter into ungreased 10-inch tube pan with removable bottom. Bake cake 30 to 35 minutes or until top springs back when lightly touched with finger. Invert cake in pan on funnel or bottle; cool completely in pan.
5. With metal spatula, carefully loosen cake from pan; place on cake plate. Sprinkle top of cake with remaining 1 tablespoon confectioners' sugar.

■ Each serving: About 120 calories, 4 g protein, 27 g carbohydrate, 0 g total fat, 0 g fiber, 0 mg cholesterol, 150 mg sodium.

Apple-Spice Snack Cake

Make this easy cake for a delicious afternoon snack. It's perfect with hot tea or coffee.

PREP *10 minutes plus cooling*
BAKE *45 minutes*
MAKES *12 servings*

- 1¼ cups unsweetened chunky applesauce
- 1 cup light (mild) molasses
- ¼ cup vegetable oil
- 1 large egg
- 2 cups all-purpose flour
- 1 teaspoon baking soda
- 1 teaspoon ground ginger
- 1 teaspoon ground cinnamon
- ½ teaspoon ground cloves
- ½ teaspoon salt

1. Preheat oven to 325°F. Grease and flour 9" by 9" metal baking pan.
2. In large bowl, with spoon, mix applesauce, molasses, oil, and egg until blended. Stir in flour and remaining ingredients until evenly mixed.
3. Pour batter into pan. Bake 45 minutes or until center of cake springs back when lightly touched. Cool cake in pan on wire rack.

■ Each serving: About 200 calories, 3 g protein, 37 g carbohydrate, 5 g total fat (1 g saturated), 1 g fiber, 18 mg cholesterol, 205 mg sodium.

Cappuccino Angel Food Cake

A sprinkling of cinnamon and confectioners' sugar makes a perfect finishing touch for this delightfully guilt-free cake.

PREP *30 minutes plus cooling*
BAKE *35 to 40 minutes*
MAKES *16 servings*

  1 cup cake flour (not self-rising)
½ cup plus 1 tablespoon confectioners' sugar
1⅔ cups egg whites (12 to 14 large whites)
  4 teaspoons instant espresso-coffee powder
1½ teaspoons cream of tartar
½ teaspoon salt
½ teaspoon plus ⅛ teaspoon ground cinnamon
1½ teaspoons vanilla extract
1¼ cups granulated sugar

1. Preheat oven to 375°F. On waxed paper, with fork, mix flour and ½ cup confectioners' sugar; set aside.
2. In large bowl, with mixer at high speed, beat egg whites, espresso powder, cream of tartar, salt, and ½ teaspoon cinnamon until soft peaks form; beat in vanilla. Beating at high speed, sprinkle in granulated sugar, 2 tablespoons at a time, beating mixture until sugar completely dissolves and whites stand in stiff peaks.
3. Sift flour mixture over egg whites, one-third at a time, folding in with rubber spatula after each addition, just until flour mixture disappears. (Be careful not to overmix or cake won't rise properly.)
4. Spoon batter into ungreased 10-inch tube pan with removable bottom. Bake cake 35 to 40 minutes or until top springs back when lightly touched with finger. Invert cake in pan on funnel or bottle; cool completely in pan.
5. With metal spatula, carefully loosen cake from pan; place on cake plate.

In cup, mix remaining 1 tablespoon confectioners' sugar with remaining ⅛ teaspoon cinnamon; sprinkle over top of cake.

■ Each serving: About 115 calories, 3 g protein, 25 g carbohydrate, 0 g total fat, 0 g fiber, 0 mg cholesterol, 115 mg sodium.

Triple-Chocolate Fudge Cake

Made with semisweet, milk, and white chocolates, this decadent cake is a chocolate lover's dream come true.

PREP *1 hour plus cooling*
BAKE *45 minutes*
MAKES *16 servings*

Cake
    unsweetened cocoa
  8 ounces semisweet chocolate, chopped
½ cup butter or margarine (1 stick)
  1 teaspoon instant-coffee powder or granules
  6 large eggs, separated
¼ teaspoon cream of tartar
  1 cup sugar
  1 cup all-purpose flour
1½ teaspoons vanilla extract
½ teaspoon salt

Chocolate Glaze
½ cup semisweet chocolate chips
  2 tablespoons butter or margarine
  3 tablespoons whole milk
  2 tablespoons light corn syrup

Chocolate Drizzles
  1 bar (1.55 ounces) milk chocolate
  2 teaspoons vegetable shortening
  2 ounces white chocolate

1. Preheat oven to 375°F. Prepare Cake: Grease 9" by 3" springform pan. Line bottom with waxed paper; grease paper and dust with cocoa. Wrap outside and bottom of pan with heavy-duty foil.
2. In small saucepan, melt semisweet chocolate with butter over low heat,

stirring frequently. In cup, mix instant-coffee powder with *¼ cup water*.
3. In small bowl, with mixer at high speed, beat egg whites, cream of tartar, and ½ cup sugar until stiff peaks form when beaters are lifted.
4. In large bowl, with mixer at high speed, beat egg yolks and remaining ½ cup sugar until yolks have thickened and become pale yellow. Stir in flour, vanilla, salt, chocolate mixture, coffee mixture, and ⅓ cup cocoa. Fold in beaten egg whites. Pour batter into pan.
5. Set springform pan in 15½" by 10½" roasting pan. Fill roasting pan with *boiling water* until it reaches halfway up side of pan. Bake cake 45 minutes (center will still be slightly soft). Remove springform pan from roasting pan. Cool cake in pan on wire rack. Remove side of springform pan; invert cake onto plate. Discard waxed paper.
6. Prepare Chocolate Glaze: In 2-quart saucepan, melt chocolate with butter over low heat, stirring often. Remove pan from heat; stir in milk and syrup until blended. Spread warm glaze over top and side of cooled cake.
7. Prepare Chocolate Drizzles: In 1-quart saucepan, melt milk chocolate with 1 teaspoon shortening until smooth, stirring often. Spoon into small self-sealing plastic bag; set aside. Clean and dry pan. In same pan, melt white chocolate with remaining 1 teaspoon shortening, stirring often. Spoon white-chocolate mixture into another small self-sealing plastic bag.
8. Cut a very small hole in corner of each plastic bag. Drizzle both chocolates over top of cake. With tip of knife or toothpick, lightly run through drizzle to make a pretty design.
9. To serve, dip knife into hot water and dry immediately (the heated blade will cut through cake without sticking). Cut cake into wedges.

■ Each serving: About 320 calories, 6 g protein, 36 g carbohydrate, 18 g total fat (6 g saturated), 2 g fiber, 81 mg cholesterol, 205 mg sodium.

Diets

Nutrition Diets

THE NEW AND IMPROVED ALL-YOU-CAN-EAT SOUP DIET

THE BEST OF THE FAD DIETS

SUPER SUMMER SLIM DOWN

15 POUNDS—GONE!

the new and improved
all-you-can-eat soup diet

Our first one was such a smash, we're back with an even tastier soup recipe and lots of new ways to prevent diet boredom. Plus: Reader success stories.

By Delia Hammock, M.S., R.D.

In 2000, we figured a new millennium deserves an epic diet, so we created Super Soup. Our seven-day meal plan and recipe for a hearty vegetable soup ran in the January 2000 issue, and the response was, well, "souper." Readers were ecstatic over dropping pounds so painlessly.

For this encore, we've jazzed up the soup a little, adding some new vegetables. It's still easy, convenient, nutritious, delicious, and filling, so you can slash calories—to as low as 1,200 per day—without being constantly hungry. Expect to lose as many as five pounds the first week, followed by one to two additional pounds each week you stay on the diet. To lose weight even faster, add exercise, aiming for 30 minutes of vigorous activity per day.

The All-New Basic Soup

5   medium carrots, peeled and cut into 1-inch slices
3   medium celery stalks, sliced
3   large onions, chopped, or 3 medium leeks, each cut into 1-inch slices
1   large garlic clove, minced
2   cans (28 ounces each) tomatoes in juice
1   small head savoy cabbage (about 1½ pounds), thinly sliced
2   medium parsnips, peeled and cut into 1-inch slices
2   packages (5 ounces each) baby spinach leaves
½   cup chopped fresh parsley
2   chicken-flavor bouillon cubes or envelopes
1   teaspoon salt
½   teaspoon freshly ground pepper

1. Coat 8-quart saucepot with non-stick cooking spray. Over medium-high heat, add carrots, celery, onions, and garlic. Cook 5 minutes.

2. Stir in tomatoes with their liquid, breaking up tomatoes with side of spoon. Add cabbage, remaining ingredients, and *12 cups water.* Heat to boiling over high heat, stirring occasionally.

3. Reduce heat to low; cover mixture and simmer, stirring occasionally, 15 minutes, or until vegetables become tender. Add more salt and pepper if desired. Makes about 25 cups.

To retain freshness and nutrients Keep a 2-day supply of Basic Soup in the refrigerator. Store remaining soup in 3-cup portions in airtight containers, leaving some headspace to allow for expansion. (If you plan to reheat soup in microwave, use a microwave-safe container.) Freeze.

To reheat frozen soup Microwave: Loosen lid on container. Heat on High (100 percent power) 8 to 12 minutes until bubbling, stirring twice. Top of stove: Place container under running cold water to loosen frozen soup from sides. Heat frozen soup in covered saucepan over very low heat about 3 minutes until soup begins to thaw. Increase heat to medium; heat about 15 minutes longer until heated through, stirring occasionally.

Note: If using frozen soup to prepare Super Soup, add ingredients during the last 5 minutes of heating. For microwave heating, use a container large enough to hold add-ins.

Seven-Day Diet Plan

DAY 1

Breakfast
1 cup high-fiber or whole-grain cereal
1 cup fat-free milk
½ banana or 2 tablespoons raisins

Lunch
Sandwich Fill 1 whole wheat pita with mixture of ½ cup drained

how to make it work

• Don't skip meals, and eat what's listed.
• You may eat as much of the Basic Soup (with no add-ins) as you wish, whenever you wish.
• You may swap a breakfast, lunch, or dinner from one day's menu for the same meal on a different day. Have a dinner meal for lunch. Then have a lunch meal for dinner.
• Drink only calorie-free beverages (tap water, bottled water, club soda, seltzer, artificially sweetened drinks, and unsweetened black coffee or tea).
• If the meal includes a piece of fruit, save it for a snack later.
• Fresh or dried herbs, spices, lemon or lime juice, mustard, nonstick cooking spray, soy sauce, vinegar, and Worcestershire sauce are OK.
• Take a one-a-day type multivitamin/mineral supplement as well as a 400- to 500-milligram calcium supplement.

water-packed tuna, 1 tablespoon light mayonnaise, shredded carrots, and finely chopped onions and celery.

Dinner

Super Soup To 2 to 3 cups Basic Soup, stir in 3 ounces skinless cooked rotisserie chicken breast, cut into chunks (⅔ cup), 3 tablespoons instant rice, 1 teaspoon soy sauce, and ¼ teaspoon thyme. Heat to boiling; then simmer until rice is tender.

4 sesame breadsticks or ½ whole wheat pita

DAY 2

Breakfast

1 split toasted English muffin topped with ¼ cup shredded Jarlsberg Lite cheese. Broil until cheese melts.

6 ounces calcium-fortified juice

Lunch

Sandwich On 2 slices whole wheat bread, spread 1 teaspoon honey mustard; layer 3 ounces skinless cooked rotisserie chicken breast or deli turkey breast, thinly sliced, with lettuce and tomato.

1 cup fat-free milk

1 small apple or pear

Dinner

Super Soup To 2 to 3 cups Basic Soup, stir in ½ cup drained canned garbanzo beans, 2 teaspoons lemon juice, and ½ teaspoon oregano. Heat through. Top soup with 2 tablespoons crumbled feta cheese.

4 sesame breadsticks or ½ whole wheat pita

DAY 3

Breakfast

1 cup cooked oatmeal topped with 6 dried apricot halves, chopped, or 2 tablespoons raisins

1 cup fat-free milk

Lunch

Fast-food meal 1 small cheeseburger,

soup galore

We know eating soup day in, day out can get tedious. That's why we've come to your rescue with four new recipes and simple accompaniments.

CHICKEN ALPHABETS To 2 to 3 cups Basic Soup, stir in 3 ounces skinless cooked rotisserie chicken breast, cut into chunks (⅔ cup); 2 tablespoons alphabet macaroni, uncooked; 1 tablespoon balsamic vinegar; and ¼ cup water. Heat to boiling; cook until pasta is tender.

4 reduced-fat Triscuits or 20 grapes

FISH CHOWDER To 2 to 3 cups Basic Soup, stir in 4 ounces cod fillet, cut into chunks; 3 slices cooked turkey bacon, crumbled; and ¼ teaspoon thyme. Heat to boiling; cook until fish is opaque throughout.

5 sesame breadsticks or 1 banana

CURRY CREAM In small pot, combine ½ teaspoon curry powder and ½ teaspoon oil. Cook over low heat 1 minute, stirring constantly. Stir curry mixture and ½ cup cooked rice into 2 to 3 cups Basic Soup. In blender, at low speed, blend soup mixture until smooth.* In saucepan, combine pureed soup and ¾ cup fat-free milk; heat through.

5 sesame breadsticks or 1 pear

HAM & CHEESE To 2 to 3 cups Basic Soup, stir in 2 ounces cooked ham, diced, and 1 teaspoon Dijon mustard; heat through. In soup bowl, sprinkle ⅓ cup shredded light Cheddar cheese and ¼ cup seasoned croutons over heated soup.

¼ whole wheat pita or 1 small apple

* If Basic Soup is hot, remove center part of blender cover.

with ketchup, mustard, lettuce, tomato slices, onions, and pickles

1 green side salad with 1 tablespoon fat-free Italian dressing (optional)

Dinner

Super Soup In small saucepan, combine ½ teaspoon curry powder and ½ teaspoon oil. Cook over low heat for 1 minute, stirring constantly. Stir curry mixture, ½ cup cooked or drained canned lentils, and ½ cup canned sweet potatoes, cut up, into 2 to 3 cups of the Basic Soup. Heat through.

2 cups bagged salad greens with 2 tomato slices and 2 tablespoons fat-free Italian dressing

20 grapes or 1 small apple

DAY 4

Breakfast

1 cup fat-free, sugar-free yogurt (plain or fruit flavored)

1 tangerine or ¾ cup fresh or frozen unsweetened berries

1 split toasted English muffin spread with 1 teaspoon light butter

Lunch

Sandwich Between 2 slices whole wheat bread, layer ¼ cup mashed avocado, 1 slice Jarlsberg Lite cheese (1 ounce), and 2 tomato slices. Season with a little salt and pepper if desired.

1 medium banana or pear

Dinner

Super Soup To 2 to 3 cups Basic Soup, stir in 3½ ounces cooked lean deli roast beef, cut up, and 2 teaspoons Dijon mustard. Heat through. Top with 3 tablespoons low-fat sour cream.

5 reduced-fat Triscuits or ½ whole wheat pita

DAY 5

Breakfast

⅔ cup calcium-fortified 1-percent-fat cottage cheese mixed with ½ cup drained, canned pineapple chunks in juice

1 slice toasted whole wheat bread spread with 1 teaspoon light butter and 1 teaspoon preserves

Lunch

Sandwich On 2 slices whole wheat bread, spread 1 teaspoon spicy brown mustard. Layer 2 ounces cooked lean deli roast beef, sliced, with tomato and onion slices.

6 dried apricot halves or 1 kiwifruit
1 cup fat-free milk

Dinner

Super Soup To 2 to 3 cups Basic Soup, stir in ½ cup drained canned corn, 2 teaspoons lime juice, and ¼ teaspoon ground cumin. Heat through. Stir in ¼ cup shredded Monterey Jack cheese with jalapeño peppers. Sprinkle with 1 tablespoon chopped cilantro.

1 ounce baked tortilla chips (about 18 chips) or 4 sesame breadsticks

DAY 6

Breakfast

2 frozen low-fat waffles, toasted, then topped with 1 tablespoon low-calorie pancake syrup and 1 cup fresh or frozen unsweetened berries

6 ounces calcium-fortified juice

Lunch

Sandwich Fill 1 whole wheat pita with mixture of ⅓ cup crumbled feta cheese, ¼ cup diced tomato, ¼ cup diced cucumber, and 2 tablespoons chopped olives. Sprinkle pita contents with red wine vinegar.

1 canned peach half in juice or 6 dried apricot halves

Dinner

Super Soup To 2 to 3 cups Basic Soup, stir in 3 ounces reduced-fat turkey kielbasa, cut up. Heat through. Sprinkle with 2 tablespoons grated Parmesan cheese.

4 sesame breadsticks or ½ whole wheat pita

1 tangerine or 1 kiwifruit

winning the weight-loss war: two success stories

DIETERS' STATS Donna Morley, 38, and Steve Morley, 43. The couple live in Charlotte, North Carolina. Donna is production manager for an advertising agency. Steve is a merchandising manager for a food distributor.

LENGTH OF TIME ON DIET Since January 10, 2000

WEIGHT LOST Donna—45 pounds; Steve—40 pounds

WHY THEY TRIED IT Steve and Donna had worrisome family medical histories that included diabetes, heart disease, and cancer. They knew the extra pounds they carried were putting them at risk. "The soup diet seemed the perfect answer," Donna says.

HOW THEY MADE IT WORK "Steve would get home from work and put the preportioned soup on the stove to warm. Then, when I got home, I would finish it up with the add-ins."

SECRETS FOR KEEPING THE POUNDS OFF "We followed the diet religiously for one month, having Super Soup every night," Donna says. "Then we started eating the other dinners three times a week and continued with soup the other four nights."

HARD-WON WISDOM Set small goals for yourself. "Plan to lose ten pounds by your birthday, instead of fifty pounds next year," Donna says.

DIETER STATS Janet Theisen, 44. Janet lives in Weston, Wisconsin, with her husband of 20 years and two teenage daughters and works as a registered nurse.

LENGTH OF TIME ON DIET Five months (February through June 2000)

WEIGHT LOST 40 pounds

WHY SHE TRIED IT An invitation to her 25-year high school reunion. All Janet could think of was the 40 pounds she'd gained in the last five years. "I was going to throw the invitation away, but then I found the *Good Housekeeping* soup diet."

HOW SHE MADE IT WORK "I am a creature of habit, so it was easy to repeat the seven days over and over. I liked being able to make the soup one day a week and freeze the portions." (Janet's husband works nights, so she doesn't have to cook for him, and her daughters eat sandwiches, heat up frozen pizza, or open a can of SpaghettiOs.)

SECRETS FOR KEEPING THE POUNDS OFF "I wish I had a secret! I'm on the scale every day, and when it goes up by five pounds, I'm back on the soup."

HARD-WON WISDOM "Get a mindset, get determined, and don't let anyone stand in your way."

DAY 7

Breakfast

½ small grapefruit or 1 tangerine
2 eggs scrambled in a nonstick skillet coated with nonstick cooking spray
1 slice toasted whole wheat bread spread with 1 teaspoon light butter

Lunch

Bake 1 large potato, top with ¼ cup salsa, ¼ cup grated Monterey Jack cheese with jalapeño peppers.

6 baby carrots

Dinner

Super Soup To 2 to 3 cups Basic Soup, stir in 4 ounces peeled raw shrimp, 2 tablespoons dry couscous, 1 teaspoon soy sauce, and ¼ teaspoon thyme. Heat to boiling, then simmer just until shrimp are opaque.

1 small pear or ½ cup canned pineapple chunks in juice

the best of the fad diets

We took what we liked best from the hottest weight-loss programs and created our own high-protein, low-carb plan. Get ready to lose pounds quickly—and safely.

By Samantha Buckanoff, M.S., R.D.

Can trendy be good for you? That's the dilemma posed by diet blockbusters such as *The Zone, Protein Power, Dr. Atkins' New Diet Revolution,* and *Sugar Busters!* Each claims to have cracked the code that makes pounds vanish, but will the weight stay off? And does following such a diet pose any health risks?

To get answers, our nutritionists examined a handful of popular plans, cover to cover. Most of them tout increasing your protein intake while slashing carbohydrates—and not without reason. Studies show protein does help suppress hunger better than carbohydrates. However, it's vitally important to take in enough carbs from whole grains and produce to meet your body's energy demands.

What we've done is take the best from the fad diets—and leave out the rest. This meal plan focuses on heart-healthy meats low in saturated fat, such as seafood, poultry, and lean cuts of beef, à la *The Zone. Protein Power: The High-Protein/Low Carbohydrate Way to Lose Weight, Feel Fit, and Boost Your Health* recommends aiming for 25 grams of fiber per day, which is a fine goal.

Sugar Busters! Cut Sugar to Trim Fat insists on whole grains instead of refined and processed starches, along with lots of fruits and vegetables, and we second that motion. *The Zone* also tells its devotees to focus on monounsaturated fats; you'll find olive oil, nuts, seeds, and oily fish on our menu. Finally, the top-sellers all suggest eliminating sugary snacks and desserts. Who can argue with that advice?

If you follow our 1,350-calorie-a-day meal plan, we guarantee you'll lose at least a pound per week—and more if you accumulate a minimum of 30 minutes of activity per day. (Exercise not only helps control weight but also improves blood pressure and cholesterol levels.) Be sure to eat all the food on the plan. Fruit, recommended at various meals, can be eaten at any time. You can swap a breakfast, lunch, dinner, or snack for the same meal on a different day and repeat meals if you wish. Drink plenty of calorie-free beverages—tap or bottled water, club soda, and artificially sweetened soft drinks. And take a one-a-day vitamin/mineral supplement to make sure you are meeting your body's needs while cutting calories.

Good Housekeeping Fad Diet

DAY 1

Breakfast

In nonstick skillet coated with cooking spray, scramble 1 egg.

2 slices cooked turkey bacon

Sprinkle 1 tablespoon shredded part-skim mozzarella cheese over 1 slice light wheat bread. Broil until cheese melts.

15 grapes

1 cup fat-free milk

Lunch

Toss 3 cups salad greens; 1 medium tomato, cut into wedges; ¼ red onion, thinly sliced; ½ cup cooked cut-up green beans; ½ cup drained water-packed tuna; and ½ cup rinsed and drained canned white kidney beans. Sprinkle salad with mixture of 2 teaspoons olive oil, 1 tablespoon red wine vinegar, and 1½ teaspoons Dijon mustard.

1 pear

Snack

10 almonds

1¼ cups vegetable juice

Dinner

Coat 9 ounces scallops with 2 tablespoons plain dried bread crumbs. In 1½ teaspoons oil, cook scallops, ⅓ cup chopped onion, and 1 minced garlic clove about 4 minutes or until the scallops are opaque throughout. Stir in 1 medium tomato, chopped. Cover and cook for 1 minute. Serve over 2½ cups cooked spinach.

1 tangerine

DAY 2

Breakfast

To 1 cup Cheerios or ¾ cup bran flakes cereal, add 1 tablespoon raisins, 1 tablespoon sunflower seeds, and 1½ tablespoons chopped almonds.

1 cup fat-free milk

Lunch

To one 14½-ounce can chicken broth, add 1 green onion, sliced; ¼ cup sliced mushrooms; and 1 cup snow peas. Heat until vegetables are tender. Stir in 4 ounces sliced lean deli roast beef, cut into strips.

Coat 1 slice light wheat bread with butter or olive-oil-flavor cooking spray; sprinkle with some Italian seasoning. Toast in toaster oven or regular oven.

1 pear

Snack

Combine 3 celery stalks, each cut into quarters; 1 red bell pepper, cut into strips; ¾ cup broccoli flowerets; and 10 grape tomatoes. Serve with ⅓ cup buttermilk-chive dressing* or 2 tablespoons low-fat blue cheese dressing.

Dinner

Spray rack in broiling pan with cooking spray. Cut 1 small eggplant (about 4 ounces) into ½-inch-thick slices. Broil eggplant, in single layer, until browned, turning eggplant once. Arrange slices in small baking dish. Top with ½ cup pasta sauce, 2 tablespoons grated Parmesan cheese, and ½ cup shredded part-skim mozzarella cheese. Bake in 350°F. oven 25 minutes.

---

* Buttermilk-chive dressing: Mix ½ cup reduced-fat buttermilk, 2 tablespoons distilled white vinegar, 2 tablespoons chopped fresh chives, 1 tablespoon light mayonnaise, ¼ teaspoon salt, and ¼ teaspoon pepper. Makes about ¾ cup.

In 1 teaspoon olive oil, stir in 1 medium zucchini, sliced; 1 minced garlic clove; and oregano, salt, and pepper to taste. Cover and cook until zucchini is tender, about 10 minutes. Top with 2 slices cooked turkey bacon, crumbled.

Coat 1 slice light wheat bread with butter or olive-oil-flavor cooking spray; sprinkle with some Italian seasoning. Toast in toaster oven.

DAY 3

Breakfast

In nonstick skillet coated with cooking spray, cook 2 tablespoons diced green pepper and 2 tablespoons diced onion until tender. Beat 2 eggs with a dash of cayenne pepper sauce; pour over vegetables. Cover and cook until set.

Sprinkle 1 tablespoon shredded part-skim mozzarella cheese over 1 slice light wheat bread. Broil until cheese melts.

1 cup orange juice

Lunch

Combine 3 cups salad greens; 3½ ounces sliced deli turkey breast, cut into strips; 1 slice Jarlsberg Lite cheese (1 ounce), cut into strips; ½ medium cucumber, sliced; and 1 orange, peeled and sectioned. Toss with a mixture of 2 tablespoons orange juice, 1 tablespoon balsamic vinegar, and 1 teaspoon olive oil.

Coat 1 slice light wheat bread with butter or olive-oil-flavor cooking spray; sprinkle with some Italian seasoning. Toast in toaster oven.

Snack

Hot cocoa made with 1 cup fat-free milk and 1 packet sugar-free hot cocoa mix

Dinner

Dot top of 6-ounce salmon fillet with mixture of 1 tablespoon plain dried bread crumbs, 1 tablespoon minced

fresh dill, 1 teaspoon light mayonnaise, 1 teaspoon Dijon mustard, and some pepper. Arrange fish in baking pan coated with cooking spray. Bake in 450°F. oven about 15 minutes or until fish is opaque throughout.

1 cup steamed mixed vegetables

DAY 4

Breakfast

Top ¾ cup calcium-fortified, low-fat cottage cheese with 1¼ cups sliced strawberries. Sprinkle with 1 tablespoon raisins and 1 tablespoon sunflower seeds.

1 slice light wheat bread spread with 1 teaspoon butter or margarine

Lunch

On 2 slices of light wheat bread, spread 1 tablespoon light mayonnaise. Layer 2 ounces sliced lean deli turkey, 1 slice Jarlsberg Lite cheese (1 ounce), 2 tomato slices, and lettuce.

1¼ cups vegetable juice

1 orange

Snack

1 apple cut into wedges with 1½ tablespoons honey-crunch wheat germ for dipping

Dinner

In ½ teaspoon oil, stir-fry 6 ounces precut beef strips 5 minutes. Stir in ½ red pepper, sliced; ½ cup sliced mushrooms; 2 teaspoons soy sauce; and 2 teaspoons balsamic vinegar. Cover and cook over low heat until beef is tender. Stir in ¾ cup frozen green peas and 2 sliced green onions; heat.

DAY 5

Breakfast

Layer 2 slices cooked turkey bacon and 2 tomato slices on 1 slice light wheat bread. Top with 1 ounce reduced-fat Cheddar cheese, sliced. Broil until cheese melts.

1 cup fat-free milk

1¼ cups strawberries

Lunch

Heat 1 teaspoon butter in small skillet. Add 4 ounces chicken breast tenders, cut into strips. Cook 5 minutes. Stir in 1 tablespoon cayenne pepper sauce. Serve chicken over 3 cups salad greens tossed with 1 tomato cut into wedges; ¼ cucumber, sliced; and ¼ cup buttermilk-chive dressing* or 2 tablespoons low-fat blue-cheese dressing.

30 grapes

Coat 1 slice light wheat bread with butter or olive-oil-flavor cooking spray; sprinkle with some Italian seasoning. Toast in toaster oven.

Snack

1 single-serve container instant Knorr's Navy Bean Soup or Corn Chowder Soup

Dinner

Sprinkle some fajita seasoning mix on top of 7-ounce catfish fillet. Bake in 450°F. oven about 15 minutes or until fish is opaque throughout. Serve over cucumber salsa (mixture of ¼ cup salsa, ⅓ cup chopped cucumber, 2 teaspoons chopped fresh cilantro leaves, and 2 teaspoons lime juice).

Combine 1 teaspoon fajita seasoning mix, 1 teaspoon plain dried bread crumbs, and 1 teaspoon oil to form a paste. Dip 8 large sweet-onion rings (each about ½-inch thick) into mixture to coat edges. Arrange in single layer, in shallow pan. Bake in 450°F. oven with fish about 12 minutes, turning once, or until onion ring edges are golden brown.

DAY 6

Breakfast

1 cup fat-free, plain yogurt tossed with 1 cup frozen blueberries, slightly thawed; 2 tablespoons wheat germ; and 1½ tablespoons chopped almonds

Lunch

To one 18.5-ounce can escarole soup, stir in 1⅓ cups rinsed and drained canned white kidney beans; 8 ounces turkey kielbasa, cut up; 1½ cups water; and 2 teaspoons lemon juice. Heat through. Makes two 2¾-cup servings.

1 pear

Snack

Combine 3 celery stalks, each cut into quarters; 1 red pepper, cut into strips; ¾ cup broccoli flowerets; and 10 grape tomatoes. Serve with ⅓ cup buttermilk-chive dressing* or 2 tablespoons low-fat blue-cheese dressing.

Dinner

In ½ teaspoon oil, cook 1 boneless pork loin chop (6 ounces) 5 minutes, turning once. Stir in 2 cups shredded cabbage; 2 sliced green onions; 1 medium Golden Delicious apple, cored and sliced; 1 teaspoon cumin; ½ teaspoon lemon juice; ⅛ teaspoon salt; and some pepper. Cover and cook over low heat until pork just loses its pink color.

DAY 7

Breakfast

To 1 cup cooked oatmeal, stir in 1 teaspoon butter or margarine, 1 tablespoon raisins, and 2 teaspoons chopped almonds.

1 cup fat-free milk

Lunch

1 Lean Cuisine Chicken Parmesan or Healthy Choice Grilled Chicken Breast & Pasta

Toss 2 cups salad greens with ½ medium tomato, cut into wedges; ¼ cucumber and ¼ red onion, sliced; ¼ cup sliced mushrooms; 8 chopped ripe olives; and 2 tablespoons buttermilk-chive dressing* or 1 tablespoon reduced-fat Italian or vinaigrette dressing.

1 orange

Snack

15 grapes

1 ounce reduced-fat Cheddar cheese

Dinner

Brush 1 boneless, skinless chicken breast (6 ounces) with mixture of ½ teaspoon Dijon mustard, ½ teaspoon soy sauce, and 1 teaspoon olive oil. Broil, turning once, until chicken is tender and juices run clear when chicken is pierced with tip of knife.

Slice 2 plum tomatoes. Sprinkle with 1 tablespoon grated Parmesan cheese and some dried basil.

1 cup steamed mixed vegetables

super summer slim down:
20 pounds by fall

Summer is the easiest time of the year to lose weight. Here's why, and how.

By Delia Hammock, M.S., R.D.

In summer, your body *wants* to be thinner. Yes, it wants to wear two-pieces and sundresses with spaghetti straps. But there's another reason. Your body responds to the season, which makes dieting simpler in the summer.

• As temperatures rise, you crave juicy fruits and fresh vegetables instead of stuffed turkeys and cassoulets.

• Sunlight from longer days spurs you to linger outdoors, which often means burning more calories.

• Sunshine also raises the brain's serotonin levels, providing a natural mood boost that renders that nightly Rocky Road unnecessary.

Why these seasonal changes? Evolution, some researchers say. In our hunter-gatherer past, we fattened up to survive winter, then spent the hot months burning off extra calories. Fast-forward to the twenty-first century, when summer is, in many ways, still the best time to drop a few.

In just ten weeks, our GH Institute diet can help take off the pounds; our travel advice will help keep them off. And the recipes are no-cook (except in a microwave or on a stovetop), so turn off that oven till September!

The No-Cook Diet

When the temperature is sweltering, fast foods beckon—but don't be tempted. This easy, drop-that-pot-holder diet can get you out of the kitchen fast and have you shedding pounds almost as quickly—up to five pounds in the first week if you choose our One-Week Quick Start (details below).

The meals Three a day, drawn from our simple plan, which includes two breakfast, three lunch, and four dinner options—and an unlimited amount of Freebies (opposite page). Mix and match meals and Freebies to create a menu for the month (daily meal total: about 1,000 calories).

The snacks Enjoy two treats per day from the list of Snacks (opposite page), each of which is about 100 calories.

The drinks Only calorie-free beverages: water, seltzer, black coffee, tea, and artificially sweetened sodas.

Essential supplements A daily multivitamin/mineral tablet and 500 milligrams of calcium.

Exercise A moderate workout three times per week.

Special one-week quick start To begin with a bang, follow the above plan but eliminate all snacks, for a daily total of about 1,000 calories. Do not continue beyond one week.

Weight loss Up to five pounds the first week if on Quick Start; up to two pounds per week thereafter.

Breakfast

- 1¼ cups bran flakes cereal; 1 cup fat-free milk; 6 medium strawberries, sliced; or ⅓ cup raspberries
- 1 cup fat-free yogurt; 2 peaches, cut up; or ¾ cup mango cubes; 1 tablespoon chopped roasted almonds or 1½ tablespoons honey-crunch wheat germ

Lunch

- 1 cup calcium-fortified cottage cheese, 2 cups cantaloupe chunks, 4 reduced-fat Triscuits or 3 sesame breadsticks
- Sandwich: 2 slices whole wheat bread or pita, 3 ounces turkey breast or lean ham, 1 tablespoon mustard, tomato, lettuce; 1 small dill pickle; 4 ounces calcium-fortified orange juice mixed with 6 ounces seltzer
- Sandwich: Stuff 1 whole wheat pita with mixture of ½ cup canned black beans, drained; 3 tablespoons crumbled feta cheese; ½ cup chopped tomato; ¼ cup diced onion; 1 tablespoon lemon juice; and ½ teaspoon olive oil.

Dinner

- Seafood salad: On lettuce leaves, arrange 4 ounces canned salmon or water-packed tuna; ⅔ cup canned white beans, drained; plus unlimited veggies from Freebies box. Sprinkle with 1 tablespoon lemon juice and 1 teaspoon olive oil.
- 4 ounces skinless roasted chicken breast or lean deli roast beef; 1 medium ear corn with ½ teaspoon butter or ¾ cup peas; 1 cup steamed green or yellow squash sprinkled with 1 teaspoon Parmesan; 1 small tomato, sliced
- 8 California rolls with soy sauce and wasabi (Japanese horseradish) or a 300-calorie frozen entrée (read label) heated in microwave. Side salad: On lettuce leaves, arrange 1½ cups shredded cabbage and 15 grape tomatoes, halved; sprinkle with mixture of 1 tablespoon rice vinegar, 1 teaspoon soy sauce, ½ teaspoon Asian sesame oil.
- Burrito: On 8-inch flour tortilla, arrange 2 ounces lean deli roast beef or skinless roasted chicken breast, ¼ small chopped avocado, ¼ cup chopped tomato, 2 tablespoons salsa; sprinkle with 1 tablespoon lime juice.

freebies

You may have an unlimited supply of the following—either raw or blanched—with any meal or between meals. May be seasoned with unlimited lemon or lime juice, wine vinegar, balsamic vinegar, or rice vinegar.

Asparagus	Onions
Broccoli	Peppers
Cabbage	Radishes
Cauliflower	Scallions
Celery	Spinach
Cucumber	Squash (green or yellow)
Endive	Snow peas
Green beans	Tomatoes
Lettuce	Watercress
Mushrooms	

snacks

Choose two per day and eat at any time.

- 1 ounce hard or semisoft cheese (American, Brie, Cheddar, Swiss)
- 9 ounces fat-free milk
- 7 ounces calcium-fortified orange or grapefruit juice
- 6 reduced-fat Triscuits
- 3 graham-cracker squares
- 1 medium banana or pear
- 1 large apple
- 1 cup (about 21) cherries
- 2 medium kiwis
- 30 grapes
- 1 wedge watermelon (about ¹⁄₁₆ of a melon)
- 12 roasted almonds
- Lettuce dressed with 2 to 4 tablespoons light or fat-free salad dressing

vote no on vacation weight gain!

On holiday, who wants to monitor every forkful? No one. That's why the typical vacationer gains weight. You can be the exception.

Lose before you leave Drop a few pounds before takeoff, and you'll return no heavier than when you left. On our No-Cook diet, you can shed up to five pounds the week before you go.

Skip the "free" breakfast Instead of the morning Danish, doughnuts, and muffins that are often included in a motel bill, opt for fruit and low-fat granola that you can stash in your room.

Drink water It's easy to confuse thirst with hunger when it's humid.

Postpone dessert If you indulge the first night, chances are you'll feel defeated—and therefore free to overeat until you go home. Instead, wait until day three or four before treating yourself.

Watch the alcohol, especially the umbrella kind What makes tropical drinks so great? Rich coconut milk and sugared syrups. Add in the rum, and you've just swallowed 400 calories or more.

Splurge, but not at every meal A "Hey, we're on vacation!" mind-set can lead you from a buffet breakfast to a three-course lunch to a six-course dinner. Each day, mentally designate one meal as special, and skimp on the others.

15 pounds— gone!

*Can small diet changes really make a big difference?
Believe it: Cut just 75 calories a day,
burn 75 more, and you'll drop the weight.*

By Kathleen Renda

Most dieters are sprinters, not marathoners. For short bursts, they can cut calories and drop pounds. Then the weight creeps back—sometimes leaving the dieter heavier at the finish than at the start. That's why many doctors now advocate a different strategy for weight loss. The key: small, consistent changes that add up to big results over time.

How small are these changes? You be the judge: If every day you can cut about 75 calories through diet and burn about 75 calories through exercise, you'll drop between 10 and 15 pounds in a year. It's practically losing weight in your sleep.

"I call it the tortoise approach," says George L. Blackburn, M.D., an associate professor at Harvard Medical School and Beth Israel Deaconess Medical Center in Boston, and an authority on obesity. "If fast weight loss has failed you, why not consider this?" Here's his advice on how to win at losing.

Good Housekeeping: Why is this plan better than other diets we've seen?

Dr. Blackburn: Fad diets—any program that promises you'll lose more than a pound per week—don't work. Why? Because there's a word for existing on 1,200 calories a day: starvation. I don't ask my patients to starve. I do ask them to cut calories—but only 75 a day, not 750 or 1,000. Seventy-five is achievable and sustainable. Do that every day, and you'll lose weight.

What's the catch—a lot of exercise?

Exercising 30 minutes a day, four days a week is great, but most people can't make that kind of commitment. Instead, ask yourself this: Can I spend just 15 minutes a day to improve my health and my looks? You don't need equipment or a gym membership—just 15 minutes of simple physical activity, such as exercising the dog or dancing to MTV videos. (The average video is three minutes long, so dance through five.) There's room in anyone's schedule for that.

How much weight can a woman lose by making those two changes?

In 25 years of medical practice and research, I've seen about 3,000 women, and the results have been consistent: On this plan, they lost 15 pounds in a year. That may not sound huge, but in terms of your health, it's dramatic. You lower your risk of heart disease, diabetes, even cancers of the breast and colon.

What's the first step?

You can't cut 75 calories unless you know how much you eat. So write down everything you put in your mouth, and how much of it, every day for three weeks. Then use a source, such as *The Complete Book of Food Counts* by Corinne T. Netzer, to figure out the calorie count for each day. Average those numbers—that's your baseline. Now you're ready to start subtracting.

But what if I don't eat the same number of calories each day?

Over the course of a week, your eating will balance out. That surprises people, but research shows your body naturally gravitates toward this baseline. If that's not the case, and your weekly counts fluctuate by thousands of calories, then getting your roller-coaster eating under control is the more immediate issue.

Suppose I eat 2,500 to 3,000 calories per day. Will cutting 75 really make a difference?

Yes. You will lose about a pound a month whether you're subtracting 75 from 1,500 calories a day or from 3,000. But if you have a lot of weight to lose, and you want to speed up sensibly, simply double the numbers: Subtract 150 calories per day from your baseline, burn 150 more with exercise, and you'll lose 30 pounds in a year.

What's an easy way to cut 75 calories?

There are many ways, because 75 isn't very many—just three quarters of a tablespoon of fat or half a can of Coke Classic will do it. Plus, you don't have to cut all 75 at one meal. Cut 50 at lunch, 25 at dinner. Start by eliminating hidden calories, such as the few bites of cake that tempted you at the office birthday party.

I hate to exercise. How can I work off those 75 calories?

Walk 5,000 steps every day, and you can burn the calories. Most women, even devoted nonexercisers, take about 2,500 steps during a regular day, so you're halfway there. To work in more steps, invest $10 in a pedometer, available at discount stores, and move at every opportunity. Pace the sidelines during the kids' soccer games, or do extra laps around the supermarket aisles. Rev up other activities: When you vacuum, get hard-core and move the sofa and beds, and clean underneath. Of course, if you can manage a 15-minute walk, so much the better.

How can I increase my chances of succeeding with this approach?

Make it a game. Every morning ask yourself, *Where am I going to trim my 75 calories today? From breakfast, from a snack, from my glass of wine at dinner?* After that, relax. You know where you're going to cut, so you won't obsess.

cut it out!

Food	Calories
13 french fries	75
6 peanut M & Ms	75
1 large egg	78
4 ounces wine	80
2 cheese ravioli	75

attack of the 75-calorie foods

If you think extra bites don't add up, do the math: All these foods deliver about 75 calories—eat just one per day, and you'll pack on almost *eight* additional pounds this year.

Breakfast
- ½ cruller, 85 calories
- 2 strips cooked bacon, 80
- 1 slice rye bread, 90
- ½ cup whole milk, 75
- ⅓ Hostess low-fat blueberry muffin, 76
- 1½ tablespoons cream cheese, 76
- 1½ sausage links, 72
- 1 tablespoon butter, 108
- ½ cup low-fat cottage cheese, 82

Lunch
- 1 tablespoon mayonnaise, 98
- 1 tablespoon peanut butter, 95
- 3½ tablespoons tuna salad, 85
- 1 slice beef bologna, 89
- 2 slices turkey roll, 84
- ¼ of a 4-ounce burger, 81
- 1 tablespoon blue cheese dressing, 77
- ½ Taco Bell beef taco, 85
- ¼ slice Domino's pepperoni pizza, 77
- 2 McDonald's Chicken McNuggets, 95
- ¼ McDonald's cheeseburger, 83
- ⅓ Subway 6-inch roast beef sandwich, 88
- ¼ cup KFC coleslaw, 72
- ½ bun-length frankfurter, 92

Dinner
- 3 tablespoons Kraft Macaroni & Cheese, 77
- 1 fish stick, breaded and fried, 76
- 4 large shrimp, breaded and fried, 73
- 2 ounces roasted chicken, 94
- ⅓ medium baked potato, no butter, 73
- 3 tablespoons sour cream, 77
- ¼ cup mashed potatoes with gravy, 75
- ¼ cup barbecue baked beans, 90
- ½ cup cream of mushroom soup, 102

Dessert/snacks
- 1 peach half, canned in syrup, 73
- 3 tablespoons whipped cream, 78
- 3 Hershey's Kisses (or ½ ounce chocolate), 79
- 10 potato chips, 75
- 4 tortilla chips, 87
- ¼ cup Breyer's vanilla ice cream, 75

Drinks
- ½ can Pepsi, 75
- 1 cup (8 ounces) sweetened iced tea, 80
- 1½ ounces hard liquor (vodka, gin, bourbon), 97
- ½ can beer, 75

Metric Equivalents

The recipes that appear in this cookbook use the standard United States method for measuring liquid and dry or solid ingredients (teaspoons, tablespoons, and cups). The information on this chart is provided to help cooks outside the U.S. successfully use these recipes. All equivalents are approximate.

METRIC EQUIVALENTS FOR DIFFERENT TYPES OF INGREDIENTS

A standard cup measure of a dry or solid ingredient will vary in weight depending on the type of ingredient. A standard cup of liquid is the same volume for any type of liquid. Use the following chart when converting standard cup measures to grams (weight) or milliliters (volume).

Standard Cup	Fine Powder	Grain	Granular	Liquid Solids	Liquid
	(ex. flour)	(ex. rice)	(ex. sugar)	(ex. butter)	(ex. milk)
1	140 g	150 g	190 g	200 g	240 ml
¾	105 g	113 g	143 g	150 g	180 ml
⅔	93 g	100 g	125 g	133 g	160 ml
½	70 g	75 g	95 g	100 g	120 ml
⅓	47 g	50 g	63 g	67 g	80 ml
¼	35 g	38 g	48 g	50 g	60 ml
⅛	18 g	19 g	24 g	25 g	30 ml

USEFUL EQUIVALENTS FOR LIQUID INGREDIENTS BY VOLUME

¼ tsp	=						1 ml	
½ tsp	=						2 ml	
1 tsp	=						5 ml	
3 tsp	=	1 tbls		=	½ fl oz	=	15 ml	
		2 tbls	= ⅛ cup	=	1 fl oz	=	30 ml	
		4 tbls	= ¼ cup	=	2 fl oz	=	60 ml	
		5⅓ tbls	= ⅓ cup	=	3 fl oz	=	80 ml	
		8 tbls	= ½ cup	=	4 fl oz	=	120 ml	
		10⅔ tbls	= ⅔ cup	=	5 fl oz	=	160 ml	
		12 tbls	= ¾ cup	=	6 fl oz	=	180 ml	
		16 tbls	= 1 cup	=	8 fl oz	=	240 ml	
		1 pt	= 2 cups	=	16 fl oz	=	480 ml	
		1 qt	= 4 cups	=	32 fl oz	=	960 ml	
					33 fl oz	=	1000 ml	= 1l

USEFUL EQUIVALENTS FOR DRY INGREDIENTS BY WEIGHT

(To convert ounces to grams, multiply the number of ounces by 30.)

1 oz	=	¹⁄₁₆ lb	=	30 g
4 oz	=	¼ lb	=	120 g
8 oz	=	½ lb	=	240 g
12 oz	=	¾ lb	=	360 g
16 oz	=	1 lb	=	480 g

USEFUL EQUIVALENTS FOR LENGTH

(To convert inches to centimeters, multiply the number of inches by 2.5.)

1 in			=	2.5 cm		
6 in	=	½ ft	=	15 cm		
12 in	=	1 ft	=	30 cm		
36 in	=	3 ft	= 1 yd =	90 cm		
40 in			=	100 cm	=	1 m

USEFUL EQUIVALENTS FOR COOKING/OVEN TEMPERATURES

	Fahrenheit	Celsius	Gas Mark
Freeze Water	32° F	0° C	
Room Temperature	68° F	20° C	
Boil Water	212° F	100° C	
Bake	325° F	160° C	3
	350° F	180° C	4
	375° F	190° C	5
	400° F	200° C	6
	425° F	220° C	7
	450° F	230° C	8
Broil			Grill

Good Housekeeping Institute
Reports and Tips Index

Look here to find every Institute report and tip box in this year's Annual Recipes. We've included all the kitchen-related reports and tips from the magazine in 2001.

Recipe Title Index

An alphabetical listing of every recipe title that appeared
in the magazine in 2001. See page 262 for the General Recipe Index.

Month-by-Month Index

*A month-by-month listing of every food story with recipe titles that appeared
in the magazine in 2001. See page 262 for the General Recipe Index.*

General Recipe Index

*A listing by major ingredient, food category, and/or regular column
for every recipe that appeared in the magazine in 2001.*

Photo Credits

Sang An cover, pages 156-157

Richard Bowditch pages 2-3, 41, 44-45, 47-49, 186, 188, 198 (bottom)

Brian Hagiwara back cover (top right and bottom left), pages 42-43, 113-115, 120, 154-155, 160, 163, 166, 233

Rita Maas pages 77-80, 151, 153 (top), 240

Alan Richardson back cover (top left), pages 1, 37-40, 116-117, 158-159, 194-197, 198 (top), 199

Mark Thomas back cover (bottom right), pages 4, 118-119, 153 (bottom), 164, 193, 200, 234-239

Favorite Recipes Journal

Jot down your family's and your favorite recipes for quick and handy reference.
Remember to include the dishes that drew rave reviews when company came for dinner.

Recipe	Source/Page	Remarks